Urban Affairs

Urban Affairs

Back on the Policy Agenda

EDITED BY
CAROLINE ANDREW
KATHERINE A. GRAHAM
and SUSAN D. PHILLIPS

McGill-Queen's University Press
Montreal & Kingston · London · Ithaca

© McGill-Queen's University Press 2002
ISBN 0-7735-2352-9 (cloth)
ISBN 0-7735-2353-7 (paper)

Legal deposit first quarter 2003
Bibliothèque nationale du Québec

Printed in Canada on acid-free paper that is 100%
ancient forest free (100% post-consumer recycled),
processed chlorine free.

McGill-Queen's University Press acknowledges the support of the Canada Council for the Arts for our publishing program. We also acknowledge the financial support
of the Government of Canada through the Book Publishing Industry Development Program (BPIDP) for our
publishing activities.

Chapter 2, "Aboriginal People in Urban Areas," is from
*Visions of the Heart: An Introduction to Canadian
Aboriginal Issues*, edited by David A. Long and Olive
Dickason, 2nd edition, © 2000. Reprinted with
permission of Nelson Thomson Learning a division of
Thomson Learning.

National Library of Canada Cataloguing in Publication Data

Main entry under title:
    Urban affairs : back on the policy agenda / edited by
Caroline Andrew, Katherine A. Graham, and Susan D.
Phillips.

Includes bibliographical references.
ISBN 0-7735-2352-9 (bound).—ISBN 0-7735-2353-7 (pbk.)

1. Urban policy—Canada.   I.   Andrew, Caroline, 1942–.
II. Graham, Katherine A., 1947–.   III. Phillips, Susan D.

HT127.U65 2002   307.76'0971   C2002-903194-X

This book was typeset by True to Type in 10/12 Sabon.

Contents

To Harvey Lithwick and Gilles Paquet,
who inspired this book

Urban Affairs
Back on the Policy Agenda

Introduction:
Urban Affairs in Canada:
Changing Roles and Changing
Perspectives

CAROLINE ANDREW, KATHERINE A.
GRAHAM, and SUSAN D. PHILLIPS

> A discussion of urban policy currently being implemented in
> Canada requires little space.
> There is in fact no such thing.
>
> (Lithwick and Paquet, 1968: 269)

Those of us interested in urban Canada are currently marking two important milestones. We have now passed the thirtieth anniversary of Harvey Lithwick and Gilles Paquet's landmark publication *Urban Studies: A Canadian Perspective*. This book was a wake-up call to contemporary researchers across many disciplines about the need to deepen our understanding of cities and to contribute, as researchers, to the sound development of urban Canada. Shortly after publication of this volume, Harvey Lithwick produced his call to policy-makers at all levels of government in a book entitled *Urban Canada: Problems and Prospects*. Lithwick's work took urban research and formulated a policy agenda designed to guide government action to address what Lithwick described as "problems *in* the city" and "problems *of* the city" (Lithwick, 1970: 19–35; our emphasis). These two publications constitute the first serious attention in Canada to urban research and policy as a political agenda. The second milestone is more commonly recognized: the wave of megacity projects controversially spreading across Canada. The role and place of Canada's cities is therefore a matter of great interest and concern.

In light of these two milestones, we think it worthwhile to examine contemporary urban policy issues in Canada and to address the question: Are urban affairs on Canada's public policy agenda? For us, this question seems particularly important because some of the public issues that have a distinctly urban dimension – for example, the issue of homelessness and the challenge of competition among metropolitan regions – are being played out in an increasingly international world.

This book had its start in a 1998 colloquium to honour the thirtieth anniversary of Lithwick and Paquet's work. Based on the interest generated at the colloquium, we expanded our network of contributors in order to illuminate more fully the inter-governmental context and the policy and fiscal environment in which urban governments find themselves as we head into the twenty-first century. We argue that this is a substantially different environment from that encountered by Lithwick and Paquet thirty years ago. Similarly, the nature of urban policy analysis and the ideas and prescriptions that emerge have changed.

This introduction attempts to provide an analytical overview of where we were, where we are, and where we might go with a policy agenda for Canada's city-regions. We begin by reviewing Lithwick and Paquet's contribution. We then identify and examine important shifts in the character of Canada's cities, in their governance, and in the resulting public policy agenda. Although the following chapters illuminate the extent to which urban affairs is back on the policy agenda, and on whose agenda, in much more depth, we suggest some preliminary conclusions about the state of urban affairs and its policy priority in Canada.

LITHWICK AND PAQUET: RATIONAL POSITIVISM AND URBAN POLICY

It is important to situate Lithwick and Paquet in context. This is not simply to bow to conservative historiography (Collingwood, 1946; Tosh, 1991). Instead, context is important so that we understand the state of social science and policy analysis thirty years ago, how Lithwick and Paquet may have been shaped by it, and how they advanced thinking at the time.

In his retrospective on thirty years of policy studies in Canada, Bruce Doern, building on Wildavsky, refers to the history of Canadian policy studies as embracing art, craft, and science (Doern, 1996: 15–26). It is reasonable to suggest that Lithwick and Paquet were writing at the crest of the wave of policy studies as science. The United States provided a particularly powerful influence to Canadians at the time. There, the best and the brightest were developing and applying rational models to deal with an urban crisis, and Canadians were watching these and other political developments (perhaps most notably the conduct of the Vietnam War) with interest and often with anxiety. The ascension in Canadian academe and government of US-trained social scientists reinforced this influence from south of the border.

Perhaps the characteristic of Lithwick and Paquet's work that most reflects this milieu is that they search for an integrated holistic approach to urban policy. This has, in our view, some lasting notable benefits. For example, they advocate a cross-disciplinary approach and advocate development of public policy for the city and its region, thereby arguing for incorporation of the dynamics of urban growth into any urban policy agenda. The ethos of the time is very much evident in their call for the rise of "urbanology," focusing on the urbanization process, work on the nature of the city, and research on the functioning of the city (Lithwick and Paquet, 1968: 10).

A second important contribution that Lithwick and Paquet make is their view of the constructive potential of urban life. This contrasts with the "city as evil" perspective embodied in the intellectual work of, among others, those writing in the tradition of Lewis Wirth and the "Chicago School" of urban sociology that focused on the disruptive character of urbanization and, at times, its pathological consequences (Wirth, 1938; Lewis, 1966; Garigue, 1956).

Lithwick and Paquet did, however, argue that there was "an urban crisis" in Canada. The source of this crisis was, in their view, the process of urbanization itself. In their words, "increasing population density has created our slum crisis, our pollution crisis, our unsafe city streets. At the same time, this process has led to our accelerating suburban sprawl, creating our transportation crisis, our municipal revenue crisis, our municipal service crisis and our housing crisis" (Lithwick and Paquet, 1968: 265). They offer prescriptions for dealing with the crisis – more urban research and urban researchers, and a national urban policy. They also recommended an infrastructure for developing and sustaining urban policy in Canada, specifically: establishment of a central urban research agency; a Senate committee on urban affairs to identify problems and begin dialogue; and "a joint federal-provincial body capable of integrating all policy instruments in all related fields, from transportation to housing" (Lithwick and Paquet, 1968: 273–4). Arguably, the establishment of the federal Ministry of State for Urban Affairs (MSUA) in 1971 and the federal government's brief flirtation with tri-level conferences on urban issues in the early 1970s were directly influenced by Lithwick and Paquet. Among observers of the period, there is consensus that this was, indeed, a rather fleeting concern for the urban on the part of the the federal government. MSUA was wound down in 1979 (Feldman and Graham, 1979: 29–58).

In light of the intervening history of urban policy, it is noteworthy that Lithwick and Paquet are silent on the role of urban governments in identifying problems, undertaking dialogue, and doing policy analysis. Urban politicians and administrators were clearly equivalent to the "hewers of wood and drawers of water" in the urban policy world. As Lithwick and Paquet acknowledge, "we felt that the urban administrators could not add very much to this rather abstract discussion of a research framework" (Lithwick and Paquet, 1968: 264).

URBANOLOGY THEN, URBAN GOVERNANCE NOW

Certainly, the urban reality in Canada is different from that of the period of Lithwick and Paquet's book. We are even more urban than we were and our large cities are even more spread out. If Lithwick and Paquet were concerned about urban sprawl, the city-regions of Canada's largest metropolitan areas would continue to be a concern. This evolving urban reality is a necessary backdrop to our analysis of the place of urban issues on the policy agenda. But rather than describe recent demographic trends in detail in this introduction, we include here a brief discussion of sources in the references for readers who wish to know more about the evolution of urban demography in Canada.

The second edition of Bunting and Filion's *Canadian Cities in Transition* (Oxford, 2000) gives an excellent overview of current processes of evolution and development of Canadian cities. It covers Canada-wide trends, patterns of development within cities and city-regions, evolution of housing and homelessness, as well as selected 1996 statistics on the twenty-five census metropolitan areas. Slightly less recent but also extremely useful is the anthology edited by Bourne and Ley, *The Changing Social Geography on Canadian Cities* (McGill-Queen's, 1993). It covers some of the same areas – gentrification, housing, homelessness, suburban development – but also includes descriptions of areas of social policy – health, day care, social planning – in Canada's urban areas.

It is also worth mentioning the impact of the Metropolis project on our understanding of the recent urban reality in Canada. The four research centres (Montreal, Toronto, Vancouver, Prairie) linked to Metropolis have produced a body of research that greatly expands our knowledge not only of immigration and processes of urban integration but also more generally about the functioning of the larger Canadian cities. The overall project produces material in a variety of forms (for examples, see the website canada.metropolis.net), including a special issue of the *Canadian Journal of Regional Science* (vol. 20, no. 1–2, 1997), which more recently produced a special issue comparing Montreal and Toronto (vol. 22, no. 1–2, 1999). And, of course, the existence of the *Canadian Journal of Urban Research*, which began publication in the early 1990s, has also contributed considerably to our understanding of urban development in Canada.

To a contemporary reader, there are some notable dimensions of the urban world that fail to appear in Lithwick and Paquet's analysis. Beyond their assessment of the relative health of Canadian cities, there is nothing about cities and city-regions in the international context. Gender-based perspectives, issues of cultural diversity, urban citizenship, and citizen engagement do not emerge, nor does one get a sense of the nature or dynamics of urban politics, even in the specific context of the period in which they were writing. Finally, a contemporary reader looking for some sense of urban policy, as emerging from a dynamic relationship among the public, private, and voluntary sectors and citizens would be disappointed. These omissions are a result of the prevailing paradigms for thinking about urban research and policy at the time when Lithwick and Paquet were writing. They are important to note because of some of the major challenges that Canadian cities have faced in the intervening years and the responses that have emerged. We proceed to summarize these challenges before examining the character of policy responses in the intervening years and the implications of those responses for the future. The challenges may be found in the broad context in which urban policy is made, in the changing context of Canadian federalism, and in the assertion of paradigms for policy analysis that compete with the rational model.

THE CHANGING CONTEXT
FOR URBAN POLICY

Perhaps the most fundamental contextual development is that urban policy issues can no longer be conceived exclusively in the context of a single nation-state. Here, Lithwick and Paquet's notion of a relative urban crisis in Canada is indeed seminal. In their view, Canadian cities were relatively well off, compared to those in other countries. The impetus for their call to action at the time was, even if Canadian cities functioned relatively well, the danger that Canadians would no longer tolerate their urban condition. But we can no longer think of major cities within Canada and our urban policy as being domestically bound. Canadian cities are now developing in an internationalized environment, part of an internationalized economy that is characterized by increasingly footloose financial and human capital. The fact that this economy is increasingly knowledge and service based, rather than dependent on natural resources and manufacturing, has social implications for our cities. Knowledge workers in Toronto or Montreal may have more in common with their counterparts in Berlin or Atlanta than they do with fellow residents who are not participating in the new economy. This bifurcation of the population is characterized not just by income differences but also by differences in mobility and commitment to place (Mayer, 1991).

A second change in the urban policy environment is the increasing ethno-cultural diversity of Canada's urban population. Canada has been home to people from different cultures for many years. Over the last twenty years, however, immigration has been characterized by the predominance of visible minorities among new arrivals. These people are highly concentrated in Canada's largest cities. More than two-thirds of the visible minority population (both recent arrivals and those born in Canada) live in the Montreal, Toronto, and Vancouver city-regions (Graham and Phillips, 1998: 267). This has resulted in a cultural richness that many Canadians (and tourists) celebrate. It has also given rise to challenges of settlement, cultural accommodation, and social harmony.

The period since Lithwick and Paquet's work has also seen a profound change in our notion of interest representation. This has also altered the urban policy environment. The rise of new social movements, advancing causes such as gender rights, environmental sustainability and human rights at the local and global levels has led to new issues emerging for debate and new conceptions of community. In political terms, we can no longer see the task of urban governance as being shaped exclusively by where in the city people reside. The rise of new social movements has contributed to the need for urban policymakers to recognize different kinds of communities, those based on physical proximity and those based on other forms of common interest. So we now see, for example, the Gay and Lesbian community, the cultural community and the environmental community playing a prominent role in urban debates.

CHANGES IN CANADIAN FEDERALISM

Changes in Canadian federalism have had an equally important impact as those in the broader environment. At the federal level, the period from the late 1960s to 2000 has been characterized by significant shifts in the way the Government of Canada interacts with provinces and in federal spending. Lithwick and Paquet were writing during the zenith of the federal government's activism; interestingly, their collection was published the year that the first Trudeau government came to power. However briefly, there was a political groundswell for creating Trudeau's "Just Society" and for the federal government to reshape the federal-provincial relationship through direct federal programming and vigorous intergovernmental negotiation. The preceding years, under the prime ministership of Lester Pearson, were characterized by a great amount of intergovernmental activity. The federal government often seemed taken aback by the assertiveness and sophistication of the provinces during negotiations on medicare and the Canada Pension Plan, which occurred during the Pearson era (for an account of federal-provincial relations during the Pearson years, see Simeon, 1972).

The tri-level process on urban issues, referred to earlier, stands out as an example of increasing federal activism in the intergovernmental arena. The government was formally engaging in an area where, from a constitutional perspective, it had no direct jurisdiction.

In the intervening years, the extent of intergovernmentalism in the Canadian federal system has certainly not diminished. But the idea that the federal government might assertively dominate the provinces has been tempered by, among other things, the events surrounding constitutional patriation and the Meech Lake and Charlottetown Accords. By 1999, the federal government had concluded the Social Union Framework Agreement (SUFA) with all provinces and territories except Quebec, which recognizes the legitimacy of the federal spending power, but limits its use in areas of provincial jurisdiction without agreement of a majority of provinces. SUFA is permeated by commitments to consult with provinces and with citizens which has prompted Roger Gibbins to refer to it as "the high-watermark of intergovernmentalism" (1999: 208). The intergovernmentalism entailed in SUFA, however, remains stuck in the federal-provincial box that has historically characterized our understanding of intergovernmental relations in Canada. In spite of the vital and growing responsibilities held by municipal governments in the development and delivery of social programs, SUFA creates no obligation for federal and provincial governments to consult with them and they remain relatively invisible in our thinking about both the federal system and about social policy.

Equally important is that the federal government has actually withdrawn from programming and financing in policy fields that require careful attention for Canada's city-regions to be sustainable and prosperous. Federal fiscal policy from the end of the Second World War until 1984 was rooted in Keynesianism and the development of the welfare state. The emergence of stagflation (inflation concurrent with high unemployment) in the mid-1970s prompted federal programming and spending on economic planning and development (Campbell, 1999: 114). From an urban perspective, the direct impact of federal spending was felt in areas such as airport construction, urban renewal, and housing, where, by the early 1970s, federal initiatives were referred to as "programs in search of a policy" (Dennis and Fish, 1972).

The biggest shift, however, began in 1984 with the election of the Conservative government of Brian Mulroney. From 1985 to 1993, successive Conservative governments grappled with the challenges of actually implementing their debt- and deficit-fighting platforms. The challenge was taken up by the Liberal government elected in 1993. The 1995 federal budget, which slashed transfers on health and social spending from the federal government to the provinces and curtailed direct federal programming on the basis of the federal government's 1995 Federal Program Review, was probably the turning point in the debt- and deficit-focused era. From 1984–99, the federal government's fiscal and policy stance has been commonly described as tilting towards the neo-conservative (Campbell, 1999).

Commenting on the impact of the federal government's neo-conservative stance, Campbell suggests that it has led us to "policy anomie and anxiety about the future," accompanied by "modest economic optimism" (Campbell, 1999: 114). Certainly, implementation of the federal restraint agenda after 1995 has sent shockwaves through Canada's other levels of government. Reduction in federal-provincial transfers has been mirrored by shrinkage in transfers from the provincial governments to their municipalities. In the wake of their straightened circumstances and propelled further by the election of neo-conservative governments in some provinces, we see provincial enthusiasm for changing the essence of their relationship to municipalities. The period since 1985 is characterized by the search for provincial-municipal disentanglement (Siegel, 1992; Sancton, 1992; Graham and Phillips, 1998).

Disentanglement is often described in terms of changes in the provincial-municipal fiscal relationship. In essence, the goal is to delineate clear and separate service responsibilities for provincial and municipal governments and to have each level assume full financial responsibility for the services it provides. The reality has been significant downloading of responsibilities to municipalities without financial compensation and a sharp reduction in provincial-municipal transfers. Disentanglement has also been accompanied by a change in provincial-municipal relations on the substance of policy. From a municipal perspective, "pay has not resulted in say." Provincial governments have asserted centralized control over policy and, in many cases, mandated the level and specifics of how services are to be delivered, while requiring municipal governments to assume full responsibility for financing and service delivery. In practical terms, there are two difficulties with this. First, the bureaucratic downsizing that has occurred across provincial governments has reduced their capacity to fulfill their policy role. The consequences of the retraction of the provincial role became poignantly evident with the Walkerton, Ontario, tragedy in the spring of 2000, when seven people died and hundreds became ill from E. coli contamination of the town's water supply. Dramatic downsizing of the provincial Ministry of the Environment, transfer of responsibility for public health and water testing to municipalities, relaxation of environmental regulations, and privatization of government water testing labs are all seen as contributing factors to the tragedy (Ibbitson, 2000: A3). Second, in the urban context, it is very problematic to divorce policy-making from delivery. What happens on the street literally informs the classic policy questions: What is the problem? What can be done? This leads us to the conclusion that contemporary provincial governments' urban policy is a chimera.

NEW POLICY PARADIGMS

There has been a reciprocal relationship between some of the broad contextual and political changes, discussed above, and the emergence of new ways of thinking about urban policy that both compete with and complement the rational positivism that characterized policy analysis in the period in which Lithwick and Paquet were writing. Increasingly, urban policy seems more art and craft than science due to two important, concurrent shifts in how we conceive of and practice public policy. First, the policy paradigm focused on "government" has been replaced by that of "governance." Hierarchy has given way to horizontality. In contrast to the top down control and relative autonomy of the former, governance implies and relies upon interdependence – among public, private, and voluntary sectors; among governments; and across departments within the same level of government. The ability to accomplish policy goals is often dependent upon collaboration among multiple players whose interests and responsibilities intersect in a fluid and contingent way. Programs or policies are themselves increasingly conceived of as "agendas" – that is as an intersecting set of policies – rather than as autonomous, stand-alone programs. This further reinforces the need for involvement of several departments or other governments working in a horizontal manner.

This move to a governance model has been accompanied by a shift in how we conceptualize urban governments as *governments*. The traditional assumption has been that the primary role of the municipal level is to provide services – to ensure that clean water flows from the tap, that the garbage gets picked up, and that kids can find enough ice time at the local arena. However, municipalities are increasingly understood to be not just service providers but democratic governments. This reconceptualization highlights the imperative of operating in a democratic, accountable, and transparent manner and brings with it expectations that governments engage citizens and communities in meaningful ways in the policy process. It also presumes that urban governments possess sufficient policy capacity and have access to appropriate policy tools to undertake strategic leadership. That such leadership may necessitate collaboration in a governance model, as described above, in no way obviates its importance. With a focus on governing rather than mere service provision comes a concern for equity: that urban governments are representative of and responsive to the needs of the diversity of communities. The implication for urban research is that the analytical methods employed are sensitive to group differences and can accommodate, for instance, a good understanding of ethno-cultural communities and gender-based analysis.

For the scholar of urban affairs, the art of analysis in this new environment has facilitated the use of many different analytical lenses, including those of the regulation/post-Fordist school, neo-institutionalism, regime theory, political economy, social movements, and feminist approaches, among others. No one perspective has a conceptual hegemony on the study of urban affairs. This is a far cry from the urbanology imagined by Lithwick and Paquet, but if we imagine urban analysis to be more art than science, it has created a healthy environment of different ways of looking at and understanding urban phenomena that arguably creates a richer composite picture. Arguably, the emergence of multiple paradigms for thinking about urban issues has enriched the world of the urban researcher and the real world of urban policy analysis.

In this introduction, in addition to the variety of theoretical perspectives adopted by the authors in this anthology, we are also using the idea of agenda-setting as a way of capturing our interest in judging the political saliency of urban issues in Canada at the present time. The idea of agenda-setting takes us to the literature on policy-making and, more specifically, to that on policy cycles (Simeon, 1976; Howlett and Ramesh, 1995).

Agenda-setting is that very preliminary stage in the policy cycle in which certain questions come to the attention of governments. As Howlett and Ramesh state it, "agenda setting is about the recognition of a problem on the part of the government" (1995: 104). Richard Simeon's categorization of public policy determinants as coming from the environment, power structure, ideas, political framework, and decision-making processes opens up the possibilities of factors involved in agenda-setting – from the huge number of potential issues, only a limited number engage the interest of government. John Kingdon's work on agenda-setting pursues this line of reasoning. He sees three sets of variables – problems, policies, and politics – that come together when problems are linked to solutions and given weight because of political pressures. Consequently, issues move on the policy agenda and the actual policy-making phases of the policy cycle begin. Following Howlett and Ramesh, this is when agenda-setting moves into policy formulation, decision-making, implementation, and evaluation (1995: 11).

A number of the chapters in this anthology are looking at specific areas of public policy and in some cases describe the full policy cycle in their particular area. This is true of Christopher Leo and Lisa Shaw's examination of inner-city decay, of David Wolfe on economic development, and of Carolyn Whitzman's examination of planning for women's safety. At the same time, these come together as the agenda-setting phase in terms of a urban policy agenda. Current specific policy initiatives run across a variety of areas; we are asking if, considered together, they suggest that urban policy as such is on governmental policy agendas. But before trying to answer this question, it is important to describe the full range of issues examined by the contributors to this volume.

CHALLENGES AND RESPONSE: THE URBAN POLICY AGENDA

Our obvious starting point in this anthology is that urban affairs ought to be back on the policy agenda. In addressing whether urban affairs are, in fact, on contemporary policy agendas, we have identified four key areas: building civil society, urban governance, planning and economic development, and fiscal challenges. We invited scholars writing from a variety of analytical perspectives and disciplines and from different parts of the country to provide their analyses of these issues and reflect on where this leaves urban policy as a political priority. In undertaking urban research, a limitation is always the specificity of urban affairs in geographic space and the extensive differences that exist across various locales. As a result, it is often difficult in this field to create a truly national discussion. Nevertheless, we have attempted to do so by asking the authors, to the extent possible, to draw out implications and issues that have relevance to urban areas beyond the immediate focus and locale of their chapters.

BUILDING CIVIL SOCIETY

This set of essays grapples with understanding the experience of particular groups within civil society in the context of the urban environment and explores how urban governments are cultivating more constructive relationships with these constituencies and with the public in general. The chapters in this section focus on the involvement and experience of four critical components of civil society in the urban context: immigrant communities, Aboriginal peoples, women, and inner-city residents. Valerie Preston and Madeleine Wong's contribution to this volume builds on their work with the Metropolis project. They argue the importance of recognizing the diversity of the immigrant experience. If we are to build inclusive urban societies we must learn to pay more attention to the diverse needs of immigrant groups. This chapter also raises the question about levels of government and responsibilities for immigration. Should municipal government play a larger role? Will they? The distinctive challenges faced by Aboriginal peoples in urban areas have historically been overlooked by both scholars and policy-makers in spite of the fact that almost half of Canada's Aboriginal peoples live in cities. Evelyn Peters focuses on how Aboriginal urbanization has been constructed as a policy "problem" and suggests ways of valuing and supporting urban Aboriginal cultures that would contribute to meeting the needs of these communities more effectively than they are met at present.

Sherilyn MacGregor's chapter is a reflection about the difficulties of making women visible in cities. The chapter looks particularly at this question in terms of urban analysis and its receptivity to feminist analysis. She looks at the recent importance of the environmental discourse and wonders whether it has pushed gender further into the background, despite the contributions of eco-feminism. Her concern for maintaining the importance of gender in urban analysis reflects an understanding of the complexity of the relations between municipal governments and social actors and those between social action and social theory.

Carolyn Whitzman looks specifically at the experiences of the recent past in trying to give voice to women in Canadian local government. This recording and evaluation of these efforts is important for our ability to learn from these experiences and to better understand the impact of social movements on urban policy. Making municipal policy more sensitive to women's needs – and to the diversity of women's needs –

has been slow and frustrating but there have been, according to Whitzman, both successes and challenges.

The final chapter in this section is by Christopher Leo and Lisa Shaw. It tackles the problems faced by inner city residents because of the deterioration of their surroundings, which can also be seen as a challenge to the resiliency of civil society. In their case study of Winnipeg, Leo and colleagues agree with Lithwick and Paquet on the symptoms and causes of the decline of the urban core, but the solutions they envisage do not emerge from the promise of an urbanology. A faith in the ability of scientific study and rational planning to revitalize Winnipeg's core has been replaced in their analysis with a recognition of the complexity of governance, the challenges involved, and the need to understand the ways in which civil society operates in the urban core.

GOVERNANCE

The section on governance addresses some of the most pressing current debates about the ways in which political structures in urban areas are being reorganized. The first chapter in this section provides background to this debate by providing an argument about the need for a sense of community in order to encourage citizen participation in urban government. The chapter was written by Merle Nicholds while she was mayor of Kanata (now part of the amalgamated City of Ottawa), one of the fastest growing urban areas in the country. For Nicholds, building a sense of community in the urban environment is vital, and she argues that citizens are not apathetic in their role in rekindling a civic society: they simply have not been inspired to believe that they have the power to make a difference to the communities in which they live. For her, this is the underlying challenge facing urban governments.

In virtually all provinces, provincial and local governments have struggled in different ways and with different solutions, to create more effective political structures for governing city-regions. Such reform has been driven largely, but not exclusively, by fiscal pressures and the ideology of "less government is better government." The result is often amalgamation within city-regions to create larger platforms that supposedly can better withstand downloading of responsibilities. It has also produced a heated debate about whether amalgamation will, in fact, reduce costs over the longer term and about what impact it will have on the sense of community. Among political restructurings, the forced amalgamation of the lower and upper tier municipalities of Metropolitan Toronto by the Harris government has been the most dramatic and the most contested to date. The process of Toronto's amalgamation is the topic of the chapter by Beth Moore Milroy. If Toronto takes the prize for most dramatic process, Montreal wins in the category of most politically complex. This unresolved case is addressed in a comparative context in the following chapter by Andrew Sancton. In comparing the development – and failure – of two-tier regional governments across Canada, Sancton raises serious concerns about the impact of creating ever larger metropolitan-scale authorities for governing city-regions.

PLANNING AND ECONOMIC DEVELOPMENT

Approaches to planning and economic development have changed significantly over thirty years. The promotion of economic development by urban governments has become not only explicitly concerned with sustainability but also with being more community oriented. Local economic development is no longer viewed as the creation of industrial parks and cutting deals with prospective tenants. City governments now see economic development as being influenced by a complex constellation of economic conditions, social circumstances, and urban quality of life. The central importance of an educated local workforce to economic prosperity is commonly acknowledged. The chapter by Barbara Levine, Paul Born, and Sherri Torjman demonstrates how community economic development (CED) is also gaining profile as districts within the city and specific segments within the urban population attempt to improve their economic circumstances. In light of these developments, urban governments' policy role has been increasingly exercised through their ability to convene other local public institutions (universities, school boards) and the private and voluntary sectors in order to develop the multi-faceted approach to economic development needed in today's world.

Another change in planning and development practices has been the greater institutionalization of consultation with the public. Pierre Hamel analyzes this through examination of the mechanisms in Montreal, a city that has established extensive formal consultative machinery. Have these mechanisms for public consultation contributed to the democratization of public policy and management? His conclusion is that Montreal's innovations in citizen involvement fell short of their potential because of their poor fit in a management system organized in a sectoral manner and in a political system that is highly centralized.

David Wolfe argues for greater recognition of the local level in his chapter on economic development policies. He looks at recent policies in Europe and argues that Canada could learn important lessons from the European examples. Two important lessons include building from the bottom up and thinking in terms of associative models of governance. These associative models imply a mixture of public and private agents and an important focus on institutional learning. In addition, these directions would allow Canadians to overcome what have been seen as the central weaknesses of our industrial policy: the lack of a strong bureaucratic state tradition and the divisive effects of our federal system.

Planning discourse is increasingly disconnected from implementation. This is the central message of Pierre Filion's chapter, in which he looks at the evolution of planning from the Second World War to the present. On the one hand, discourse has become increasingly focused on an ideal of intensification, whereas practice remains firmly rooted in low density suburban development. Filion explains the growing disconnection by the fact that the discourse is being marked by vocal environmental advocacy groups, whereas practice is increasingly influenced by the lessening capacity of governments to intervene.

FISCAL CHALLENGES

This section starts with the chapter by Michael Fenn, written when he was CEO of the Regional Municipality of Hamilton-Wentworth. The fiscal challenges are crucial and Fenn argues that urban governments must proceed with a focus on innovation rather than mere preservation. Ken Cameron's chapter continues with the theme of fiscal challenges by looking at the changing intergovernmental context over the past thirty years. Social problems have gotten worse, community solutions are popular, and there is a growing sense of entitlement on the part of citizens. His answer to the question "Who governs Canadian cities?" is double: in the formal sense it is the provincial governments but, in the political sense, it is the people living in these cities and the people they elect locally. The fiscal challenges therefore lead us back to the challenges of building civil society.

Finally, Enid Slack argues that fiscal pressures and global competition have ensured that urban affairs are on the policy agenda. She examines the three primary ways in which provincial governments have been addressing these pressures – through local service realignment; municipal restructuring; and property tax reform. Although she suggests that these changes are necessary to the creation of a sounder financial footing for municipalities, she also notes that they are not sufficient to meet the complex needs of large city-regions.

URBAN AFFAIRS AND DEMOCRACY:
COMING FULL CIRCLE

The successful creation and promotion of policy agendas hinges large-ly on the art of managing increasingly complex, interdependent poli-cies and players, as well as the craft of getting the attention of the pub-lic and governments and convincing them as to what action should and should not be taken. In the concluding chapter, Warren Magnusson reminds us that "when we speak of 'policy agendas,' we always have a politics in mind." In responding to our request to reflect on whether urban affairs is on the policy agenda at the start of the millennium, Magnusson notes that, as a prerequisite, a clarification of terms is required. The first is our understanding of what constitutes "urban." In a globalized environment, the world in which we live has been deter-ritorialized in significant ways and the hierarchy of place – city, region, nation, globe – has collapsed. Thus the ways in which a Canadian city is connected to a region are now very complex, involving connections to international economies and to nationalities that are themselves global rather than limited to a single nation-state. Second, thinking about urban policy "agendas" presupposes a concept of the state and an understanding of the nature of relationships between state and soci-ety. The development of Canadian cities has been characterized by a particularly strong provincial state and most approaches to the study of urban policy, including that of Lithwick and Paquet, have been high-ly statist. The relationship between states and society has undergone significant change in thirty years, largely because, as earlier chapters note, social movements and other civil society actors have reinvented politics, whether governments wanted them to or not. "In this sense," Magnusson concludes, "urban affairs is always already on the policy agenda, even if it is not exactly where our managers would like it to be."

IS URBAN AFFAIRS
ON THE POLICY AGENDA?

Our review of the thirty years since the first foray into urban policy analysis by Lithwick and Paquet and our assessment of where we are now leads us to two conclusions. First, urban affairs – as urban affairs – are not back on the national policy agenda. The urban dimension of analysis and policy formulation is weak within the fed-eral milieu. Neither has it been particularly strong at the provincial level. In terms of Ottawa's development of an urban agenda, little progress has been made. Even in the supposedly more collaborative atmosphere engendered by the Social Union Framework Agreement, the federal government still defines intergovernmental relationships largely in terms of the provinces. The provinces still jealously guard their urban creatures, discouraging direct federal involvement. Nevertheless, a few openings have been created in recent years where tripartite co-operation has worked effectively, notably the federal government's infrastructure program known as Canada Works, the initiative to alleviate homelessness, and several federal-provincial-municipal agreements to address specific problems such as the development of the Forks project in Winnipeg. But these are the exception, not the norm. If the federal government is serious about promoting social cohesion, it will need to figure out how to do this where diversity is the greatest, in the metropolitan areas. And this will involve thinking about how these areas operate.

There are perhaps some recent indications that the federal government is becoming more interested in urban questions. There has been newspaper speculation in early 2002 that the federal government was thinking about a major commitment of funds for urban transportation or even the creation of a ministry concerned with urban questions. Federal activities in relation to homelessness have also increased federal awareness of the urban agenda.

In exercising their constitutional responsibilities for municipal institutions and affairs, provincial governments continue to rely on a "one size fits all" approach, maintaining a presumption of the equity of place. They have been reluctant to tackle the real differences between major cities and small towns or rural areas. Consequently, legislative frameworks and funding policies tend to treat all municipalities equally, which often results in the provision of inadequate policy tools for urban governments or under funding for their human services. The weakness of the urban dimension is disquieting. Most of the major issues currently seizing policy-makers in both Ottawa and provincial capitals – issues such as immigrant settlement, homelessness, and environmental issues – clearly merit attention through an urban lens.

Our second conclusion is that there has been real policy action at the urban level. Urban governments in Canada have shown remarkable resilience and capacity to innovate in the wake of the challenges of the last thirty years. They have also become the locus of urban policy capacity among Canadian governments. Our city governments have been propelled into their policy role, in part because of the vacuum at the federal and provincial levels. Ironically, their traditional role in service delivery, which led Lithwick and Paquet to conclude that municipal officials had little to offer in deliberations about urban research and policy, has been a springboard to more sophisticated policy research and analysis at the local level. Changing and more complex service needs have led to innovations in service delivery that carry policy overtones. Perhaps most significantly, urban governments have been in the forefront in working within the governance paradigm, working in collaboration with the voluntary and private sectors and with citizens to rise to the challenges of creating healthy and prosperous cities.

PART ONE

Building a Civil Society

1 Immigration and Canadian Cities: Building Inclusion

VALERIE PRESTON and
MADELEINE WONG

To prepare for the millennium, *The Toronto Star* published a series of articles entitled "Beyond 2000: Home to the World." The articles that examine the city's transformation into a multicultural city are only one indication that contemporary immigration is transforming Canada's cities. Currently, Canada admits between 200,000 and 250,000 immigrants per year, expecting them to settle permanently[1] (Citizenship and Immigration Canada, 1998).[2] The sustained pace of current immigration is faster now than at any time since the Second World War. Newcomers are distinguished by their concentration in Canada's largest cities. In 1996, 85 percent of all immigrants lived in large urban centres compared with just 57 percent of the Canadian-born population (Statistics Canada, 1997). Recent immigrants, those who arrived between 1991 and 1996, are even more concentrated; three quarters have settled in Canada's three largest urban areas: Toronto, Vancouver, and Montreal.

The immigrants who are concentrating in Canada's largest cities are extremely diverse. They include wealthy business investors, family members being reunited, and refugees torn from their societies of origin. Despite differences in their migration histories and in the resources they bring to facilitate settlement in Canada, recent immigrants share many challenges during the settlement process. Growing numbers are members of visible minorities who often face barriers to full participation in contemporary Canadian society. Language barriers, lack of recognition of previous work experience and credentials, and unfamiliar social and cultural norms are challenging to all immigrants.

Newcomers settle in urban areas undergoing rapid economic and political change. The implementation of the Free Trade Agreement and subsequently the North American Free Trade Agreement in a period of fiscal constraint has accelerated the restructuring of Canada's urban economies. At the same time, provinces have altered urban boundaries, amalgamated a number of municipalities, revised the division of responsibilities between provincial and municipal levels of government, and altered funding for local services, often shifting costs from the property tax base to user fees (Frisken, 1997). Social services designed to facilitate settlement have been reduced, reorganized, and reconstituted at the same time as the diverse backgrounds of immigrants place even more demands on them (Social Planning Council of Metropolitan Toronto, 1997). Confronted with the increasing divergence of urban economies and municipal policies, immigrants' decisions about where to live in Canada have profound implications for their experiences and for their impacts on Canadian society.

In this context, the concentrated settlement of recent immigrants in Canadian cities raises urgent policy issues. Some of the most pressing include evaluating the contributions of immigrants to Canadian cities, documenting the challenges that immigrants encounter in their efforts to participate fully in Canada's urban society, and discerning the impacts of contemporary immigration on the social, political, and economic fabric of Canadian cities (Abu-Laban, 1997; Citizenship and Immigration Canada, 1998). Local governments and settlement agencies are also anxious to identify successful models of service delivery so that scarce resources can be allocated more efficiently (Municipality of Metropolitan Toronto, 1995; Mwarigha, 1997).

This chapter examines the urban nature of contemporary immigration and the public issues it raises to develop a research agenda intended to advance our understanding of contemporary social change in Canadian cities. We begin with a very brief review of current literature about citizenship that clarifies the meaning of this term in an urban context. The second section reviews current immigration trends. In section 3, we concentrate on some of the policy issues associated with immigration in Canada's large cities, commenting on relevant research findings. The theoretical and policy implications of the research agenda are then discussed in the last section.

CITIZENSHIP: CONTESTED TERRAIN

The transformation of Canadian cities by contemporary immigrants reflects and simultaneously illustrates changing notions of citizenship and changing conceptions of Canadian identity that underpin our ideas about citizenship. By virtue of their decisions to cross international borders, migrants immediately confront changes in citizenship obligations and rights (Sassen, 1996). Less well recognized is the fact that within Canada, citizenship rights and obligations at the provincial and municipal levels are in flux as provincial governments alter municipal governance. Indeed, the Canadian situation currently illustrates how citizenship flows from membership in a community rather than solely from membership in a nation-state (Yuval-Davis, 1996). For contemporary immigrants, citizenship is now a multi-tier construct that reflects their membership in a variety of collectivities that operate at different geographical scales. Immigrants are increasingly involved in transnational communities that engage actively in social networks in countries of origin and destination. At the same time, the federal Canadian state sets out specific rights and responsibilities for its members. The actions of provincial and local governments along with those of other local institutions such as school boards also affect citizenship. As a result, the settlement experiences of immigrants and their impacts on Canadian society depend very much on where immigrants settle. Examining the various ways in which citizenship is experienced by immigrants to Canada provides a prism to examine recent changes in Canadian citizenship.

Discussion of citizenship in the urban context necessarily focuses on the distinction between "formal" citizenship and "substantive" citizenship. By "formal" citizenship, Marshall (1964) refers to political rights – for example, the rights to vote and to stand for political office – all of which are conferred normally by a nation-state on those considered to be full members of the community, usually legal nationals of the country. "Substantive" citizenship is a broader topic that involves the potential to exercise a full set of civil, political and social rights (Fincher, 1997). Civil rights are rights to individual freedom, normally enforced by the rule of law and the courts, whereas political rights refer to the exercise of political power. Social rights include rights to a decent standard of living and the social heritage of society provided by the welfare state (Smith and Blanc, 1996).

Immigrants' presence in Canadian cities challenges our taken-for-granted notions about formal and substantive citizenship. Canada is one of a small number of traditional countries of immigration in which formal citizenship is ascribed to all those born within their territories and in which it is assumed that immigrants will become full citizens (Garcia, 1996).[3] Despite these expectations, as landed immigrants, refugee claimants, and illegals, immigrants' formal citizenship rights are more limited than those of the Canadian-born. Moreover, critics have argued persuasively that the substantive citizenship rights of

Table 1
Local Influence on Citizenship

Rights	Definition	Local influence
Civil	rights to individual freedom	minor
Political	exercise of political power	somewhat
Social	rights to standard of living and social heritage	major

Source: Garcia (1996), modified by author.

immigrants continue to be less than those of the native-born even after they become formal citizens (Ng, 1996; Li, 1998).

In the Canadian context, municipal governments and other local institutions affect the abilities of immigrants to exercise fully their civil, political, and social rights (table 1). Civil rights are largely the purview of federal and provincial governments in Canada; municipal governments may facilitate them, however. For example, the Equity and Access Committee of the government of the former regional municipality of Metropolitan Toronto has developed purchasing guidelines intended to increase business with minority firms. Although discrimination on the basis of race is illegal, the guidelines recognize that positive steps are needed to promote business with minority enterprises.

Political rights are relevant at multiple geographical scales. At a local level, once immigrants become citizens their votes are solicited and some immigrants have also participated actively in local social movements (Abu-Laban, 1997; Stasiulus, 1997). Again, the actions of local institutions can facilitate or impede immigrants' abilities to exercise their political rights. Another example, this time from the former city of Toronto: until the 1997 municipal election, the city had allowed candidates to be identified by number as well as by name on the ballot, aiding the participation of immigrants who were not completely fluent in English. In the new, amalgamated city of Toronto, this type of accommodation is not permitted, increasing the odds that some immigrant groups might be excluded from participating successfully.

Finally, local governments and other local institutions, such as school boards, play a crucial role in immigrants' achievement of social rights. The availability of services intended for immigrants is affected directly by local policies. Although federal and provincial policies set the broad parameters for provision of many services, implementation occurs at a local level. One result is wide variation among municipalities. Again, drawing on a Toronto example, adjacent regional municipalities pursued different policies with regards to adult immigrants who were enrolled as full-time students in high school. In the regional municipality of Metropolitan Toronto, students were eligible for welfare during the summer months when schools were closed, whereas in the regional municipality of Peel, all adult students were dropped from the welfare rolls on the last day of high school when they were deemed employable.

The impact of local institutions on citizenship is changing in many Canadian cities where provinces are delegating more responsibilities for some services to municipal governments and other local institutions, at the same time that the provinces are centralizing control over other services or assigning responsibility to special purpose agencies. Recent changes in governance have increased the diverse responses of local institutions to immigration issues. Variations among municipalities in Ontario may be particularly marked because of the shared municipal and provincial responsibility for social assistance and other income-support programs.

The recent divergence among Canada's largest urban economies has accentuated the differences in local capacities and willingness to provide services for immigrants. During the 1980s and 1990s, the economies of Canada's largest cities had very different trajectories. While Toronto boomed from 1986 to 1990, Vancouver struggled to overcome a deep recession that began in 1980. Around 1990, their situations reversed: Vancouver's economy began a period of steady growth, while Toronto suffered the worst recession since the Depression. Montreal has never recovered completely from the recession of the early 1980s, experiencing persistently high unemployment. Calgary and Edmonton, two other important immigration destinations, have had equally varied and complex economic histories. Economic circumstances affect the individual capacities of immigrants to participate fully in Canadian society, but the economic context has an even greater influence on the capacities of local institutions.

Confronted with the increasing divergence of urban economies and growing variation in the nature and quality of urban services, immigrants' decisions about where to live in Canada profoundly affect their integration into Canadian society and the extent to which they can exercise full citizenship rights. Immigrants' decisions also alter everyday life in contemporary Canadian cities in varied ways.

CURRENT IMMIGRATION IN CANADIAN CITIES

Growth in the numbers of immigrants to Canada has been accompanied by marked changes in their countries of origin and social backgrounds. These factors are linked to the increasingly transnational character of contemporary immigration. Since the 1970s, the proportion of immigrants from Europe and the United States has decreased steadily, while the number of immigrants from Asia, the Middle East, Latin America, Africa, and the Caribbean has increased. Asian immigrants have seen the largest increase now accounting for more than half (57 percent) of all recent immigrants, up from 33 percent of immigrants in the 1970s and 12 percent in the 1960s. Nearly a quarter of all recent immigrants are from Eastern Asia, where Hong Kong, the People's Republic of China, India, and Sri Lanka are major source countries.

European-born immigrants are the second largest group of recent immigrants, accounting for only 19 percent of all immigrants who arrived from 1991 to 1996. The proportion of European-born immigrants has declined steadily since 1961, when they represented 90 percent of immigrants. As a result, the European-born are still the largest group of immigrants in Canada, but in 1996, for the first time in Canadian immigration history, the European-born accounted for less than half of the foreign-born in Canada, only 47 percent. Within this European group of immigrants, there have also been significant changes in source countries. Prior to 1961, most European immigrants came from the United Kingdom, Italy, Germany, and the Netherlands. More recently, they have come from East European countries such as Poland, Romania, and the new Russian Federation (Statistics Canada, 1997). In order of their relative importance, Central and South America, Africa, the Caribbean, and Bahamas were the remaining sources of immigrants.

The social characteristics of immigrants have also changed. The shift from a manufacturing-based economy to one dominated by service sectors has affected the type of immigrants that Canada is willing to accept. Under current legislation, Canada admits immigrants for three purposes: economic development, family reunification, and humanitarian obligations. In the past three years, the federal government has responded to research suggesting that immigrants admitted to Canada on the basis of family ties had difficulties establishing themselves in the restructured economies of Canada's large cities (DeVoretz, 1995). The government has increased the proportions of immigrants admitted on economic grounds as independent and investor immigrants, people whose qualifications, work experience, and occupations are in demand in the Canadian economy or who have financial resources and entrepreneurial expertise to invest in the Canadian economy. In 1997, these entrepreneurial and skilled immigrants (with their families) accounted for approximately 58 percent of all newcomers (Citizenship and Immigration Canada, 1998). Family class immigrants, people admitted because of relatives and kin who are permanent residents of Canada, are a declining share of all immigrants, accounting for less than 28 percent of immigrants admitted in 1997. This is a rapid decline from their share of approximately 46 percent in 1994. Refugees who are admitted for humanitarian reasons are the smallest group, about 14 percent in 1997.

As the proportions of immigrants admitted under each class have changed, government resources to assist settlement have declined. Independent and investor immigrants, along with family-class immigrants, are expected to settle without benefit of much government assistance. It is expected that independent and investor immigrants are well endowed by virtue of their education, financial resources, skills, and work experience, while family class immigrants are expected to have access to financial and social assistance from family and other members of their ethnic group. Refugees are now the only class of immigrants who are eligible for social assistance upon arrival in Canada. Current settlement policies assume that the vast majority of immigrants will settle successfully without direct income support; however, in the rapidly restructuring economies of Canada's large cities, the validity of this assumption varies geographically and temporally. In the early 1990s, the economic prospects for recent immigrants were likely to be better in Vancouver than in Toronto. In 1999, economic advantage lies with Toronto.

Transnational Immigrants

Local circumstances have heightened the transnational nature of contemporary migration. Growing numbers of immigrants try to maintain social links and identities in their countries of origin and in the new country of settlement (Nolin-Hanlon and Kobayashi, 1998; Basch, Schiller, and Blanc, 1994). From the Ghanaian refugee women who enter Canada intending to accumulate funds to finance their returns to Ghana to the businessmen and businesswomen from Hong Kong who have set up astronaut households in which children and one parent remain in Canada while the other continues to live and work in Hong Kong, immigrants are actively negotiating new forms of immigration that have important implications for their citizenship rights in Canada (Man, 1997; Wong, 1998).

Technological improvements in transportation, communication, and economic and social marginalization simultaneously facilitate and encourage transnationalism.[4] As the costs of moving people, goods, and information have decreased and as television and other mass

Table 2
Top Metropolitan Regions of Recent Immigrants to Canada, 1991–1996

Metropolitan Region[1]	Number of recent immigrants	Percentage of total number
Toronto	441,030	45
Vancouver	189,660	20
Montreal	134,535	14
Ottawa-Hull	38,040	4
Calgary	33,755	3
Edmonton	27,270	3
Other	106,750	11
TOTAL	971,040	100

[1]Metropolitan Region is the Census Metropolitan Area as defined by Statistics Canada.
Source: Statistics Canada Daily, November 1997

media keep migrants in touch with events in their countries of origin, it is easier for immigrants to maintain ties to their homelands. Social, political, and economic conditions in Canadian destinations may also encourage the maintenance of close ties. Many immigrants face systemic barriers in the labour market and in the social and political spheres of Canadian life (Nolin-Hanlon and Kobayashi, 1998). Unable to exercise fully their citizenship rights in Canada, marginalized immigrants may redirect their limited resources to maintaining social networks and social identities in their countries of origin. This response to marginalization creates a cycle in which immigrants who feel marginalized in Canada have few resources with which to struggle against barriers to full citizenship in Canada. As a result, marginalization may persist, at least among the immigrant generation itself. We know little about the impact of these new behaviours and attitudes on immigrants themselves or on the cities where they settle. However, the transnational behaviour of recent migrants has raised public concerns about their commitment to Canada that will be discussed shortly.

URBAN CONCENTRATION

A very uneven geography of immigration in Canada adds to the diversity of contemporary immigration. From 1991 to 1996, Toronto was the destination for 45 percent of Canadian immigrants. Vancouver came in second taking in about 20 percent of Canadian immigrants, with another 14 percent going to Montreal. Smaller numbers of immigrants went to Ottawa-Hull, Calgary, and Edmonton (table 2).

A close relationship exists between recent provincial economic per-

Table 3
Top Five Origins and Total Recent Immigrants to Canada, 1991–1996

Country of Origin	Toronto # (Rank)	Vancouver # (Rank)	Montreal # (Rank)
Hong Kong	48,535(1)	44,715(1)	–
Sri Lanka	36,735(2)	–	–
People Rep. China	35,330(3)	22,005(3)	6,650(4)
Philippines	33,210(4)	13,610(5)	4,640(7)
India	33,185(5)	16,185(4)	4,380(8)
Taiwan	–	22,315(2)	–
Haiti	–	–	9,995(1)
Lebanon	–	–	9,610(2)
France	–	–	7,540(3)
Romania	–	–	5,225(5)
TOTAL	441,035	189,660	134,535

Source: Statistics Canada Daily, November 1997

formance and the number of immigrants. Metropolitan areas that dominate their respective provincial economies attract the majority of immigrants. Metropolitan variations in immigrants' places of origin accentuate the diversity in settlement patterns. Toronto is home to an increasing number of immigrants from Asia and the Middle East, as well as from Latin America, the Caribbean, and Africa (table 3). A similar trend is apparent in Vancouver where those born in Asia and the Middle East made up eight of every ten recent immigrants, with 50 percent coming from Hong Kong, People's Republic of China, and Taiwan. In contrast, the largest numbers of recent immigrants to Montreal came from Haiti, Lebanon, and France.

Issues

The diversity of contemporary Canadian immigration and its spatial concentration in a few large urban centres creates new challenges and opportunities. Although many of these are longstanding, they are manifested differently in each urban region. The various forms in which issues emerge reflect the migration pattern to each city, its contemporary political economy, and its unique social, economic, and political history.

Since immigration is transforming Canada's largest urban regions and, by extension, the hinterlands that they influence, almost every aspect of urban life is affected by immigration. Our discussion is necessarily selective, focusing on residential concentration, economic

mobility, service provision, and public tolerance. We have concentrated on issues that are linked directly to the changing nature of citizenship in contemporary Canadian cities. They are also the subject of public concern as expressed in various consultations, public forums, and a
scan of relevant literature. Finally, the urban aspects of these issues
have only been touched on in recent discussions of immigration and
citizenship.

RESIDENTIAL CONCENTRATION

Complementing the uneven geography of immigrant settlement among
urban areas is a complex and varied geography of residential concentration and dispersion within urban areas. Historically, in each of
Canada's large cities, multi-ethnic neighbourhoods near the downtown
centre have welcomed immigrants. Celebrated in prose and film, these
neighbourhoods have served as traditional ports of entry for immigrants arriving with few resources. It was assumed that social and economic mobility would lead to dispersion of the immigrant community
whose members would assimilate (Darroch and Marston, 1971).

Several other patterns of concentration have emerged in Canadian
cities (Balakrishnan and Hou, 1996). Some enclaves persist, despite the
economic success and social mobility of the immigrant group. In
Toronto and Montreal, for example, Portuguese immigrants are still
concentrated in areas adjacent to downtown, although second concentrations are developing in the suburbs. Economic success has enabled
the immigrant community to relocate rather than disperse (Teixeira,
1998). Other immigrants are locating directly in the suburbs, often
creating a complex geography of multi-ethnic residential districts in
which no single immigrant group is the majority of the population (Li,
1998). Recent Chinese immigrants, who come from several different
source countries, are concentrated in the suburban margins of the
Toronto metropolitan area, congregating in Mississauga, Markham,
and Richmond Hill (Lo and Wang, 1997). Other groups of immigrants
are dispersed, locating wherever affordable housing is available. For
example, Caribbean immigrants are scattered across different bor-
oughs of metropolitan Toronto with significant clusters in Scarborough, North York, and Etobicoke (Mercer, 1995). Their dispersal
reflects the availability of apartments in Toronto's rental market as
well as cultural and social differences among immigrants from the
Caribbean, who are a heterogeneous group that would not necessarily
live together (Henry, 1994). Finally, the tendency of Caribbean immigrants to live in apartments reflects a history of chain migration that
began with women entering Canada as domestic workers. As women,

their wages tended to be lower than those of men, and, as single mothers, they bore the additional burden of sole support for their families, so rental housing has often been their only option.

Although the forms of residential concentration are similar in Canada's other cities, the ethnic composition of concentrations reflects the unique immigration history of each city. For example, in Vancouver, the largest immigrant group is the Chinese, who are concentrated in West Vancouver, Richmond, and Burnaby (Ray, Halseth, and Johnson, 1997). In the Montreal area, Haitians are among the most dispersed of the immigrant groups who tend to live in neighbourhoods dominated by francophones, whereas Jamaicans live in the most segregated concentrations, mainly in the city of Montreal itself (Ray, 1998).

The persistent residential concentration of immigrants raises several important policy issues. The reasons for persistent concentration are not well understood. Is it the result of a discriminatory housing market, as in the United States? Alternatively, does concentration result from decisions about the location and levels of provision of social housing, as European experience suggests?

In general, Canadian research has emphasized that concentration is a voluntary phenomenon reflecting the desire of each immigrant community to retain its culture and identity. Recent evidence, however, suggests that residential concentrations of specific immigrant groups are not necessarily voluntary. Social housing policies and discriminatory practices on the part of landlords and managers have contributed to the concentration of some immigrants in suburban areas of Toronto. The availability of subsidized housing units at suburban locations within the former regional municipality of Metropolitan Toronto when Vietnamese immigrants arrived and the subsequent decisions to cease construction of most socially assisted housing have contributed to the persistent concentration of the Vietnamese population in specific suburban residential areas (Murdie, 1993). Although federal and provincial policies may influence the provision of socially assisted housing, municipalities are the final arbiters. In the Toronto region, several municipalities have successfully resisted efforts to increase the availability of low-cost, socially assisted housing within their jurisdictions (Frisken, 1997). The limited supply of socially assisted housing increases opportunities for discrimination in the private rental housing market. A chronic shortage of affordable units enables landlords and managers to discriminate among potential tenants on the basis of immigrant status, race, gender, and social class (Hulchanski, 1998).

The meanings and impacts of residential concentrations vary as widely as the factors contributing to residential concentrations (Peach,

1998; Ray, 1998; Hiebert, 1998). Income directly affects the extent to which residential concentration is voluntary or involuntary, but the perceived acceptance of an immigrant group is also crucial. The persistent residential segregation of Jewish-Canadians has been attributed to their efforts to maintain and support a distinct culture and to anti-Semitism that previously restricted the residential alternatives available to them (Balakrishnan and Hou, 1996).

The impacts of residential concentration are currently under intense investigation. In European cities, there is growing concern that residential concentration has deepened the exclusion of some immigrant groups from the mainstream (Madonapour, Cars, and Allen, 1998). Residential segregation of African-Americans and Latinos in American cities is also associated with deepening poverty and social malaise (Wilson, 1996; Massey and Denton, 1993). The empirical evidence linking residential concentration of immigrants with poverty in Canada is mixed. Some recent immigrants are overrepresented in residential areas where 40 percent or more of the population lives in poverty (Kazemipur and Halli, 1997). Nevertheless, country of origin and visible minority status are not related as closely to the poverty rate as are more conventional predictor variables such as unemployment rates and percentage of single-parent households (Ley and Smith, 1997). Moreover, there are marked differences among Canadian cities in the strength of the relationships between the concentration of immigrants and poverty rates. Until we have more longitudinal research describing how the relationship between residential concentration of immigrants and poverty rates is evolving in different Canadian cities, we can only speculate on the effects of residential concentration. Moreover, any speculation must take account of the different immigrant populations in each city. For example, in Toronto, only 2.4 percent of the Chinese population lives in census tracts where 40 percent or more of the population lives in poverty, whereas 16.4 percent of the Chinese population in Winnipeg lives in areas with high poverty rates (Kazemipur and Halli, 1997). Toronto's appeal to a large influx of well-educated immigrants from Hong Kong, Taiwan, and China is apparent in these figures (Lo and Wang, 1997).

Marginalization may be a more subtle process, rooted in the everyday experiences of living as an immigrant within a residential concentration of other immigrants. Starting with the experience of searching for appropriate housing, immigrants may experience discrimination that reinforces their identities as newcomers who are considered to be different from other Canadians. A recent study of the housing careers of refugees in Toronto found that experiencing discrimination from landlords on the basis of race, class, and gender played an important role in Somali women's construction of their Canadian identities as visible minorities (Hulchanski, 1998).

Every day life in a residential concentration influences immigrants' settlement in Canada in myriad ways, both beneficial and adverse. Initially, daily life is facilitated by living in a residential concentration where people speak one's language and where familiar services and goods are available (Ray, 1999). Residential concentrations also provide markets and employees for ethnic businesses that are often the first employers of immigrants (Li, 1998). In the long run, the lack of opportunities to learn and practice French and English is perceived as a major disadvantage of a residential concentration (Preston and Man, 1999). Aware of the isolation of living in a residential concentration, immigrant women value learning how to navigate the city on public transit (Rose and Ray, 1998).

Residential concentrations also affect public views about immigrants and immigration. As formerly immigrant neighbourhoods are transformed into enclaves of ethnic restaurants and festivals, the meaning of the residential concentration is also transformed (Jacobs, 1998). Certainly, the success of Little Italy, Chinatown, and Greektown in Toronto has been noticed. Other business improvement districts in the city are trying to emulate them by establishing a unique and often "ethnic" identity. Less well received are concentrations of businesses that take new forms to serve a mainly immigrant population. In the same way that "monster homes" have generated controversy about Chinese and East Indian immigrants in Vancouver (Abu-Laban, 1997; Ley, 1995; Li, 1998), "Asian" malls developed to reproduce the commercial environment of Hong Kong have become the flash point for some residents' concerns about the growing concentrations of recent immigrants in Toronto's suburbs (Preston and Lo, 1997; Qadeer, 1998).

ECONOMIC MOBILITY

In the restructured economies of Canadian cities, immigrants are encountering increasing difficulties entering the labour market. In the 1980s, newcomers had markedly lower earnings than new arrivals in the 1970s (DeVoretz, 1995; Reitz, 1997). Although the Canadian government has responded to these trends by an increasingly selective immigration policy that places more emphasis on independent and investor migrants, recent census data suggest that immigrants continue to encounter difficulties entering the labour market. Between 1990 and 1995, the average earnings of newcomers continued to decline relative to those of Canadian-born workers (Statistics Canada, 1998).[5]

The reasons for these economic difficulties are not well understood.

The original explanation that Canada was admitting too many immigrants who were not qualified for the labour market no longer holds true. Newcomers are now more likely to have a university degree than Canadian-born workers of the same age (Badets and Howatson-Lee, 1998; Reitz, 1997); however, a large number of older immigrants who arrived in the post-War period are not well educated. The age-adjusted rates for the proportions of adults with less than a grade nine education are still higher for immigrants than for Canadian-born, 15.1 percent versus 12.7 percent in 1996. Some economic difficulties of immigrants are likely due to this large number of less educated older workers – whose economic livelihoods have been particularly hurt in the recent round of restructuring – because the manufacturing jobs on which this group of workers relied have relocated and disappeared from Canada's large urban economies (Rutherford, 1997).

Others have suggested that visible minority immigrants are encountering discrimination in the labour market so that racism is impeding their economic mobility (Carey, 1999a; Infantry, 1999). One study in the 1980s demonstrated that employers distinguished among equally qualified applicants on the basis of colour and accent (Henry and Ginzberg, 1985). Recently, Reitz (1997) has suggested that recent arrivals need better institutional support. Among other suggestions, he argues for efforts to inform Canadian employers about the qualifications and work experiences of newcomers and government programs to facilitate accreditation. Acutely aware of the economic difficulties facing newcomers, non-governmental organizations have recommended more programs to encourage entrepreneurship among immigrants.

All of these recommendations to warm up the economic welcome for recent immigrants will only succeed if they are implemented locally. Municipal agencies and nongovernmental organizations that are familiar with the changing dynamics of their local economies and the resources of specific groups of newcomers are best situated to facilitate immigrants' labour market experiences. Moreover, it is at the local level where the problems of immigrants' limited economic mobility will also be borne. Particularly in Ontario, where social assistance is a shared cost program between the province and municipalities, municipalities are very interested in ensuring that immigrants succeed economically.[6]

Immigrants' economic difficulties are important in and of themselves because economic success remains the main criterion by which people are judged in Canadian society. As a result, the economic performance of immigrants has important implications for public opinion. During periods of economic prosperity, immigrants tend to be viewed with favour, while the opposite is true during periods of high unemployment

(Knowles, 1992). The attention given to the perceived, often ill-conceived, disadvantages of immigration encourages us to overlook its many advantages. Many migrants bring social connections, knowledge of foreign markets, and linguistic abilities that facilitate trade. With their efforts to maintain social ties in their countries of origin, recent immigrants can be an important source of information that will promote economic growth. Although policy-makers and analysts often refer to the beneficial contributions of immigrants (Municipality of Metropolitan Toronto, 1995), these benefits are rarely documented and celebrated.[7]

SERVICE PROVISION

For many immigrants, full participation in Canadian society depends on the provision of appropriate services at a local level. Even among affluent immigrants, settlement services ease their integration into a new and unfamiliar place. In addition to services targeted directly at immigrants, income support programs and social services such as health, housing, and education affect the well-being of immigrants. Local public services are funded by complex and variable arrangements that involve all three levels of government (GTA Task Force, 1996). In Ontario, an additional layer of complexity is added by the presence of two tiers of municipal governments: regional and local municipalities. For example, the Greater Toronto Area consists of four regional municipalities, twenty-four local municipalities and the amalgamated City of Toronto. School boards and other special purpose districts are also involved in the provision of local services that affect immigrant settlement. During the 1990s, the federal government dealt with the fiscal deficit by reducing transfers to individuals and provinces. Both actions affected immigrants. Reductions in transfers to individuals adversely affected immigrants, who had greater difficulty qualifying for income support and who then received less income from the various programs when they did qualify. Many provinces responded to reduced federal transfers by redrawing municipal boundaries, reallocating responsibilities, revamping decision-making processes, and altering financial arrangements for local services (Evans, 1997). As a result, the availability and quality of local services have deteriorated. In Toronto, agencies providing services for immigrants were among the agencies most likely to report reductions in the number and quality of services offered to their clients (Social Planning Council of Metropolitan Toronto, 1997).

Services for immigrants have been affected doubly by the federal government's efforts to reduce the deficit. Direct funding from the federal government for settlement services declined at the same time that provincial governments reduced funding for immigrant services and, more generally, for local services. Until recently, funding for school boards and municipalities had declined steadily in Ontario, Alberta, British Columbia, and Québec, the locations of the five cities that are the main immigrant destinations. Québec is the only province where provincial funding for immigrant settlement services has been maintained and slightly increased during the 1990s (Reichhold, 1998).

In this context, school boards, municipalities, and other special purpose districts are reconsidering the provision of services for immigrants. For example, the Toronto School Board has hired interpreters to facilitate parent-teacher meetings, however, the practice may be discontinued. Parental involvement in schools is a crucial predictor of immigrant children's academic success, so any decision to reduce interpretation services places immigrant children at a disadvantage (Bernhard, Nirdosh, et al., 1998). Reductions in general services also place additional burdens on immigrants. The Toronto Board's recent decision to close all its adult education schools, where adults could study full-time, has significant impacts upon immigrants who must complete high school to qualify for college, university, and technical training.

For immigrant service agencies, the ongoing challenges of serving a changing population are now compounded by the impacts of funding cuts and economic downturns in Toronto at the beginning of the decade, in Vancouver recently, and persistently in Montreal. The agencies have adapted by narrowing the range of services that they offer, just at the time that research suggests immigrants need additional institutional support to settle successfully[8] (Richmond, 1996; Reitz, 1997).

Even where funding has been maintained, immigrant service agencies find that cuts in other parts of the welfare state mean that immigrants who are not eligible for their services return seeking help. As one Montreal service provider recently said "we help them because who else will?" (Reichhold, 1998). Despite the efforts of many institutions to provide services in immigrants' languages and in culturally appropriate ways, health, education, and other services are still not available in their first languages for many immigrants (Weinfeld, 1997). Current funding reductions have overtaken questions about how to provide services to immigrant communities. The mix of services that should be provided by ethno-specific agencies versus those that are provided most effectively and cost-efficiently by mainstream agencies is still being debated (Wayland, 1992). Nevertheless, there is no question that limited access to social services provided in their own languages and in culturally appropriate ways will hinder successful settlement of newcomers (Weinfeld, 1997).

The question of how to pay for the services that immigrants use has resurfaced (Immigration Legislative Review, 1997). In one of its most controversial recommendations, the Immigration Legislative Review suggested that any immigrant over the age of 5 years who requires language training should be required to pay its full costs. The rationale for this recommendation states that Canadians expect people to pay their way (Immigration Legislative Review, 1997). The recommendation flies in the face of research suggesting that, in aggregate over their lifetimes, immigrants pay more in taxes than the value of all the public services that they consume. The growing propensity for user fees to finance local services reflects the unwillingness of municipal politicians and school board trustees to maintain and improve local services when they are increasingly dependent on property taxes as their main revenue source (Frisken, 1999).

The changing fiscal arrangements between municipalities and provinces and between the provinces and federal government are altering the availability of services, their suitability, and their terms of payment. In Toronto, reductions in social services combined with the economic difficulties of recent newcomers have renewed concerns that an immigrant underclass living in concentrated poverty areas may be emerging for the first time in Canada (Kazemipur and Halli, 1997; Ley and Smith, 1997). In Vancouver and Montreal, there is only a weak link between poverty areas and immigration, perhaps because of better economic conditions in Vancouver during the first half of the decade and stable funding for immigrant services in Montreal.

TOLERANCE

Without sufficient services, struggling to participate successfully in restructured urban economies, and concentrated in specific neighbourhoods of Canada's largest cities, immigrants still fight for tolerance and public acceptance. Until recently, surveys had shown that tolerance for difference defined on the basis of skin colour, accent, and place of birth was increasing steadily in Canadian society. The most tolerant attitudes were expressed by the residents of Canada's largest cities where society was most diverse and everyday life brought newcomers into contact with the Canadian-born (Economic Council of Canada, 1991). A new report suggests that residents of large cities are still more favourably inclined towards immigration than other Canadians (Palmer, 1997). The ratios of positive to negative views of immigration in each city range from 3.41 in Vancouver to 1.91 and 1.33 in Montreal and Toronto, respectively. In each city, positive views outnumber negative views, although the margin is smaller in Toronto than elsewhere.[9]

Toronto residents' views about immigration are more like those of other residents of Ontario than the views of residents of Montreal and Vancouver are similar to those held by residents in the rest of their respective provinces. Outside Toronto, the majority of Ontario residents hold positive views of immigration by a ratio of 1.18. In contrast, residents of Québec and British Columbia who live outside their respective metropolitan centres are less favourably inclined towards immigration. In Québec, positive and negative views are almost equal with a ratio of 0.99 for positive views to negative views, while the ratio of positive to negative views for British Columbians outside Vancouver is 0.84. While the survey results suggest that Torontonians hold less positive views about recent immigration than residents of Canada's other metropolitan centres, the majority of views are still positive. Moreover, the broader provincial context in Ontario is more receptive for immigrants than in either Québec or British Columbia.

The diversity of views among residents of Canada's three largest cities suggests that local events and local circumstances shape public opinion. In Toronto, governments at all levels and the business community have promoted an image of ethnic harmony despite a series of events pointing to deep social inequalities, some of which are rooted in race and immigrant status (Croucher, 1997). Relatively less support for immigration in Toronto, compared with Montreal and Vancouver, may reflect popular discomfort about growing inequality in Toronto, however. Although many social groups are vulnerable in Toronto's less equal society, immigrants may be the most visible group. Historically, Canadian tolerance for difference has declined during periods of economic difficulty (Knowles, 1992). Recent economic restructuring in Toronto, where real family incomes fell 10 percent between 1991 and 1996, may have contributed to less tolerance. Certainly, the recent reductions in services that are expected to impede immigrants' integration are unlikely to improve popular opinions. Indeed, the integration of the most vulnerable immigrants is likely to be hampered at a time when residents of Toronto are less willing to tolerate difference.

The growing social diversity of Toronto, Vancouver, and Montreal raises questions about Canadian identity. In Canada's largest cities, increasing diversity has been accompanied by popular debate about the defining characteristics of the Canadian identity. Recent immigrants do not always fit popular conceptions. With our highly selective immigration policy, growing numbers of educated, middle-class, and sometimes very affluent immigrants are settling in Canada's largest cities. The newcomers are accustomed to participate fully in their societies of origin, while some Canadian-born and established immigrants may assume that immigrants must work their way into Canadian society.

Metropolitan variations in the meaning and salience of identity issues are also evident. One legacy of Québec's Quiet Revolution is a more coherent and hegemonic identity for Québécois to which immigrants who concentrate in Montreal are expected to conform (Ray, 1999). In Vancouver, some commentators are less sanguine, stating that residential and commercial concentrations of Chinese and other South Asian immigrants indicate that "assimilation has been superseded by the reality of cultural takeover" (Brunet, 1997). Similar concerns have been expressed about recent immigrants from many countries of origin in Toronto (Carey, 1999b).

Current disputes and discomfort centred around the transformation of Canadian cities by recent immigrants pale in comparison to the conflicts that have occurred in the past (Knowles, 1992). Nevertheless, in a recent survey, 38 percent of a sample of Chinese immigrants in Toronto reported that they had experienced discrimination, despite their middle-class status and relative affluence (Carey, 1999a). While public expressions of animosity about recent immigration are more muted than in the past, its persistence and the discrimination experienced by immigrants suggests that full participation in Canadian society still eludes many.

The transnational nature of contemporary migration adds to the urgency of identifying the factors that enable local institutions to encourage urban societies to negotiate difference and accommodate the diverse members of municipal populations. Contemporary migrants are more likely than their predecessors to actively maintain social ties with their countries of origin. The impacts of transnationalism are ambiguous. On the one hand, the societies where immigrants settle benefit from their knowledge and social contacts in countries of origin for economic and social purposes (Municipality of Metropolitan Toronto, 1995). On the other hand, for many immigrants who are suffering economically in Canada's restructured urban economies, the resources devoted to maintaining transnational ties may reduce those available to facilitate settlement in Canada (Nolin-Hanlon and Kobayashi, 1998).

CONCLUSION

The diverse backgrounds of current immigrants and the diversity of their experiences in different Canadian cities call into question the wisdom of making generalized statements about immigrants. Even within a single metropolitan area, there are significant variations in geographical patterns of residential concentration, economic opportunities, the provision of services, and social history that influence immigrant settlement. The varied settlement patterns, needs, and interests of diverse immigrant populations must be taken into serious considera-tion in any meaningful discussion of civil society. Changes in metro-politan areas take particular social and built forms in diverse neigh-bourhood settings that require locally sensitive policy-making and citizen response (Mercer, 1995). With the increasing numbers and diversity of immigrants entering various socio-economic sectors of Canadian society and the concomitant increase in public concern over competition for access to social services and Canada's capacity to absorb immigrants, the challenges of diversity to civic society need to be addressed.

Diversity originates in the specific social, political, and economic his-tories and geographies of Canadian cities. For immigrants, the selec-tion of a destination city has a crucial impact on their abilities to par-ticipate fully in Canadian society. Despite a national immigration policy and provincial settlement policies, the diverse ways that local institutions respond to immigrants play a critical role in their settle-ment in Canadian society and the extent to which they can exercise cit-izenship rights.

For municipal governments, the challenge of building inclusive urban societies requires that local governments and other local institu-tions take account successfully of diverse interests and needs. Tradi-tional municipal responsibilities and practices, such as land-use plan-ning, must be modified to accommodate the wishes and interests of culturally and socially diverse urban populations (Qadeer, 1997). Awareness of the diverse needs of the local population is a prerequisite for designing and delivering inclusionary local services. A recent study of Australian municipal governments showed that many municipal politicians and government officials lack knowledge of the diversity of local populations and the ways that diverse needs can be accommo-dated in planning and service provision (Thompson et al., 1998). In the Canadian context, similar research is needed to establish municipal governments' awareness of diversity, to evaluate the best practices for promoting inclusionary urban societies, and to identify the resources needed by municipal governments and other local institutions to imple-ment best practices. Additional research is also needed to determine the barriers encountered by immigrants and design effective policies to reduce and remove barriers. This research will have to compare the experiences of immigrants among Canadian cities, taking account of the local knowledge of immigrant and Canadian-born residents in each city.[10]

In addition to additional research, some analysts have called for reconsideration of the current division of responsibilities and powers among municipalities, the provinces, and the federal government. The former Regional Municipality of Metropolitan Toronto went so far as to suggest that the federal government should direct funds to the municipal level to finance public services for immigrants (Municipality of Metropolitan Toronto, 1997). Others have advocated disentanglement of federal, provincial, and municipal responsibilities in which the provincial government would assume all responsibility for social services, while physical services would be a municipal responsibility to be funded from the property tax (GTA Task Force, 1996). The challenges of building inclusionary cities may very well spur revision of the powers and responsibilities of each level of government.

This chapter has argued that contemporary immigration, with its urban focus and its transnational character, challenges universal notions of citizenship within a single nation-state. Citizenship emerges as a multi-tiered, fluid relationship between an individual and a number of communities. While we have concentrated on communities defined geographically by political boundaries, communities based on other social characteristics, such as gender and ethnicity, may also cross political boundaries (Yuval-Davis, 1996). Exploration of the evolving nature of citizenship for immigrants in various urban societies will contribute to ongoing debates about emerging forms of citizenship and their significance (Garcia, 1997; Smith and Blanc, 1997). The research will also contribute to current debates about the rise of city-states, debates that have mainly concentrated on the economic aspects of city-states, overlooking their social and political significance.

Immigration is transforming Canadian society in distinct urban places. Contemporary urban change can only be understood by taking account of recent immigration and its impact. In the same way, the social issues raised by immigration can only be understood as urban issues, warranting a return to a policy agenda that takes cities seriously.

NOTES

1 In 1997, Canada also admitted more than 200,000 temporary migrants – mainly students, executives and other temporary workers, and refugee claimants – whose cases have not been decided (Citizenship and Immigration Canada, 1998).

2 Recent data show that the foreign-born share of the Canadian population has increased from an average of 15 percent between 1951 and 1991 to 17.4 percent in 1996, the highest proportion in over fifty years (Statistics Canada, 1997).

3 The extent to which immigrants are ever able to participate on equal footing with the native-born is hotly debated (Ng, 1996; Li, 1998).

4 Transnationalism has a long history. Immigration historians have documented the efforts of earlier immigrants to North America to maintain social ties with their societies of origin; however, technological change has altered the quality and intensity of ties that can be retained. At the same time, increasing economic disparities between developed and less developed countries, which encourage migration in the first place, heighten the necessity for many migrants to send remittances and other forms of economic support back to their countries of origin.

5 These are preliminary findings that require much more detailed analysis taking account of the structure of the Canadian-born and immigrant workforces; nevertheless, the raw data suggest that the declines in immigrants' economic success that were observed in the 1980s are continuing.

6 In some jurisdictions, this interest has translated into enforcement measures. The regional municipality of Peel is the location of a pilot program to monitor sponsorship agreements for family-class immigrants. Since the last recession, when real family incomes fell 10 percent in the Toronto Census Metropolitan Area, many families have been unable to fulfil their sponsorship obligations. This is a pilot project that is being closely watched by local governments in the rest of the Greater Toronto Area and elsewhere.

7 For an exception, see the recent articles in *The Toronto Star* series entitled "Beyond 2000."

8 For an example of the roles of local services and intraurban variations in their provision, see Permezel (1999).

9 The survey results were interpreted negatively by Palmer (1997), who highlighted the disparities in ratios of positive views to negative views between residents of Toronto and residents of Vancouver and Montreal. This interpretation has been highlighted in the media (Lungren, 1997), where reporters have overlooked the fact that positive views still outweigh negative views in Toronto.

10 A recent analysis of the municipal government of Franfurt-am-Main (Lehrer and Friedmann, 1997) illustrates the benefits of a comparative approach grounded in careful analysis of local viewpoints.

2 Aboriginal People
    in Urban Areas

EVELYN PETERS

Urban Aboriginal people have been weakly and problematically incorporated into Canada's urban policy scene. This is true whether one looks at individual cities or at the national impact of federal and provincial policies affecting Aboriginal peoples. There have always been Aboriginal people living in urban areas in Canada, though for much of Canada's history since contact, non-Aboriginal Canadians have tended to view their presence in cities with misgivings. This chapter addresses the source of these misgivings and suggests alternative views of Aboriginal people and urban life.

The largest increase in the urban Aboriginal[1] population has occurred since the early 1950s. After 1960 a substantial literature emerged that addressed the implications of the movement to cities. While attention to the issue had declined by the late 1980s, the urban Aboriginal population had not, and the 1991 census suggested that many cities had substantial numbers of people with Aboriginal origins living in them. Now public attention seems to be drawn to urban Aboriginal people again. In 1992, the Royal Commission on Aboriginal Peoples identified urban Aboriginal people as an important emphasis in their research. Urban Aboriginal people have been featured in chapters in recent books on Aboriginal people generally (Comeau and Santin, 1990; Frideres, 1993; Richardson, 1994), a bibliography (Kastes, 1993), and a book of "life stories" (Shorten, 1991). The establishment in 1997 of the federal government's Urban Aboriginal Strategy and a recent book on urban reserves (Barron and Garcea, 1999) also demonstrate a growing interest in urban Aboriginal peoples.

There has been very little writing by Aboriginal people on the experience of migrating to and living in urban areas (but see Armstrong, 1985; Culleton, 1983; Maracle, 1992). Most of the available literature comes from non-Aboriginal academics, consultants, and researchers. From the beginning, Aboriginal urbanization has been presented as problematic in this literature. The way this "social problem" was defined provided a framework for identifying appropriate policy responses. There is evidence that this framework is increasingly being challenged by Aboriginal people. In this context, it is appropriate to provide a critical assessment of non-Aboriginal writing about Aboriginal urbanization.

The primary object of this paper is not to explore the situation of Aboriginal people in urban areas. The work cited above is available to interested readers. Moreover, I am not an Aboriginal person. I am an academic of Dutch and Ukrainian origins, who is not qualified to speak about the urban experience for Aboriginal people. What I do feel qualified to write about, in a critical way, is how I and my peers have conceptualized the situation of urban Aboriginal people, what some of the implications have been, and what are some possible ways forward.[2]

The chapter begins with a brief profile of Aboriginal people and organizations in urban areas. Next, it compares Aboriginal urbanization patterns to cycles of public interest in their situation. The chapter moves to an exploration of how Aboriginal people in cities have been labelled problematic, and how this problem has been characterized. The final sections of the chapter present an alternative approach and identify some ways to make cities better places for Aboriginal people and cultures.

A PROFILE OF CONTEMPORARY URBAN ABORIGINAL PEOPLE

Population Characteristics

A brief profile of the characteristics of Aboriginal people in urban areas cannot possibly do justice to all the important issues facing this population, nor can it depict the diversity of urban Aboriginal populations or of urban areas. The following paragraphs highlight five themes: urbanization rates; socio-economic, legal, and cultural characteristics; and urban institutions.

In 1991,[3] about half (49.5 percent) of those who identified themselves as Aboriginal people in Canada lived in urban areas (table 1). Urbanization rates varied for different groups of Aboriginal people.

Table 1
Location of Residence, Aboriginal Identity Population[1], 1991

	Total Aboriginal[2]	Registered North American Indian[3]	Non-Registered North American Indian[4]	Métis[5]	Inuit
Total	625,710	351,590	104,260	135,260	36,215
On-Reserve	183,600 (29.3%)	173,655 (49.4%)	3,600 (3.5%)	4,535 (3.4%)	620 (1.7%)
Off-Reserve	412,105 (70.7%)	177,940 (50.6%)	100,660 (96.5%)	130,725 (96.6%)	35,590 (98.2%)
Urban,[6] Off-Reserve	309,940 (49.5%)	143,910 (40.9%)	72,150 (69.3%)	87,850 (64.9%)	7,151 (21.9%)

Source: Privy Council Office, Royal Commission on Aboriginal Peoples, Research Directorate, Customized Data from the 1991 Aboriginal Peoples Survey, pp. 20–1. Ottawa: Minister of Supply and Services, 1994.

Notes:

[1] These data have not been adjusted for non-enumeration or under-counting.

[2] Because some respondents (approximately 1 percent) gave multiple Aboriginal identities, summing identity categories will result in overcounting. The "Total Aboriginal" category does not double count those giving multiple Aboriginal identities.

[3] The North American Indian population registered according to the Indian Act of Canada. This category *excludes*: 4,830 North American Indians with registration status not stated in the APS; 17,060 Metis who reported being registered according to the Indian Act (they are counted as Metis); 2,080 Inuit who reported being registered according to the *Indian Act* (they are counted as Inuit); an estimated 58,000 persons residing on unenumerated Indian reserves or settlements.

[4] Those who identified themselves as North American Indian.

[5] Those who identified themselves as Métis.

[6] This number does not include urban reserves.

Slightly more than 40 percent of Registered Indians lived in cities. In comparison, the majority of non-registered Indians and Métis live in urban areas. The Inuit were the least urbanized of all the Aboriginal groups.

Until recently, there was very little statistical information available on the socio-economic characteristics of urban Aboriginal people across the country. Surveys conducted in 1978 and 1982 by the Institute of Urban Studies in Winnipeg provided information about Aboriginal people in Winnipeg, Saskatoon, and Regina (Clatworthy, 1980; Clatworthy and Hull, 1983), but there was little in the way of more recent information that provided wider geographic coverage. Data from the 1991 Aboriginal Peoples Survey demonstrated that many of the attributes highlighted for urban Aboriginal people in these prairie

Table 2
Socio-Economic Characteristics of People Who Identify Themselves as Aboriginal in
Selected Census Metropolitan Areas[1]

	Aboriginal Population (%)	Total Metropolitan Population (%)
Ages 0–14	35.9	19.8
Females in 25+ Population	57.5	52.1
Unemployment Rate	23.4	9.4
Adults 15+ With Total Income Less Than $10,000	48.4	25.3
Adults 15+ With Total Income Greater Than $40,000	6.4	19.0
Residence Needs Major Repairs	12.8	6.9
Moved between 1986 and 1991	46.1	50.4
Moved in Last 12 Months	20.4	17.6
Total Population	159,945	16,665,360

Sources: Statistics Canada, 1991 Census, cat. nos. 93-339 and 93-340, Ottawa, Minister of Industry, 1991; Statistics Canada, Aboriginal Peoples Survey, cat. no. 94-327, Ottawa, 1993.
Note:
[1]Data are available for Halifax, Montreal, Ottawa-Hull, Toronto, Winnipeg, Regina, Saskatoon,
  Calgary, Edmonton, Vancouver, and Victoria.

cities held in other urban areas and in more recent years. Table 2 shows
that the urban Aboriginal population tended to be younger than the
total urban population, with a higher proportion of women, particularly in the main child-bearing years. Unemployment rates were much
higher for Aboriginal people than for total metropolitan populations,
and many more Aboriginal people had relatively low incomes. While
there were some Aboriginal people earning incomes of $40,000 or
more, the proportion was much lower than the total metropolitan population. Because of their low incomes, Aboriginal people were more
likely to live in poor housing. As other researchers have found, migration rates were similar for Aboriginal and non-Aboriginal people.
   It is important to recognize, however, the variation in the characteristics of the Aboriginal population in different urban areas. Table 3
compares major Canadian cities with respect to some characteristics of
Aboriginal residents. Information concerning the number of individuals who identified themselves as Aboriginal is available from the 1996
Canadian census. The remainder of the data in the table are based on
the population that identified itself as Aboriginal pursuant to the 1991
Aboriginal Peoples Survey. In 1996, the number of Aboriginal people
varied from slightly more than two thousand in Halifax, to more than

Table 3
Selected Characteristics of People Who Identify Themselves As Aboriginal in Major
Metropolitan Areas, 1991

	1996 Census			1991 APS		
	Number Who Identify As Aboriginal	City Popu-lation (%)	Metis (%)	Understand Aboriginal Language (%)	Unemploy-ment Rate (%)	Moved since 1986 (%)
Halifax	2,110	0.6	-	-	-	38.2
Montreal	9,960	0.3	24.7	14.1*	13.1	42.1
Ottawa-Hull	11,605	1.1	20.6	22.2*	12.7	47.0
Toronto	16,100	0.4	5.6*	25.3*	11.2	36.1
Winnipeg	45,750	6.9	21.3	49.1	27.3	44.1
Regina	13,605	7.0	33.8	49.2	25.8	57.8
Saskatoon	16,165	7.4	46.9	61.1	32.7	44.2
Calgary	15,195	1.8	30.4	37.3	18.1	52.5
Edmonton	32,820	3.8	46.2	50.2	28.1	46.1
Vancouver	31,140	1.7	16.3	39.6	29.0	49.4

Source: Statistics Canada, 1991, Census, cat. no. 94-327, Ottawa: Minister of Industry, 1993; Statistics Canada, Aboriginal Peoples Survey, cat nos. 94-327, 89-533, and 89-534, Ottawa: Minister of Industry, 1994; Statistics Canada, Census, cat. no. 95-206-XPB, Ottawa: Minister of Industry, 1998.
* The coefficient of variation of the estimate is between 16.7% and 33.3%. These estimates should be used with caution to support a conclusion.

forty-five thousand in Winnipeg. Aboriginal people comprised the largest proportion of the metropolitan populations of Winnipeg, Regina, and Saskatoon. Cultural characteristics also varied. Prairie cities contained the largest number of Métis people. They also contained the most people who understand an Aboriginal language. The latter dimension varied from 14.1 percent in Montreal to 61.1 percent in Saskatoon. With respect to socio-economic characteristics, unemployment rates were highest in Saskatoon (32.7 percent) and lowest in Toronto (11.2 percent).

Aboriginal people living in urban areas are subject to a complicated legal regime. According to the 1991 Aboriginal Peoples Survey, Indians registered under the *Indian Act* of Canada constituted the largest legal category. The federal government has held that it was responsible only for Registered Indians and that these responsibilities were limited to reserve borders (Morse, 1989). Only a few federally funded services are available to Registered Indians generally, no matter where they live. The most notable of these are non-insured health benefits and post-secondary educational assistance. The federal government has regarded non-registered Indians and Métis as a provincial responsibility. In

Table 4
Origins of the Aboriginal Population, Regina, Saskatchewan, 1982

First Nations	
Reserve origins:	27 reserves in Saskatchewan plus others in other provinces.
Treaty area of origin:	Treaties 1, 2, 3, 4, 5, 6, 7, 9.
First Nation of origin:	Assiniboine, Blackfoot, Cree, Dakota, Ojibwa and possibly others.
Provincial origins:	BC, Alberta, Saskatchewan, Manitoba, Ontario, Nova Scotia.
Countries of origin:	Canada and the United States.
Métis	
Provincial origins:	BC, Alberta, Saskatchewan, Manitoba, Ontario.
Countries of origin:	Canada and the United States.

Source: Peters, 1994.

1939, the courts ruled that the Inuit would be considered as Indians for the purposes of clarifying federal jurisdiction.

These categories are further complicated by differences between registration status and band membership. Under Bill C-31, passed in 1985, registration and band membership were separated. After Bill C-31, bands were given the opportunity to draw up and adopt codes governing membership, while registration continues to be governed according to (revised) *Indian Act* regulations. Band membership involves a variety of rights and privileges with respect to an individual's band of origin, including rights of residency on the reserve. Some urban Aboriginal people are registered but not band members, while some are band members but not registered.

The complex amalgam of legal categories that has emerged has created inequalities for and among urban Aboriginal people. Registered Indians living on reserves have access to federally funded programs not available to urban Indians. Registered Indians in urban areas have access to some federally funded programs unavailable to other Aboriginal people. Band members have opportunities to participate in self-government through their bands of origin. These opportunities are denied to Aboriginal people who do not have band membership.[4] While some urban programs have been established through federal, provincial and municipal funding, these initiatives are unevenly distributed, with short-term and often limited funding.

The cultural diversity of Aboriginal people in urban areas is not often recognized. Employing data from the 1991 Aboriginal Peoples

Survey, the Royal Commission on Aboriginal Peoples (1996: 592–7) found that large metropolitan areas were extremely complex in terms of the cultural composition of Aboriginal people living there. Vancouver, for example, had residents from more than thirty-six different First Nations cultures and Toronto had residents from more than sixteen. Even in Winnipeg, which was relatively homogeneous, the population was composed of 5 percent Chippewyan, 25 percent Cree, 2 percent Dakota, 68 percent Ojibwa, and a less than 1 percent from other Nations. Other characteristics point to even more diversity among urban Aboriginal populations. In Regina in 1982, for example, First Nations people living in the city came from twenty-seven reserves, eight treaty areas, at least five First Nations, six provinces, and two countries. Métis people came from five provinces and two countries (table 4).

Researchers in the past commented on the paucity of Aboriginal institutions representing or providing services for urban Aboriginal people (Clatworthy and Gunn, 1981; Falconer, 1985 and 1990; Frideres, 1984). At present, however, many large urban areas have a considerable number of organizations controlled and staffed by Aboriginal people and that focus on the permanent urban Aboriginal population. Winnipeg appears to be among urban centres with the most well-developed set of urban Aboriginal institutions (table 5).[5] While some of these organizations have a very long history, many have been established in recent years. Collectively, these organizations provide a fairly broad range of services to Aboriginal people.

There are several features of the Winnipeg situation that appear to be unique. Unlike most urban areas with large Aboriginal populations, Winnipeg has two organizations, the Aboriginal Centre Inc. and the Winnipeg Native Family Economic Development Corporation (WNFED), that have focused on community development and attempted to provide inter-agency links and networks. In 1992 a non-profit board representing a variety of Aboriginal service organizations purchased and renovated Winnipeg's CPR Station in the heart of the city's core area (Winnipeg Free Press, 29 December 1992 and 4 January 1995). The station, renamed the Aboriginal Centre of Winnipeg, brought under one roof a variety of Aboriginal organizations. It attempted to provide a place for Aboriginal activities and to serve as a focal point for the urban Aboriginal community. The Aboriginal Centre has acted as an anchor for the development across the street of the Neeganin ("our place" in Cree) complex, the first phase to include the construction of a spiritual and cultural centre – the Circle of Life Thunderbird House (Neeginan Development Corporation, 1999). WNFED is

Table 5
Aboriginal Institutions in Winnipeg, 1994

Organization	Primary Focus	Year Established
A-Bah-Nu-Gee Child Care	Child & Family Services	1984
Aboriginal Centre Inc.	Social Service, Community and Economic Development	1990
Aboriginal Council of Winnipeg	Political	1990
Aboriginal Literacy Foundation	Education	1990
Aiyawin Corporation	Housing	1983
Anishinabe Oway-Ishi	Employment	1989
Anishinabe RESPECT	Employment	1981
Bear Clan Patrol Inc.	Safety	1992
Children of the Earth High School	Education	1991
Indian Family Centre Inc.	Religious/Social Service	1973
Indian Metis Friendship Centre	Cultural/Social Service	1959
Iwkewak Justice Society	Justice	1986
Kinew Housing	Housing	1970
Ma Mawi Chi Itata Centre	Child and Family Services	1984
Manitoba Association for Native Languages	Language	1984
MMF – Winnipeg Region	Political	?
Native Clan	Inmates	1970
Native Employment Services	Employment	1972
Native United Church	Religious	?
Native Women's Transition Centre	Housing	?
Nee-Gawn-Ah-Kai Day Care Centre	Child-Care	1986
Neechi Foods Community Store	Economic Development	?
Original Women's Network	Women's Resource Centre	?
Payuk Inter-Tribal Housing Co-op	Housing	1985
Three Fires Society	Cultural	1982
Winnipeg Council of First Nations	Political	1991
Winnipeg Native Families Economic Development Corporation	Social Service, Community and Economic Development	

Sources: Clatworthy et al.,1995; Peters, 1995.

an umbrella organization created to bring together a number of different projects in order to provide linkages and a support network within the Aboriginal community. Winnipeg also appears to be unique in that it has Métis, First Nations and pan-Aboriginal political organizations presently functioning simultaneously. Like many other Aboriginal political bodies, these organizations are exploring self-governance options (Helgason, 1995).

Table 6
Total and Off-Reserve Registered Indian Population, 1959-1996.

	Registered Indian Population	Off-Reserve		Enfranchisements[1] Per 5-Year Period	
		Number[2]	Percent	Number	Percentage
1959[3]	179,126	30,372	16.9		
1961	191,709			2077	1.1
1966	224,164	43,746	19.5	3216	1.4
1971	257,619	69,106	26.8	3009	1.2
1976	288,938	79,301	27.4	1094	0.4
1981	323,782	96,290	29.6	40	0.01
1986[4]	415,898	123,642	31.9	14	0.00
1991	511,791	207,032	40.5		
1996	610,874	256,505	42.0		

Sources: Information Canada, Perspective Canada: A Compendium of Social Statistics, p. 244, Ottawa: Minister of Industry, 1974; DIAND, Indian Affairs: Facts and Figures, Ottawa: Indian Affairs Branch, 1967; DIAND, Basic Departmental Data, p. 5, Ottawa: Minister of Supply and Services, 1992; Powless, J., DIAND, personal communication, 1994; DIAND, Basic Departmental Data, p. 5, Ottawa: Minister of Supply and Services, 1997.

Notes:
[1]Figures for 1961 and 1966 are estimates based on DIAND's fiscal year, figures for 1971 to 1986 are based on the calender year.
[2]Not including those living on crown land.
[3]Statistics on off-reserve residency began to be collected only in 1959 (Bradley, 1993).
[4]In 1985, the *Indian Act* was amended to allow, through Bill C-31, the restoration of Indian status to those who had lost it due to discriminatory clauses in the *Indian Act*.

Urbanization Patterns

It is difficult to build up a reliable historic picture of the movement of Aboriginal people to Canadian cities. Changing definitions of ancestry in census data (Goldman, 1993) make it difficult to compare population numbers over time. The Indian Register kept by the Department of Indian Affairs omits Métis and non-registered Indian people, dates only from 1959, and identifies residence on or off reserves, but not in particular cities.[6] Despite problems with finding accurate, comparable data, it appears that Aboriginal urbanization is a comparatively recent phenomenon. In this section, data from the Indian Register, the Aboriginal Peoples Survey and the census provide information on Aboriginal populations in urban areas.

While early studies show that, even in the 1950s, some Aboriginal people had been relatively long-term residents of cities (Boek and Boek, 1959: 20; Davis, 1965: 372; Lurie, 1967), overall urbanization rates

Table 7
Aboriginal People in Major Metropolitan Centres, 1951–1991.

	1951	1961	1971[1]	1981	1991[2]	1996[3]
Halifax	–	–	–	–	1185	2110
Montreal	296	507	3215	14450	6775[4]	9960
Ottawa-Hull	–	–	–	4370	6915	11605
Toronto	805	1196	2990	13495	14205	16100
Winnipeg	210	1082	4940	16575	35150	45750
Regina	160	539	2860	6575	11020	13605
Saskatoon	48	207	1070	4350	11920	16165
Calgary	62	335	2265	7310	14075	15195
Edmonton	616	995	4260	13750	29235	32820
Vancouver	239	530	3000	16080	25030	31140

Sources: Statistics Canada, Census and Aboriginal Peoples Survey, cat. no. 94-327, Ottawa: Minister of Industry, 1993; DIAND, Customized Data, 1981; Information Canada, Perspective Canada: A Compendium of Social Statistics, p. 244, Ottawa: Minister of Industry, 1974; Statistics Canada, Census, cat. no. 95-206-XPB, Ottawa, Minister of Industry, 1998.
Perspective Canada, 1974:244.
Notes:
[1]The 1971 data do not include the Inuit.
[2]Individuals who identified with an Aboriginal group pursuant to the Aboriginal Peoples Survey.
[3]Individuals who identified with an Aboriginal group in the 1996 Census.
[4]The population for the Kahnawake and Kanesatake Reserves which are in the Montreal CMA
  boundaries were not enumerated in 1981, 1991 or 1996. Population estimates (5,218 and 618
  respectively) were included in 1981 counts but not included thereafter.

appear to have been low. There is no statistical information available about Métis urbanization trends, but it appears that relatively few Registered Indians left their reserves between the turn of the century and the 1950s. In 1959, only 16.9 percent of Registered Indians lived off-reserve, with probably an even smaller proportion resident in cities (table 6). In 1981, 29.6 percent of Registered Indians lived off-reserve, and, by 1996, that proportion had increased to 42 percent.

Table 7 shows census statistics on the changing number of people with Aboriginal ancestry in major metropolitan centres. Data for the years 1951 to 1981 in this table are based on answers to the census question on ethnic origin or ancestry. While the data for various years are not directly comparable because of changing definitions and questions on census forms (Goldman, 1993), they present some rough estimates of the size of the urban Aboriginal population. Changes in the census question on ancestry make it impossible to compare 1991 data to data for earlier years.[7] The 1991 statistics are from the Aboriginal Peoples Survey, which asked individuals who reported Aboriginal ancestry in the census whether they identified with an Aboriginal group. If the 1981 method of collecting information about ancestry had been used, these numbers would probably be greater.

In interpreting these statistics, it is important to remember that changes in census statistics on urban Aboriginal populations are not only a function of migration, but also reflect changing patterns of self-identification as Aboriginal, natural increase, and the addition of Bill C-31 populations,[8] as well as changing definitions of ancestry and methods of data collection. Despite these caveats, it is clear from table 7 that, while the number of people with Aboriginal origins in major cities was very low in 1951,[9] numbers have steadily increased over the decades from 1951 to 1996. By 1996 several prairie cities had very substantial populations of Aboriginal people.

WRITING ABOUT ABORIGINAL URBANIZATION

Changes in the degree of public interest in urban Aboriginal people do not reflect changes in their numbers in cities. While issues concerning Aboriginal people were very much in the public eye in the late 1800s, they seemed to fade in importance after the turn of the century (Tobias, 1983). As public interest in Aboriginal issues revived in the mid-1900s, federal and provincial governments commissioned an array of studies into the conditions of Aboriginal people (Davis, 1965: 519; Hawthorn et al., 1958: 84; Hawthorn, 1966–67; Lagasse, 1958). An overriding theme in many of these studies was the depressed social and economic conditions of reserves and rural Métis settlements. As these conditions came to public attention, policy-makers looked to urbanization for at least a partial solution. Even without public policy intervention, rapid population growth on reserves made out-migration seem inevitable.

The prospect of the rapid migration of Aboriginal peoples to cities challenged academics, citizens' groups, and policy-makers to formulate what the "urban experience" meant for migrants and for cities. A large body of literature on the topic – academic and policy oriented – emerged after the late 1960s and continued to the mid-1970s. A number of studies appeared in the early 1980s, many associated with statistical surveys of Aboriginal people in Winnipeg, Regina and Saskatoon conducted by the Institute or Urban Studies, University of Winnipeg. Relatively little was published on urban Aboriginal people after 1985. As a result, there is little current work available with respect to urban Aboriginal people, and Kastes's (1993: 56) overview of the literature on Aboriginal urbanization concluded that:

The literature on urban Aboriginal issues in Canada is sparse, limited in scope, largely dated in relevance ... Given the significant changes which have occurred in Canada, as well as within the Aboriginal communities themselves since the mid 1980s, the existing literature is of limited use for contemporary policy and program development.

"Large numbers appear threatening," states Larry Krotz (1980: 50) in his journalistic account of urban Aboriginal people in prairie cities. However, the interest in urban Aboriginal issues does not appear to be related to numbers, nor is the declining interest due to the integretaion of urban Aboriginal people into the economic mainstream of urban areas. These factors suggest that it is not only the objective conditions and numbers of urban Aboriginal people that contribute to public interest in Aboriginal urbanization but also interpretations of its significance and frameworks of meaning through which Aboriginal peoples' migration to cities was understood. In what follows, I suggest that cycles and themes in writing about urban Aboriginal people reflect ideas about the relationship between Aboriginal culture and urban life.

DEFINING THE RELATIONSHIP
BETWEEN ABORIGINAL AND URBAN CULTURES

From the earliest writing on Aboriginal people in cities, their presence was constructed as a problem.[10] Even in the 1950s, when very few Aboriginal people lived in Canadian cities, many employers, municipal governments, and members of the general public viewed Aboriginal migration to cities with apprehension. On the basis of his Manitoba survey, Lagasse (1958: 167) concluded that: "the belief that an Indian's place is on the reserve is still very strong among the Canadian people." The Saskatchewan Government's 1960 submission to the Joint Committee of the Senate and the House of Commons warned that: "the day is not far distant when the burgeoning Indian population, now largely confined to reservations, will explode into white communities and present a serious problem indeed" (Canada, JCSHCIA, 1960b: 1083). Buckley's (1992: 72–6) review of attitudes towards Aboriginal employment in Northern prairie resource towns in the 1950s and 1960s concluded that, in public opinion, there was no place for them in these communities. Other writers also noted the intense hostility of townspeople in the mid-1900s to Aboriginal residents and visitors (Braroe, 1975; Brody, 1983; Lithman, 1984; Robertson, 1970; Shimpo and Williamson, 1965; Stymeist, 1975).

While materials from mid-century on, demonstrate agreement that migration to the city would create problems for Aboriginal people

(Canada, JCSHCIA, 1960a: 369; Canadian Corrections Association, 1967: 7–8; Regina Welfare Council, 1959) there were also worries about the state of cities – about how to maintain property values, keep down welfare rolls, and prevent inner-city decay (Hirabayashi, 1962; Indian-Eskimo Association, 1960; Lagasse 1958: 167).[11] John Melling, former Executive Director of the Indian-Eskimo Association, chastised federal, provincial, and municipal governments for being concerned about First Nations peoples only when the conditions of inner cities were seen to be threatened. His statement, however, also reflects attitudes towards Aboriginal urbanization at the time.

One hundred and sixty thousand Indians may wither in their reserves ... But bring even one-quarter of that number into our towns, or to fester in city tenements and shanty slums ... and that situation is quite intolerable. If the rot can be confined to the lives of Indians alone and if it can remain hidden from the rest of us, that is one thing; if it begins to affect the lives of others and becomes an open eyesore, that is another thing (Melling, 1967: 72).

Aboriginal people were still conceptualized as a threat to cities in the 1970s. The introduction to a 1977 report for the City of Winnipeg stated:

[A] major in-migration of generally low skilled, minimally educated ... and relatively impoverished people will serve to exacerbate the increasing expenditure and services demands. Beyond this, native urbanization will pose specific and unique problems and situations for both the City of Winnipeg and native people themselves (Reiber-Kremers, 1977: 1).

The Government of Saskatchewan's urban Native initiative in the late 1970s linked urban Aboriginal people and inner city deterioration (Saskatchewan, 1979). More recently, Kastes (1993: 83) argued that the situation of Aboriginal people constituted a serious challenge for prairie cities.

In recent years, Aboriginal urbanization issues have received little attention from researchers despite the fact that the social, economic and political problems within the urban Aboriginal community represent, by all accounts, one of the most serious and complex set of issues currently affecting urban environments.

The nature or source of the problem as identified by researchers and policy-makers has changed over time. A common theme in the literature on Aboriginal urbanization before the 1980s is that Aboriginal culture[12] presented a major barrier to successful adjustment to urban society. A 1957 Calgary conference on Aboriginal people in urban areas, organized by the National Commission on the Indian Canadian (later the Indian-Eskimo Association), clearly enunciated this view. Delegates representing churches, labour, government, and community groups concluded that:

Our [sic] Indian Canadian is faced or hampered with ... his [sic] own personality. The Indian Canadian is different from his fellow Canadians of European descent ... These differences are from his cultural heritage ... For instance, his concepts of time, money, social communication, hygiene, usefulness, competition and cooperation are at variance with our own and can prove a stumbling block to successful adjustment (Canada, DIAND, 1957: 3).

In *Indians in the City*, a book based on his Ph.D. research in Toronto, Nagler wrote that:

While urban living is not foreign to most European immigrants, it is a completely new way of life for the Indian. The highly generalized characteristics described as "being Indian" affect the Indian's ability to urbanize ... Indians thus experience difficulty in adjusting to a new environment because their conceptions of living do not involve punctuality, responsibility, hurry, impersonality, frugality, and the other social practices which are a part of the urban environment (1970: 25).

Zeitoun's (1969) review for the Department of Manpower and Immigration contrasted reserve and urban cultures and identified these differences as underlying the dislocation of urban Indians (table 8). Adaptation to the urban environment, according to Zeitoun and others, required a change in cultural values and orientation.[13]

These views were still current in the late 1970s. A consultant's report (Reiber-Kremers, 1977: 2) to the City of Winnipeg, for example, indicated that the problems of Aboriginal people "stem from major cultural differences, lack of familiarity with wage economy participation as well as urban lifestyles." While some writers challenged these interpretations (e.g., Elias, 1975; Lurie, 1967; Price and McCaskill, 1974), the overriding emphasis in the literature of the 1960s and 1970s was on the incompatibility of Aboriginal culture and urban life and the need to abandon cultural values in order to adapt to the urban setting.

The "problem" of Aboriginal urbanization was largely redefined in work after 1980,[14] and explicit mention of issues concerning Aboriginal culture virtually disappeared. Much of the work on urban Aboriginal people during this period framed the issue as a problem of poverty

Table 8
Reserve-City Cultural Differences

Reserve Characteristics	City Characteristics
• cultural homogeneity.	• cultural heterogeneity.
• economic activity requires generalized skills.	• occupational specialization.
• natural environment.	• manufactured environment.
• social life characterized by primary relationships, community, informality, personal relationships.	• social life is characterized by class structure, formal relationships, anonymity
• work is task oriented. It is one aspect of life and does not confer status. It is independent and unsupervised.	• work is time oriented, separate from personal life, and is the main source of status and satisfaction. It is supervised and directed.
• ties with kin and to the land result in a deep attachment to place and may interfere with geographic mobility.	• nuclear families and occupational specialization result in a weak attachment to place and do not inhibit economic and geographic mobility.

Source: Zeitoun, 1969.

stemming from lack of education and unemployment. The emphasis of Comeau and Santin's (1990) chapter on urban Aboriginal people is primarily on their poverty. A series of studies based on statistical surveys of Aboriginal people in prairie cities and published by the Institute of Urban Studies in Winnipeg demonstrated low incomes and high levels of unemployment and dependence on transfer payments. Summarizing much of this work, Kastes (1993: 78) illustrates that the needs of urban Aboriginal people were seen to derive from their socio-economic status.

Most studies describing the needs of the urban Aboriginal population develop a common integrated description of needs. They stem from a relative lack of formal education leading to unemployment or low-wage/low-skill jobs, insufficient levels of income, poverty and ultimately dependency on social assistance. The vast majority of needs in much of the urban Aboriginal population related to housing, health care, recreation and child care are not that dissimilar from other disadvantaged groups which make up the urban poor.

According to this perspective, the main factors differentiating the urban Aboriginal population from the other urban poor were the services required to adapt to urban life, the degree of their poverty, and the extent of their housing needs (Kastes, 1993: 79–80).

Another approach to typifying the nature of the problem emphasized structural elements. One thread of this analysis identified the confusion about federal and provincial responsibility for making policy and funding programs for urban Aboriginal people as an important element (Breton and Grant, 1984; Comeau and Santin, 1990: 43; Falconer, 1985).[15] Analysts noted the inconsistency in relationships between the federal government and various provinces, the inequities between various groups of Aboriginal people, and the wrangling among governments about policy-making and financial responsibility. In their analysis of government programs for urban Indians in Manitoba, Breton and Grant (1984: ix–xx) warned that:

The past ten years of circular jurisdictional squabbling have permitted the situation of Manitoba's Indians to become progressively worse. If we have ten more years of inconclusive action, the results, in human terms, will be too disastrous to contemplate.

Another theme was the inability of public service organizations to meet the needs of urban Aboriginal people (Falconer, 1985; Frideres, 1988; Maidman, 1981; Reeves and Frideres, 1981). Frideres (1988) argued that public service organizations failed to adequately serve urban Aboriginal peoples because of their assimilationist objectives, limited target groups, unclear mandates, and uncertain funding. While Aboriginal organizations were more successful in providing culturally appropriate services, they had relatively little success in "graduating" their clients.

The themes of the 1980s provide an important context for efforts to make urban areas better places for Aboriginal people. However, they do not address the essential question of the relationship between Aboriginal culture and urban life. In fact, the invisibility of Aboriginal culture in this literature suggests that it has no role in urban life – that it is irrelevant. In this context, urban Aboriginal people become just another socio-economically marginalized group in Canadian inner cities, with no distinct rights, needs, or characteristics.

Changing frameworks for interpreting Aboriginal urbanization may explain cycles of public interest in Aboriginal people in cities. When the source of the problem is defined as a cultural mismatch between Aboriginal and urban cultures, there is a substantial literature that focuses on urban Aboriginal issues. When urban Aboriginal people are viewed primarily as a socio-economically disadvantaged population, their situation can be subsumed under the general literature on urban poverty.

ALTERNATIVE CONCEPTIONS OF
ABORIGINAL CULTURE IN URBAN LIFE

How Aboriginal people have been defined in Western thought has set up a fundamental tension between the idea of Aboriginal culture and the idea of modern civilization (Berkhoffer, 1979; Francis, 1992; Goldie, 1989). While the geographic implications of these deeply held images have not been well developed, Goldie (1989: 16–17, 165) points out that, in non-Aboriginal writing, "true" Aboriginal cultures are seen to belong either to history or to places distant from urban centres. The failure to address critically how researchers conceptualize Aboriginal culture in relation to the city helps to reproduce a framework that defines Aboriginal people as problematic and potentially disruptive of city life.[16] In this context, assumptions about the incompatibility between urban and Aboriginal culture persist (Peters, 1991). The Native Council of Canada noted that: "There is a strong, sometimes racist, perception that being Aboriginal and being urban are mutually exclusive" (1992: 10).

In contrast to views of Aboriginal culture as either incompatible with, or irrelevant in, an urban environment, Aboriginal people have argued that supporting and enhancing Aboriginal culture is a prerequisite for coping in an urban environment. These perspectives recognize that Aboriginal cultures and the Euro-Canadian cultures that dominate Canadian cities are distinct in many ways, but they insist that Aboriginal cultures can adapt to, and flourish in, urban areas and that supporting Aboriginal cultures will enrich cities as well as making them better places for Aboriginal people.

Urban Aboriginal people who spoke to journalist Lynda Shorten (1991) in Edmonton identified the process of regaining their cultural heritage as essential for survival in the city. At the National Round Table on Aboriginal Urban Issues sponsored by the Royal Commission on Aboriginal Peoples, speakers emphasized the importance of maintaining their cultural identities in urban areas and passing them on to their children (1993a). Aboriginal participants at a 1994 workshop on urban self-government identified the process of healing from the effects of colonialism on their cultures as a priority for urban residents (Peters, 1995).

In their submissions to the 1992–94 public hearings of the Royal Commission on Aboriginal Peoples, participants stressed the need to enhance Aboriginal cultures in urban areas. Nancy Van Heest, working in a pre-employment program for Aboriginal women in Vancouver, told the Commissioners:

Today we live in the modern world and we find that a lot of our people who come into the urban setting are unable to live in the modern world without their traditional values. So we started a program which we call "Urban Images for First Nations People in the Urban Setting" and what we do is we work in this modern day with modern day people and give them traditional values so that they can continue on with their life in the city.[17]

Urban Aboriginal people spoke to the Commissioners of the need for a strong foundation in Aboriginal culture for healing the urban Aboriginal community. In Orillia, Ontario, Harold Orten outlined the relationship between recovering Aboriginal cultures and healing.

Recovering our identity will contribute to healing ourselves. Our healing will require us to rediscover who we are. We cannot look outside for our self-image, we need to rededicate ourselves to understanding our traditional ways. In our songs, ceremony, language and relationships lie the instructions and directions for recovery.[18]

In Saskatoon, Margaret King, representative for the Saskatoon Urban Treaty Indians, argued that:

[O]ur cultural heritage ... formed the basic elements of individual empowerment, a solid foundation of cultural values and the knowledge of our history and traditions, our basic needs in the development of an individual before he or she becomes a productive member of society. As an assembly we believe in the value of individual self-esteem and will strive to empower our people through the development of culturally appropriate programs and services.[19]

The assault on Aboriginal cultures does not originate only in cities. It is part of the colonial legacy of our country. Yet, urban areas present special challenges for the survival of Aboriginal cultures. These challenges come in part because many of the traditional sources of Aboriginal culture – contact with the land, elders, Aboriginal languages, and spiritual ceremonies are difficult to maintain in cities at present. Moreover, Aboriginal people must be continuously exposed to perceptions, either consciously or unconsciously held, that cities are not where Aboriginal cultures belong and can flourish (Royal Commission, 1993a: 2). At the public hearings, David Chartrand, then President of the National Association of Friendship Centres, told the Commissioners:

Aboriginal culture in the cities is threatened in much the same way as Canadian culture is threatened by American culture, and it therefore requires a similar commitment to its protection. Our culture is at the heart of our people, and without awareness of Aboriginal history, traditions and ceremonies, we are not whole people, and our communities lose their strength ... Cultural education also works against the alienation that the cities hold for our people. Social activities bring us together and strengthen the relationship between people in areas where those relationships are an important safety net for people who feel left out by the mainstream.[20]

CHANGING CITIES TO WELCOME
ABORIGINAL PEOPLES AND CULTURES

Making cities places where Aboriginal cultures are welcomed and enhanced will require sustained effort. Aboriginal people must be involved in identifying and putting into place appropriate initiatives. The following, however, puts forward some suggestions to illustrate what it means to change long-standing views about the relationship between Aboriginal cultures and urban places. These include cultural programming, building urban Aboriginal communities, supporting urban self-government, and improving the representation of Aboriginal people in urban areas.

SUPPORTING CULTURAL PROGRAMMING
AND EDUCATION

At present, there are many urban Aboriginal institutions that attempt to meet the needs – including the need to strengthen cultural identity – of urban Aboriginal people. However, a survey of urban Aboriginal institutions in Winnipeg, Toronto, and Edmonton (Clatworthy et al., 1995) showed that, while organizations attempted to meet the cultural needs of their clients by incorporating Aboriginal philosophies and cultures into their structures and program delivery, relatively few had as their primary mission the promotion or support of Aboriginal culture and identity. Moreover, while organizations reported flexibility in delivery style and administrative matters, their activities were highly circumscribed by funding relationships with other parties, mostly non-Aboriginal governments.

Friendship Centres, which have existed in Canada's urban centres for more than thirty years, have often become the main focus of cultural and social events and activities for Aboriginal people living in cities. In many urban areas, the Friendship Centre has been the only major voluntary association available to meet the needs of Aboriginal people for social and cultural development. Yet, funding to Friendship Centres for activities that support Aboriginal cultures such as celebrations, access to elders, and language education are limited. The cultural work Friendship

Centres currently carry out is chronically underfunded and relies heavily on the work of volunteers who are already overcommitted.

In the context of the sustained assault on Aboriginal cultures in cities and the poverty of much of the urban Aboriginal population, there is a need for substantial new institutional support to assist Aboriginal people to maintain and enhance their cultural identity in urban areas. Teaching Aboriginal languages is one area that needs to be stressed. The Aboriginal Peoples Survey showed that only about 15 percent of urban Aboriginal people could speak their Aboriginal language of origin. Yet 71 percent of Aboriginal people who could not speak an Aboriginal language would like to learn or relearn one. Providing space for Aboriginal activities and ceremonies and cultural education for children, youth and adults are also priorities. In its final report, the Royal Commission on Aboriginal Peoples emphasized the need to support cultural programming in urban areas, indicating that "Aboriginal, municipal, territorial, provincial and federal governments [should] initiate] programs to increase opportunities to promote Aboriginal cultures in urban communities" (Royal Commission, 1996: 537).

BUILDING ABORIGINAL COMMUNITIES

The evolution of strong Aboriginal communities in urban areas remains largely unfulfilled after forty years of urbanization. In many cities, Aboriginal people exist as an impoverished minority, without a collective cultural identity. While there are now many cities with a variety of Aboriginal organizations, they do not reflect and have not been able to create group solidarity and cohesion. A study of Aboriginal organizations in Edmonton, Toronto, and Winnipeg found that only a small portion of the total urban Aboriginal population participates as members or receives benefits or services from existing organizations (Clatworthy et al., 1995). The study also found that there were relatively few formal and effective inter-organizational structures with a focus on community building and consolidation.

Community building through the establishment of networks, institutions, and collective identity can enhance political strength and visibility and provide the support for resilient cultural identities. Community building can also contribute to economic development and begin to address the pressing poverty of many Aboriginal people living in cities (Rothney, 1992). In this context, some urban Aboriginal people have emphasized the need to engage in a process of healing and of consensus and community building in urban areas.[21] David Chartrand, then President of the National Association of Friendship Centres, told the Royal Commission on Aboriginal Peoples that the most effective way to solve problems Aboriginal people face in the city was to catch them before they start through strengthening individuals' identities and awareness of the urban Aboriginal community.[22]

The challenges to community building in urban areas are considerable. One source of the challenge comes from the cultural diversity of urban Aboriginal people. In his report for the Native Council of Canada, Morse (1993: 88) pointed out that:

In the urban setting, asking the individual members of the potentially very diverse urban group [sic], each with their own unique identity, traditions, language and culture, to put aside their differences and build a new community is a formidable task. It requires the rejection of the long history of federal intervention, and for the urban Aboriginal population to come to terms with their diversity.

Many people who live in urban areas retain ties with their non-urban communities of origin, and these ties represent an important component of their cultural identities. Moreover, some land-based First Nations communities are currently exploring ways of extending their jurisdiction over their members living in urban areas.

At the same time, urban Aboriginal people have the need for local access to places, people, and activities that support the celebration and enhancement of their cultures. In cities where there are a relatively small number of people from any particular cultural group, these opportunities can only exist through co-operation and collective activities. The challenge for Aboriginal people then, urban and non-urban, is to explore ways of creating urban communities that will support a variety of cultural origins and, at the same time, protect the ties some people have to their non-urban communities of origin. These approaches can only be designed by Aboriginal people themselves, and they may vary from place to place.

Another challenge for creating urban communities comes from the extreme poverty of many urban Aboriginal people.[23] Poverty and economic marginalization work against community building, which could begin to alleviate that condition. The majority of urban residents do not possess the financial resources to support institutional development. Moreover, many are faced with enormous daily challenges in trying to obtain an adequate standard of living, which leaves little time or energy for participation in community building. These struggles take place in the context of a political environment that does not support urban community building. Representatives to the Royal Commission on Aboriginal Peoples' National Round Table on Aboriginal Urban Issues pointed out that: "any sort of co-operative urban Aboriginal movement has been hamstrung by scarce resources, fragmented populations, unclear mandates, and a lack of ... federal or provincial encouragement and support" (Royal Commission, 1993a: 79). In many cities, then, the processes of urban Aboriginal community building require the infusion of financial resources from other levels of government. The Royal Commission recommended that federal governments give priority to making Aboriginal services delivery more comprehensive, with more secure and stable funding (1996: 557).

SUPPORTING SELF-GOVERNMENT

Until recently, most of the literature on the nature of and possibilities for Aboriginal self-government focused on land-based populations. While there was some consideration of urban applications (see Dunn, 1986; Reeves, 1986; Weinstein, 1986), most researchers pointed out the difficulties of implementation off a land base and concentrated on land base arrangements (see for example, Penner, 1983; Royal Commission, 1993b: 44).

Urban Aboriginal peoples' demands for self-government contradict the colonial legacy that views Aboriginal cultures, communities and values as incompatible with or inappropriate in the urban industrial milieu. Self-government is also essential for the enhancement of Aboriginal cultures in urban areas. In their study of Aboriginal organizations in three major urban centres, Clatworthy et al. (1995) found that their activities were highly circumscribed by the interests of funding organizations that were, for the most part, non-Aboriginal governments. Opekokew (1995) argues that cultural preservation and enhancement only take place when Aboriginal people have control over their institutions.

A number of models of urban self-government for Aboriginal peoples in urban areas have been put forward in recent years (Graham, 1999). Many First Nations support the extension of jurisdiction of land-based governments to urban citizens (Opekokew, 1995). The Native Council of Canada (now the Congress of Aboriginal Peoples) suggested options, including governance over urban reserves or Aboriginal neighbourhoods, self-determining Aboriginal institutions, and pan-Aboriginal governing bodies in urban areas (Native Council of Canada, 1993). Tizya (1992: 8) described an approach in which urban residents would fall under the jurisdiction of the First Nation in whose traditional territory the urban centre lies. Métis organizations place governance for urban residents in a structure with urban and rural locals nested in provincial and national organizations (Young, 1995).

The issue is complex. In addition to debates over the scope of an inherent right to self-government in urban areas, some approaches to governance cannot be implemented in conjunction with others, and setting up different structures for each cultural group could result in impossible complexity (Peters, 1994). Yet, extending opportunities for self-government is crucial for the large number of Aboriginal people living in urban areas. The Royal Commission on Aboriginal Peoples recognized the importance of access to self-government for urban Aboriginal people and, without recommending specific approaches for particular situations, emphasized the need for urban Aboriginal people to be involved in decision-making concerning urban governance initiatives (1996: 599).

REPRESENTING ABORIGINAL PEOPLES IN URBAN LANDSCAPES

Initiatives to change public perceptions about the relationship between Aboriginal cultures and urban life are needed in addition to support for community building, cultural programming, and self-government. These initiatives must occur in a wide variety of areas, and they must be sustained because they are part of changing very deeply held ways people have of organizing their view of the world. In this context, changing presentations of Aboriginal peoples and histories in educational materials and the media would benefit urban Aboriginal people. However, some initiatives that focus specifically on urban landscapes are also needed. The Royal Commission on Aboriginal Peoples recommended that "all governments co-operate to set aside land in urban areas dedicated to Aboriginal culture and spiritual needs" (1996: 537).

Another important strategy in this regard has to do with changing the way Aboriginal people are represented (or not represented) in urban landscapes. Symbols in urban landscapes reflect and reproduce societal values about what is and what is not valued and important. Contemporary urban landscapes offer little to valorize Aboriginal cultures, affirm their relevance to contemporary life, or admit their continuing existence. There is little recognition that most cities are on Aboriginal peoples' traditional territories or that urban development may affect sites that are important for spiritual or historic reasons.[24] There are few attempts at historic preservation of significant sites or at bringing to public consciousness the Aboriginal heritage of the lands on which urban areas are built. There are few streets, parks, or buildings named after significant Aboriginal people, historic or contemporary. Aboriginal heroes do not often appear in monuments dedicated to their memory. Making Aboriginal people and cultures visible in urban landscapes would signal that they have a valued place in contemporary urban areas.

CONCLUSION

Support for the maintenance and enhancement of Aboriginal cultures is not the only challenge facing Aboriginal people in urban areas. Aboriginal people have also stressed other pressing needs. Participants at the Royal Commission on Aboriginal People's National Round Table on Aboriginal Urban Issues identified the need for economic development, more appropriate services, changes in government policies and jurisdiction and a voice in governance and decision-making (Royal Commission, 1993a). I have focused on cultural issues in this paper for two reasons. The first has to do with a long history of denying that Aboriginal cultures have an appropriate place in urban areas – a place that has challenged the identities of many urban Aboriginal people. The second has to do with my sense that valuing and supporting urban Aboriginal cultures in cities would contribute to meeting some of the other needs of urban Aboriginal communities.

Approximately half of the Aboriginal people of Canada live in urban areas. Taking measures to support and enhance their cultures will make cities better place for Aboriginal people and for non-Aboriginal residents.

NOTES

1 By Aboriginal peoples I mean the indigenous peoples of this country, including First Nations peoples, Métis, and Inuit. First Nations peoples are people who identify themselves as such, including people who are and are not registered pursuant to the *Indian Act*. I use the term "Indian" when I refer to Euro-Canadian constructions of First Nations peoples. Registered Indians are registered under the *Indian Act*.

2 The paper takes a social constructionist approach to the issue of Aboriginal urbanization (see Best, 1989; Spector and Kitsuse, 1987), which argues that people's sense of what is and what is not a problem is not simply the result of objective conditions but has also been produced or constructed through social action and events. Typically, the social construction of an issue characterizes it as a certain type of problem. This characterization serves as a framework for identifying appropriate strategies for its management or solution.

3 Aggregate data on Aboriginal urbanization rates are not available for more recent census years. The census question that collects information on Canadian's ethnic or cultural origins asked: "To which ethnic or cultural group(s) did this person's ancestor's belong?" The 1991 Aboriginal People's Survey (APS) asked individuals who indicated they had Aborigi-

nal ancestry whether they identified with an Aboriginal group. This "identity" population is smaller than the population that has Aboriginal ancestry or cultural origins.

4 To date, federal negotiations have been with bands and groups of bands.

5 This list does not represent all Aboriginal organizations in the city, but only those that are managed by Aboriginal people, are autonomous, and are both urban-based and urban-focused.

6 Other limitations include changing definitions (Gerber, 1977: 4), the location of a number of reserves in urban centres, and failure to regularly update records (Canada, DIAND, 1991).

7 Before 1981 only one ethnic origin was captured in the census. In 1981 more than one origin was allowed, but respondents were not encouraged to identify more than one.

8 By 1991, about 87,000 people had been added to the Registered Indian population, increasing the total population by about 21 percent between 1985 and 1991. A substantial proportion of the peoples added to the register would have lived in urban areas.

9 There are no published statistics on urban Aboriginal people before 1951.

10 John MacLean, a missionary with a doctorate in history and author of *The Indians of Canada* (1889) and *Canadian Savage Folk* (1896), was considered to be an authority. Describing the Sarcees on a reserve near Calgary, he wrote (1896: 18):

"Their close proximity to Calgary is injurious to the morals of the white people and Indians, as the natives of the plains always find the lower stratum of society ready to teach the willing learner lessons of immorality, and degradation is sure to follow any close relationship of Indians with white people in the early stages of their training."

11 While I recognize that some of the concern may be spillover from events in inner cities in the US during the 1960s, the definition of Aboriginal urbanization as problematic substantially predates these events, and the themes and explanations are too persistent to be simply a reflection of the US experience.

12 There is little recognition of the diversity of Aboriginal cultures in this literature.

13 These quotes do not represent isolated opinions taken out of context, but reflect a general framework within which writers understood the nature of the urban experience for Aboriginal migrants. See also, for example, Asimi, 1967: 94; Bond, 1967; Currie 1966: 14; Indian-Eskimo Association, 1971: 6; Melling, 1967; Canada, JCSHCIA, 1960b: 1034–9; Trudeau, 1969; Vincent, 1971: 13; Zentner, 1973: xii. At the same time, it is also important to note that there were writers who argued that urbanization did not represent a rejection of Aboriginal culture (Lurie, 1967; McCaskill, 1981).

14 Clearly these dates are approximate, and there are works that fit into neither time period nor subject category as I have organized them. Moreover, some of the themes I associate with the post-1980 period were also present before then.

15 Ryan (1975) made similar points earlier.

16 It is important to note that Aboriginal people are not the only group who have been so defined (see Ray, 1992; Sibley, 1981).

17 Nancy Van Heest, Vancouver, BC, Public Hearings, Royal Commission on Aboriginal Peoples, 2 June 1993: 14. Available from the Royal Commission on Aboriginal Peoples, 1993, *The Electronic Series: Public Hearings* CD-ROM, Minister of Supply and Services, Ottawa, Ontario.

18 Harold Orten, Public Hearings, Royal Commission on Aboriginal Peoples, Orillia, Ontario, 13 May 1993: 66. Available from the Royal Commission on Aboriginal Peoples, 1993, *The Electronic Series: Public Hearings* CD-ROM, Minister of Supply and Services, Ottawa, Ontario.

19 Margaret King, Saskatoon Urban Treaty Indians, Public Hearings, Royal Commission on Aboriginal Peoples, Saskatoon, Saskatchewan, 28 October 1992. Available from the Royal Commission on Aboriginal Peoples, 1993, *The Electronic Series: Public Hearings* CD-ROM, Minister of Supply and Services, Ottawa, Ontario.

20 David Chartrand, Public Hearings, Royal Commission on Aboriginal Peoples, Toronto, Ontario, 26 June 1992: 565. Available from the Royal Commission on Aboriginal Peoples, 1993, *The Electronic Series: Public Hearings* CD-ROM, Minister of Supply and Services, Ottawa, Ontario.

21 See, for example, presentations by Sylvia Maracle and Wayne Helgason to a workshop on urban self-government (Peters, 1995).

22 David Chartrand, Public Hearings, Royal Commission on Aboriginal Peoples, Toronto, Ontario, 26 June 1992: 565. Available from the Royal Commission on Aboriginal Peoples, 1993, *The Electronic Series: Public Hearings* CD-ROM, Minister of Supply and Services, Ottawa, Ontario.

23 It is important to emphasize that the economic marginalization of urban Aboriginal people is not of their own making. Instead it comes from a long history of their exclusion from the mainstream of society.

24 Rosalee Tizya, co-coordinator, Urban Perspectives, Royal Commission on Aboriginal Peoples, made this point at a workshop on Self-Government for Urban Aboriginal Peoples held at Queen's University, 25–26 May 1994.

3 Bright New Vision or Same Old Story? Looking for Gender Justice in the Eco-city

SHERILYN MacGREGOR

In what might be called a key feminist "click moment" of the 1980s, Canadian sociologist Mary O'Brien (1986: 430) looked at Marx's ideal communist society wherein "men could be fishermen in the morning, farmers in the afternoon and critics in the evening" and wondered "who will be minding the kids?" More than a decade later, the dream of a communist utopia may be over, but the utopian impulse in progressive North American thought is alive and well and living in the eco-city. In the ideal ecological society, a man will be free to be a self-employed environmental consultant working at home online in the morning, a community organic gardener in the afternoon, and a Greenpeace activist in the evening. This leaves me wondering not only who will be minding the kids but also who will be sorting the recyclables and taking out the compost?

Evidence of the development of an eco-city vision can be found in many different fields from political theory to urban planning and architecture as part of a general consensus on the desirability of environmental sustainability. In the Canadian context, interest in sustainable development has grown rapidly since the early 1990s, when public concern for the environment was at its height and when governments at all levels were compelled to incorporate green strategies into their policy agenda.[1] While concern for the viability of natural ecosystems and resource conservation has tended to dominate, there is a growing community of scholars, activists, policy-makers, and professionals for whom the quality of urban environments is paramount. Many of the leading models for sustainable urban development in the world have been developed in Canada (cf. Royal Commission, 1992; Tomalty et al., 1994; Wackernagel and Rees, 1996; Roseland, 1998) and the ability of these environmental advocates to place urban issues on the policy agenda, particularly at the municipal level, has been rather impressive. Insofar as urban issues are on the public agenda today, they tend to be implicated in governmental efforts to improve Canada's environmental record in the eyes of the world. For example, municipal governments throughout the country have made environment-related changes to their official plans since the late 1980s, and in 1997 the Canada Mortgage and Housing Corporation (CMHC) released a report titled *Changing Values, Changing Communities*, which advocates a number of strategies for the development of sustainable and healthy communities. So what kinds of issues and strategies are being promoted, and what kinds of effects are they likely to have on the diverse populations in Canadian cities?

My interest in this chapter is to assess what I will call the "urban sustainability agenda" itself, with an interest in the amount of attention that has been given to social equity in general and gender relations in particular. Feminist critic of gendered spaces Daphne Spain (1995) has argued that the emergence of interest in the sustainable community concept may offer hope for the realization of utopian visions of the ideal feminist city. But I am not so optimistic. My review of the recent literature on urban sustainability in Canada leads me to believe that, while some aspects of urban sustainability appear to be similar to feminist goals for a non-sexist city, others have the potential further to intensify gender inequality. This is because the majority of eco-city visionaries – like mainstream urbanists in general and despite several decades of feminist urban scholarship – have been blind to the myriad ways in which gender identity affects urban experience and civic engagement. Although they may pay lip service to the goal of social equity, what they offer us is "so frequently, so unimaginatively, patriarchal" (Massey, 1991: 31).

In this chapter, I interrupt the ongoing conversations about "greening the city" among urban sustainability scholars to challenge their oversights on issues relevant to a diversity of urban women. In the first part of the discussion, I provide an overview of the discourse of urban sustainability, its principles, assumptions, and proposed strategies, and assess them from a feminist urbanist perspective. I then provide some concrete examples of the gender implications of some of the more popular eco-city visions that seem to suffer from an acute case of gender blindness. In response to these, in the last part of the paper, I offer some alternative or expanded urban sustainability principles that better incorporate the critical insights and analyses of feminist urban scholars.

THE DISCOURSE OF URBAN SUSTAINABILITY
IN CANADA

The discourse of urban sustainability most often involves questions about how to improve the quality of urban life while minimizing human impact on the ecosystem. For the past several decades there has been a growing consensus that the state of Canadian cities is ecologically unsustainable (Rees and Roseland, 1991; Paehlke, 1994; Roseland, 1998). Reports of declining urban air and water quality, increasing environmental health problems, inability to manage municipal solid and hazardous wastes, and the endangerment of urban wildlife habitats (among other problems) have led to an increased sense that we have an urban crisis on our hands. Much of this is seen to be the result of conventional urban planning and policies that have facilitated resource and land intensive forms of urban development, with little or no regard for long-term ecological implications. Indeed, the typical design of the post-war Fordist city has a number of built-in problems such as the separation of industrial and residential zones leading to (sub)urban sprawl, mass consumption of single family homes, and overreliance on the private automobile. Such aspects lead to levels of ecological degradation that affect more than just the local quality of life: cities are increasingly seen as a major contributor to ecological problems of global proportions such as climate change and ozone depletion (WCED, 1987; White and Whitney, 1992).

Analyses of the interconnections between – and the desire to do something about – the local and the global, urban development, and environmental problems have given rise to a number of different discourses of urban sustainability. These range in tone and substance from technical and reformist to the ideological and revolutionary. For the purposes of explication, one might draw a distinction between the approaches to urban sustainability held by urban planners and policymakers on the one hand and those held by urban scholars in the fields of geography, political economy, and environmental studies on the other. While this is neither an exhaustive list nor a watertight categorization, it offers a provisional mapping of the main currents in the contemporary discourse. I shall describe them each briefly, as follows, and then go on to draw out some of their common themes and strategies.

ECOSYSTEM PLANNING AND
SUSTAINABLE COMMUNITY PLANNING

Local governments have become especially active in undertaking policies for sustainability (Roseland, 1998; ICLEI, 1996). Among planners and municipal policy-makers, two approaches to dealing with the urban environmental crisis have gained popularity in recent years. These are ecosystem planning and planning for sustainable communities. Both provide, in slightly different ways, concrete strategies for the creation of urban places that facilitate more harmonious human-nonhuman relationships. One of the first Canadian publications to discuss specifically the ecosystem approach is *Watershed*, the interim report by the Royal Commission on Toronto's Waterfront headed by former Toronto mayor and former federal cabinet minister David Crombie (Royal Commission, 1990). In the Commission's final report, titled *Regeneration* (1992: 32), the underlying premise of ecosystem planning is articulated: "that, unless we regain an awareness of humans as being part of ecosystems, and unless we respond to that awareness by changing the process and criteria of decision-making, we will not be able to improve, and will even lose, the quality of life for which so many generations laboured." The report goes on to list some of the fundamental principles of ecosystem planning, which include the notion that "everything is connected to everything else" and an understanding of sustainability much like that reached in the Brundtland Report, titled *Our Common Future* (WCED, 1987): that humans have a moral responsibility to minimize their impacts on the environment and their costs to future generations.

Since the work of the Crombie commission, planning practitioners and academics have taken up and applied the ecosystem approach in a number of Canadian cities. Tomalty, Gibson, Alexander, and Fisher (1994) examine the many examples and case studies of ecosystem planning initiatives that can be identified across Canada.[2] According to these authors (1994: 7) "the essential contribution of the ecosystem approach to planning is its recasting of relations between humans and the rest of nature." This is a significant departure from conventional planning wherein an overtly anthropocentric and instrumental epistemology has prevailed. With ecosystem planning, on the other hand, the concern is to "design with nature" rather than against it, meaning that planners should respect biophysical boundaries, like watersheds or bioregions, and should work to restore biodiversity (Taminga, 1996).

Various ecosystem planning tools and methods have been developed in the last decade. These include scientific approaches to ecosystem management such as those dealing with hydrological cycles, soils remediation, and ecosystem and habitat restoration (cf. Hough, 1995). There are also various management and regulatory strategies that municipalities can use to protect local ecosystems, such as the Environmentally Sensitive Area (ESA) bylaws and State of the Environmental reporting done in Burnaby, British Columbia (Roseland, 1998). Perhaps the best-known ecosystem planning tool is the "ecological foot-print" analysis developed by William Rees and Mathis Wackernagel from the University of British Columbia (Wackernagel and Rees, 1996). Using the basic principles of ecological economics, the concept "accounts for the flows of energy and matter to and from any defined economy and converts these into corresponding land/water area required to support these flows" (Wackernagel and Rees, 1996: 3). When applied to urban areas, the ecological footprint analysis can measure the overall impact of present city forms on our "natural cap-ital" and assist planners and policy-makers to chart the progress of efforts to move towards sustainability.

The literature on planning for sustainable communities takes a slightly different, perhaps less technical, perspective on the ecological crisis and on the role of planners as enablers in the process of urban environmental change. More attention is paid to the socio-political aspects of community and to a normative, "social learning" approach to transforming societal values than is apparent in most of the ecosys-tem planning literature. The underlying analysis is that the same kinds of problems that have led to the ecological crisis have also contributed to the erosion of a sense of community in Canada. In particular, the concentration and centralization of power in the hands of a few – who are not well informed about or responsive to the needs and traditions of local people – has led to many socio-economic problems such as poverty and alienation (Nozick, 1992). In a federal system that gives limited power to the local level, the argument goes, it is no coincidence that the poor management of resource industries by faraway bureau-crats is a major cause of environmental problems in and economic dis-parities among Canadian regions (cf. Plant and Plant, 1995).[3]

The sustainable community literature is closely tied to the healthy community movement and to the growing field of community eco-nomic development. Mark Roseland (1998: 2), who is perhaps the best-known proponent of sustainable community planning, defines the approach as "a synergistic approach [that] will enable our com-munities to be cleaner, healthier, and less expensive; to have greater accessibility and cohesion; and to be more self-reliant in energy, food, and economic security than they are now." Similarly, Marcia Nozick (1992) believes that, in response to the "breakdown of community" in Canada, planners, entrepreneurs, and activists should contribute to the building of ecologically sound and self-supporting communities that have a better sense of local culture and respect for the needs of individual residents. There is a range of strategies for bringing about these changes, most of which are based on the direct and active involvement of citizens in the revisioning and reconstruction of their communities. Planners and other community-based professionals are seen as facilitators or enablers of the process by providing resources, by helping to organize and promote demonstration projects, and by designing processes through which communities might realize their own needs and desires from the ground up (Gurstein and Curry, 1993). The assumption is that, given a choice and the power to implement their own policies, local people will redesign their environments in more sustainable ways than far away politicians and corporate elites.

URBAN POLITICAL ECOLOGY

The trouble with cities and their impacts on the planet has been exacerbated in recent years by economic restructuring and globalization, two trends that have led to problems like unemployment, the widening of the gap between rich and poor, eroding social services, and inner-city fragmentation and decline. In Canada, major urban areas like Toronto, Vancouver, and Montreal are gradually becoming more closely tied into the global economy than their smaller counterparts, and have come to be regarded – and promoted – as the engines of national economic growth. Many urban scholars have developed an analysis of "global cities" (Sassen, 1991) but only a few have looked at the links between environmental problems and globalization at the urban level (Keil, 1995 and 1996). Those who have done so have theorized the connections between socio-economic, spatial, and ecological problems – typically from a Marxist or political economy perspective. According to urban political ecologists, the current period of global capitalist restructuring is bringing about dramatic changes in the shape of the city – from Fordist to post-Fordist – accompanied by many negative ecological implications (Esser and Hirch, 1994). Stemming from a shift in human relationships with the natural world (due in part to the dislocation of relations of production from environmental effects), the "environmental problematic in world cities" (Keil, 1995) consists of an intensification of pollution and exurban growth. Writes Roger Keil (1995: 289): "The construction of a built environment for global capital in these cities and the transnational pressures on local land use have in most cases exacerbated the stress on residential communities, green spaces, and public spaces used by the majority of citizens."

The response from the left has been to develop a new red-green agenda for urban research. In a recent issue of the journal *Capitalism, Nature, Socialism* on urban ecology, for example, the editorial collective outlines an "urban ecological politics" that entails a critical analysis of urban ecology [which] lends itself to a spatialized red-green critique of capitalist urbanization. Such a spatialized eco-Marxism would insist that, given the urbanization of capital, a red-green challenge of capitalism must extend to a claim for the "right to the city." Claiming urban space for transformational socio-ecological purposes might include imposing development controls on landed capital and building alternative economic networks, for example, organic food regimes, as a way of loosening the burden of capitalist urbanization on regional, continental, or even global hinterlands. This may be achieved by binding local states to self-managed labour and community controlled sectors to promote democratic planning, to decommodify work, and to boost use-value oriented production (Kipfer, Hartmann, and Marino 1996: 15).

Along with such strategies, urban political ecologists conceive of a central role for urban social movements for environmental and distributive justice in the achievement of local democratic governance and sustainability (cf. Keil, 1996; Kipfer, Hartmann, and Marino, 1996).

HOW TO BUILD THE MOST APPROPRIATE HUMAN HOME: FIVE COMMON THEMES

Unlike many environmentalists who have a strong anti-urban bias, suggesting that urban ecology may be a contradiction in terms (Trepl, 1996), ecosystem planners and urban sustainability advocates embrace the city as "the most environmentally appropriate human home" (Paehlke, 1994: 106). In the wake of social and spatial changes brought about by post-Fordist economic restructuring, they propose innovative ways to redesign urban spaces and urban practices with ecological limits and socio-economic justice in mind. These proposals differ depending on the fields of literature upon which they draw or where their proponents lie on the green political spectrum. Some are clearly more pragmatic and incremental, while others are radical and utopian. Ecosystem planners, on the one hand, are more concerned with redesigning and "retrofitting" the city to be more in tune with natural systems, while on the other hand urban political ecologists (red-greens) seek to integrate alternative and more radical economic and political approaches into their visions in order to address the ecological and economic crisis simultaneously. The range of strategies that have been proposed is too broad to cover in detail here. Instead, I shall highlight and briefly explain five common themes or principles that can be found in much of the recent work on urban sustainability.

Compact Urban Form

The most widely embraced strategy for making urban areas more sustainable is to reduce urban sprawl by planning for intensification and "infill" – meaning that new development should take place within the already existing city limits rather than continuing to expand out into the hinterland. This will have the environmental benefit of conserving remaining agricultural land and undeveloped areas. It will also result in more efficient use of space and resources in the city – from the design of housing complexes (co-housing) to the renovation of abandoned buildings. Compact cities are also meant to be mixed-use cities; that is, there will be a convenient mix of residential, commercial, and recreational facilities, as well as green space, within the neighbourhoods in which people live. This will result in a significant reduction in car dependency, a problem that is built into the present design of large urban places.[4]

Minimal Waste and Consumption of Resources

In order to tackle the enormous environmental problems of resource depletion (e.g., energy, water, wood) and waste production, urban sustainability advocates and ecosystem planners have included in their vision the principle that cities should be designed and managed in ways that ensure minimal strain on "stocks and sinks" (Wackernagel and Rees, 1996). Designs and technological applications for energy and water efficiency is a prominent feature of urban sustainability literature. Many sustainability proponents advocate more humble energy conservation approaches. These involve appropriate technologies that are "low tech" and that rely heavily on human power – doing things by hand, for example (cf. Roberts and Brandum, 1995). Perhaps most successful has been the widespread implementation of municipal waste management programs based on the proverbial 3 Rs (reduce, reuse, recycle). In her study of sustainable urban development in Canada, McLaren (1992) found that waste management programs are the most prominent urban sustainability strategy. The mainstreaming of residential recycling programs is a testament to the success of environmentalists at putting environmental issues on the urban agenda.

Minimal Use of the Automobile

Closely related to the above two principles, a drastic reduction in the use of private automobiles and all fossil fuel powered vehicles is an integral part of all urban sustainability visions. The problems of traffic congestion and smog caused by CO_2 emissions are often held up as evidence of the environmental guilt of major cities. This most commonly translates into promotion of mass transit through improved and expanded services and into urban designs that foster greater reliance on alternative forms of transportation, such as cycling and walking. Some planners favour the move to a car-free city, which is to be initiated by, among other things, the implementation of gas taxes and the elimination of inner-city parking lots.

Community- and Self-Reliance

A fourth principle of urban sustainability is that communities and individuals should become less reliant on the global capitalist marketplace and state-sponsored services that engender dependency and apathy. This emanates from critiques of the culture of mass consumption and the disempowering nature of the welfare state. As an antidote, urban sustainability advocates tend to promote the redesign of urban communities in ways that facilitate greater local production of food, services, and specialty craft items (cf. Perks and Van Vleit, 1993). For example, community gardens are regarded as a way to provide healthy and affordable produce at the same time that they bring community members together for a common project. Local currencies and Local Employment and Trading Systems (LETS) are seen as a way to subvert the money economy while encouraging individuals to develop their skills. Nozick's study (1992) gives an excellent overview of the range of possibilities for increasing community and self-reliance. Several texts now exist that give "how-to" tips on how to plan and implement such practices (cf. Roseland, 1998; Roberts and Brandum, 1996).

Decentralization and Participatory Democracy

Among environmentalists, the desire to "put power in its place" (Plant and Plant, 1995) is part of a long-range strategy to solve the underlying causes of the ecological crisis: the centralized control of resources and political processes by elites with vested interests in the global rather than the local economy. Almost all urban sustainability visions incorporate some form of community participation – ranging from greater involvement in decision-making at the local level to co-operative and communal living. Ecosystem planners are in favour of inclusive public processes and seek ways to encourage greater community stewardship of the local environment. More radical visions for urban political change are advocated by red-greens and anarcho-greens who believe that simply increasing participation in the current system is not enough (Dobson, 1995). Bioregionalists, for example, believe that small, non-hierarchical, and co-operative communities are the most natural and sustainable way for humans to live (Sale, 1992). Libertarian municipalism, a concept developed by social ecologist and anarchist Murray Bookchin (1992), would entail the local control of policy-making through the direct, face-to-face participation of citizens of autonomous municipalities that are organized into a coordinated network of municipalities.

THE FEMINIST CITY VS THE ECO-CITY

These five principles and the strategies they inspire seem to follow logically from a careful analysis of the urban ecological problematic. Without a doubt all, if implemented, would yield dramatic improvements in the quality of life for urban dwellers. Who can argue with making the city more livable for all? Why quibble about feminist political aims when "we lay gasping for a clean breath of air on our devastated earth?" (Eichler, 1995b: 1). The answer to the question is this: while feminists may heartily endorse many urban sustainability strategies in principle, it is in the anticipated implementation stage that things seem to get a little dubious – and a lot political – particularly when it comes to who does what, when, and how.

Visions of a feminist or non-sexist city have been an important part of feminist urban scholarship. As a critical-visionary perspective, feminist urbanism has always highlighted the effects of androcentric and gender-blind nature of planning practices on women's experience of cities, as well as developing innovative alternatives that promise to be of benefit to all urban dwellers (MacGregor, 1995). One of the most celebrated examples of this literature is Dolores Hayden's "What Would a Non-sexist City be Like? Speculations on Housing, Urban Design and Human Work" (1980), in which she outlines a program for reorganizing public/urban and private/household life in the context of American society. In Canada, feminist urban scholars have been very active in contributing to the development of a feminist urban agenda that includes radical changes in housing, social service, transportation, and land use policy (MacGregor, 1995). For example, Gerda Wekerle's work since the late 1970s has not only consistently been critical of the gender-blind nature of the environmental professions but also has documented the role of women as academics, bureaucrats, and activists in the reshaping of urban policy and urban form in Canadian cities (1980, 1993, and 1996; Wekerle and Whitzman, 1995; Wekerle and Peake, 1996).

Recently, several books and articles have kept up Hayden's tradition by imagining what a "feminist city" would be like (Andrew, 1992), what a "safe city" would be like (Wekerle and Whitzman, 1995), and what a "non-sexist sustainable city" would be like (Eichler, 1995a). Drawing on Andrew's piece, Margrit Eichler (1995b: 16) summarizes the feminist city to include some of the following dimensions: "a wide variety of services; elimination of public violence against women ... a first class public transportation system that is safe, cheap, and efficient; active encouragement of community-based, economic development, with meaningful jobs for women, co-ordinated with daycare; [and] a close physical relationship between services, residences, and work-places, encouraged by mixed urban land uses."

There is also a small but growing feminist critique of municipal amalgamation, gentrification, and urban restructuring in the current context of the new right globalization agenda – a context that sub-stantially alters the terms of the debate and the latitude for making gender-friendly urban policy changes (cf. Bondi, 1991; Jezierski, 1995; Kofman, 1998; Fincher and Jacobs, 1998; Milroy, this volume; Whitz-man, ibid). This literature looks at the restructured, post-industrial division of labour, the socio-spatial impacts of globalization, and "important structural and political changes [that] have affected women's roles in [paid] work, in the community, and at home" (Jezier-ski, 1995: 61). There is also greater recognition of the intersections of gender, race, class, nationality, and ability than there has been in the feminist urbanist scholarship that once portrayed women as a univer-sal category (MacGregor, 1995). And now along comes the discourse of urban sustainability. What might feminist urbanists have to say about the gender implications of this new vision with a putative con-cern for nature, equality, democracy, and freedom in North American cities?

At first blush, observers may in fact find some interesting overlaps between feminist and urban sustainability approaches on points relat-ing to urban form. For example, increased urban density and mixed land use would be beneficial not only environmentally, but would also help to transcend the work-home dichotomy that has made life in the Fordist city so problematical for women (Jezierski, 1995). In addition, feminists will see the benefit of higher urban density in the potential to increase the use of public spaces thereby making them safer – although the safety of parks and green spaces, something about which feminist planners have been quite vocal (cf. Whitzman, 1995; Whitzman and Wekerle, 1995), is seldom mentioned. Housing intensification and co-housing designs are not only more resource and space efficient; they may accommodate a greater diversity of family forms, facilitate the sharing of appliances, and perhaps even the collectivization of child care and domestic work – providing, of course, that housing development proceeds with a commitment to affordability and collectivization rather than following the New Urbanist model, which maintains the single family model and is accessible mainly to the affluent (Leher and Milgrom, 1996). Infill and intensification should also not lead to gentrification, which also tends to reduce the supply of affordable inner-city housing (Bondi, 1991). Features such as intensification, co-housing, and the accomodation of diverse family forms are central to Hayden's (1981) non-sexist city, and something about which Spain (1995) is particularly hopeful when she looks to urban sustainability discourse.[5]

These things considered, it seems possible that physical or design changes that would make the city more ecologically sustainable might also make them more livable and socially equitable. However my suspicion is that, given that transforming traditional gender roles is a concern for neither eco-city planners nor red-green visionaries, any potentially positive benefits relating to women's specific needs may simply be the unintended consequences of efforts to reduce the "ecological footprint" of the city (Wackernagel and Rees, 1996). Meanwhile there are several aspects of the urban sustainability and sustainable communities literature that threaten to intensify gender inequality because there remains little understanding of the gender division of labour and little recognition of the fact that women's experience of urban life is qualitatively different than men's experience because of the persistence of gender inequality (Birkeland, 1991; MacGregor, 1995).

SUSTAINABLE FOR WHOM?
GENDER IMPLICATIONS OF URBAN
SUSTAINABILITY

I will now give some specific examples of what might happen if strategies for urban sustainability fail to take feminist concerns into account. Given that so much of feminist urbanist analysis has been premised on a critique of the gender division of labour, an obvious way to start is to look at the implications of assumptions made about the nature and division of the work required to live sustainably. As alluded to in the opening paragraph of this chapter, this issue undercuts many of the critiques I have of the eco-city vision. In the urban sustainability literature, "work" almost always refers to productive, monetarily remunerated labour in the public sphere and stands in opposition to non-work activities commonly referred to as leisure. If people are not at work, then they are at leisure. There is little recognition of the "continuum of work" that includes full and part-time, paid employment, and community and household managing (unpaid) work (Milroy, 1996). When planners fail to accept all types of work along the continuum as significant, they are highly unlikely to make plans that accommodate them (Milroy, 1996).

We find this to be the case in the recent conversations about how "the end of work" is bringing about opportunities for a socially and environmentally responsible third sector or civil society (Rifkin, 1995). For example, French political ecologists like Alain Lipietz (1992) and Andre Gorz (1993) promote the move to a shorter work week on the grounds that it will bring about the growth of non-consumptive leisure and environment-related voluntarism. Similarly, Canadian environmental theorist Robert Paehlke (1994 and 1998) gives a list of social and environmental benefits that could be felt with the limitation of overtime, the four-day work week, and early retirement schemes: better family relations, higher productivity, lower unemployment, less pressure to extract resources, and more personal time to make environmental lifestyle changes. Many red-greens regard changes in the political economy and organization of "work" as central to the search for sustainability.

As feminists have been arguing for decades, however, the narrow understanding of work as only that which is paid has led to the invisibility and devaluation of the necessary labour performed largely by women (Armstrong and Armstrong, 1994). As a consequence, there is little recognition of the implications of plans for sustainable societies for those who will be compelled, by virtue of their socially constructed gender roles, to perform the extra work required to live sustainably in everyday life. In a 1992 article titled "Who Takes out the Garbage?" sociologist Randy Stoeker writes that social reproduction activities like cooking, cleaning, and caring are often overlooked in research on new social movements (of which the environmental movement is a prime example) and taken for granted by male activists.[6] As Margo Huxley (1994: 187) observes, "usually the gender dimension [of urban environmental change] has been neglected, so that being environmentally sound ends up being 'more work for mother.'" Take, for example, the eco-city principle of minimizing the consumption and waste of resources and the various strategies proposed for realizing this goal.

Insofar as environmentalists and sustainable community planners have realized that changes in living habits are a necessary part of the search for sustainability, they advocate initiatives that demand particular responses from household and community members, such as waste reduction and energy conservation strategies. These kinds of changes in daily living are no doubt important, but what must be challenged is the lack of awareness that they will intensify the burden on unpaid labour. Strategies for minimizing the consumption and waste of resources tend to be targeted at the private sphere. Household recycling, precycling, and composting campaigns are growing in popularity in many Canadian cities. In London, Ontario, for example, a sustainable community initiative is to send experts into private homes to conduct "Home Check-ups" and provide residents – ironically called homeowners – with helpful tips on living green (Vodden, 1997). Many environmentalists recommend the switch to appropriate technologies like solar ovens and composting toilets, and other low-tech, energy-efficient gadgetry in order to reduce energy use and waste production (Roberts and Brandum, 1995).

A feminist critique of this is that all of these strategies demand extra time and effort from those responsible for household maintenance and provisioning. When people no longer rely on household appliances, they must do things by hand. Recycling depends on the diligence of individuals to collect, wash, sort, and transport recyclables, and composting requires increased effort on the part of cooks and gardeners. Precycling involves, one, the reduction of waste by avoiding overpackaged convenience goods and environmentally unfriendly household cleaners and, two, purchasing more fresh foods. Research conducted in German households by Schultz (1993) found that precycling alone adds at least 20 percent more work time for the two-person household. Given the typical gender division of household labour, we can guess who will do the work. Like Huxley (1994), Schultz argues that feminists could quite reasonably see the goal of an environmentally friendly household as simply more work for women.

Canadian ecofeminist sociologist Catriona Sandilands (1993) has argued that placing responsibility for sustainable living on the household can be seen as a form of "environmental privatization." The focus on household waste management programming takes the onus off corporate polluters and municipal regulators who continue to get away with ecological murder. Few urban sustainability visions place a priority on making corporate polluters pay or banning all forms of toxic waste production at the mouth of the pipe. Instead, the majority of attention is placed on residential waste production, which is only a fraction of the problem but is perhaps easiest to target for legislated and/or voluntary compliance. The responsibility is then shifted or downloaded to domestic managers (the majority of whom are women) under the assumption that the ability to provide and serve is elastic and infinite. Rarely is mention made of the work required or who will do it, because unpaid housework is taken for granted (or "externalized" in the language of economics). The same writers who argue that there are biophysical limits to human use of the earth seem to forget that there are also limits to the use of human labour.

Certainly, we need to reconsider the range of energy-, resource-, and waste-intensive practices that we rely on to sustain us, but part of the discussion must be how to ensure an equitable redistribution among men and women of the work that will take their place. This has been an important principle of feminist utopian visions since the material feminists of the nineteenth century who attempted to establish built environments that would free women from shouldering an unfair share of domestic burdens (Hayden, 1981). This has carried over into the contemporary feminist co-housing literature that advocates the kind of spatial and social arrangements that facilitate – and even mandate – collective responsibility for necessary life-sustaining labour. With the sustainability agenda in mind, we might add a commitment to green household practices and the universal right to leisure time that might be used for self-development, physical fitness, intellectual, and spiritual pursuits. It stands to reason that a major part of this alternative vision is a reconsideration of the standards of "good housekeeping" that are embedded in Western culture.[7]

The narrow understanding of work also leads to problems in the strategies designed to reduce automobile use in sustainable community literature. Eco-city planners promote sustainable forms of transportation as a way to reduce "dependency" on private cars and sometimes even as an alternative to public transportation. Many Canadian cities have implemented policies and programs to address air pollution, calm traffic, and promote alternative forms of urban mobility, such as walking and cycling (cf. Roseland, 1998; CMHC, 1997; Roelofs, 1996). These may be viable options for able-bodied people who have fairly uncomplicated travel patterns, but what is frequently not addressed is the logistical problems for those who need private cars to get around the city: those whose family responsibilities have them getting around the city with children and groceries in tow and those whose mobility is limited due to age and/or physical ability. Nowhere is there mention of the relationship between the fear of violence and the avoidance of public forms of transportation, nor are there initiatives to enable children to have independent means of mobility (Huxley, 1997).

Greens sometimes advocate the move to more home-based employment and telecommuting in order to minimize the need to journey to work by car (Paehlke, 1994; Perks and Van Vleit, 1993; Rees and Roseland, 1991). "Telecommuting has potential to substitute for some of the commuting that goes on in and between our communities, and so may lead to a reduction in vehicle trips generated" (Roseland, 1998: 110). Such strategies have been adopted in Portland Oregon and Vancouver, BC, among other places (Rees and Roseland, 1991). Clearly this demonstrates a failure to consider what it means for those workers who already see the home as a twenty-four-hour-a-day workplace. From a feminist perspective, it is important to consider how people are likely to combine domestic and paid work under one roof. Given that women do the majority of the housework, which, in a sense, "is never done," it stands to reason that home-based employment will cause great difficulty for women workers. Sherry Ahrentzen's (1997) research has found that home-based employment can be extremely isolating for women and that many women enjoy the escape from domestic responsibility that going outside the home to work provides.

The apparent enthusiasm for telecommuting, it seems to me, is a product of a rather elite understanding of the so-called informational city taking shape in the globalization discourse (Castells, 1989). How many workers in the new global economy actually perform the kind of labour that can be accomplished in cyberspace? How many urban sustainability writers have in mind making jeans for the Gap and getting paid by the piece in an unventilated basement as an example of working at home? In the global city, there has been an increase in flexible, casual, and subcontracted work, and in work performed at home. It is well known that women and racialized people (particularly new immigrants) are concentrated in poorly paid "bad jobs" (Kofman, 1998). Further, recent movement toward spatial fragmentation of urban areas will make women's efforts to combine employment and family life more difficult than ever before (Jezierski, 1995).

Sustainable community planners have embraced the principle of self-reliance as integral to the eco-city vision (cf. O'Hara, 1993; Nozick, 1992; Roseland, 1997). Urban agriculture – the production of food in community gardens (also know as community shared agriculture) – and permaculture initiatives are seen as ways to reduce the need to import food from other regions, improve energy efficiency, and give urbanites a new respect for natural processes. The benefits are great, writes Roseland (1998: 47): "as people reconnect with one of nature's most basic processes, save money on food bills, and enjoy greater local self-reliance." The same is often said for local craft production, which can bring people into touch with their cultural heritage, increase community pride, and boost the local economy.

Community economic development initiatives like Local Employment and Trading Systems (LETS) and worker-owned businesses are promoted as a way for local communities to circumvent the pressures of the global capitalist system, foster personal empowerment, and promote ecological sustainability. One writer sees the LETS as a way for low-income people to meet their needs without money and thereby get off welfare (Burman, 1997). Co-operative daycare centres and community kitchens are promoted as a way to decrease reliance on state-delivered social services and to make more efficient use of community space (Rees and Roseland, 1991). A consistent theme throughout the CMHC sustainable communities report is the development of self-help, volunteer, and co-op programs as part of a program of economic change.

This leaves me wondering who is doing the work required to plan, manage, and maintain these collective projects. While collectivizing socially necessary work can be (and has been) seen as a positive change from a feminist perspective, it does not automatically lead to the dismantling of gender roles or expectations about who should perform certain tasks. This is demonstrated in the literature on intentional communities and 1960s communes (cf. Kanter, 1972). I have personally visited many community kitchen and garden projects where all the participants were women. I also wonder how the goal of self-reliance fits into the efforts of New Right governments to download the work of caring to the community. The Harris government in Ontario has attempted to cut its social service costs by promoting "community care" and restoring a greater sense of personal responsibility for poverty (MacGregor, 1997). The notion that community and self-reliance is, in part, the answer to sustainability appears dangerously close to playing into such an agenda due to the failure to deconstruct the concept of "community" or problematize the amount of work required to maintain collective projects.

A central part of feminist urban scholarship has been the destabilization of homogenizing uses of community that mask diversity and inequalities (cf. Garber, 1995; Young, 1990). With such an understanding in mind, feminists might wonder how women will be able to engage in paid work if they depend on child care that they also have to organize or for which they must pay with the exchange of more work (as might happen with LETS). Can a bartering system ensure universal access to services? Sometimes people are too busy, poor, or are physically unable to be self-reliant, that is in part why feminists have embraced the welfare state and concept of social citizenship throughout the second wave of the women's movement. An alternative feminist vision of a sustainable community would include universal access to affordable and professional services that alleviate the private responsibilities of homemakers, thereby ensuring them the right to truly "free" time (Schor, 1997). After all, as feminist ecological economists have been active in pointing out, the work done to reproduce and nurture the next generation is a public good that ought to be counted as the core of the human economy and ought to be supported as such (cf. Waring, 1989; Pietilla, 1997).

Finally, if we look at the principle of decentralization and participatory democracy in the sustainable community vision, we see more demands on unpaid time with little or no thought as to how "citizens" can do it all. It seems that the ideal inhabitant of a sustainable community is someone who has the time, energy, and resources to practice green household strategies, engage in local development projects, and take an active part in the decision-making processes required to manage the community.

Most sustainability advocates envision a greater role for citizens in the planning and administration of local communities and neighbourhoods (Dobson, 1995; Rees and Roseland, 1991). Citizen advisory boards, task forces, and roundtables on environmental issues, community-based environmental impact assessments, and other forms of participatory democracy are thought to be an essential element of a sustainable society.

While feminists are likely to support participatory democracy and more inclusive decision-making processes, this should be tempered by concerns for disparities in the ability to participate between men and women. Feminist political theorists argue that it is about equality of condition, not just equal opportunity to participate (Young, 1990). They have been extremely critical of masculinist notions of politics and citizenship that take for granted or/and completely ignore the role of the private sphere in the functioning of the polis. Indeed, the very notion of citizenship – heartily embraced by Bookchin and Sale – is based on the Athenian model of politics, wherein citizens had women and slaves (who were denied citizenship status) to care for their basic needs. Rarely do advocates of citizen participation and social movement activism take into account that these activities are incredibly time-consuming and require a range of conditions that only a small and relatively privileged segment of the population enjoy (Stoecker, 1992). For women who already perform a double or triple day of work, taking an active role in the planning and ongoing management of their community adds an additional burden to their already overburdened lives (Milroy, 1996). And, if women are not able to participate in public decision-making, it is doubtful whether issues of concern to women will make it onto the political agenda of the sustainable community (Zillman, 1996).

A feminist approach to urban sustainability would qualify the notion of political participation and direct democracy with the principle that the realm of necessity also must be democratized and that the line between the public and the private is up for constant negotiation and contestation. So far, the discussion does not seem to be moving very quickly in this direction. Feminist scholarship on women's urban activism needs to continue to challenge conventional meanings of politics and to show how central this work is to the quest for sustainability (Wekerle and Peake, 1996). At the same time, however, we need to be careful not to romanticize this work to the point where gender roles are reinscripted and the overburdening of individual women is portrayed as a sacrifice necessary for the common good. Instead, feminist urbanists need to develop a definition of local citizenship that puts up front community power dynamics and the relationships between gender, race, class, place, and politics. As Chantal Mouffe (1992: 376) argues, feminists ought to strive for a redefinition of radical democratic citizenship that addresses the pervasive postmodern questions of identity and pluralism and for a degendered notion of citizenship that " would create the conditions for a new hegemony articulated through new egalitarian social relations, practices and institutions." Only through the development of this kind of overtly eco-political analysis, I would argue, will feminist urban sustainability advocates be able to combat the persistent blind spots and stay-sharp double-edged swords of patriarchal urban theories and practices.

CONCLUSION: PUTTING GENDER ON THE URBAN SUSTAINABILITY AGENDA

I want to conclude by pointing out that many of the criticisms I have made about eco-city visions are not exactly new. In fact, Rebecca Peterson made similar criticisms in 1979 of what was then called the "Conserver Society." Obviously, despite more than twenty years of feminist critiques of man-made environments and man-envisioned utopias, we haven't had much success in persuading non-feminist scholars to put the specific gender-based concerns of women on the urban agenda. Why is this the case?

In a similar kind of critical (and frustrated!) discussion, British feminist geographer Doreen Massey (1991) posits that the continued loyalty to the Marxist narrative of class conflict and the unwavering belief that capitalism is the root of all evil are to blame for the nasty case of "flexible sexism" plaguing the discipline of geography. This appears to be the case with many urban political ecologists, who seem to tack "gender" on to their list of themes for a new urban research agenda only reluctantly and then never follow through with that aspect of the research. (They are likely confident that some feminist somewhere will do it for them.) There also the problem of the persistent disagreements/misunderstandings over what constitutes public and private space. As Elizabeth Wilson (1995) notes, recent discussions about the privatization of space through electronic monitoring technologies – typified by the work of Mike Davis (1990) – have complicated the efforts of feminist urbanists to address the gendering and dichotomizing of space evident in non-feminist urban theory. Eleanor Kofman (1998) suggests that the global cities discourse is too concerned with the city as a place of capital accumulation, too apt to classify people based on their location in the global economy, and not concerned enough with the significance of race, ethnicity, political status, and gender in the analysis of globalizing cities. "What is clear," she writes, "is that gender makes a difference to the nature of stratification and widening inequalities, a difference that cannot be measured in terms of the neutered and decontextualized individual" (Kofman, 1998: 280).

The addition of environmental concerns to an urban research and policy agenda may have pushed gender and feminism even further into the background. In the critique of the current state of cities there is a nostalgic vision of community and self-reliance that does not bode well for women's liberation. There is also now a prevailing assumption that "we're all in this together": since we all face the threat of ecological collapse, then we humans stand to benefit equally from efforts to avert it. Little attempt is made to understand the diversity within the universal "we" or that some of "us" may stand to win more than others in the process (Marcuse, 1998, is an exception). And if this is given consideration, the urgent threat of global destruction seems a valid excuse for putting equality off until the time when we can breathe easily again. This is reminiscent of the "wait till after the revolution" line that women have been given in most socialist struggles (Sargent, 1981).

Ecofeminist theory provides the tools to critically analyze the false universalism of masculinist environmental and planning discourse that leaves little room for the particularities of gender, race, or class experience (Birkeland, 1991 and 1993). Some have gone so far as to find explanations for gender-blindness and sexism in male psychosocial development and the deeply rooted traits of masculine identity (cf. Plumwood, 1994). How else are we to account for the fact that if feminists do not raise issues of importance to daily life, like who takes out the garbage, they simply go unmentioned (Eichler, 1995)?

Leaving aside this difficult and perhaps unanswerable question, it seems clear that in the face of current priorities in Canadian urban affairs, as tenuous as they may be, there is a need for feminist urban scholars and activists to remain vigilant in their struggle to keep gender on the urban agenda. While it may be tempting to engage in the rather fashionable academic discussions on topics like sustainability, globalization, and cyberspace, by their very nature, such topics seem very far removed from the necessary details and basic requirements of survival in the places where people live. As such, they may obscure the fact that a great proportion of people's everyday lives remains the same in the face of vast economic, technological, and environmental change. People still need affordable homes, safe places to play, help with their chores, decent wages, and friendly support in order to lead a meaningful and healthy existence. There is a great amount of labour that will never be mechanized or made obsolete by artificial intelligence. It is therefore impossible to speak about the "end of work." With projected changes in demographics and in light of the erosion of the welfare state, life-sustaining labour is arguably a growth sector in Canadian cities. Since, with few exceptions, feminists are the only ones who are concerned with the conditions and distribution of this work – and their implications for the spatial arrangements in which we live – there remains a lot of work left to do to ensure that gender justice is part of the urban sustainability agenda and indeed *any* urban agenda.

NOTES

Author's Note: This chapter is based on a paper presented at the World Congress of Sociology, International Sociological Association, in Montreal in July 1998. I would like to thank Gerda Wekerle for her assistance in preparing and presenting the original paper. This research was supported by a doctoral fellowship from the Social Science and Humanities Council of Canada.

1 By most accounts, the ascendance of environmental concern was ignited by the release of the World Commission on Environment and Development (WCED) report *Our Common Future* in 1987. In Canada, the federal government responded by drafting a Green Plan in 1990 and establishing a National Roundtable on the Environment and Development (NRTEE) in 1992. For more information of the history of the Canadian environmental agenda, see Dalal-Clayton, 1996.

2 These case studies include the Fraser River Estuary Management Program (BC), the Fraser Basin Management Board (BC), the Georgia Basin Initiative (BC), Alberta's Integrated Regional Planning System, the Meeswasin Valley Authority (SK), Cumulative Effects Monitoring on the Niagara Escarpment (ON), Oak Ridges Morain (ON), Laurel Creek Watershed (ON), Regional Municipality of Ottawa-Carleton (ON), the Waterfront Regeneration Trust (ON), the Hamilton Harbour Remedial Action Plan (ON), the St Lawrence Action Plan (PQ), and the St Croix Estuary Project (NB/US); Tomalty et al., 1994.

3 The collapse of the East and West Coast fisheries is a prime example of this situation (cf. Rogers, 1994).

4 Models of high-density Compact City design are promoted in planning circles throughout North America. In the US, Peter Calthorpe has developed the notion of "pedestrian pockets" that allow residents to meet most of their daily needs without using a car. Urban intensification initiatives have been popular in Canadian municipalities as well. For example, the official plan of the now-defunct Metropolitan Toronto included a commitment to the concept of housing intensification.

5 The emergence of feminism and ecofeminism has been seen as a response to the fact that women activists in the New Left and environmental movements were left to do the dishes while their male counterparts were out fighting the establishment (cf. Mellor, 1992).

6 Others do recognize the problems associated with such a strategy (Roseland, 1998).

7 We might also question who is the "self" in "self-reliance" – it may very well be code for greater household sufficiency, which typically translates into a greater burden of work for women.

4 The "Voice of Women" in Canadian Local Government[1]

CAROLYN WHITZMAN

INTRODUCTION

Mobilizing at the local government level has been relatively peripheral to the contemporary feminist movement in Canada.[2] One reason for the low level of importance accorded by the feminist movement to local governments is that priority issues such as poverty, childcare, violence against women, and access to abortion were under senior government jurisdiction, and senior governments were also major sources of funding for feminist organizations. Another, equally powerful, reason is that local government has traditionally been seen by both women and men as a matter of technical administration – "roads, rates, and rubbish" – rather than political choices (Andrew, 1992). "Women's issues" or more precisely, a gendered analysis of urban issues such as housing, transportation, public safety, and social services, have also been quite peripheral to Canadian mainstream urban planning, governance, and academeme.[3] Nevertheless, a significant body of academic work over the past thirty years has elaborated on ways that local government policies, programs, and services have a gendered impact, and there is a harder-to-find but equally significant current history of how women have tried to make an impact on urban planning and governance. The focus of this chapter is on these attempts to give women a "voice" at the local political arena in Canada: who these voices were (and were not), what the voices have said (and have not), where the voices have had impact (and where they have not), and how recent changes at the local government level may have an impact on these voices.

It is impossible within the limits of a chapter to fully describe all of these attempts,[4] especially since there are so many potential areas where local government could make a positive change in women's lives: housing, transportation, income, policing, urban environment, food, provision of services, childcare, recreation, etc. I am using as case studies three mechanisms that women have used to try to locate "voices" in local government discourse and influence local government policies, programs, and services:

1   institutionalized "women's committees" and "safe city committees" operating as part of local governments;
2   the "Women's Safety Audit Guide," a community or "grassroots" organizing tool on improving public safety for women, originally developed in Toronto ten years ago, but now used nationally and internationally;
3   participatory research on women's planning needs, with an emphasis on a research and advocacy organization called Women Plan Toronto, which has remained active for more than fifteen years.

In all of these case studies, there has been some academic literature on the subject, but as is often the case, feminist activism or praxis and feminist academe have not necessarily been well connected. I am focusing on these three case studies partly because they hold lessons about getting voices "inserted" in local government discourse, but also in order to validate hitherto unwritten histories by including them in a book. Part of the lesson I have learned over fifteen years of feminist activism is that, in Canadian society, stories that do not get written down get lost. In fact, as these case studies will illustrate, even writing stories down on paper is no guarantee that the lessons from these stories will not get lost or misconstrued.

THE INTELLECTUAL BACKGROUND: WHAT ARE THESE WOMEN ON ABOUT?

Since the early 1970s, "a small group of feminist academics, planners, and grassroots activists in developed countries have been critically analysing the role of the built environment in the perpetuation of gender inequality and other forms of social and environmental justice" (MacGregor, 1995: 26).

Beginning with a tentative exploration in an American "radical journal of geography" in 1973 (Burnett, 1973), and elaborated throughout the 1980s,[5] a socialist feminist analysis of the North American city began to develop, especially in relation to housing, transportation, and social services. The gist of this analysis was that urban policy focused on what socialists would call "production," on paid work; but what about "reproduction," the unpaid work such as childrearing and household management that was necessary for the smooth functioning and generational continuation of paid work? As women enter the paid job market, they still are generally responsible for unpaid caring of children, elders, and home. Moreover, urban policy assumed a spatial divide between (paid) "work" and "home," and this divide has increased as urban planning has increasingly emphasized car-based transport (Mackenzie and Rose, 1983; Hayden, 1984; Wekerle, 1984; Michelson, 1985). There is also increasing concern that the gendered workload of "caring" is increasing as governments cut back on health care and social services: volunteer services and families are expected to step in to fill up the slack (Milroy, 1991a: 5–6).

Using categories developed by Adamson, Briskin, and McPhail (1988) as a template, the empirical research could be summarized this way:

1 the challenge of difference: looking at ways, for instance, that women's experience of housing access might be different than men's because of generally lower incomes and greater family obligations (e.g., McClain and Doyle, 1984);
2 the sexual division of labour, especially within the household: for instance, different transportation patterns because of household obligations such as grocery shopping or dropping children off at childcare (e.g., Michelson, 1985);
3 the role of the state in reproducing power relationships (along with the workplace and family): the ways, for instance, that local government zoning has encouraged the separation of home and work, and has made suburban services ranging from home-based childcare to small business incubators more difficult to access (e.g., Ritzdorf, 1986);
4 a challenge to the public/private divide: the rejoinder to these empirical studies might be that it is a private choice whether to have children, or how household labour is divided. The implicit challenge in this literature is that "private" lives, in part, are determined by the constraints of public space, and that the impact on these "private" lives was a legitimate concern for public policy (McDowell and Pringle, 1992).

The analysis went beyond empirical research on the *products* of urban policy and planning – what is wrong – to *process* and *theory* – why things have gone wrong and how we can think of cities in a new way in order to correct these wrongs (MacGregor, 1995). Literature on these subjects includes historical research on forgotten alternatives to current urban policy and form (Hayden, 1984), development of alternative futures – what might a non-sexist city be like (Hayden, 1981; Andrew, 1992; Eichler, 1995b) – and an increasing emphasis on how urban planning and policy might be retheorized so that these "private" concerns might be seen as less marginal (Milroy, 1991a; Sandercock and Forsyth, 1990 and 1992a; Planning Theory, 1992; Hendler, 1994).

A second, and secondary, stream of feminist literature on the gendered city flows from a 1974 article by two French radical feminists, Enjeu and Save. This literature takes as its central fact women's different use of public space because of male violence against women. In contrast to the socialist feminists, who focus on material barriers to women's equality such as inadequate public transit, housing choice, or social services, feminists who write about violence against women focus on less tangible but no less significant barriers to full participation in public life. As will be discussed below, women are more likely to avoid public spaces such as parks and downtown streets, especially after dark, because of fear of crime, and this fear of crime, which is commonly labelled by urban decision-makers as "irrational," is actually based on real experience and knowledge (METRAC, 1990; Valentine, 1990 and 1992; Whitzman, 1995).

Despite some differences in organizations and emphasis between these two feminist streams, they share both an overriding epistemology and an underlying weakness. Epistemology is a daunting term that means simply "how we learn what we know." In the case of a feminist critique of how cities are built and run, the importance of *listening to the voices and lives* of everyday women cannot be overemphasized. Drawing on criticism of urban planning dating back to Jane Jacobs (1961), the critique directly challenges the idea of objective expertise in urban planning and policy (e.g., Ritzdorf, 1992). Instead, it posits that one's understanding of what is important or legitimate is a result of personal experience and that experience itself may be a form of expertise. In other words, not only is including a gendered analysis of housing, urban transportation, public safety, and social services important in the creation of local government policy and programs, but developing this analysis through talking with women, listening to women, using women's own knowledge and experiences, even creating pictures or other symbolic forms with women is equally important (Sandercock and Forsyth, 1992b: 45).

The weakness of feminist writing on the city is inherent in its epistemology, and that is its exclusivity. If knowledge is based on understanding of personal experience, then the personal experiences drawn upon in this literature have been mostly those of middle-class, white, heterosexual, able-bodied women living in large cities of the overdeveloped world (MacGregor, 1995: 41). Other than gender, there have been more social similarities than differences between those making local government decisions and those feminists criticizing these decisions. Although some recent Canadian feminist empirical research attempts to address difference based on race, ethnicity, sexual orientation, and ability[6] – and other research on urban experience has certainly attempted to "reach out" to more marginalized women – the majority of those writing and advocating on "women's" behalf have represented a relatively small and privileged group of women. The emphasis on differences between men and women, as opposed to differences *between* women, may obscure as much as it explains (Lugones and Spelman, 1983; Young, 1990; Sandercock and Forsyth, 1992a: 50).

FROM KNOWLEDGE TO ACTION: WAYS OF GETTING WOMEN'S VOICES HEARD IN CANADA

Women have worked, individually and together, in hundreds of ways to make their voices heard at the political level. Demonstrating, lobbying, voting, running for political office, working for a political party, working within the system as a "femocrat," boycotting, demanding funding for services from government, autonomously organizing services not provided by government, and publicizing injustices or successes are all ways that women have used to actively influence politics (Wekerle and Peake, 1996). These activities are sometimes put on a scale, with "mainstreaming" or working within existing structures on one end and "disengagement" or ignoring structures such as government on the other (Adamson, Briskin, and McPhail, 1988: 180–5). However, the realities of working "in and against the state"[7] are increasingly complex. For instance, many women's services that developed autonomously in the early 1970s, such as rape crisis centres and battered women's shelters, now depend on government funding to operate. Conversely, many socialist feminists now question the idea that state organizations are immovable objects and are exploring the extent to which social change can be brought about via the institutions of the state (Halford, 1992; Watson, 1992).

In the limited literature on feminist work within local government, women's committees have received the most ink, especially in Great Britain, Australia, and Canada.[8] However, basic information, such as which Canadian cities have or have had women's and/or safe city committees, is not readily available. I approached the Federation of Canadian Municipalities (FCM), the National Action Committee on the Status of Women, and YWCA-Canada with the request for a list or at least some contact names, to no avail. The information of women's safety audits and on participatory research on women's planning needs is even more sketchy: although METRAC, the originator of the Safety Audit Guide, has received hundreds of requests for guides in Canada, they have no list of who is doing safety audits where, nor does the National Crime Prevention Centre. Similarly, Women Plan Toronto has sent out hundreds of copies of its original report, *Shared Experiences and Dreams* (1986), but does not keep a list of who ordered what from where. Fortunately, in my ten years as coordinator of the Toronto Safe City Committee, I had also received requests for information on safety and planning issues from staff and/or community activists in many of the larger cities in Canada. From following up by phone or email with these contacts, as well as contact names given by the YWCA and FCM, I was able to assemble a "snowball" sampling of twenty-five cities and their experiences with women's committees, safety audits, and participatory research on women and planning.[9] Contacts for Guelph, St. John, and St. John's were out of service or unreturned.

Finally, an apology. The stories told below emphasize work accomplished in Toronto, Canada's largest city. This is partly because of the personal experience of the author, but mostly because Toronto's initiatives have had a large influence on other Canadian cities. There are certain regions of Canada that are underrepresented, and I wish I had more stories from the East and the North.

WOMEN'S COMMITTEES AND SAFE CITY COMMITTEES IN CANADA: THE INSIDE-OUT DILEMMA

In Canada, as elsewhere in the Western world, there is a long history of women's involvement at the local government level: in school boards, welfare committees, and settlement houses and housing initiatives.[10] To give one example, the Regina Council of Women has been in existence for 102 years; its initial concerns with immigrant settlement and health services continue to be strong themes.[11] The involvement of middle-class women in local governance did not necessarily have benevolent impacts on other women with less social or economic power. Margaret Little (1998), for instance, details the "moral regulation of single mothers" in Ontario by volunteer welfare committees appointed by local government. But the idea of a local government committee that might represent women as a collective subject is relatively new (Wekerle, 1991).

The first Canadian local government women's committee that has received any attention in the literature is Toronto's Mayor's Committee on the Status of Women, which existed from 1972 to 1975 (Wekerle, 1991; Whitzman, 1992). In the late 1980s and early 1990s, women's committees sprang up in larger Canadian cities such as Montreal, Québec, and Toronto (again), along with committees on race relations, seniors, and people with disabilities. These "equity" committees were both a product of these communities' advocacy for a "voice" at the local level of government and of local government's resultant desire to provide a visible example of responsiveness to the concerns of the vocal marginalized. Often, however, identity-based committees have provided only the appearance of inclusivity and have had little impact on the policies, programs, and process of local governments.

In Toronto, for instance, the Mayor's Task Force on the Status of Women was established soon after a reform council was elected in 1972, with a membership consisting of three city councillors and representatives of women's organizations. It was given an impossibly broad mandate: to report back to the Mayor within a year of its establishment, having:

[inquired] into the status of women in the City of Toronto to determine what action should be taken to ensure women have equal opportunities to men in all aspects of society and equal access to employment, recreation, housing, information, social services and other prerequisites of residence in the City of Toronto without regard to age, marital status, sexual orientation, or the age and number of children (City of Toronto, 1973, cited in Wekerle, 1991: 6–7).

Although the Task Force did generate reports on equal pay for work of equal value, childcare, abortion, venereal disease, recreation opportunities, and affirmative action, the "Final Report" of the City of Toronto Task Force on the Status of Women in 1976 was highly critical of the lack of support from the City Council and the potential for action on its recommendations. It was underresourced, with only one full-time staff person assigned, while being expected to comment on every city policy that might have an impact on women. The end result, it felt, was that it was distrusted both inside and outside City Hall (City of Toronto, 1976). Although a recommendation in the final report led to the establishment of an Equal Opportunity Office within the City of Toronto's bureaucratic structure, it is difficult to determine whether the work done by the Mayor's Task Force had an impact on the status of women in Toronto (Wekerle, 1991: 8–9).

The idea of a "women's committee" in Toronto was revived on the eve of another election, in 1991, although again the precise reasons for its creation are unclear, even for people quite close to the action. Wekerle (1991: 17) contends that it was intended as a more conservative counter-balance to the overtly feminist Safe City Committee, a City of Toronto committee that was working on issues of public violence against women; certainly, the politicians supporting the 1991 Mayor's Committee on the Status of Women were not the feminists on council who had supported the establishment of the Safe City Committee. Although this women's committee had a longer life than the first Toronto women's committee – and it again commissioned research on issues related to women's equity – it repeated the exact same mistakes as its predecessor and had as little impact on policy. In the course of research for this article, I asked both the present coordinator of the Committee and another staffer who knew the Committee's work for a summary of recommendations made by the Committee and any follow-up on these recommendations: these documents do not exist. Then I asked both women what the Committee had accomplished in the years they had acted as part-time staffers to it, and they were both hard-pressed to answer.

In contrast to the Toronto experience, where the impetus to create a women's committee came from inside city government, both Montreal and Québec's women's committees grew out of ad hoc advocacy groups. Montreal's Collectif Femmes et Ville (Women and the City Collective) was formed by eight women, planning students and professionals, who were angered that the 1988 background documents for the City of Montreal's Official Plan made little mention of gender. Together, they developed a document that demonstrated how feminist concerns about safety, housing, social services, and childcare could be incorporated into a planning document. After making a presentation at a public meeting, the group was convinced that their recommendations would be ignored. But the new left-leaning party in power, the Montreal Citizens Movement, wanted to distance itself from the previous administration. A powerful feminist councillor, Lea Cousineau, asked them to re-present their proposals to the Standing Committee on Urban Planning. By 1989, the Mayor had released a report drawing on the Femmes et Ville document and created a committee within the Planning Department to implement their recommendations (City of Montreal, 1989; Lahaise and Whitzman, 1990; FCM and FVM, 1997).

Québec City's initiative was inspired by the Montreal example. There, too, a small group of feminist academics and activists created a

Femmes et Ville document that was adopted by local government. The Québec City initiative has had a particular focus on achieving equality in political representation. In 1993, half the seats on the City's executive committee were filled by women. In 1996, seats were reserved for women on neighbourhood councils (FCM and FVM, 1997).

Among the few other Canadian cities with women's committees, the City of Saskatoon commissioned a series of focus groups on "women's issues" within the community, which led to an advisory committee on women's issues; the committee remains active.[12] In Hamilton, a Status of Women Committee was established in 1994, but after an unsuccessful attempt to create a safe city committee, staffing support was cut back as part of a review of standing committees.[13]

Women's committees were the exception rather than the norm in Canadian cities of the 1980s and 1990s: a recent survey by Wekerle of 112 Canadian cities found only six formal Status of Women Committees (Wekerle, 1997). This contrasts with Great Britain, where, in 1989, Halford found fourteen full women's committees, eight women's subcommittees, and ten related initiatives such as women and planning groups (cited in Little, 1994: 79), although Little noted that no new women's initiatives had been established since 1990 and that eight committees had folded. The most successful women's committees, in Montreal and Québec City, have perhaps been more influenced by developments in Europe than by their English Canadian counterparts. In the Netherlands, women's emancipation officers became a statutory local government requirement in the late 1980s (Penrose, 1987), and a number of other European countries, including Norway, have adopted a similar course (FCM and FVM, 1997). Québec representatives have actively participated in the Federation of Canadian Municipalities' International Office and the International Union of Local Authorities, who have recently developed a declaration on Women in Local Government (IULA, 1998). In contrast, an American presence in international discussions on women and the city has been notably absent (OECD, 1995; FCM and FVM, 1997), and English Canada seems to be obsessed with following the bad example of the USA in this as in other political issues.

Although generalized local government women's committees have not been strong in Canada, women-led committees that focus on community safety in general and violence against women in particular have gone further than in most countries (OECD, 1995: 98). In 1982, a series of rape/murders proved the galvanizing force behind the establishment of a Task Force on Public Violence Against Women and Children at the Metropolitan or regional level of government in Toronto. Violence against women, which had been virtually ignored by the 1973-75

Toronto Status of Women Task Force, was the exclusive issue for this committee (Wekerle, 1986). The feminist terms of reference – emphasizing "women and children victims of crime," pornography and sexist imagery as a root cause of violence, and improved funding for rape crisis centres and shelters as a means of dealing with crime – were a result of lobbying by women's advocacy groups as well as the presence of feminists within the local power structures (Whitzman, 1992: 171). For instance, Jane Pepino, a conservative feminist development lawyer who was a member of the Police Services Board in 1982, became the chair of the Task Force, and Pat Freeman Marshall, who was active in the Liberal Party, became the first Executive Director of the organization that resulted from the Task Force.

Once again, the work of a task force led to the establishment of an advocacy organization. Instead of an office within the bureaucracy, however, the advocacy organization was to be government-funded but separately incorporated. Whether it was because of this "arms-length" relationship, because the timing was right, or because of the talents and connections of the individuals involved, METRAC – the Metro Action Committee on Public Violence Against Women and Children – became extremely effective at mobilizing the energies of grassroots organizations, academics, and bureaucracies. With Women Plan Toronto and York University's Faculty of Environmental Studies, METRAC conducted a series of workshop with a variety of diverse women's groups, asking the simple but potent question, "Where do you feel unsafe and why?" This information was supplemented by a questionnaire, distributed selectively through women's centres and other women's gathering places. The results helped pinpoint areas of concern, including public transit and parks (Sterner, 1987), which in turn helped set further directions for METRAC's activism (Whitzman, 1992; Klodowsky, Lundy, and Andrew, 1994).

In the meantime, the City of Toronto was engaged in a long-term planning process for its largest centre city park, High Park, and the Toronto Transit Commission (TTC) was engaged in a study of its accessibility to the growing elderly and disabled population. The City's Parks Department commissioned a user survey of High Park in 1987, which found that twice as many men used the park during the day as women and three times as many men used the park during the evening as women. Of the respondents concerned about their safety, 93 percent were women (City of Toronto, 1987: 8). The 1996 TTC Public Attitude Survey found that 45 percent of women felt uncomfortable riding TTC vehicles after dark, as compared to 13 percent of men (Toronto Transit Commission, 1988). Both entities called in METRAC to act as consultants, which led to reports on improving safety

(METRAC, 1989a; Grant, 1989). While there has been no formal evaluation of either report's effectiveness, many of the recommendations in both reports have been implemented, including better staff training and public information on harassment and assault in the TTC, increased evening parks programming, and a new signage system in High Park. The TTC and the Parks and Recreation Department also committed to some systemic changes in the way they planned. The TTC has paid groups such as Women Plan Toronto to consult on safety and security concerns while planning their new subway stations, and the Parks and Recreation Department established safety guidelines for park design and maintenance (Coates, Guberman, and Orsini, 1992). By keeping their involvement focused and specific, by making connections with specific powerful organizations who showed vulnerability on safety issues, and by being able to mobilize individual women and women's organizations to show up at public meetings (the Dis-Abled Women's Network was especially effective in making their concerns known to the TTC during their consultations), METRAC was able to set the wheels in motion to create small but significant changes in women's lives in Toronto.

Out of the High Park and TTC experiences, METRAC developed a checklist of questions that women could use to assess the safety of public places and how they could be improved (see below for a detailed discussion of the safety audit guide). Unfortunately, in the ten years since 1989, METRAC's work has been more and more identified with that single product. Although a CD-ROM has recently been published on sexual assault and harassment in schools, and there has been considerable coalition work on sexual assault legislation, there have been no reports with the impact of *Moving Forward: Making Transit Safer for Women, Planning for Sexual Assault Prevention: Women's Safety in High Park,* and *The Women's Safety Audit Guide.*

METRAC has also had sometimes tense relationships with more grassroots violence against women organizations, who feel that it is overly reformist and does not adequately address the root causes of violence against women. As in Ottawa-Carleton and London, there is a parallel coordinating committee on wife assault (the Toronto Woman Abuse Council, the London Coordinating Committee to End Woman Abuse, and the Ottawa Coordinating Committee to End Violence Against Women) supported by the regional government. The two groups are often set against one another by local government funders, who do not see the reason for funding two groups working on violence against women. But the coordinating committees most often work on local protocols to ensure good communication between agencies and government services and with senior levels of government on reforms to law, justice, health, and socio-economic support systems, while the "action" committees work on immediate local government responses from planning, police, and other agencies. While the partnerships are different, it could be argued that the existence of these parallel organizations helps perpetuate the public/private divide.

A hallmark of work in Toronto in the 1980s was the mutual reinforcement of women's initiatives. Behind the scenes, advocacy by METRAC and Women Plan Toronto, activism by grassroots women's groups formed in the wake of three separate serial rapists in the City of Toronto, and support from left-leaning and/or feminist city councillors led to the development of a report called *The Safe City: Municipal Strategies for Preventing Public Violence Against Women* (City of Toronto, 1988). This report went before Toronto City Council immediately prior to the 1988 municipal election, and led to the creation of a Safe City Committee to monitor the report's implementation.

Unlike the earlier Mayor's Task Force on the Status of Women, but like METRAC in its early days, the Safe City Committee had a focused mandate and a strong network of "outside" women's advocacy groups to guide it. The first years of the Safe City Committee saw notable successes, with a policy in the Official Plan that mandated the inclusion of safety concerns when reviewing development applications; the development of guidelines, workshops, and forums on safer parks, businesses and underground garages; free women's self-defence courses in all thirty city-run recreation centres; and, most ambitiously, a new grants program entitled Breaking the Cycle of Violence, which for the past nine years has disbursed approximately $500,000 annually to community organizations working to prevent violence against women and other vulnerable groups (Whitzman, 1995). The grants program was the product of a consultation with 120 diverse community groups, again asking a simple set of questions, "What are you doing to prevent violence? What would you like to be doing? How can local government help you?" This second consultation led to a two-fold expansion of the Safe City Committee's mandate: to take on "private" as well as "public" violence, and to look at other definitions of vulnerable groups as well as "women": including language, ethnicity, disability, and sexual orientation (Wise-Harris, 1991).

The committee's success generated a backlash from two directions in 1991. The mayor and a right-wing councillor announced a high-profile "Crime Inquiry" that would examine the causes and prevention of crime, with a budget for a six-month inquiry that exceeded the Safe City Committee's allocation for the previous three years. Almost simultaneously, the mayor announced the formation of a Mayor's Committee on the Status of Women. Both of these announcements involved no prior consultation with the Safe City Committee, METRAC, or grass-roots organizations such as the Toronto Rape Crisis Centre, Women Plan Toronto, or any of the neighbourhood women's groups fighting sexual assault in their communities (Wekerle, 1991: 16–17). Despite the inevitable move to disband the Safe City Committee once these two "similar" committees existed, the Safe City Committee held its own in the mid-1990s, organizing a conference on community safety "success stories" in 1994 (Catallo, 1994), developing public education on "what men could do about violence against women" in eleven languages, and working with the race relations and drug abuse prevention committees on issues of common concern. The Committee was also able to galvanize community organizations during a crisis. For instance, in 1991, the report that recommended the Breaking the Cycle of Violence Grants was "tabled" – recommended to be shelved indefinitely – by a City Council subcommittee. The community members of the Safe City Committee swung into action, and by the time the report went on to City Council two weeks later, all seventeen members of council had been personally lobbied, there were dozens of letters of support, and more than two hundred people showed up at the Council Chambers. The report was adopted by City Council with a 16–1 vote. The 1994 election of Barbara Hall as Mayor, at least partly based on her reputation as the Chair of the Safe City Committee, was another highlight for the initiative.

However, the fiscal and organizational pressures created by the amalgamation of the City of Toronto with five adjacent suburban municipalities and the regional level of government in 1998 created almost insurmountable difficulties for both the Safe City Committee and METRAC. The Safe City Committee was reconstituted as the Task Force on Community Safety, with a minority of women's groups as members. It was difficult to interest committee members in violence against women as an issue, especially after less than 1 percent of the five hundred community organizations who responded to a survey identified it as a priority issue (see City of Toronto, 1999). In the meantime, METRAC's funding from local government was converted from an annual operating grant of approximately $200,000 to project-by-project funding of no more than $50,000 per project. The funding cuts by all levels of government had finally resulted in a loss of the infrastructure of community support that made these two organizations effective as women's initiatives.

Immediately following the establishment of the Safe City Committee in 1989, there was a flurry of interest in establishing similar committees in other Canadian cities. Following the election of a female mayor and a progressive council, the City of Edmonton established a Mayor's

Task Force on Safe Cities in 1990. Montreal created a Women's Action Committee on Urban Safety (comite d'action femmes et securite urbaine – CAFSU) in 1991, the same year that the regional government of Ottawa-Carleton established the Women's Action Committee Against Violence (WACAV) and that the City of Winnipeg commissioned its Social Planning Council to develop a report on A Safer Winnipeg for Women and Children, which led to a Safe City Committee in that municipality. In Dartmouth, a 1992 Task Force on Family Violence developed recommendations that led to changes in senior government handling of incidents, after the Mayor of Dartmouth became Premier of Nova Scotia.[14] By 1993, there were also Safer Cities initiatives in Calgary, Guelph, St. John, Regina, and Vancouver. In the province of Québec, long the most progressive part of the country on both feminist and crime prevention issues, the "Gateway to a Safer City" project organized twelve municipal initiatives in cities like Granby, Joliette, Rimouski, Québec City, Sherbrooke, and Valleyfield. All of these organizations worked on at least some of these elements: integrating safety concerns in planning, design and management, supporting and promoting networks among local agencies working to prevent violence against women, public/school/workplace education on the prevention of violence, increasing community involvement in violence prevention (FCM, 1993).

From this high-water mark in the mid-1990s, safe city initiatives have quietly petered out and/or lost a gendered perspective in many Canadian municipalities. Calls to the coordinators of the St. John, Winnipeg, Regina, and Guelph Safe City Committees in May 1999 found out-of-service phone numbers; follow-up searches of those city's websites found no mention of safe city committees.[15] Kitchener has an active Safe City Committee (whose work on safety audits will be summarized below), and is part of a larger Kitchener-Waterloo Region Community Safety and Crime Prevention Council, but both organizations do little specific work on violence against women. Kitchener's Safe City Committee has no representation from women's groups, although some of the neighbourhood committees are women-led. Like Kitchener-Waterloo, the City of Edmonton does work on family violence that includes some wife assault issues, but its initiatives on safer housing, children and youth, and urban planning include no consideration of gender. In Vancouver, the safe city initiative deals with safety and planning issues from a gender neutral standpoint (Rondeau, 1999). Calgary's Action Committee Against Violence has a domestic violence subcommittee with strong representation from feminist service providers, but, again, the safety and planning work does not have a gendered perspective (Arthurs, 1999). London has both a Coordinating Committee on Community Safety, which has a gender-neutral focus on violence prevention in the downtown area, and a Community Safety and Crime Prevention Advisory Committee, which looks at injury prevention as well as violence prevention, but has no representation from violence against women groups. There seems to be little relation between these two committees and the London Coordinating Committee to End Woman Abuse. WACAV's funding from the regional municipality of Ottawa-Carleton has been reduced, and the City of Ottawa's Crime Prevention Committee (which had a gender-neutral perspective and was often in an oppositional relationship to WACAV) no longer exists.

There are many possible reasons for this decline. Unlike Great Britain, Australia, South Africa, the Netherlands, Belgium, and many other countries, Canada has no national program that promotes safe city initiatives. Several local safe city initiatives, including those in Ottawa and Montreal, developed out of consultations funded by the federal government's women's program in 1989–91 (MacLeod, 1989); this work petered out as women's programs were cut at the federal level. The Canadian Panel on Violence Against Women, which was marked by controversy both inside and outside the feminist movement, developed recommendations on local mobilization that virtually disappeared the moment their final report was published (Canadian Panel, 1993). While the National Crime Prevention Centre has begun to fund local crime prevention initiatives and one of its three priorities is violence against women, safe city committees as such are not a priority for funding. The Federation of Canadian Municipalities, which developed an organizing handbook for community leaders on building safer communities in 1993, now does not have safer communities as a priority concern. Outside of Québec, the BC Coalition for Safer Communities is the only provincially funded organizing and networking initiative for local government safety initiatives, only some of which have a gendered perspective. Of local initiatives started in the early 1990s, only Montreal's CAFSU retains a strong gender perspective, with recent projects including a high-profile campaign against male violence and the redesign of a neighbourhood as the result of a series of safety audits (Paquin, 1998).

Perhaps the greatest reason for success, both in Toronto and Montreal, of safe city initiatives, was their grounding in strong grassroots advocacy groups by and for women. The report on the first year of the Québec mobilizing project made this point:

the women's groups, women's centres and CALACS (women's crisis centres) that took on the project hold key positions in their respective communities. Because

of the nature of their mission, they have an understanding of women's experience of violence and the benefit of many alliances over the years (Développement Québécois, 1994, cited in FCM, 1993).

When and where this grassroots energy became eroded by funding
cuts, funders' demands to cut back to "core services" and give up
advocacy work, infighting, or just plain exhaustion, safe city initiatives
have declined or lost their gender perspective.

WOMEN'S SAFETY AUDITS: THE DIFFUSION/DE-FUSION OF A FEMINIST IDEA

As mentioned above, the Women's Safety Audit Guide developed out
of participatory research on where Toronto women felt unsafe and
why, particularly in relation to public transportation and parks. In a
larger sense, women's safety audits were the result of four influences
that converged in the late 1980s:

1 the growth of feminist organizations pressuring government for
   women's equal rights;
2 the radical feminist analysis that violence against women was a significant barrier to women enjoying equal rights to the city;
3 the investigation of environmental design as a possible factor affecting urban crime;
4 the work by women's committees and grassroots women and planning advocacy groups to take women's safety concerns into account
   in urban design and planning (WACAV, 1995: 2, summarizing Whitzman, 1991).

The women's safety audit guide, as initially published by METRAC
and modified in 1992, was a short booklet (forty-five pages) that
included a six-page checklist of design factors that help make a place
safer or less safe, including lighting, signage, sightlines, and nearby
land uses, along with suggestions for organizing and following up on
safety audits. METRAC offered assistance in organizing safety audits,
but the guide was intended to be simple enough that first-time community activists could bring together a small group of three to seven
women to carry a safety audit out themselves (METRAC, 1989b;
Klodowsky, Lundy, and Andrew, 1994). While the format was simple,
the underlying notion was radical: that "women have expertise about
cities -and what causes problems in them – that traditional experts
don't have" (METRAC, 1989b: 3).

METRAC publicized its new safety audit guide in a special issue of *Women and Environments* magazine (METRAC, 1990), but no-one involved really knows how and why the safety audit idea caught on so quickly. Less than five years after its development, the Ottawa Women's Action Centre Against Violence was able to identify 250 individuals and organizations in Canada that had carried out safety audits (WACAV, 1995: 6), and safety audit programs were taking place in Great Britain (Korn, 1993), Australia (VCCAV, 1995), and New Zealand (Manakau, 1995). By the late 1990s, the European Forum on Urban Safety had distributed safety audit guides in English, French, Spanish, and Portuguese.[16] The lines of diffusion seem to have occurred along sectors: for instance, the Ontario Ministry of Colleges and Universities hired METRAC to modify their guide for use by colleges; this campus audit guide then became known by colleges and universities in other countries.

There is considerable anecdotal evidence of safety audits' effectiveness. One of the first safety audits was carried out by the DisAbled Women's Network at Toronto City Hall. As the result of their concerns, City Hall staff were directed to escort users to the Wheeltrans (public transportation for people with disabilities) stop, and the stop was eventually relocated to inside City Hall, next to an emergency telephone (METRAC, 1990: 8). Also in Toronto, a group of women, mostly single mothers, in a public housing project known as Blake Boultbee, organized a safety audit in 1991. Their recommendations were supported by the housing manager, who herself was a former tenant of public housing, and by the local city councillor. In less than a year, there were considerable modifications to the development, including changes to a problematic parking garage and a reorganization of the entrances and open spaces of the buildings. The women were so heartened by the audit's success that they went on to other community development projects (Catallo, 1994: 8–9; Wekerle and Whitzman, 1995: 173–81, has a copy of the audit report). The City of Montreal has developed safety audit guides for multi-unit residential buildings and parking lots and garages and has redesigned a neighbourhood as a result of safety audits (Paquin, 1998). Recently, in Duncan, BC, women from the Cowichan Valley Intercultural and Immigrant Aid Society audited the local bus depot. Despite initial resistance from the depot manager, the owner of the regional bus company said he would use their recommendations as the basis for a one-million-dollar renovation of the depot. Once again, exhilaration and a sense of empowerment was noted by participants (Hallatt and Dame, 1999).

But something basic often got lost as the women's safety audit guide was distributed, modified, and utilized. Part of the problem can be summarized in an anecdote. In 1995, I received some email correspondence from an acquaintance at the Queensland University of Technology (QUT). The University of Queensland had attempted to copyright its security-related materials, including a campus safety audit guide that made no specific reference to women. The original "safety audit guide" was said to have been produced by the University of Ontario, a non-existent institution. The entire origin of the *women's* safety audit guide had been lost, and, along with it, any gender analysis.

There is however, a more serious underlying concern with safety audits. This concern was reiterated by an informal evaluation forum in Melbourne in 1995 and a similar Canadian evaluation done by the Ottawa Women's Action Committee Against Violence that same year. At best, safety audits:

- are a good first step for organizations;
- validate participants' experiences, especially women participants who have been excluded from decision-making;
- increase awareness of how different people perceive the same space and of women's fear of violence;
- increase recognition of women's safety as an important issue;
- develop a sense of participants' ability to create change;
- *sometimes* lead to practical, concrete, visible, and publicized changes in the urban environment;
- *sometimes* involve a wide range of people who then have a common basis to work together;
- *sometimes* develop both short- and long-term solutions.

But, in practice, safety audits have had certain problems, including:

- not being based in a broadly supported problem-solving process, but organized by a particular group with a particular agenda;
- "neutralizing" safety audits by removing any references to gender and other sources of vulnerability – including income, disability, and ethnicity – and making no efforts to attract these groups to the audits;
- increasing fear and frustration, especially if nothing is changed as the result of an audit;
- most importantly (concluded both studies), creating unreal expectations in the community that safety would magically "happen" because a safety audit had occurred, which both ignores the real challenge of the safety audit – bringing about the sometimes systemic changes recommended by the audit – and possibly diverting energy from more substantive community issues related to violence and crime (WACAV, 1995: 21-2; VCCAV, 1995).

Ironically, Toronto – where safety audits originated – has never implemented a city-wide program to respond to safety audits. The few cities
that have – Kitchener, Ottawa, Calgary, Montreal – have found it difficult to make safety improvements a priority, as cities cut back funding for capital improvements as a result of downloading from senior
governments. Of these four cities, only Ottawa and Montreal emphasize bringing women into the safety audit process, and both CAFSU and
WACAV acknowledge that this is an uphill battle.[17] In Québec City, the
deletion of gender in its French-language safety audit guide is especially galling, since this leaves all references to participants as male.[18] The
few cities who have attempted to involve people from diverse ethnic
origins have not been very successful. WACAV (1995: 23) gives the following examples:

In Vancouver, representatives from the Indo-Canadian and Chinese-Canadian
communities participated in the organizing committee, and the safety audit
guide was translated to facilitate participation by these communities. However, no audits were sent into Vancouver's planning department. In Ottawa, residents of Cambodian background participated in a safety audit with the assistance of interpreters, but their participation was limited by not understanding
the process and not feeling they had the right to complain. Several groups in
Québec organized safety audits specifically for women of particular cultural
groups but very few women participated.

Safety audits are a seemingly simple solution to a complex problem.
But, in reality, the implementation of recommendations from an individual safety audit, let alone a comprehensive municipal safety audit
program, requires considerable commitment, both from grassroots
organizations and from local government. When women "get lost,"
either because the safety audits become a top-down gender-neutered
process, or because the women involved have no way into the power
structure (the kind of "in" that might be created through an effective
women's committee or a safe city committee), then safety audits lose
their initial radical potential and become part of the problem instead
of part of the solution.

WOMEN PLAN TORONTO:
SINGING BY THE SKIN OF HER TEETH

Although public consultation is a requirement for urban planning, the
extent to which planners and planning theory has dealt with gender
concerns in consultation processes has been extensively critiqued by
feminists. Beth Moore Milroy, for instance, points out that

matters that draw women into collective action – safe neighbourhoods, decent housing, help for society's cast-offs, childcare – have rarely been designated political. Local politics seem to deal mostly with matters related to making and investing money. Planning takes the same general clues (1991B: 8).

In the 1980s, participatory action researchers, especially in England (Greater London Council, 1985; Matrix, 1984), took the radical step of directly asking women what they liked, disliked, and wanted to see in their cities. The consultation process in London, UK, called "Women Plan London," inspired a group of women in Toronto to try a similar exercise in 1985 (Taylor, 1985; Modlich, 1988).

Women Plan Toronto, as the group called itself, conducted workshops with twenty-five groups of women, chosen to represent a range of life situations: women who were income earners and also mostly responsible for housework and/or nurturing dependents, full-time homemakers, sole support mothers living in subsidized housing and getting by with limited incomes, women who were living with very unstable housing and/or income, immigrant women in linguistic-based support groups, young women, elderly women, and women with physical disabilities. WPT was unable to organize a workshop with native women, but consulted with leaders of two native women's groups (WPT, 1986: 12–13). Women Plan Toronto also made a point of going to the women, getting themselves invited to regular drop-in sessions for mothers with children or socially isolated low-income women, rather than expecting them to come to a workshop. The workshop itself was very simple in format. Women were asked to share some of the problems they experienced when trying to carry out their everyday and weekly activities, then were asked to brainstorm on possible solutions to the problems they experienced. Both the workshop facilitators and the participants used drawings as well as words to convey their "experiences and dreams." Each group ended by evaluating the workshop's process (ibid.: 7).

Like the WISE report and the Safe City Committee consultations, the simplest questions often provoked the most profound answers. Ideas were categorized under "my place," "my community," "getting around," and "finding understanding and support." Throughout, the emphasis was on transcribing women's words, rather than "analysing" or otherwise rephrasing what women had to say. The overall tone of the report was one of respect: for the experiences of the participants, for the way they chose to express those experiences, and for the participants' ability to develop "new and creative responses to the issue or problem" (ibid.: 6).

Women Plan Toronto then transformed itself from a project to a research and advocacy organization, with a mandate to tackle the issues raised by the consultation. The originators of the project had been members of a group called Women in/and Planning, but by 1985 there was a split between those women who considered the group a network for female professional planners (women in planning) and women who were interested in planning advocacy by and for women (women and planning). Over the next fifteen years, the majority of the women involved in Women Plan Toronto, including myself, had a professional background in urban studies and were involved in the group both to make change and to have a place where mutual support was possible (MacGregor, 1994: 62–9). The sometimes "clubby" atmosphere of Women Plan Toronto, common to volunteer organizations, may have been a contributing factor to its relative homogeneity; while WPT has included and continues to include a range of ages, sexualities, and racial and ethnic backgrounds, most of the women involved have a university degree and were thus in status if not income middle class (ibid.: 75).

Given the small number of people involved – no more than fifty active members at its height – and extremely shaky funding status – occasional project funding from local and senior governments, never any core funding – Women Plan Toronto has had a great impact on local government policies and programs. It was central to the Women in Safe Environments project, the TTC and High Park safety work, and the development of the Safe City Committee. It developed and distributed pamphlets explaining planning in layperson's terms (Women Plan Toronto, 1987 and 1990) and successfully lobbied for the inclusion of women, children and seniors as "special needs groups" in the 1993 City of Toronto Official Plan. Housing intensification has been a particular concern, with WPT lobbying suburban municipalities to change their zoning bylaws to allow as-of-right second units in houses, accessory apartments and house-sharing, and working to support an intensification-supportive regional Official Plan. In 1988, WPT developed a widely distributed pamphlet of gender-related questions for candidates on housing, transportation, urban safety, and childcare (Women Plan Toronto, 1988). WPT also conducted twelve workshops with grassroots women's groups to give them information on how local government affected women and how women could affect local government. Finally, "ward watchers" were organized in almost all fifty local government wards to ask questions at all-candidates meetings and contribute towards a "report card" of elected officials' voting records. The "election projects" were repeated on a somewhat smaller scale in 1991, 1994, and 1997 (MacGregor, 1994: 72–107; City of Toronto, 1997).

Throughout Women Plan Toronto's history, the emphasis has been on respectful listening and the elimination of unnecessary jargon. For instance, when WPT conducted workshops with suburban ratepayers' groups on housing intensification in 1993, participants were asked what their definition of intensification was. One workshop facilitator described hearing about problems ranging from

illegal rooming houses to no parking and so on until people eventually come around to the benefits such as you need a certain amount of density to have subways ... shopping you like ... recreation and educational centres that we'd like to have – and within the city walking is better ... you'll find out that there's something in each area ... which has largely blocked intensification in some ways, [but also] something that people are interested in that suits the goals of intensification (MacGregor, 1994: 93).

While local government has statutory requirements to consult with the public, this element of respectful listening and inclusionary language is often lacking (Sandercock and Forsyth, 1990 and 1992a). Moreover, WPT's emphasis on constant open-ended consultation helps avoid members drawing only from their own, necessarily limited, personal experience.

The longevity of WPT is due, as much as anything, to one woman: Reggie Modlich, who has provided continuity since the days of Women in/and Planning, and in whose house WPT is presently based. In recent years, WPT's project funding has grown more and more scarce, and there is no money left even to support the tiny office that WPT shared with *Women and Environments* magazine, another organization whose reputation far exceeds its resources.

Women Plan Toronto has inspired a few similar projects across Canada. In British Columbia, the Women in Planning Group developed a community plan for a suburban neighbourhood and published a "tool kit" on Women and the Community Planning Process (Planning Ourselves In, 1994). The City of Saskatoon used a similar methodology to WPT in its 1992 focus groups on women and urban planning: approaching "young women in schools, working women, retired women, women who were single, married, parents, aboriginal women, physically challenged" and asking them what they liked, disliked, and would like to see in order to make the city a safer place. Suggestions were explicitly linked to policies in the Development Plan (City of Saskatoon, 1993). The examples of Montreal and Québec City, where feminist planning documents became incorporated into their respective city's official plans, has been discussed above. But, in my interviews with planners in Vancouver, Hamilton, Ottawa, Kitchener, and Calgary, no other grassroots women and planning organization were noted, and none of the "vision exercises" being developed for Official Plan documents included specific consultations with women.

CONCLUSION:
SMALL FISH IN A RAPIDLY DRAINING POND

Women's activism at the local government level involves both the dangers of "mainstreaming" – reaching out to the majority of the population with popular and practical feminist solutions – and of "disengagement" – critique of the system from outside the system (Briskin, 1991: 30). On the one hand, working within existing structures, even when they involve a new kind of committee or a safety audit, limits the ability to critique from the inside. There is always the threat of co-optation and compromise. Women end up "appealing" and "negotiating," rather than "demanding" change. The work is often discouraging and slow (Adamson, Briskin, and McPhail, 1988: 180). On the other hand, organizing as women and relying on personal resources and personal experience can result in "unarticulated norms [making the organizations] inaccessible and uncomfortable to women on the outside," especially women who are focusing on personal survival and do not have the financial or emotional resources to work on systemic change (Briskin, 1991: 31). Developing a "voice for women" requires taking infinitely complex issues and prioritizing, simplifying, and concretizing them to the point where piecemeal transformation can take place. This in turn requires positively Herculean (Xenian?) efforts to build coalitions while collectively making choices as to what to tackle first. While, at best, the work results in the opportunity to learn skills in political organizing, lobbying, presenting deputations, and public speaking (Adamson, Briskin, and McPhail, 1988: 236), it always involves time taken away from other work, family, and self – an often frustrating process, and a questionable end result. Most significantly, the choices are rarely simple, the way ahead usually unclear, and the ability to learn lessons from past experience limited.

A primary focus on the contemporary Canadian women's movement has been "to get the state working for women, not against us" (ibid.: 115). Women's initiatives at the local level government level are

those activities and programs that promote new and positive policies for women through the use of the resources and sphere of influence of the local state. They establish women as claimants in new policy arenas, changing ideas of what is legitimate for policy and legislation at the municipal level (Wekerle, 1991: 2).

At the local state, the attempts to insert the "voice of women" through a range of initiatives have resulted in both successes and challenges. As Canadian local government reaches the point of "sink or swim," women will have to individually and collectively decide whether local government matters. If local government does still matter, then the challenge is to ensure that the voices of women – as local government workers, community activists, users of services, politicians, and advocates – are heard, loud and clear.

NOTES

I would like to acknowledge the financial assistance of the Canadian Association of University Teachers and the Australian Federation of University Women in supporting research related to this article.

1 "Voice of Women" is a Canadian peace group that has been in operation for forty years. I have appropriated its name, but not, I hope, its voice.
2 For instance, a history of Canadian feminism from the late 1960s to the late 1980s (Adamson, Briskin, and McPhail, 1988) has no direct references to feminist organizations working at the local government level and only two indirect references: a provincial funding cut to the Vancouver Status of Women Committee (p. 85) and an failed attempt to unite feminist organizations in Toronto (p. 82).
3 Some Canadian examples: McClain and Doyle (1984) talk about the exclusion of gender analysis in housing policy up to the mid-1980s; Klodowsky, Lundy, and Andrew (1994) give several case studies of how violence against women has been ignored in housing and community planning; Eichler (1995a) contains examples of the exclusion of gender analysis in housing, public health, and transportation policy and in contemporary university planning programs.
4 Wekerle (1986), Ross (1995), Andrew (1992), Wekerle and Whitzman (1995), Novac (1995), Guberman (1995), Zielinski (1995), and Wekerle and Peake (1996) all contain current examples of Canadian women's activism at the local level, particularly in the field of housing. I am not including the current example of "Women Vote," a project of the Ontario Coalition for Social Justice, or other projects that mobilize locally for changes at senior levels of government.
5 A trio of books published in 1980-81 were especially significant to the development of this analysis: Stimpson et al. (1981); Wekerle, Peterson, and Morley (1980); Hayden (1981). Milroy (1991b) provides a good summary of the first fifteen years of the literature; Andrew and Milroy (1988) and Eichler (1995a) are two relatively recent collections of articles that focus on Canadian examples.

6 See, for instance, Novac (1995) on the intersection of racism and sexism in housing, Chouinard (1999) on the challenge of disability to women's movements, and Ross (1990) on diverse lesbian organizing on housing issues.

7 Phrase from London Edinburgh (1979).

8 See, for instance, Watson (1990 and 1992), Halford (1992), Little (1994), and Wekerle (1986 and 1991).

9 The following interviews were held (by telephone and email) in May and June 1999:

YWCA Canada: Karen Takacs, Director of Advocacy

National Crime Prevention Council: Barbara Hall, Chairperson;

Duncan, BC: Terri Dame, Coordinator, Cowichan Valley Safe Community initiative;

Vancouver, BC: Mary Beth Rondeau, Development Planner, City of Vancouver Planning Department; and Ali Grant, British Columbia Coalition for Safer Communities;

Calgary, AB: Chris Arthurs, Planning Assistant, City of Calgary Planning and Building Department;

Edmonton, AB: Pijush Sarker, Coordinator, Edmonton Safer City Initiative;

Yellowknife, NT: Lyda Fuller, Executive Director, YWCA of Yellowknife;

Saskatoon, SK: Elizabeth Miller, Safe City Coordinator, City of Saskatoon;

Regina, SK: Mayor's Office and Shirley Liebel, President, Regina Council of Women;

Winnipeg, MB: Jenny Gerbasi, City Councillor, Chair, Committee for Safety;

London, ON: Mandy Alvares, Coordinating Committee for Community Safety; Nancie Inving, City of London;

Hamilton, ON: Vanessa Grupe, City of Hamilton Planning and Development Department;

Toronto, ON: Sue Kaiser, Grants Coordinator, Breaking the Cycle of Violence; Priscilla Cranley, Healthy City Office; and Catherine Leitch, Status of Women Committee, City of Toronto; and Reggie Modlich, Women Plan Toronto;

Ottawa, ON: Caroline Andrew, former Chair, Women's Action Committee Against Violence; and Betty MacGregor, Coordinator, WACAV;

Montreal, QC: Anne Michaud, Coordinator, Femmes et Ville, City of Montreal Social Development Department;

Halifax-Dartmouth: Stella Lord, Nova Scotia Women's Directorate.

10 Hayden (1981) provides a good history of early US "material feminism"; Mackenzie and Rose (1983) review women's organizations in Great Britain over the past hundred years; Valverde (1991) provides a history of Canadian woman-led "moral reform" in the late nineteenth and early twentieth centuries.

11 Shirley Liebel, President of Regina Council of Women (conversation with author, May 1999).

12 This is based on a 1999 conversation between the author and Elizabeth Miller, the City of Saskatoon Safe City Coordinator, and on City of Saskatoon (1993).

13 Vanessa Grupe, City of Hamilton Planning and Development (conversation with author, 1999).

14 Stella Lord, Nova Scotia Women's Directorate (emails with author, June 1999).

15 Winnipeg's Safe City Committee was disbanded in 1996, but a new "Committee for Safety" was formed in May 1999. It is too early to tell whether there will representation by women's groups or a focus on violence against women (Gerbasi, 1999).

16 Anne Michaud, Community Development Officer, Social Development Department, City of Montreal (conversation with author, 1999).

17 Betty MacGregor, Coordinator, Ottawa-Carleton Women's Action Centre against Violence (conversation with author, 1999) and Anne Michaud, Community Development Officer, Social Development Department, City of Montreal (conversation with author, 1999).

18 Anne Michaud, Community Development Officer, Social Development Department, City of Montreal (conversation with author, 1999).

5 What Causes Inner-city Decay, and What Can Be Done about It?

CHRISTOPHER LEO and LISA SHAW with
KENNETH GIBBONS and COLIN GOFF

EXECUTIVE SUMMARY

This paper[1] discusses the problem of urban decay, presents Statistics Canada data to explore it, and discusses a variety of remedies. The primary focus is on Winnipeg, but throughout it is emphasized that the problem is North America-wide, and that there are many commonalities in the solutions available to different cities.

Causes of Decay

In this section we consider how the process of inner-city decay works in North American cities and investigate two of the causes of this troublesome phenomenon:

Sprawl development at the urban fringe, which escalates the cost of infrastructure and services, undermining the financial viability and physical well-being of the city.

Ghettoization, a term we use to refer to the social isolation of poor people in ghetto neighbourhoods, which multiplies their problems as inadequate shelter and nutrition are compounded by poor-quality education and by exposure to violence.

Consequences

Next we investigate four inner-city neighbourhoods at various stages of the process of decay in Winnipeg, using both firsthand observation and statistical data to gain a more concrete understanding of how those neighbourhoods are changing. Our findings make it clear that they are caught up in a process of decline that is evident from deteriorating incomes and deteriorating condition of homes and strongly suggested by a variety of other signs. At the same time, it is obvious, both from the visual inspection and from statistical data, that the neighbourhoods still offer much to build upon.

Dealing with Decay

Finally, we focus on the growing efforts in many communities across North America to deal with growth-related problems that help cause inner-city decay and consider briefly some of the tools that are available in Winnipeg and other Canadian cities. We discuss five measures that could contribute to the inner city's recovery from some of the problems associated with decay:

Growth boundaries
Housing measures
Pricing of new development
Overcoming regulatory rigidities
Transit-oriented development.

INTRODUCTION

Inner-city decay is a much-lamented reality in Winnipeg, and efforts to address the problem have so far proven futile. The elements of Winnipeg's situation mirror those of many North American cities. The population of the inner city is shrinking, and there has been substantial deterioration of buildings and public facilities. Despite heroic efforts on the part of all three levels of government and the local business community, once-bustling Portage Avenue, one of Winnipeg's two main arteries, is now a problem area, and Selkirk Avenue, the former commercial heart of the historic North End, is moribund. Unoccupied retail premises are a common sight on Portage and are virtually ubiquitous on Selkirk.

There has been substantial housing deterioration in the inner city, and boarded-up residences are becoming an increasingly common sight in some of the worst neighbourhoods. Some neighbourhoods are beset by gangs. The entire inner city north of the Assiniboine River has been redlined by insurance companies: homeowners applying for insurance may be refused, or may be required to pay more than the standard premium (Redekop, 1996a and 1996b).

All three levels of government have, within the past decade, committed substantial sums of money to the preservation of the inner city and the establishment of such facilities as Portage Place, the Forks Market, and an extensive system of parks and riverfront walkways. There have been programs of housing construction, preservation, and rehabilitation; job-training and job-creation schemes; and a wide range of initiatives offering counselling, recreation, personal assistance and companionship in attempts to address a daunting array of social problems (Clatworthy, 1987a and 1987b; Epstein Associates, 1987; Marshall, 1987; Winnipeg Core Area Initiative, 1992).

In recent years, business people and private citizens have become increasingly involved in efforts to save the inner city. Throughout the downtown area, business improvement zones draw on neighbourhood business people for funds to promote commerce and provide public facilities. Individual business people, inspired by both the search for profit and intrinsic motivations, have sought to breathe new life into the inner city by participating in a wide variety of proposed or actual business ventures, including sport promotion and other forms of entertainment, as well as conventional retail ventures.

Despite all that, the decline proceeds apace. A steady parade of committees, public participation exercises, consultants, and individual rescue efforts, accompanied by cheery predictions, serve, in many citizens' eyes, mainly to demonstrate that there is no plan and no real leadership. The parade of self-appointed saviours seems endless: one group promises to secure the continued presence of the Winnipeg Jets to keep Winnipeg "on the map" (they are now putting Phoenix on the map); someone else wants to make Winnipeg the country music capital of North America. More recently, there are renewed attempts to salvage the downtown portions of Portage Avenue and Main Street – which were supposedly salvaged previously by the Portage Place Mall, a new City Hall, a concert hall/museum/planetarium complex, numerous renovations of heritage buildings, and more. Repeated optimistic and well-intentioned pronouncements ring hollow against the background of continuing deterioration.

Winnipeg is not alone. Indeed, its dilemma is more nearly the rule than the exception in North America, at least among slower-growing metropolitan areas. But there is a ray of hope on the horizon. Across North America in recent years, there have been efforts to gain a more fundamental overview of the problem and to address it more seriously.

The most credible of these efforts are ones that treat inner cities not as problem areas to be revitalized with programs disconnected from the wider urban area but as the heart of a metropolitan area that must be managed as a coherent whole. Such efforts are underway, or under discussion, in such diverse locations as Oregon, Florida, Minneapolis-St Paul, Toronto, Montreal, New Jersey, California, Colorado, Washington State, and more (Leo with Beavis, Carver, and Turner, 1998). The purpose of this paper is to apply to Winnipeg's problems the kind of thinking that has gone into some of these other efforts.

We begin with a discussion of the causes of decay, drawing on materials from a variety of sources and applying them to Winnipeg's situation. Next we present the results of a study, drawing on Statistics Canada data to gain some insights into the process of decaying neighbourhoods beyond the obvious vacant storefronts and abandoned houses, and, more generally, to get to know these neighbourhoods a little better. Finally, we draw on documentation of metropolitan growth management efforts throughout North America, as well as a variety of other sources in the city-planning literature, to present some examples of measures that could be taken by Winnipeg.

CAUSES OF DECAY

Why are inner cities all over North America turning into funereal landscapes marked by boarded-up buildings, ruined public facilities, and gang graffiti? Urban decay can be explained in terms of such disparate elements as economic distress, unemployment, crime, drug abuse, family break-up, widespread anomie, housing decay and abandonment, failure of the education system and social supports, and more: The Fraser Institute argues that rent control is to blame (Block and Olsen, 1981).

However, it is our argument that the single most important key to understanding much of what is involved is the progressive abandonment of the inner city by middle-class residents through suburban development. The result is *de facto* class segregation and the concentration of social problems in one area of the city, even as the material, social, and political resources for dealing with them dwindle. In order to see how that happens, we need to follow the development process step by step and trace its consequences. The best way to start is by looking at a typical subdivision approval process and then, separately, at exurban development, where a different set of political and financial considerations applies.

Urban Expansion

For decades, Winnipeg has been permitting sprawl within its boundaries that undermines its financial viability. When a developer puts a proposal to city planners for a new suburban subdivision, according to Winnipeg's Land and Development Services Department,[2] it is responsible for expenses incurred in three areas: any new road construction, any additions to the water and sewer system, and any new parks. After the developer has agreed to compensation in these areas, the new subdivision is typically touted by City Council as a rich new source of tax revenues, at no expense to the city. But there are more expenses to come, none of which are included in the original development charge.

Residents of new subdivisions justifiably demand levels of servicing similar to those enjoyed by other residents of the city. Like everyone else, they want a conveniently located community centre, a reasonable level of bus service, a library branch within reasonable distance of home, and levels of fire protection comparable with other areas of the city. Political pressure and the demands of simple justice force the city to provide these extra services, but they must be paid out of general revenues. They are not covered by the subdivision's development charge.

As the city is forced to cover servicing to ever more far-flung subdivisions at lower and lower densities, costs of municipal government services escalate, and taxes with them. At some point, homeowners and business people begin to calculate that it does not pay to live and do business in the city. Growing numbers realize that the much lower servicing costs in adjacent municipalities allow for substantial property-tax savings; and the city remains readily accessible through commuting.

Winnipeg has reached this point, and in recent years population growth within the city has all but ground to a halt, while municipalities bordering the city have grown at rates at least twice as fast, and in some instances more than five times as fast.

Municipalities adjacent to Winnipeg are growing at an accelerating rate, while Winnipeg's growth declines sharply. Winnipeg grew only 3.7 percent from 1986 to 1991, but even that low rate plummeted to 0.3 percent from 1991 to 1996, for a ten-year average annual rate of less than 0.5 percent. Meanwhile, the other municipalities – including all but two of those adjacent to the city[3] – grew at rates ranging as high as 46.8 percent over the ten-year period.

Winnipeg's property values are stagnant or declining. Because of slow growth and decline of property value, the revenues of the city are shrinking and, unless something happens to reverse the trend, the shrinkage will accelerate. This state of affairs signifies a critical shift in the political situation faced by city council. Once adjacent municipalities are open to urban residential, commercial, and industrial development, the city's power to insist on favourable financial terms, as well as locations and densities that can be serviced without undue cost to taxpayers, approaches zero. With growing desperation, city council realizes it often faces a stark choice: approve whatever the developer asks for or lose the development (Martin, 1994). Even confident politicians are prone to decision-making that does not look beyond the next election.

The Process of Decay

Long before things got to that point, problems were piling up for the City of Winnipeg and other North American cities. For more than a generation, urban sprawl has been taking a terrible toll. Those who can afford to leave the inner city are drawn by the lure of modern housing, more plentiful land, and – if their destination is outside the city limits – lower taxes. As more middle-class residents leave, and the business-es that serve them follow, the inner city is increasingly perceived – outside a few upper-income enclaves – as the place to live only for those who cannot afford anything else.

What are the signposts on the road to decay? Uncontrolled suburban growth, as we have seen, typically forces the provision of similar quality services over ever larger areas at lower and lower densities – that is, at a growing per capita cost. Exurban development produces a population that typically remains dependent on the city for a wide range of services, while spending less money there than residents do and contributing nothing to the property-tax base.

In time, most people who can afford to live outside the inner city do so. Predominant among those left behind are the people who cannot afford to move out. Poverty is not necessarily accompanied by social problems, any more than wealth guarantees the absence of social problems. But when a metropolitan area is divided into neighbourhoods where poverty predominates and others where comfortable circumstances are the rule, it is inevitable that there will be a concentration of social problems in the poor areas. At the same time, the exodus from those areas makes it inevitable that, as the problems escalate, the resources for dealing with them will dwindle.

Where social problems predominate, crime follows. As crime grows, law-abiding people are faced with the Hobson's choice of becoming accomplices or victims. Thus crime spreads. At about this point, down-town neighbourhoods begin to be redlined. Insurance companies refuse fire and theft insurance; banks become reluctant to lend money for mortgages or renovations. That, roughly, is as far as Winnipeg has travelled on the road to inner-city decay, but that is not where the decline ends.

Sprawl and Ghettoization

What is the reason for the seeming inevitability of inner-city decay? Two answers leap to the eye: first, continuing outward development at lower and lower densities gradually escalates the costs of infrastructure and service-provision to the point where the viability of service-delivery, especially in the inner city, is undermined; second, the social isolation of poor people in ghetto neighbourhoods multiplies their problems, as inadequate shelter and nutrition are compounded by poor-quality education and by exposure to violence. What seems obvious from a survey of the situation in North American cities, however, does not come through at all clearly in the literature on urban growth and development. Neither the problems of sprawl or ghettoization have received the analysis they deserve. We can consider each of these in turn.

Sprawl.   Sprawl has been under indictment since at least 1974, but as recently as 1996 a thorough and careful review of the literature still portrays it as being bedevilled by question marks (Bourne, 1996). However, if we look at the available studies, instead of keeping score on the wide variety of carefully hedged conclusions, a clear, if fragmentary, picture does emerge.

Blais (1996), one of the most thorough studies yet conducted, cites five earlier studies (Wheaton and Schussheim, 1955; Isard and Coughlin, 1957; Stone, 1973; Real Estate Research Corporation, 1974; Essiambre-Phillips-Desjardins Associates et al., 1995) that, among them, calculated the infrastructure costs associated with different densities and settlement patterns, as well as the differences between uniform and mixed-use developments. Among them they make it clear beyond reasonable doubt that the low-density, single-land-use development that is typical of North American suburbs and exurban areas carries a heavy price tag.

The CMHC study (Essiambre-Phillips-Desjardins Associates et al., 1995) calculated the seventy-five-year life-cycle costs for two less sharply contrasting developments – a conventional subdivision at twenty-two units per net hectare and one developed along fashionable "new urbanist" lines at forty-three units – but still found that the more compact development produced savings of $10,977 per unit. Another interesting finding dealt with the costs of centralized and decentralized employment sites. According to Stone (1973), when other variables were held constant, the regional road capital costs associated with centralized employment were always higher than for patterns of decentralized employment, by about 19 percent on average.

Persuasive as these studies are, they barely scratch the surface of the true cost differences between conventional sprawl and more compact, mixed-use development. As Blais (1996: 19–20) points out, these studies do not, for the most part, consider the costs of infrastructure outside the immediate sites under study, nor do they consider non-residential infrastructure costs or revenues produced by different types of development, including not only the obvious property tax receipts, development charges, and user fees but also such things as linkage fees and transit revenues.

In short, if we look at studies that make a serious attempt to compare the costs of sprawl development with those of more compact forms of urban growth, it is impossible to escape the conclusion that the viability of cities is being undermined by their patterns of expansion.

Ghettoization.   American research has documented the growth of high poverty rates in cities since the 1970s. The best way to deal with this problem would be the abolition of poverty, perhaps through a judicious combination of social supports, job training, and job creation. It is urgent that such an agenda be pursued seriously, but in this study we are pursuing a different line of reasoning, having to do with social isolation.

There is growing interest in the question of whether social isolation exacerbates the ills associated with poverty (Wilson 1987, 1991, and 1996; Wacquant and Wilson, 1993; Holloway et al., 1998; Van Kempen, 1997; Marcuse, 1997a and 1997b; Enchautegui, 1997; Massey and Denton, 1993; Mincy and Wiener, 1993; Harrell and Peterson, 1992). That line of investigation invites the suggestion that crime is one of the social ills exacerbated by social isolation, and there is plenty of basis for considering that suggestion plausible, as well as the broader suggestion that social isolation promotes a variety of social ills.

We are not arguing that it is impossible for socially isolated poor neighbourhoods to organize, and deal with their problems, only that special measures for protection of the community are more likely to be necessary and more difficult to implement. Likewise neighbourhoods where there is a mix of poor and better-off people are more likely to have schools that produce high levels of educational attainment than neighbourhoods where only poor people reside. Good schools and safe streets, in turn, reduce the likelihood that the poverty of one generation will reproduce itself in the next. An alternative development vision for the metropolitan area could have the effect of providing resources to inner-city residents for such things as libraries, swimming pools, and better-financed community centres.

If our line of reasoning is accepted, it becomes clear that urban sprawl, as we know it in North America, promotes social isolation and that sprawl and social isolation are significant contributors to inner-city decay. It follows that one of the remedies for decay is to rethink conventional Canadian urban development practices. This would not address the problem of poverty itself, nor would it address the direct links between poverty and crime – the myriad ways in which the struggles, dilemmas, and conflicts of being poor can be manifested as anti-social behaviour – but it could affect the intensity – and possibly the incidence – of poverty-related problems and open new possibilities for the mobilization of community support in the battle against poverty. Our intention here is not to offer a comprehensive solution to the problem of poverty but to show some of the adverse consequences of urban sprawl and social isolation.

Demographic evidence on this point is somewhat mixed, but not on balance encouraging. The numbers of aboriginal people are growing rapidly in Winnipeg as a whole, increasing from 2.7 percent of the population in 1981 to 7 percent in 1991 and reaching a total of more than forty-three thousand people. The inner-city aboriginal population has grown much faster, increasing by 60.9 percent between 1986 and 1991 alone, and the aboriginal percentage of the inner-city total reached 16.4 in 1991, or 18,725 people. Still, less than half of the aboriginal population lived in the inner city. In other words – and contrary to many a stereotype – the majority of aboriginal people live in suburban settings (Social Planning Council of Winnipeg, 1995: 25–6).

That certainly does not resemble the classic American ghetto pattern of the 1950s and earlier, in which African Americans often had no choice but to live in ghettos. But it may well be that growing numbers of *lower-income* aboriginal people are left with no choice other than the inner city, and, without additional evidence, we have no way of knowing to what degree, if any, their practical choices are limited only to certain inner-city neighbourhoods. If lower-income aboriginal people are being steered toward certain inner-city neighbourhoods,[4] even while their middle-class counterparts are able to live in the suburbs, the situation faced by aboriginal people in Winnipeg is generally similar to that faced by urban African Americans.

Is that all bad? It could be argued that socially – or even racially – exclusive neighbourhoods offer good opportunities for the establishment of a network of community supports and government services appropriate to a particular population. That is a question worth discussing – though a full discussion would take us beyond the scope of this paper – but, in brief, we take the position best articulated by Marcuse (1997a and 1997b), who distinguishes between ghettos and enclaves. Ghettos are neighbourhoods that are socially isolated primarily because their residents cannot afford to live elsewhere.

Enclaves, by contrast, are neighbourhoods that are socially isolated because people of a particular category choose to gather there, usually for mutual support and companionship. These can be either racially or economically defined, or defined by some combination of both characteristics; examples would be a Chinatown; a Little Italy; a favourite location for writers' artists', and musicians' lofts; or a gay district. Such neighbourhoods may be primarily or exclusively low-income, but whether they are or not, they offer support, opportunity, and choice to their residents.

Ghettos, by contrast, tend to imprison their residents and limit their opportunities. It is our argument that these are the neighbourhoods most likely to be plagued by inadequate education, crime, social disorganization, and community instability. That said, we are not suggesting that these neighbourhoods are helpless victims. Numerous community development efforts in the inner city – including Neechi Foods, Children of the Earth school, Andrews Street Family Centre, the Native Women's Transition Centre, North End Women's Centre, Nee Gawn Ah Kai childcare centre, and a variety of housing initiatives, to name only a few items on a longer list – testify that inner-city residents can organize institutions and provide support for their communities. We will also note below that the inner-city neighbourhoods in our study are by no means hopeless cases.

Nevertheless, the overriding reality is that we are systematically developing the metropolitan area in such a way as to isolate a lower-income population from most of the metropolitan area and from the most active job markets, while placing their safety and the education of their children at risk. That some of them are able to organize themselves to fight back against this constriction of their opportunities in life is a tribute to their resilience, but a rapidly growing proportion of Winnipeg's inner city more closely resembles ghetto neighbourhoods than enclaves.

INNER-CITY NEIGHBOURHOODS

So far, we have established the connection between inner-city decay and a particular mode of suburban and exurban expansion and considered the role that social isolation may play in the decay. But, although some degree of decay is a virtual certainty in inner cities surrounded by low-density development, it does not take the same form everywhere. In understanding the differences, it is most useful to distinguish between the patterns typical of cities that are growing slowly, or not at all, and those found in fast-growing magnets for economic development.

Differences among Cities

The kind of decay we are focusing on in these pages is more typical of slow-growth centres – for example Edmonton; Winnipeg; Omaha; Duluth; Dubuque and Des Moines, Iowa; and Grand Forks, North Dakota – where the pace of inner-city decay is not matched by the rate at which commercial development expands (Leo and Brown with Dick, 1998). It is in such centres that we are most likely to find large numbers of boarded-up storefronts as well as decayed and abandoned housing.

The Neighbourhoods: A Cyclist's View

The data in this study on decay in downtown Winnipeg are based primarily on collection of and extrapolation from Statistics Canada[5] data on four 1961 census tracts in downtown residential neighbourhoods, one of which was divided to form five 1991 census tracts with boundaries that coincided exactly with those of the 1961 tracts. Hereafter they will be referred to as four neighbourhoods, three of which consisted of one tract in both 1961 and 1991. The fourth neighbourhood was one tract in 1961 and was divided into two by 1991. Figures for 1991 are derived by adding those for the two tracts in question. The 1991 neighbourhoods varied in population from 3,758 to 10,397 people. In 1961 those same neighbourhoods's populations varied from 4,496 to 13,147 people.

The tracts were selected for inclusion in the study, partly to satisfy the need for 1991 boundaries that were congruent with those of 1961, but mainly on the basis of close familiarity with downtown Winnipeg. The use of direct observation as a supplement to a body of data that are primarily statistical is an unusual feature of this study. Conventionally, statistical data are presented as a self-contained body of evidence that must be kept separate from direct observation. Indeed, authors of such studies sometimes leave the impression that they are pretending not to have direct knowledge that they in fact possess.

Such a pretence would have appeared quixotic to a pre-behavioural social scientist, and it may appear so again once behavioural techniques of observation have been part of the social science arsenal long enough to have been placed in perspective.

To be sure, it is important to keep the direct observation and statistical data separate – not to confuse one with the other, or to mix them up so that it is no longer clear which evidence supports which conclusion – but it is hard to see why an investigator who knows downtown Winnipeg well should somehow appear "more scientific" by pretending not to. Direct observation and statistics are both valuable sources of information, each with its own strengths and weaknesses, and there is no reason why they cannot supplement each other.

Therefore, we begin with a brief description of the neighbourhoods studied, based on firsthand observation by bicycle.[6] The objective of the inspections was to scan for signs of decay and abandonment, as well as signs of vitality. The intention was to observe as any alert citizen would, not to tick off the items on a predetermined checklist. Among the things that attracted the inspector's attention were the visible condition of houses and yards; apparent age of dwellings[7]; liveliness or otherwise of the streets, including presence or absence of children (or such signs of children as plastic toys and small bicycles); graffiti, "Beware of Dog" signs, and barred or heavily screened windows; presence, absence, and condition of such public facilities as parks, community centres, and park benches; signs of maintenance work, either complete or underway, or the absence of such signs; and evidence of either multiple- or single-family occupancy of homes.

The selection of census tracts was based not on seeking out those apparently most decayed, but on trying to choose areas that seemed to be in a process of transition, with the idea of trying to capture some sense of not only what happens when a neighbourhood decays, but also how the process of decay moves forward (or downward). For convenience, the neighbourhoods chosen for the study are designated by names in common use in Winnipeg.

West End (Downtown).[8]   Bounded east and west by Sherbrooke and Ingersoll Streets and north and south by Notre Dame and Ellice Avenues, this area is located immediately northwest of an area known to journalists and police as Murder's Half Acre, an area notorious for crack houses, after-hours drinking havens, and street violence. The West End (downtown) neighbourhood itself is generally considered less seriously decayed. It is predominantly residential, but contains a fair amount of commercial development, and includes both individual homes or duplexes – primarily of pre-Second World War designs, with little space between houses – and apartment buildings. The majority of yards are reasonably well-kept, and there is much evidence of continued efforts to maintain many buildings.

North End.[9]   Located just north of another of the city's seemingly most decayed neighbourhoods, this area is bounded east and west by

Salter and Arlington Streets and north and south by Church and Burrows Avenues. Just four blocks south of Church – outside the study area – is Selkirk Avenue, the commercial heart of Winnipeg's historic North End, formerly the main street of a neighbourhood that was home to two generations of predominantly Ukrainian and Jewish immigrants. The study area itself is more of a patchwork than any of the other study areas, featuring a colourful mixture of older and newer, larger and smaller, more decayed and better-kept areas, the overwhelming majority appearing to be either single-family residences or duplexes.

The only really uniform area is the southeast corner, which is dominated by visibly decayed residential properties, many of them boarded up. In the rest of the study area, patches of decay alternate with patches of well-kept homes, some of them almost suburban in appearance. Generally, the best-kept areas are to the north and the most decayed to the south, but decay is evident throughout the study area.

Elmwood.[10]   This neighbourhood ought, by some criteria, to be "better" real-estate than it is. Its south boundary is the Red River and Ernie O'Dowda Park, a spacious, attractive, well-kept stretch of public riverbank and flower beds. In the southwest corner, facing onto Henderson Highway, is Concord College, a Mennonite post-secondary college affiliated with the University of Winnipeg. In addition, a community centre features an attractive children's playground and a wading pool.

Housing is a mixture of single-family residences; duplexes; functional, obviously lower-rental apartment buildings; and a tract of well-kept public housing in the form of a row-house complex. The single family residences are a mixture of pre-war and post-war housing on small lots. Most houses and yards appear well-kept, giving the neighbourhood the overall appearance of modest circumstances, rather than poverty. A few houses, however, are little more than shacks and, towards the northeastern corner, lawns and homes are generally somewhat less well-kept, and gang graffiti is visible. "Beware of the Dog" signs are substantially more in evidence than in the West End and North End neighbourhoods.

West End (Suburbs).[11]   This is the next neighbourhood to the west (i.e., farther away from the city centre) of the downtown West End, bounded on the east by Ingersoll Street and on the west by a single rail line one block beyond Wall Street with the same north and south boundaries as the downtown West End. As one moves west from Ingersoll, houses and yards appear progressively better kept, commercial development is less in evidence, and there is a noticeably greater concentration of apparently single-family homes. Near the western end of the neighbourhood is Sargent Park, as well as spacious grounds belonging to Winnipeg School Division #1, with school and education administration buildings deployed across copious green space. On a visual inspection of a city map, these grounds take up about one-quarter of the neighbourhood's total area, and many of the properties bordering them would not look out of place in a moderate-income, outlying suburb.

The Neighbourhoods Statscan Sees

Turning to Statistics Canada census data, we offer a series of indicators of the condition of these neighbourhoods without making any assumptions about what they indicate. Our indicators are income decline, population decline, condition of homes, ownership rates, mobility of residents, and immigrant/aboriginal presence in the neighbourhood.

These statistics are not necessarily all suggestive of decay. It is reasonable to assume that declining incomes and deteriorating condition of homes tell a tale of decay, but population and stability statistics are more problematic. For example, population decline is often associated with conditions unsuitable for families and even abandonment of homes, but, if rooming houses are being converted to single-family homes, a decreasing population could be symptomatic of the opposite circumstance, gentrification.

That said, the census data seem generally compatible with our firsthand observations. They suggest that the neighbourhoods all suffer from substantial decay and that they are more decayed than in 1961, but that the West End suburbs are in different circumstances from the other three neighbourhoods, as we noted in our visual inspection. The data also suggest a spreading malaise, that has had its worst effect on the neighbourhoods nearest the centre and that presumably is continuing its spread. Finally, they suggest that there is a lot of life left in these neighbourhoods and much to build upon if the malaise can be arrested.

Relative Income Decline.   Table 1 shows the family average income[12] in each of the four neighbourhoods, expressed as a percentage of the income in the Winnipeg census metropolitan area (CMA).

Except for the West End suburbs, all the neighbourhoods were already well below the CMA average income in 1961, with the North End the poorest of the neighbourhoods. The West End suburban median was actually a bit higher than the median for Winnipeg. By 1991,

Table 1

Year	Winnipeg CMA	West End (downtown) (%)	North End (%)	Elmwood (%)	West End (suburbs) (%)
1961	$5,222	86.6	81.9	88.9	105.3
1991	$46,619	64.1	60.4	67.6	80.0

Table 2

Population	Winnipeg CMA	West End (downtown)	North End	Elmwood	West End (suburbs)
1961	475,989	13,147	9,200	4,788	4,496
1991	652,354	10,397	6,016	3,823	3,758
Change (%)	37.1	–20.9	–34.6	–20.2	–16.4

Table 3

Need major repair	Winnipeg CMA (%)	West End (downtown) (%)	North End (%)	Elmwood (%)	West End (suburbs) (%)
1961	5.3	5.4	8.5	12.3	0.0
1991	8.4	15.9	17.9	11.4	10.3

all the neighbourhoods were poor areas relative to the city as a whole, with medians ranging between three- and four-fifths of that of the CMA. Again, it was the North End that was the poorest and the West End suburbs that were least beset by poverty.

Population Decline.   All of the neighbourhoods under study have suffered substantial population declines since 1961, with declines sharpest in the North End and the West End suburbs least affected. (See table 2.)

Condition of Homes.   The percentage of dwellings in need of repair – 8.4 percent for Winnipeg as a whole – is higher for all the neighbourhoods under study, but by far the highest in the downtown West End and North End, with homes in Elmwood and the West End suburbs in markedly better condition overall. (See table 3.)

Table 4

Owner-occupied	Winnipeg CMA (%)	West End (downtown) (%)	North End (%)	Elmwood (%)	West End (suburbs) (%)
1961	70.3	63.2	66.7	79.5	84.6
1991	62.0	45.7	58.2	53.8	74.1

Interestingly, Elmwood was in roughly the same condition in 1991 as 1961, while the other three neighbourhoods have deteriorated markedly. The West End suburbs, where homes are now a little more in need of repair than dwellings in the city as a whole, passed Statistics Canada's 1961 inspection with a clean bill of health.

Ownership. In 1961, the percentage of owner-occupancy in the downtown West End and North End was lower than that for the city as a whole, while in both Elmwood and the West End suburbs it was markedly higher. By 1991, only the West End suburbs still had a higher owner-occupancy rate than the CMA. (See table 4.)

In the downtown West End and Elmwood, the owner-occupancy rate was down substantially from 1961 and also considerably lower than the figure for the city as a whole. Interestingly, the North End suffered the smallest absolute decline in home ownership, remaining very close to constant in relation to the percentage for the city as a whole. In 1961, the North End's total was 3.6 percent less than that of the city and, in 1991, 2.8 percent.

A possible explanation is that the North End has always been a low-income district, thus has perhaps changed less relative to the rest of the city than the other neighbourhoods. Another relevant factor is that housing remains very affordable in Winnipeg, and especially so in the neighbourhoods that are considered less desirable from a real-estate agent's perspective.

Stability. Winnipeg as a whole has become a great deal more mobile since 1961. In 1961, 95 percent of the residents had been in the same home for at least a year and 88 percent for more than five years. By 1991, those totals were down to 80 and 48 percent respectively. However, in three of the four neighbourhoods under study, the declines in stability were greater.

In 1961, all the neighbourhoods except the suburban West End were as about as stable as the city as a whole, but in 1991 the downtown West End, North End and Elmwood were all less stable than the city as a whole. The West End suburbs, which in 1961 had had a lower

Table 5

Resident in the same home for:		Winnipeg CMA (%)	West End (downtown) (%)	North End (%)	Elmwood (%)	West End (suburbs) (%)
1 year	1961	95.4	94.7	94.5	95.7	96.4
	1991	79.8	72.8	77.7	73.6	83.3
5 years	1961	88.0	86.9	85.5	84.5	81.8
	1991	47.7	38.0	44.0	45.9	51.8

percentage of five-year residents was, in 1991, more stable than the city as a whole. (See table 5.)

Interestingly, although the North End was the poorest neighbourhood, with the heaviest population decline and the houses most in need of repair, it was slightly higher than the West End in terms of both homeownership and stability. The reason for that might be the fact, observed in the visual inspections recounted above, that multiple-family dwellings were more in evidence in the downtown West End.

As for the suburban West End's decline in stability, it is possible that some parts of this neighbourhood were still under construction in 1956, five years before the collection of the 1961 data. Overall, however, the differences between these relatively low-income neighbourhoods and the CMA as a whole are not very striking. On balance, they suggest that, in these instances, stability and poverty do not have a great deal to do with each other.

Immigrants and Aboriginal people. The figures in table 6 represent percentages of the total population in Winnipeg and each of the neighbourhoods. The 1961 figures are the percentage born outside Canada and the 1991 figures are the percentage who are classified as either immigrants or of aboriginal origin. The rationale for organizing these statistics as we did was to gather evidence bearing on the widely held popular conception that immigrants – especially from poorer countries – and aboriginal people bear a good deal of blame for the problems that are associated with inner-city decay.

The comparison is an awkward one because the 1961 census does not provide data on aboriginal origin. Thus the best comparisons are between neighbourhoods, rather than between time periods. If the vertical comparisons are of any value, they are interesting. They suggest that, while the combined immigrant and aboriginal presence in Winnipeg in the North End has remained largely unchanged between 1961 and 1991, the proportion of this population in the West End has

Table 6

Immigrants and Aboriginals	Winnipeg CMA (%)	West End (downtown) (%)	North End (%)	Elmwood (%)	West End (suburbs) (%)
1961	23.8	33.6	28.3	38.0	28.8
1991	20.6	58.5	36.8	22.6	38.2
Immigrants 1991	17.3	47.8	21.3	18.4	33.4
Aboriginals 1991	3.3	10.7	15.5	4.2	4.8

increased noticeably, especially downtown, and that in Elmwood it has decreased sharply.

We have no data to help us explain these disparities, but they suggest tantalizing questions for further research. Has Elmwood changed in a way that makes it more resistant to people perceived as outsiders, or is it perhaps perceived as a good place to live by people of European origin, but not by others? In other words, is some form of racial steering (see note 6) being practiced as part of a wider pattern of ghetto formation? Our study does not help us in answering these questions.

Turning to the more reliable horizontal comparisons, they suggest that, while newcomers seek out the moderately priced housing of these neighbourhoods, there is no correlation between an aboriginal and immigrant presence and indicators of neighbourhood decay. If aboriginal people and immigrants produced decay, we would expect that the least decayed neighbourhoods would have the lowest visible minority presence. That is not the case.

The figures suggest nothing more or less than that each neighbourhood has its own character and that place of origin has little or nothing to do with stability, home ownership, or condition of dwelling. In 1991, the West End, both downtown and suburban, were home to large, and apparently growing, populations of aboriginal people and immigrants, while the percentage of this population in Elmwood, which was high in 1961, approximated the figure for the city as a whole in 1991.

In addition, Elmwood, one of the more decayed of these neighbourhoods, had by far the lowest percentage of aboriginal people, indeed only a bit more than the percentage for the CMA. The North End, always a centre for immigrants, was home to even more aboriginal people and immigrants in 1991 – but not as many as the economically better-off suburban West End.

Summary.   These are not the most notoriously declining neighbourhoods in Winnipeg, but all of them have experienced substantial population declines while the rest of the city grew. All but Elmwood suffered substantial increases in the percentages of dwellings in need of
repair. Home ownership rates were markedly down both absolutely
and in relation to the city as a whole in the downtown West End and
Elmwood. In the North End they were also down absolutely, but
remained fairly constant in relationship to the city as a whole. In the
West End suburbs, owner-occupancy rates remained higher than for
the city as a whole.

If owner-occupancy were a reliable sign of neighbourhood vitality,
therefore, the West End suburbs would not appear to have decayed by
1991, even though the population of the neighbourhood had declined
while the condition of dwellings deteriorated. A similar picture
emerges in considering the stability of the neighbourhoods, with the
West End suburbs actually more stable than the rest of the city in 1991,
while the stability of the other three neighbourhoods had declined
since 1961.

It seems reasonable to read these statistics as indicating that the
degree of decay in these neighbourhoods, from least to most, lines up
as follows: West End suburbs, Elmwood, West End downtown, and
North End. If so, then visual inspections, carried out independently of
the statistical analysis, produced the same result. A final finding is that,
whatever is happening to these neighbourhoods, evidence is lacking
that in-migration from outside Canada and aboriginal residence have
anything to do with it. Two of the more decayed neighbourhoods and
the least decayed one were centres of immigration and aboriginal residence. The other more decayed one was no more so than the city as a
whole.

More broadly our findings make it clear that these neighbourhoods
– not the most notoriously decayed in the city – are in trouble. They
are caught up in a process of decline that is evident from deteriorating
incomes and deteriorating condition of homes and strongly suggested
by a variety of other evidence. At the same time, it is obvious, both
from the visual inspection and from statistical data, that these neighbourhoods still offer much to build upon. Even in the North End,
where the condition of dwellings was the worst in this study, more than
80 percent of the properties were found by the Statistics Canada census not to be in need of major repair. In all the neighbourhoods, the
visual inspection produced many signs of well-maintained properties.
The pride of ownership and resilience of community that is evident in
such signs tells us that much will be lost if these neighbourhoods are
written off.

DEALING WITH DECAY

Whatever we make of some of our statistics, it is clear that decay is a problem, that the neighbourhoods surveyed in this study, and others like them, are in a state of decline. Anyone who doubts that the decline can continue, and accelerate, need only survey some of the numerous examples of American cities that have been through a similar sequence of events, brought on by similar policies.

If Americans are ahead of Canadians in suffering the effects of inner-city decay, however, they are now also pulling ahead in the search for means to deal with the problem. The idea of attempting to develop policies designed to check urban sprawl and its impact on inner cities is gaining wider acceptance than would have been thought possible a scant few years ago, especially in the United States, but in Canada as well (Leo with Beavis, Carver, and Turner, 1998).

Action is underway in numerous jurisdictions. The best-known case is that of Oregon, where stringent measures for the control of metropolitan growth have been in place for more than two decades. Oregon is no longer an exceptional case. Initiatives of varying degrees of seriousness are also underway in Florida, Washington State, New Jersey, British Columbia, Maryland, Minnesota, Colorado, Massachusetts, Pennsylvania, Vermont, and San Jose and Santa Clara County, California. Politically influential support for urban growth management, in addition to the cases already cited, has surfaced in Michigan, South Carolina, Montreal, and Salt Lake City (Turner, 1990; DeGrove with Miness, 1992; Orfield, 1997; Baker, Hinze, and Manzi, 1991; Smith, 1996; Leo with Beavis, Carver, and Turner, 1998).

In this section, we survey some of the policy instruments that are in use elsewhere and that could play a role in addressing the problem of decay in Winnipeg's inner city. We begin with a word of clarification. In much of the literature, the term "growth management" has been equated with "growth controls," meaning attempts to limit or exclude either new development in suburban areas or large-scale commercial development in the inner city.

Such efforts have been widely criticized on a variety of grounds: they are associated with NIMBYism (the "not-in-my-back-yard" syndrome), exclusion of lower-income people from suburbs, and the desire to enjoy the benefits of urban life without having to help pay for them. It has been argued that growth controls drive up the price of housing by limiting the locational options available to developers (Babcock and Bosselman, 1973; Mallach, 1984; Fishel, 1990; Logan and Zhou, 1989), that they have the effect of shifting the costs of development from one community to another (Rosen and

Katz, 1981), and that they exclude the poor from suburbs (Downs, 1988).

It is important to emphasize, therefore, that meaningful metropolitan-wide growth management is a far more ambitious undertaking than local growth control. It involves the attempt to set out rules for development that are designed to preserve the livability, viability, and attractiveness of an entire urban area and especially to preserve the inner city from deterioration as suburban and exurban areas expand.

Necessarily, such a venture is far-reaching and difficult. It involves the achievement of a complex set of political trade-offs that, together, address the conditions for the vitality and health of the metropolitan area. These necessarily include a concern with inner-city and suburban communities, rural areas beyond city limits, and inherently far-ranging environmental and social considerations. Furthermore, the aim of growth management must be not to stop growth, but to accommodate it where it is occurring while checking its destructive potential.

Not only is genuine regional growth management ambitious, it requires patience. We have spent at least several decades mismanaging the growth of our cities. There is no quick fix that will reverse this history in a year, or even five years. But once we start, significant results will be visible within five years, and the benefits will accelerate with the passage of time. The alternative is to stand by while decay takes over many inner cities and spreads into the suburbs.

Growth Boundaries

Growth boundaries are as simple and straightforward in conception as they are difficult to achieve in practice. They are unlikely in most cases to be feasible without the intervention of a senior government (Leo with Beavis, Carver, and Turner, 1998). Typically, it begins with the establishment of a set of mandatory planning goals, to which local governments must comply. An enforcement mechanism is created to ensure this outcome. Such plans are then required to include a growth boundary – or green line, as it is called in California – a line drawn around the edge of the metropolitan area, separating areas available for urban development from those that are reserved for agricultural, resource, or recreational use.

In Oregon, where this process has been in place for almost two decades, the experience has been that successful establishment of a growth boundary requires a mixture of local initiative and state supervision. If there is not a participative process at the local level, leading to decisions acceptable to many about the location of the growth boundary, the political viability of the boundary is in question. By the same token, without a final, authoritative determination at the state level, the motivation to go through the participative process would probably not materialize.[13] Of course, a solid base of popular support is essential.

Throughout the 1980s, Winnipeg had a so-called urban limit line, which bore a superficial resemblance to the growth boundary, but was not the same thing. In the first place, it did not separate agricultural from urban development, but only set limits on how far Winnipeg would extend its infrastructure, leaving entirely open the question of what would happen outside city limits. Secondly, it was an artifice of the planning department, a sensible idea to be sure, but without either provincial or popular sanction. Even the commitment of City Council, which included the urban limit line in its official plan, proved less than sincere. During the period in which the line was supposedly in force, it was not always honoured, and in the end it was unceremoniously dropped from the official plan.

At the same time, however, it is important that the regulations connected with growth management not become a series of onerous bureaucratic obstacles to development. If that happens, they will escalate the cost of development and incur the opposition not only of developers, but also of prospective homebuyers. Oregon's approach has been to combine a series of stringent but well-understood regulations with provisions to ensure that enforcement mechanisms are transparent, readily negotiable, and, especially, quickly negotiable.

Housing Measures

For any city suffering from inner-city decay, affordable housing is a major concern, whether recognized or not. The presence of affordable housing for people of all income levels is a priceless asset, and not just for the obvious social reasons. It populates the inner city and thereby makes it safer. Thus it helps to make inner-city residence a live option for better-off people and bolsters the stability of neighbourhoods that badly need the boost. In the process, it helps to keep the inner city from being abandoned in a flight to the suburbs and provides a crucial support for inner-city commerce.

Over the past two decades a great deal of new housing has been developed in Winnipeg's inner city, and older housing renovated, some with the help of government grants and loans, some through private initiative, thanks to the much-criticized Winnipeg Core Area Initiative, together with a welter of other federal, provincial, and local programs. As a result, new and renovated housing for people of all income levels was created throughout the inner city and homeowners renovated their properties with partially forgivable loans from the government. Co-operative housing for elderly people, immigrants, and others offered the stability of homeownership, together with a sense of community, to people for whom these benefits might otherwise have been out of reach. These programs helped to keep the inner city marginally viable and supported business, as well as providing support for people who needed help. Winnipeg's inner city may be in a parlous condition, but it would be a great deal worse without the housing that was added and renovated in the 1980s.

Such programs could still be in place and – since the prices of inner-city housing remain very low – they could be managed in such a way as to avoid a significant drain on government resources (Leo and Brown with Dick, 1998). A discussion of how such programs could be structured and implemented would take us beyond the scope of this study. Suffice it to say that what we are recommending is not gentrification of the inner city but the renovation and development of housing at all income levels.[14]

There are two reasons for this sprawl. The obvious one is that land along major roads and land zoned for agriculture is inexpensive. A less obvious reason is that suburban subdivisions closer to the city centre are often zoned to exclude moderate-income housing. Such restrictions are motivated partly by a perhaps self-fulfilling prophecy that the proximity of lower-income housing will reduce property value in adjacent, higher-income areas. In suburban municipalities with their own tax base, they are motivated, in addition, by the desire to bolster the tax base.

A growth boundary cuts off much of the opportunity to overcome these obstacles through sprawl development. As a result it may incur the wrath both of moderate-income residents who aspire to a home of their own and developers of moderate-income housing. However, a different outcome is possible, and, once again, Oregon is a case in point.

In the mid-1970s, when Oregon's system of growth management was still in the process of becoming established, it was opposed by developers. 1000 Friends of Oregon, an environmentalist group, and a key supporter of the growth boundary, considered the problem of developer opposition and concluded that developers faced too many obstacles to the development of new housing. An accommodation became achievable after 1000 Friends decided to match its support for the growth boundary with opposition to restrictions on the development of housing within the growth boundary.

After that, environmentalists and builders frequently appeared as allies in the advocacy of standards that required municipalities throughout the metropolitan area to accept housing at a variety of densities and designed to serve various income levels. The support of builders played an important role in defeating a 1978 initiative against land-use planning and has remained important in the maintenance of the growth boundary since then (Leo, 1998).

Wherever a political configuration such as the one in Oregon is achievable, growth boundaries and affordable housing, far from being at odds with each other, can become compatible and mutually re-enforcing objectives. Growth boundaries can serve as a spur to modest increases in urban density,[15] and density, in turn, can supplant cheap land as a means to affordable housing.

Pricing of New Development

The discussion of the costs of sprawl development in a previous section of this paper implies that fringe development is not paying its share of the bills – i.e., its share of what it costs to keep the metropolitan area as a whole viable and attractive. That implication is made explicit in Orfield's (1997) study of Minneapolis-St Paul, in which the sources of money spent on new development are analysed.

If we accept the premise that newer and more prosperous communities are not paying their share of the costs of maintaining the infrastructure and services of the metropolitan area as a whole, then the obvious solution is some combination of development levies that hit lower-density subdivisions harder, together with tax equalization measures. Given exurban development, these would have to be mandated by the provincial government, and the mandate would have to include provisions to ensure that the proceeds of the taxes are used to provide support where it is needed.

Minneapolis-St Paul already has a system whereby commercial industrial tax base is shared. Orfield (1997: 87) argues that this is a step in the right direction, but points out that the heavy dependence on commercial tax base has the effect of ensuring that some poorer jurisdictions, which happen to have a significant commercial tax base, pay in, while some prosperous, largely residential suburbs do not.

Measures that add to the costs of establishing and maintaining low-density subdivisions would have the added benefit of influencing the incentive structure facing developers. Costs added on to the development of suburban and exurban subdivisions might begin to stimulate re-evaluation of development locations, densities, and mixes.

Overcoming Regulatory Rigidities[16]

Canadian suburbs are often thought to be quintessentially individualist, but in fact they have been profoundly shaped by interventions from all three levels of government, interventions that today are limiting the options open to consumers, developers, and hard-pressed municipalities. It helps if we understand how this happened. At the end of the Second World War, the federal government anticipated that the return to civilian life of large numbers of veterans would pose a problem of housing supply and decided to meet it head-on by stimulating private enterprise. Federal, provincial, and municipal governments all became involved in a massive program of government support for suburban development.[17]

To be sure, this was not a case of the state imposing its will on a reluctant public. The suburbs and cities we have today are the product of a complex mix of corporate initiative, popular preference, and state action. The state was responding not only to popular opinion but also to the demands of E.P. Taylor and other development magnates of the time, the professional biases of bureaucrats in the Department of Finance and the Central Mortgage and Housing Corporation, the sensitivities of Liberal party contributors and the international financial community, and more.

Whether or not we judge these actions to have been appropriate to the political circumstances of the late 1940s and 1950s, the problem we face today is that the actions of those years has left us saddled with the same regulatory apparatus that produced the suburbs of the 1950s and 1960s. They have long since become a monolith that limits everyone's choices, including those of developers. Since the 1970s, with the size of family units shrinking and the cost of housing escalating, developers have repeatedly identified market opportunities for more compact forms of housing – or for neighbourhoods where the proximity of stores and public facilities encourages more walking and less driving – only to be thwarted by planning regulations affecting such things as lot sizes, widths of rights-of-way, or separation of uses.[18]

This regulatory apparatus, therefore, is not only deepening the distress of decaying inner cities. By sustaining a bias in favour of the very kinds of development that are contributing to the inner cities' declining viability, it is also limiting the ability of developers to respond to new market opportunities. One way of supporting the revival of inner cities, therefore, would be to attack this regulatory apparatus, an attack which should be capable of gaining some support from developers. In fact, a recent initiative does seem hesitantly to be moving in this direction.

The Canada Mortgage and Housing Corporation is financing a program called Affordability and Choice Today (ACT), the purpose of which is to encourage provincial governments to reform the regulations governing land development, including land development standards, the development approval process, and residential renovation. It makes small grants to municipalities to expedite programs working towards those objectives. This is an initiative of three national groups: the Canada Homebuilders' Association, the Canadian Housing and Renewal Association, and the Federation of Canadian Municipalities (FCM). The initiative has been underway for several years, and CMHC reports suggest that the kinds of changes it is looking for will be favourable to housing intensification and therefore to a reversal of some of the worst aspects of existing development patterns. A recent crop of grants, for example, deals mainly with regulatory changes designed to facilitate the development of affordable housing, extra rental units in single-family housing, and seniors' housing (Canada Mortgage and Housing Corporation, 1994).

This appears to be constructive, but a more widespread public understanding of the damage conventional development patterns are doing could lay the basis for a much more concentrated, frontal attack on the outmoded regulations that are shackling our cities. This need not be as difficult as it may sound. The regulations that limit development options today were put in place very rapidly after the Second World War, once the government decided that housing development was an important priority. Given a favourable climate of public opinion, a similar decision today might well be capable of producing similarly swift results. The need, after all, is not for new regulations but for greater freedom from unreasonable and counter-productive regulations. In the 1990s, that should be a saleable proposition.

Transit-oriented Development

If the above recommendations were implemented, we would find ourselves living in cities that were gradually becoming denser,[19] less dependent on automobiles, with a greater mixture of incomes within residential districts and of different kinds of land uses. Such development would reinforce the need for and viability of transit. By the same token, the development of transit would reinforce the viability of such development.

CONCLUSIONS

A modern city is as complex and multifaceted as modern society itself, and any attempt to understand it is bound to lead us down many paths. Our own attempt, in these pages, to gain purchase on the problem of inner-city decay, and to consider ways of addressing it, has taken us from social ills of the inner city, through a look at the complexities of inner-city society and built form, to a consideration of some of the ways in which different systems of urban land use and urban transportation interact to produce problems and some ways in which they can be altered to produce solutions instead.

In the past, we have avoided these complexities, relied on the advice of experts and hoped that they would not lead us astray. That hope has not been fulfilled, because experts tend to think in terms of their own narrow specialties. Road engineers get us to finance more extensive road systems, suburban developers encourage us to permit the opening of new land for ever more far-flung subdivisions, downtown developers explain the difficulties of preserving older buildings and neighbourhoods, while social workers impress upon us the urgency of providing more extensive support networks for the isolated, inner-city poor.

In order to avoid thinking about the complex interactions that cause urban problems, we have concentrated on fixes. Each fix, however, causes new problems, and all of them together exacerbate each other's shortcomings and cause still more problems. We will do better with our cities if we rely less on experts and devote more attention to them ourselves. The problem of inner-city decay, along with the many other problems that interact with it, is complex, but it is comprehensible. In many North American cities, a new determination to grasp the problems and start addressing them is becoming visible. In some places it is starting to produce results. The process requires public understanding of the problems and the engagement of citizens in addressing them.

There is much we can do to deal with inner-city decay that is not covered in these pages, especially in the area of inner-city housing and community development. The purpose of this paper is to open up a topic that requires much further thought and discussion, and requires it urgently. If we do not begin to address our growth problems now we will be forced to face the financial and social costs of overextended and deteriorating infrastructure and services, accelerating social segregation and isolation of the poor, and inner-city decay that spreads inexorably into the suburbs. The choices are ours. Whatever choices we make will have momentous consequences for ourselves and our children.

NOTES

1 Thanks to the University of Winnipeg and the Social Science and Humanities Research Council, as well as Jim Silver and the Canadian Centre for Policy Alternatives, for supporting the research and writing of this article.

Lisa Shaw did invaluable and complex analytical work in gathering, analysing, and working out the significance of the data; Ken Gibbons provided crucial support for the analysis; and Colin Goff played an important role in developing the ideas on which the study is built. Neither Colin Goff nor Ken Gibbons bear responsibility for the conclusions.

2 Personal communication, 4 October 1996.

3 Not included are Headingly – which seceded from Winnipeg in 1992, rendering comparable five- and ten-year figures unavailable – and Macdonald.

4 A tacit agreement among real-estate people and homeowners to try to ensure that racial minorities are restricted to certain neighbourhoods is referred to in the United States as racial steering.

5 Known as the Dominion Bureau of Statistics in 1961, but we will refer to all data as Statistics Canada Census data.

6 Christopher Leo has worked in downtown Winnipeg for more than twenty years and has lived in one of the remaining predominantly middle-class neighbourhoods downtown for much of that time. In the summer, he regularly rides a bicycle through all parts of the inner city, for enjoyment and exercise, but also because he has found it a useful means of observation, less obtrusive than being on foot and far more instructive than driving or riding. Either a stranger on foot or a slow-moving vehicle is bound to attract attention in a ghetto neighbourhood. In the eyes of locals, however, cyclists – like letter carriers – fade into the background. Before writing the following descriptions, he rode through each neighbourhood, systematically visiting all parts of it.

7 In North American cities, a particularly important historical watershed is the Second World War. It is usually easy to distinguish post-war from pre-war neighbourhoods by the design and placement of houses. For any single house, such evidence might be questionable, since there would be nothing to prevent, say, a post-war builder from copying pre-war styles. However, when one travels through a section of Winnipeg and observes a transition from two-storey clapboard and brick homes with little space between them to bungalows on spacious grounds, there is little doubt where post-war suburban development began.

8 Tract 25 in 1961, 28 and 29 in 1991.

9 Tract 6 in 1961, 45 in 1991.

10 Tract 15 in 1961, 39 in 1991.

11 Tract 26 in 1961, 30 in 1991.

12 Median household income would have been a better figure to use in this table, but the only direct 1961-91 comparison available in the Statistics Canada census data was the one we have used.

13 These issues are discussed in more detail in Leo (1999).

14 The term "gentrification" refers to a situation in which a formerly lower-income neighbourhood is transformed rapidly, leading the prices of housing and services to escalate so quickly that the low-income neighbours are priced out of their homes and neighbourhood and are forced into more expensive and/or inferior accommodation or onto the streets. It is a situation, in other words, in which a neighbourhood becomes uniformly upper-income.

The kind of program we have in mind, by contrast, could include a variety of measures for assisting low-income earners to acquire modest homes, renovating abandoned and decaying homes and finding purchasers or tenants to occupy them, building new homes appropriate to their surroundings in marginal neighbourhoods, offering new locational choices to people who feel trapped in decaying neighbourhoods and wish to escape, and more. It would also include encouragement for middle-class people to live in the inner city while taking steps to avoid – or at least to avoid subsidizing – gentrification.

15 Densities that would be effective in meeting regional growth management objectives can be achieved without drastic alterations in familiar development patterns. Downs (1998: 146) says "relatively high average residential densities can be attained in new-growth areas even if most residential land there is developed with low-density, single-family units. And this would not require constructing high-rise housing."

16 This section draws on Leo (1995).

17 The story was broadly similar in the United States, though it differs in some details that are significant in contexts other than that of this article (Leo, 1995; Weiss, 1987).

18 Since the late 1980s, the cause of compact housing and mixed-use neighbourhoods has been taken up by proponents of the so-called "new urbanism." A perusal of the postings on the email list of the Congress for the New Urbanism produces numerous examples of the frustrations posed by conventional planning regulations.

19 It is worth reminding the reader that more effective utilization of urban infrastructure can be achieved without a large increase in densities, without high-rise apartment buildings and without infringing on the majority preference for single-family homes with large lots. All that is required is to provide incentive structures for developers that are more appropriate to the reality of urban land markets, more cost-effective location of new subdivisions, and the provision of greater choice to the consumer.

PART TWO

Governance

6 Is Urban Affairs a Priority on the Public Agenda?

MERLE NICHOLDS

There is no doubt that urban affairs has moved to the forefront on the public agenda. With greater pressures both at work and at home, people are feeling a loss of control over the events that shape their lives. As a result, there has been a shift of focus back on the community. People are recognizing that the urban environment is a key determinant of overall quality of life. High on the public agenda is the desire to live in safe, healthy communities with a high quality of life. Local issues related to traffic, crime, youth, property taxes, declining services, and loss of green space have taken on even greater importance. As the public feels increasingly powerless and alienated from government, they feel that they can at least exert some direct influence over the issues closer to home that have a direct impact on their everyday lives.

With governments at all levels under pressure to reduce expenditures, communities and volunteer groups are being called upon to fill in the gaps in the delivery of some basic community services. Government can no longer afford to be all things to all people. Citizens are now starting to take action for themselves to prevent crime in their neighbourhood. Communities are starting to reconnect with their traditional values and methods for solving problems. The most desirable communities are the ones with very active citizen involvement.

In spite of this renewed focus on community, there is a community-building crisis within urban areas. First of all, citizen involvement in civic affairs and volunteer work has been significantly impacted by increased demands in the workplace, which leave little time or energy for commitments outside the home. On top of that, sprawling, automobile-dominated suburban development has created communities with little focus or identity. It is very difficult to feel a sense of community when your neighbourhood is physically divided from the rest of the city by a multilane arterial road.

In rapidly growing communities, people feel the additional stress of coping with a constantly changing community. The emergence of both strip malls and big box stores and the associated traffic congestion threaten their quality of life. People feel an even greater loss of control over the community around them when trees are cut down and green space is paved over to clear the way for more subdivisions. Many people are drawn to areas with that traditional "small town" sense of identity. They invest in the community with the expectation that nothing will change. Many municipal politicians have heard this well-worn message: "When I bought my house, you didn't tell me this was in the plans." Massive opposition arises even when a road that has been planned for years comes forward for construction. People strongly resist changes in their neighbourhood for which they feel a sense of ownership. It should come as no surprise, then, that in fast-growing communities there is an even greater feeling of powerlessness and less interest in getting involved.

Local government is confronted with quite a dilemma. At a time when citizen involvement is needed to deliver some of the community services that government can no longer afford to provide, volunteer participation is declining. While the public demands more open, consultative local government, fewer people are participating in the consultative process. Even though there is strong resistance to change in their community, people demand to have the convenience of new amenities and services. Just as there is a growing recognition of the need to focus on rebuilding communities, it is more difficult than ever to motivate people to take some ownership for the community around them. The predominant view is that responsibility for what goes on beyond their property line belongs to someone else.

Democracy is strongest at the local level, where government is closest to the people. As the public feels alienated and frustrated with big government at higher levels, they demand that municipal politicians respond to all of their needs and concerns and be held accountable for the actions of all other government bodies. They do not accept the arguments from municipalities that provincial downloading has seriously impacted their ability to hold the line on taxes while maintaining the same service levels. Unfortunately, the role of local government, in the view of the public, is all too often reduced to that of a service provider. What many have forgotten, including local politicians, is local government's responsibility to govern and to provide leadership in building communities.

There is, however, a crisis of leadership at the local level. Politicians are not rewarded for making tough decisions that are good for the long term. While the public says that they want better long-term planning and fiscal responsibility, they lobby for decisions that bring short-term benefit. Special interest groups pressure politicians into making ad hoc planning decisions. It can be very difficult to advocate increasing contributions to reserves, which are set aside for the maintenance and repair of aging infrastructure, when the public is demanding to put that same money into the construction of a new arena. Politicians have the dual responsibility of making decisions in the best interests of the whole community in addition to representing the wishes and concerns of their constituents. These two responsibilities can pose real conflicts at times. A decision for the overall long-term good of the community, which results in a negative impact on one segment of the population in the short term, is the toughest to deal with. It is a sad reality that the views of the majority, who have the most to lose, are very rarely heard in the debate.

As mayor of one of the fastest-growing cities in the country, I have learned first hand about the vital need for both leadership and public involvement in building healthy communities. I am constantly challenged to find innovative methods to engage the community in civic affairs. This is particularly challenging with a population of predominately highly educated professionals in very demanding jobs. People who spend much of their workplace time in meetings are not interested in attending traditional public meetings at night. They demand to be kept informed, but have no time or inclination to read the city notice page in the local newspaper. In addition to dealing with low public interest, politicians in rapidly growing cities must balance all of the competing and conflicting demands of growth. They must make decisions that reflect the community's interests while at the same time recognizing their limitations to impose restrictions on development. For example, a municipality cannot satisfy residents' demands to freeze all development until a school is built. High levels of growth put great strain on a municipality's ability to meet the need for new roads and facilities to service its expanding population. The resulting decline in service levels only makes the public more frustrated and cynical about their local government. It is a vicious cycle that only further exacerbates the problems in building communities. In order to reclaim our communities and get the situation back on track, we are going to need strong community leadership.

It is difficult for me to completely separate the discussion on leadership and public participation because the two are so closely intertwined. The public is not going to get involved unless it is inspired behind a vision and clear sense of purpose, and leaders cannot be effective unless their community cares about their future.

BOOSTING PUBLIC PARTICIPATION

Let me focus first on the lessons that I have learned on how to increase public participation. It is important to recognize and accept that the traditional methods of public consultation are no longer working. To reverse this situation, municipalities must take the risk of experimenting with a variety of innovative approaches that will attract the involvement a broader segment of the population. Municipalities must take the time to strategically plan their consultation process and make a sincere commitment to really listen to what the community has to say.

Most people today are very selective about how they spend the little free time that they have. In my experience, people are very generous about volunteering if they are assured that their efforts will have an influence on achieving a desirable outcome. Participation levels drop dramatically when the municipality is perceived as "just going through the motions" of public consultation. Municipal leaders must clearly demonstrate that they are listening to the public's advice and show in very tangible ways the value that is placed on volunteer contribution.

While increasing public participation is the objective, municipalities must also take precautions to avoid citizen "burnout." It is a well-known fact in many communities that it is the same small group of citizens who show up for every public meeting or volunteer to take on community projects. A city can certainly "wear out its welcome" if it consults extensively on every issue it deals with. This does not mean that a consultative approach to decision-making should not be taken. What is does mean is that, in order to open up the process to a wider range of new participants, innovative consultation methods need to employed. It also means that more attention should be paid to previously received public feedback on community priorities and concerns. The public has a right to feel skeptical about whether their politicians are really listening if they keep going out to them with the same questions. The public expects their political leaders to consult them about their priorities, expectations, and concerns. They also have great respect for politicians who can take this direction from the community and apply it decisively and consistently to many issues. In fast-growing cities, politicians and staff are frequently forced to respond to many big issues all at one time. Citizens reasonably object if they are barraged with requests to participate on too many issues at once. This can be avoided with careful planning to design a more strategic and inclusive consultation process.

In order to involve a broader range of the population, municipalities need to rethink their consultative approach and tailor it to the needs of the public they are trying to reach. For example, if people have no time to attend a public meeting, then consultation should be taken to where people are already gathered, such as at the grocery store or at a community event. Youth are usually overlooked in the consultation process but will offer clear opinions and suggestions if anyone takes the time to ask. It can be as simple as going to the classroom or taking some pizza over to their local hangout. Seniors too have the time to offer an incredible amount of insight and experience to any debate. All it requires is making the process flexible enough to meet their particular needs. Most people want to be more informed and involved in their community. Participation has to be made relevant and accessible to them. A large segment of the population considers the usual bureaucratic type of information to be meaningless and irrelevant. The strategy is to convey the message in a way that clearly communicates exactly how this issue affects them and why they should care. I have successfully involved seven-year-olds in problem-solving on several major community issues. I have worked with a youth advisory group who gave me advice on everything from site plan applications to priorities on the city's future strategic directions. It does require creativity and extra effort to make the message relevant to a variety of different groups, but the results pay off great dividends.

Municipalities get most of their feedback from special interest groups, residents' associations, and developers but very little from the business sector. With their focus on maintaining the viability of their business, most business people give little attention to community issues. As major contributors to the local economy, their needs and concerns should be considered in community decision-making. This may involve taking the consultation process directly into the workplace and holding focus groups with both management and employees. Many business owners are interested in providing input on civic issues as long as the process is well managed and efficient and they are assured that their feedback will make a difference.

There is no prescribed course of action that will guarantee public participation in every situation. Achieving effective public consultation requires a municipality to be adaptive and creative, to tailor the process to meet the needs of each situation and target audience. A municipality cannot be successful, however, unless its politicians and staff are completely committed to the fundamental importance of public involvement in decision-making.

THE IMPORTANCE OF LEADERSHIP AND VISION

Residents will get involved if they feel a sense of community ownership and identity. In order to have a real identity, a community has to have a clear vision of what kind of community it wants to be. A community cannot move forward to fulfill that vision without a leader who is committed to those same objectives. Communities need leaders to inspire them behind a vision and common sense of purpose. A fast-growing municipality can easily fall prey to haphazard development and a declining quality of life unless it has strong leadership to steer and shape it in accordance with its community vision. Market forces and short-term thinking can change a community's direction almost overnight. The cumulative effects of ad hoc decisions can be quite devastating on community life. It requires strong and committed leadership to manage and steer growth in the desired direction. It can be a very difficult to stay focused on the big picture in fast-growing communities when you are completely preoccupied with "putting out the fires" from issues arising from all directions.

If we are to reclaim our sense of community, we need to give careful attention to community planning and development. It is our physical built environment that is the biggest factor in determining our urban quality of life. Cities that have an abundance of green spaces and lively public spaces are very desirable places to live. Human-scale development that fosters an attractive environment for pedestrians engenders a real sense of place. People are longing for that traditional town centre and main street that create a real focus and identity. We can prevent the sense of isolation felt in most urban centres with public spaces and streets that are filled with people instead of cars. We need to pay more attention to the social needs of the community by designing the built and natural environment around the need for human interaction. People are looking for a community with a heart and soul.

The importance of community is certainly a high priority on the public agenda. If we are going to meet the challenge of rebuilding that sense of community, then we are going to have to completely rethink our traditional methods of managing urban affairs. We are going to have to be innovative and creative in order to foster community participation and civic pride, which are fundamental to our future as healthy communities. It is critical that we find strong leaders with both vision and commitment to move us forward on the right path towards having more livable and vibrant communities. The public is not apathetic. It has simply not been inspired to believe that it has the power to make a difference to its community. It is high time we rekindled the spirit of local democracy.

7 Toronto's Legal Challenge to Amalgamation

BETH MOORE MILROY

At the heart of the massive struggle that Toronto residents engaged in against their provincial government in 1997 was this issue: what rights do citizens have to shape their city? That year, the more senior Ontario provincial government challenged city governments as never before, and did so on several fronts at once. One of the most dramatic battles was the forced amalgamation of six otherwise separate cities and the elimination of the regional government that had held them together in a metropolitan arrangement since 1953. "Metro," as the regional government was called, had collectively provided certain services such as police, transportation, and welfare and spread the costs proportionately across the six cities. Amalgamation blew apart these arrangements and also the citizenry's expectations about their capacity to influence the city's evolution.

The case of Toronto's amalgamation is used in this chapter to explore the powers that municipalities and their citizens ultimately have. Through political action and ultimately court challenges to the amalgamation legislation, Torontonians found that their rights to shape their city as citizens of the city were highly circumscribed. Given the etymology of "citizen," it is ironic that citizen rights and responsibilities do not reside at the city-scale but in Canada, at least, derive only from residence in the country and a province. During a brief, poignant period Torontonians came face-to-face with what Isin has described as "cities without citizens" (1992). His phrase refers to the British practice, repeated in Canada, of more senior governments constituting cities as corporations responsible to them, legal entities with rights and obligations distinct from their citizens. This is in contrast to medieval cities in which "citizens were *collectively* the city" (Isin, 1992: vii).

Torontonians discovered that their city was unquestionably just a municipal corporation and they were not its governors. Their presence, voices, actions, and demands had no effect at all upon a provincial government unwilling to pay attention. The outcomes of other cases of this type may vary across nations; however, the results elsewhere in Canada and in other countries built on British traditions could in principle be the same: cities without citizens, citizens without a city.

Other analyses of Canadian cities support Isin's point. Andrew (1995) notes that there is wide agreement among those who write on local government in Canada that the initial creation of municipal institutions had to do with provincial, not local, actions. Before confederation, Ontario set up municipal governments "as a way of increasing public expenditures on infrastructure without increasing the provincial debt burden. Ontario then tried to "sell" this model to other provincial governments and, indeed, the confederation agreement of 1867 accepted the Ontario model of provincial–municipal relations" (Andrew, 1995: 138–9). More broadly, the formal political arrangement in Canada is that powers are shared between the federal and provincial levels of government as set out in the *Constitution Act, 1867*. Local government falls within the provincial sphere and exists only because provincial governments establish municipalities and devolve tasks to them. Local government is not guaranteed within the *Constitution*. A second formal locus of power is the *Canadian Charter of Rights and Freedoms* (the *Charter*), which in some circumstances can support citizens who argue their rights are infringed by peremptory or imperious actions of governments.

The orientation toward infrastructure and services continues to define what local governments in Canada do. But, as Andrew says, even though local-provincial relations oscillate between local structural and administrative reforms demanded by the provincial government, this back-and-forth is somewhat influenced by the political costs that could come from local unrest (Andrew, 1995: 137–8). There have therefore been periods when citizens have been invited to greater and lesser degrees into the decision-making processes affecting the structure and functions of cities. Thus, informally, powers devolved by provincial governments to municipalities are exercised with varying degrees of autonomy. An expectation has grown that local governments will be consulted when provinces contemplate major changes affecting them. In Ontario, extensive consultation practices have evolved. There were two examples showing that quite a sophisticated level of consultation was being practiced in the province when the amalgamation issue was thrust on the cities: the processes associated with developing a new provincial *Planning Act* in the period 1992 to 1994 (Sewell, 1998) and with studying governance in the Greater Toronto Area by the provincially appointed task force in 1995–96 (Ontario, GTA Task Force, 1996). This tension between local government as a provider of services on the one hand versus an expression of collective goals on the other is regularly noted in writings about Canadian local government or local/provincial relations (see, for example, Tindal and Tindal, 1995; Graham and Phillips, 1998b; Cooper, 1996), and is key to understanding the amalgamation struggle in Toronto in 1997.

The forced amalgamation of Toronto's municipalities and regional government by the province was strongly contested by citizens, using both political and legal means. Documents from the legal challenges to the amalgamating statute are used in this chapter to illuminate how the powers that local governments and citizens have were interpreted by all concerned – citizens, cities, the provincial government, and the courts. These are analysed below, and legacies from the experience are described. Before discussing the legal documents themselves, however, I will first outline the context for the *City of Toronto Act, 1997*, also known as Bill 103. Among other things, the background shows some of the roads not travelled by the government in its intention to fix Toronto and why its actions so baffled and angered citizens.

BACKGROUND

From about 1988 there had been focused discussion about governance in the Greater Toronto Area (GTA), an area that included five regional governments of which Metropolitan Toronto was one. The GTA had thirty municipalities in about 7,200 square kilometres and a population of about 4.5 million. There was widespread agreement that the problem in the GTA was fragmented regional government: there were no formal mechanisms to tie the regions together, even though population growth and settlement had made the whole area increasingly interdependent. Consequently, solutions were being proposed at the scale of the GTA (see, for example, Frisken, 1993; IBI Group, 1990). The last study prior to amalgamation had proposed eliminating the five regional governments and creating a Greater Toronto Council with authority over a limited range of activities, while developing even stronger local municipalities (Ontario, GTA Task Force, 1996: chapter 5). It incorporated the principle of subsidiarity: "the idea that services are most efficiently and effectively delivered by the most local level of government capable of providing them," an idea the task force had adopted from European experience (Graham and Phillips, 1998a: 180). The GTA Council's primary responsibility would be to integrate infrastructure and land use planning in the region (Ontario, GTA Task Force, 1996: recommendation 36). More specifically it was envisioned that the Council would undertake complementary planning and co-financing initiatives in the following areas: regional planning, environmental protection and conservation, transportation planning and development, sewer and water works and waste treatment and disposal, and economic development and investment (Ontario, GTA Task Force, recommendation 47).

In Metro Toronto's cities, major services in which economies of scale could be reaped had already been amalgamated at the metropolitan level, and it was expected these service arrangements would continue at that scale or, where appropriate, be bumped up to the scale of the GTA. No study had recommended eliminating the six cities of Metropolitan Toronto,[1] nor had citizens been asking for this. In the midst of a discussion dominated by studies recommending the reconfiguration of the *regional* governments, then, came legislation to amalgamate *city* governments without any solid evidence produced by the provincial government as to why this was a good plan (Milroy, 1997; Tindal, 1997). It was not clear that money would be saved,[2] and it did nothing to solve the long-identified problem of the GTA, which was the actual urban region that needed fixing. It created a government both too large and too small. The megacity was argued to be too large in the sense that its size made it a regional-scale government in Canadian experience, not a local government that attends to the minutiae of daily life in a city. And it was too small because the area over which coordination was required was the GTA or some approximation of it. It was a decidedly paradoxical solution in terms of urban and regional practice.

The new city was described in the government's background information to the legislative bill in financial and economic terms, especially as a tool of economic development for the province. It seemed to have nothing at all to do with its citizens and their desires. Importantly, it did not appear related to any vision of Toronto, the GTA, or the province, whether a newly minted vision from this government or one cobbled together out of the many GTA studies.

Since the idea for amalgamation was not evident in the Common Sense Revolution (CSR) election manifesto (Conservative Party of Ontario, 1994; see, for example, Harrison, 1998) and did not emerge from reasoned studies, a minor industry has grown up locally to search for the explanation. As tempting as it is to engage in that speculation, let me leave that to political scientists and journalists (for some examples see the sleuthing of Ibbitson, 1997; Sancton, 1998; Drainie, 1998) and turn instead to the events that happened next.

Discussion about amalgamation took place from about the end of October 1996, when the province let the six mayors know its intention to consolidate their cities into one. At no time was formal notification given to mayors, councils, or city clerks about the substance of Bill 103 or the timetable for its introduction to the legislature (Scarborough, 1997: para. 43). The minister of municipal affairs and housing had two meetings with the six mayors and, at the end of October, gave them thirty days to come up with an alternative to amalgamation (Mayors' Proposal, 1996). They proposed eliminating the metropolitan level of government and introducing a Local Municipal Coordinating Board with elected representatives from each city who would deal with amalgamated services and matters properly dealt with at the larger-than-city level. But thirty days to redesign a city for 2.4 million people was nonsensical. Further, the mayors did not have time to consult their councils concerning the report, and so the report was considered questionable even by local elected officials. It was created under duress. The provincial government apparently paid no attention at all to it except to use certain aspects of it (such as its recommendation to reduce the number of elected representatives) as ammunition against the cities in their subsequent objections to Bill 103, including during the court challenges.

Nineteen days later the Bill received first reading. It was formally announced first on the morning of 17 December 1996 at the Board of Trade of Toronto and later the same day in the legislature.[3] Having learned about the legislation only days before, and with the Christmas holidays about to start, the response by citizens took a short while to build but by early January had reached an astonishing momentum. The citizen response reminded some long-time residents of Toronto of a similar response in the early 1970s, when the metropolitan government attempted to build an expressway through the heart of some of Toronto's most cherished neighbourhoods. But even that massive struggle was overshadowed by the sheer numbers of citizens involved in expressing their hostility to Bill 103.

Opposition took many forms: dozens of meetings were held in all six cities (on one hectic Wednesday there were twenty-three Bill 103-related meetings scheduled in the six cities), six city umbrella organizations coordinated responses to the Bill, letters were sent to the newspapers, experts on the relationship between amalgamation and costs of government were hired, and deputations were made to a legislative committee. There were marches, parades, postering, leafleting, speeches by the politicians in the opposition parties, filibustering in the legislature, threats of legal challenges by all the cities and by citizens, and referendums in each of the six cities. Five of the six mayors were solidly opposed to amalgamation, including the man who would subsequently be elected the first mayor of the megacity; one mayor and the chair of Metro were either equivocal or in favour. John Sewell, a former mayor of Toronto and its most active defender against Bill 103, started a network named Citizens for Local Democracy, usually referred to as C4LD. It was remarkable for several reasons, one being that its meetings attracted around 1,200 people every Monday night for almost three months and several hundred for most of the rest of 1997. It was also special because it was the first major protest organization in Toronto to employ asynchronous listservs and the internet, together with the synchronous Monday meetings, to keep a huge population informed and its actions somewhat coordinated in the massive effort to stop the Bill from passing.[4]

None of this had much effect on the government. A few battles were won, none of them major.[5] The Bill received Royal Assent on 21 April 1997 and the next day three legal challenges were launched against it in the Ontario court. These are the documents we turn to next.

THE LEGAL CASE: ARGUMENTS FOR AND AGAINST AMALGAMATION

This research is presented from the point of view of a participant in the citizen struggle rather than a scholar. I was on the board of directors of the citizens' group that challenged the *Act* in court. While obviously not disinterested, I try to offer an objective analysis of the legal case that was taking place beside the political citizens' movement. One set of sources is analysed for this chapter – the documents associated with the legal challenges to Bill 103, the *City of Toronto Act, 1997*. Readers should be aware that I am an urban planner, not a lawyer, and so the emphasis will be more on gaining a better understanding of the status of cities and citizens' political engagement and less on the state of the law, which I am not qualified to assess.

The Documents

The legal documents describe what the provincial government, the cities, and the citizens thought local government should be like in Toronto. The parties put their issues forward, framing them within their interpretation of the distribution of powers available to them formally and in conventional practice. The documents are therefore an important source of information about local governance, particularly

Table 1

Document source	Level 1 Divisional Court	Level 2 Appeal Court	Level 3 Supreme Court Canada
CLC Inc. et al. Applicants/Appellants	factum (1997a)	factum (1997b)	memo of argument (1997c)
East York et al. Applicants	factum (1997)	–	–
Scarborough et al. Applicants	factum (1997)	–	–
Attorney General of Ontario Respondent	factum (1997a)	factum (1997b)	memo of argument (1998)
Borins J.	decision see: Corporation of the Borough of East York et al. v. Attorney General for Ontario ...	–	–
Abella, Rosenberg, Moldaver, JJ.A.		decision see: Citizens's Legal Challenge Inc. et al. v. Attorney General of Ontario	–

the struggle over who controls the government of the city and what it provides its citizens.

At the first court level, the cases of the three applicants were heard together before the judge. Since the attorney general of Ontario (hereinafter A.G.Ont.) was the respondent in all the cases, that office submitted a single reply factum to the three applicant parties. One applicant was a group of four citizens organizations and 125 individual citizens called Citizens' Legal Challenge Inc. (hereinafter CLC); another was the City of Scarborough and a resident, Alan Carter (hereinafter Scarborough); the other by East York, Etobicoke, Toronto, and York (hereinafter East York et al.). A sixth city, North York, did not participate in the legal challenges. The five cities dropped their legal actions after losing at the first level. CLC carried on to the Appeal level and then, unsuccessfully, sought leave to be heard by the Supreme Court of Canada. (See table 1.)

These eight documents by the applicants and respondent, plus the replies by the lower and appeal court judges, have all been used for the analyses that follow. The case and statute law called upon are neither analysed nor judged for their appropriateness. Here we focus on selected points.

The Method

The ten documents were read and annotated in their totality. Distillation generated four "pillars" on which the applicants had based their arguments and to which the attorney general responded.

In summary, the pillars are these. First, the applicants argued that there are conventions surrounding provincial/municipal relations that lend reasonable autonomy to municipalities or, when major changes are foreseen, the conventions include a process of *consultation*. For the province not to honour those is to step outside its jurisdiction under the *Constitution*. Second, the actions proposed by the province in its legislation will create *harm* to individuals as interpreted through the *Charter of Rights and Freedoms*. Third, the province is using its *power* in a cavalier manner and, fourth, is attempting to give credence to its actions via strictly *utilitarian justifications*, which neither logic nor evidence support.

Elaboration of the Four Pillars of Argument

Consultation.   The applicants argued that the wording of the *Constitution* must be seen in context. There is a tradition of strong local government in Canada, predating even the *British North America Act* of 1867. It derives from English tradition, extending as far back as the *Magna Carta* of 1215. Furthermore, the settlement of the six cities threatened with dissolution predates 1867. Implicit in the preamble to the *Constitution* and the first section of the *Charter*, the applicants argued, is a "strong case for recognizing a degree of democratic autonomy for local municipal government as an implicitly entrenched legal component of the *Constitution of Canada*" (Scarborough, 1997: para. 164; CLC, 1997c: para. 37–42).

The interpretation the applicants sought from the court was that, once created by provinces, cities have traditionally exercised a reasonable autonomy in running their affairs; that this tradition harkens back to pre- as well as post-confederation practice; and that it underlies the *Constitution* as its interpretive context. They were not arguing that cities are a "third order of government," or that provinces do not have the power to "create, destroy, or amalgamate particular municipal institutions." Rather, their point was that when provinces exercise their powers they are subject to constitutional constraints including constraints derived from the *Charter* and stemming from "constitutional norms such as the implicit guarantee of reasonable municipal autonomy" (CLC, 1997c: para. 41). They attempted to show that municipal councils are not "mere administrative agencies" of a province but that their "roots are deep in our constitutional history and heritage" (Sancton, 1997: para. 83). Specifically, the *Act* was said to infringe the reasonable autonomy of the local governments because it:

- provided significant powers, including financial powers, to appointees rather than elected officials (this referred to the Financial Advisory Board and the Transition Team, which were described in the legislation as bodies of appointed officials given extensive authority to oversee and conduct the transition and whose decisions could not be appealed);
- violated the territorial integrity of the existing Metro municipalities without the consent of the citizenry and without meaningful consultation with the citizenry;
- provided a form of municipal institution that did not accord with the democratic wishes of the citizenry (CLC, 1997a: para. 72b).

A key argument was that major provincial actions affecting cities are by tradition preceded by a process of consultation. Because Bill 103 represented the most massive action ever taken towards Ontario cities, there should have been a public consultation process. Failing that, the provincial government should have paid attention to the unsolicited massive objections raised by the citizens and elected officials of Metro to Bill 103 (Scarborough, 1997: para. 14–15; East York et al., 1997: para. 50, 63–5, 85–97). For example, the government should have paid attention to the plebisites held in March in each of the six cities, following guidelines established by the province the previous autumn. The results showed 76 percent of those voting were opposed to Bill 103. The attorney general argued that the *question* posed in the plebisites (the same question was used in each of the six cities) was outside the competence of municipalities. While it used to be that municipalities could ask *any* question in a referendum, new legislation decreed that they were permitted to ask only questions that were within their assigned powers to act upon. Because changing their boundaries was a provincial, not a municipal, prerogative the cities should not have held the plebisites in the first place, said the province.

The attorney general argued that the province clearly had the jurisdiction and that the applicable section of the *Constitution* is clear that there is no municipal autonomy. The attorney general argued further that legal precedents show that the preamble to the *Constitution Act, 1982* does not apply British traditions to powers that are not in the *Act* itself. Neither municipal autonomy nor reasonable autonomy – that is, some degree of autonomy in specific matters – exists. The provincial government can delegate to municipalities or withdraw from them any powers the province has had delegated to it via the *Constitution* (A.G.Ont., 1997a: para. 77–8). The province argued that these powers are confirmed by both academic and judicial authorities based on the following principles:

- municipal institutions lack constitutional status;
- municipal institutions are creatures of the legislature and exist only if provincial legislation so provides;
- municipal institutions have no independent autonomy and their powers are subject to abolition or repeal by provincial legislation;
- municipal institutions may exercise only those powers that are conferred upon them by statute (A.G.Ont., 1997a: para. 79).

On the matter of consultation, the attorney general asserted that the *Act* was passed "after extensive public consultation," which began in 1995 (A.G.Ont., 1997a: para. 45–63). The attorney general failed to mention, however, that at no time was amalgamating the six cities discussed in that consultation (see note 1). More audaciously still, legal counsel for the attorney general said in oral argument that consultation had been going on since around 1953 because amalgamation was just the logical completion of service integration that began when metropolitan government was first introduced. The audience in the court gasped in astonishment at this claim. If this was true, why had there been almost a decade of study about how to revise governance in the GTA, no moment of which had, to their knowledge, been given to contemplating eliminating the six cities? But, just in case the judge did not agree with the government's claims of having held an extensive public consultation, the backup argument to the court by the attorney general – and the clincher – was that the province has no formal obligation to consult prior to passing legislation. A judgement of the Supreme Court of Canada, in which American practice was used as a precedent, was cited (A.G.Ont., 1997a: para. 158).

The judge's decision at the Divisional Court level said that no convincing evidence for reasonable autonomy was put forward by the applicants and that the province did not exceed its powers (Corporation of the Borough of East York et al. v. A.G. Ont., 1997: 795g, 798d). Further, while he agreed with the applicants that the consultation was inadequate, it was the prerogative of the government to act without consultation. The judge's view was not tempered; he said the applicants provided no support for their alternative position "that there is a constitutional convention which requires the province to consult with, or obtain, the consent of a municipality before it can legislate the restructuring of a municipality" (ibid.: 798d). The Appeal Court decision had a similar observation that no case "has ever diluted this fundamental authority" of provinces over municipalities (*Citizens' Legal Challenge Inc. et al. v. A.G.Ont.*, 1997: 738d).

Harm. The existing two-tier government structure in Metropolitan Toronto has been remarkably successful, as shown by the accolades it has received from experts and other sources (Scarborough, 1997: para. 21-2; CLC, 1997a: para. 59). Nonetheless, no party to the case was arguing against change. However, any change should retain the best features reaped from excellent experience with the two-tier system, the applicants said. One feature is citizen manageability – the sense of responsiveness of the local government and of the capacity to understand the complexity that is the city (CLC, 1997a: para. 23, 28). Another feature to guard is the potential for small municipal governments to be innovative and creative. This would suggest dismantling Metro; putting a Local Municipal Coordinating Board in place to manage the already-shared service delivery among the six cities; and folding these cities into a GTA region with an overarching government to deal with major tasks such as economic development, transportation, regional planning, and environmental conservation – as described in the 1996 GTA Task Force report (CLC, 1997a: para. 24). Instead, the legislation wiped out the much-lauded cities and erased the equally lauded two-tier approach because it did not tie the megacity to the GTA. The government thereby legislated the most harmful option of all those available to it, argued the applicants (East York et al., 1997: para. 171).

Specifically, the *Act* causes harm in several ways, according to the applicants. First, it dramatically increases the ratio of elected representatives to residents. Where there had been 107 elected officials spread over six cities and the metropolitan government, there would now be 57. This would make the ratio of residents to councillors abnormally high in a Toronto, GTA, Ontario, or Canadian context. It would further mean that the 57 officials in one government would have to do the work of 107 in seven governments. Because the work load for all councillors will be so heavy, some of their customary activities will have to slide. The loss will be in the attention councillors can give to their committee work and to citizens in their wards (East York et al., 1997: para. 69–71).

Table 2

Jurisdiction	Elected REGIONAL Representatives	Elected MUNICIPAL Representatives	Total no. elected Representatives	Population	Ratio ALL Representatives to Population
(Chair)	1	–	1	–	–
East York	1	9	10	102,696	1:10,270
Etobicoke	4	13	17	309,993	1:18,235
North York	7	15	22	562,564	1:25,571
Scarborough	6	15	21	524,598	1:24,981
Toronto	8	17	25	635,395	1:25,416
York	2	9	11	140,525	1:12,775
TOTALS Metro Toronto (before 01.01.99)	29	78	107	2,275,771	[not applicable]
Amalgamated Toronto (after 01.01.99)	–	57	57	2,275,771	1:39,926

This means a fundamental shift in the way municipal politics takes place. Voting power is diluted, and access to elected representatives is reduced. The ratio of elected representatives to population in the pre-amalgamated City of Toronto was 1:25,416, and in the megacity 1:39,926, up 57 percent; representation for a given metropolitan resident was diluted somewhere between 56 percent and 289 percent. Professor Andrew said in her affidavit: "[i]n its purported effort to improve efficiency, the *Act* clearly impairs the goal of citizen access, and clearly will have a detrimental impact on citizens' direct contact and ability to have an impact upon local government" (1997: para. 9).

Second, it was claimed that a council of fifty-seven would make the Canadian local government tradition of face-to-face debate in council chambers unworkable, a system where honourable compromises were meant to be made in the full light of public scrutiny. There would be too many councillors to conduct business in that way (Scarborough, 1997: para. 54). An executive committee system would therefore be needed to move along the business of the city, a form of government that (a) diminishes the influence of councillors who are not on the executive and (b) places the business of local government out-of-sight and outside the influence of ordinary citizens (Scarborough, 1997: para. 57b, c). An executive committee works against representation by population (East York et al., 1997: para. 45).

Third, the applicants claimed that party politics would surely be needed to exert discipline over debate in City Council and that this inserts party discipline between a citizen and his or her councillor. While it is the model of provincial and federal politics, it does not normally occur in local government, the main Canadian exception being Montreal. This again diminishes the direct impact of citizens on elected councillors.

Fourth, a single, very large bureaucracy would be less responsive to the needs of individual citizens and require extra layers of expensive management to run it. Both complexity and cost would thereby be increased (CLC, 1997a: para. 18–23). And fifth, because of the size of the council and the bureaucracy, standardized solutions, which are insensitive to diversity and community specificity and which are resistant to innovation, are more likely. Jane Jacobs, well-known for her analyses of cities, was an expert witness for CLC. She used examples to illustrate this last point about bigness encouraging standardization in her affidavit (1997a: para. 24–5, 27) and responded extensively to her critics in her reply affidavit, especially to Professor Bourne, who testified for the attorney general (Jacobs, 1997b, passim; Bourne, 1997: para. 62–74).

The applicants claimed these inferior democratic institutions would violate several sections of the *Charter*: freedom of expression, freedom of association; right to basic political liberty, security against unreasonable seizure, and equality without discrimination. With respect to equality without discrimination, the applicants' position was that citizens have *Charter*-protected rights over and above those that cities have and that a province cannot violate these in the process of exercising its powers whether to create, destroy, or modify municipal institutions. The applicants' saw their task as two-fold. First, they had to show there were disproportionately higher numbers of disadvantaged people in Metro compared to the rest of the GTA or the province, that is, people who are in the so-called enumerated or analogous groups recognized by the *Charter* as having been historically disadvantaged because of sex, age, race, national or ethnic origin, and so on. Second, they needed to demonstrate that the new, inferior municipal institutions would have disproportionate impact on these groups. The applicants could not argue disproportionate impact using empirical evidence from elsewhere because no studies could be found, and they could not use evidence from Toronto because, of course, the presumed damage was yet to occur. Thus they relied on logic; for example, they argued that democratic institutions are relied upon more heavily by those suffering historical disadvantage than others and, therefore, if the institutions are made inferior, those groups will suffer more (CLC, 1997a: para. 112–23). Thus the CLC argued that the *Act* entrenches disadvantage.

The attorney general said that the applicants failed to demonstrate any harm would result from the *City of Toronto Act, 1997*, whether to the cities, to citizens generally, or to disadvantaged citizens in particular. They maintained that the arguments were in the realm of theory and conjecture. The Courts agreed with the respondent that "[t]here is neither jurisprudential nor evidentiary support" for the arguments concerning potential harm (*Citizens' Legal Challenge Inc. v. A.G.Ont.*, 1997: 736d) and that "the *Charter* was not intended to alter or limit the Legislature's jurisdiction over municipal institutions, or bestow upon municipal institutions any constitutional status" (Corporation of the Borough of East York et al. v. A.G.Ont., 1997: 799h).

Power: There were a few explicit references to the exercise of power, and plenty of implicit references in the attorney general's factums. One theme was the relationship between the size of government and its power. The CLC argued that, all things being equal, smaller governments are more accountable, more attuned to communities and neighbourhoods, and more amenable to local control (1997a: para. 28). The government said the opposite, that the creation of a very powerful political structure (as contrasted with the current amorphous power structure) will improve control by politicians of the staff/administration serving a municipality (A.G.Ont., 1997a: 23). The affidavit evidence to support these positions was very weak on both sides. *[margin note: sort of corporatist perspective]*

Another explicit theme was the different treatment Toronto received compared to other Ontario cities where amalgamation was concerned. This was widely thought to be because the provincial government wanted to put Toronto in its place (Ibbitson, 1997: 242–3). The applicants noted the approach in Simcoe in 1990, in Kingston in 1997, and concurrently in Ottawa and Hamilton, where the province chose to delay intervention in order to permit local debate and consultation. For instance, when Ottawa requested provincial involvement in the restructuring, the province refused on the ground that local solutions would be preferable (CLC, 1997a: para. 42–4, respectively). Local approaches had been a public theme: the current government said in its CSR manifesto that it would sit down with the municipalities to create solutions because local decisions were better than those from the province (CLC, 1997a: para. 46; Downey and Williams, 1997). Toronto was not offered a process of consultation and, worse, was mainly dealt with through the media on its amalgamation (East York et al., 1997: para. 52–7). *[margin note: unfair treat't]*

The four cities argued that "the Respondent chose to unilaterally dissolve democratic institutions that have played a fundamental role in the development and maintenance of local government within the province and to replace them with a system of government that will drastically undermine their right to effective democratic representation" (East York et al., 1997: para. 141). They said this infringes the right to political liberty guaranteed by the *Charter* by peremptorily dissolving municipal institutions that convey effective democratic representation (ibid.: para. 127(i); 141).

In the closing paragraphs of his decision, Judge Borins referred to the government's display of power as megachutzpah. But, he observed, "there is no guarantee under the *Charter* that individuals will live free from government chutzpah or imperiousness" (Corporation of the Borough of East York et al. v. A.G.Ont., 1997: 799h). He used a passage from a decision almost a century ago to refer, by association, to this government's actions as "somewhat of a reversion to an older type of paternal or autocratic rule" (ibid., 804g). The Appeal Court decision notes that notwithstanding the "public disapproval with the methodology employed prior to the passage of the *City of Toronto Act, 1997* ... [w]hat is politically controversial is not necessarily constitutionally impermissible" (*Citizens' Legal Challenge Inc. v. A.G.Ont.*, 1997: 738a).

Utilitarian Justifications

The applicants contended that the province's reasons for amalgamating the seven governments did not justify overturning the conventions on consultation, infringing *Charter* rights, and suspending local self-government. For them, the government had set out only utilitarian purposes, making the city into a tool for global competition and reducing the cost while increasing the administrative efficiency of municipal government in Metropolitan Toronto (Scarborough, 1997: para. 140; and cf. Machimura, 1998, on the use of globalization rhetoric in Tokyo's urban politics). These, they said, were inadequate arguments for such an amalgamation. When Metro Toronto was created in 1953 as a federation of cities, the then chair of the Ontario Municipal Board hearing, Lorne Cumming, Q.C., who was responsible for introducing that model, rejected the City of Toronto's bid to consolidate surrounding cities under its control because it would not provide government close to the people. His decision included the following observation:

The practical and technical advantages of complete consolidation must be frankly admitted. They are comparable with similar advantages in a completely centralized totalitarian form of national government. Local government in a democracy, however, at least to the great majority of Ontario people, means a government that is very close to the local residents (East York et al.,1997: para. 38).

Thus, at that time, utilitarian justifications were not sufficient to override democratic claims as adequate grounds for amalgamation.

The attorney general asserted the province had a right to establish the purposes for the City of Toronto and to impose a structure it deemed would achieve those purposes. The government argued that the strength of Metro Toronto was of great significance, not only for Metro but also for the GTA and the rest of Ontario, and the *City of Toronto Act, 1997* was the only way to achieve its objectives. The attorney general's factum said the purposes of the *Act* were to:

• provide improved governance for Metropolitan Toronto and strengthen the fiscal and economic position of Toronto and the Greater Toronto Area;
• strengthen Toronto's position for global economic competition;
• remove an extra tier of government and reduce the number of elected representatives in order to create greater accessibility and accountability of municipal government;
• complete the unification of service delivery begun in 1953, using one budget and tax base and to stop municipalities within Metro-

politan Toronto from competing with each other at each other's expense;

- address the needs of local areas and neighbourhoods through community councils and neighbourhood committees;
- eliminate duplication and waste and ensure cost-effective government (A.G.Ont., 1997a: para. 10). → *selling point of amalgamation*

However, the province did not use affidavit evidence to show how the *Act* would achieve these purposes (CLC, 1997b: para. 25). By contrast, the applicants ploughed one-by-one through the six purposes using affidavit and other evidence to demonstrate there was little likelihood any of them would be realized through amalgamation. The applicants assumed that if they could show that the purposes would not be achieved, and that harm would come from attempting them through this *Act*, then there would be grounds for the court to disallow the *Act*. However, because no crack could be opened up in the constitutional rights that provinces have over municipalities, the province was not obliged to give solid justifications for the legislation. And because the arguments concerning harm were dismissed, so too was any onus on the respondent to justify its legislative aims. The judge noted that, "[i]n presenting Bill 103, the government expressed its view of the appropriate model of government. Counsel for the respondent, in my view, correctly, submitted that in doing so the province did not exceed the powers conferred on it by s. 92(8) of the *Constitution Act, 1867*" (Corporation of the Borough of East York et al. v. A.G.Ont., 1997: 795g). Later on in his decision he pointed out that: "[i]t is not the role of the court to pass on the wisdom of the legislation. Specifically, it is not for the court to determine whether the megacity will be good, or bad, for the inhabitants of Metro Toronto" (ibid.: 797c).

WHAT WAS LEARNED?

The applicants argued that the Bill was wrong from the perspective of history, experience, ethics, logic, academic evidence, policy-making practices, and conventions on consultation – all to no avail. It may have been shown to be wrong on all those grounds, but the arguments were no match for the *Constitution Act*. In such a case, constitutional law became all-important. This serves as a reminder that there indeed has been a revolution in Ontario. In 1953, when the creation of Metro Toronto was being discussed, the chair of the Ontario Municipal Board hearing, Lorne Cumming, placed the weight of his judgment on the democratic function of cities when he said that he would deny Toronto's wish to consolidate all the surrounding cities under its wing. Instead he called for the confederal form of Metropolitan Toronto.

Thereafter, local restructuring was associated with studies and political input. But in 1997 Premier Harris reversed this, putting the weight fully on service provision, and did it without studies or citizen input. Ontario is right back to pre-Confederation thinking on the matter of cities. Any balance that had existed between the service and the political expression functions of cities has been lost.

A number of lessons are left from the court challenges. First, by forcing amalgamation on strongly opposed local governments, the actual distribution of power between the province and municipalities did not change; the line of demarcation just became more evident. The future is foggy. Graham and Phillips (1998b: 176–7) suggest that Ontario's strict control over municipal autonomy may not be a weathervane for Canadian practice elsewhere. They point to recent legislation and tabled proposals in the provinces of Alberta, British Columbia, Manitoba, and Nova Scotia, which appear to give greater room to municipalities to act independently from their provincial masters and suggest that there is a trend toward "greater municipal autonomy and less restrictive provincial control." By contrast, Donald Lidstone (1998), a lawyer specializing in municipal legislation, argues that on key matters these acts and proposals do not leave Canadian municipalities better off. He analyses the proposed or legislated reforms in Newfoundland, Nova Scotia, Ontario, Manitoba, and Alberta to see if they provide for: "consultation on matters affecting local government; amending local government legislation; joint decision-making powers in areas of shared responsibility; provincial compliance with municipal regulations; and delegation of adequate powers." He finds them wanting in most respects and far out of step with what citizens acting locally need.

It is not even clear that globalization will create the conditions for Canadian cities to be able to act with greater autonomy. It is often claimed that globalization puts a city in a position to interact directly with other cities, bypassing its more senior governments. Andrew (1995: 151) looks at some of the evidence and concludes that given the status of cities in Canada it is not obvious that this will occur and that empirical research is badly needed. One completed study about Ontario would suggest that the provincial government has already taken hold of the globalization agenda, not so much to facilitate globalization for the likes of Toronto but rather to transform the whole province from the heartland of Canada into a highly competitive North American economic region state (Courchene, 1998: 172).

A second lesson is that expectations from practice certainly changed, even though the power distribution did not. After such a long history of generally consultative policy-making around municipal matters, the provincial government's refusal to engage in any debate whatsoever about the amalgamation legislation shocked citizens and city governments alike. "Undemocratic" was the word most often heard and read in conjunction with the Bill. But it did not matter if the majority believed the action was undemocratic. That was from the perspective of practice, not law, where practice counted for naught. Ontario citizens are forced to accept the reality that participation in local decision-making truly *is* at the pleasure of the provincial government and not wishfully hope otherwise. Citizens have been redefined in terms of customers and have no guaranteed access to citizen rights to use local government to express themselves politically. In the amalgamation fiasco, citizens were treated as a nuisance by the government, especially by Premier Mike Harris and Minister of Municipal Affairs and Housing Al Leach (Rusk, 1997). The imperiousness of the government resulted in "killing the spirit of citizens," as one columnist described the situation at the end of the political and at the start of the legal struggle (Barber, 1997b). An impassioned plea even went out in November 1996 from the usually sanguine Federation of Canadian Municipalities to some of the more senior governments saying: "we are not your liabilities, we are your assets. And assets must be developed with wisdom and care. If you torpedo the flag ships of your fleet, then you will not have much of a fleet left" (*Municipal World*, 1997).

Third, if a city is defined as a tool of a province's interests, its residents cannot successfully demonstrate harm from the province's actions. Toronto was defined by the province as a tool it wanted to sharpen so that it could use it aggressively to make Ontario as a whole more globally competitive. The applicants were unable to show the potential harm associated with the particular government structure the province imposed because of lack of data. But they were also technically unable to do this within the law because in effect the government had declared a provincial interest in Toronto serving a specific role.

Fourth, residents have no constitutional right to a vision for their city. This is another facet of the tension between the interpretation of cities and their local governments as representative of citizens' political expression versus service providers. The province's vision of the new city was utilitarian, focused on service provision. It has been characterized as an "Economy First" vision based on analysis of the province's position put forward during the amalgamation struggle (Milroy et al., 1999). There was no recognition of the metropolitan region's multiculturalism, of its arts, of the quality of its neighbourhoods, or of its civic activism – all of which make it the kind of place it is.

Based on another analysis of a wide range of documents from 1997, it is clear that citizens had very different, non-utilitarian visions of their city in which (a) citizens need some control over civic space and institutions through participating in decision-making; (b) it is understood that the city and its citizens are interconnected, the one influencing the other, continuously; (c) the economy is contextualized within the whole business of living, not isolated and placed prior to other activities; and (d) it is understood that certain spatial practices such as inattention to the public realm exacerbate the marginalization of certain socio-economic and cultural groups (Milroy et al., 1999: 27–8). In the legal challenge, the cities and citizens made no headway at all in arguing for the right to an encompassing vision of their city and the right to a set of municipal institutions that would foster good civic practices such as a reasonably sized city council, a reasonable ratio of representatives to population, special accommodations for disadvantaged people, and so on.

more research needs to be done. [handwritten margin note]

Fifth, the court challenges show where research is needed. Some of the data gaps that emerged directly from trying to mount the legal arguments are: what are the costs of municipal government and services at different scales; under what conditions do higher ratios of residents to elected representatives affect both what representatives are able to achieve and the degree of possible local control; what are the effects of higher and lower ratios of elected representatives to residents where high percentages of the residents are disadvantaged? Another area that needs research in the face of the "customer revolution" is the importance of overlap and interplay among levels of government. These concepts are roundly denounced by the current government as inefficient yet demonstrated as essential in Leo's (1998) rich study of metropolitan growth management in Portland, Oregon.

Summary [handwritten margin note]

The case of Toronto's amalgamation starkly shows the effects of a constitutional and legal regime in which cities are tools of more senior governments to be used in their service delivery, fiscal, and economic interests *without* an equally strong counterweight in local citizenship rights. Balance is missing. Here is where citizens need to apply pressure for change.

NOTES

1 Recent studies that did not recommend amalgamating the six cities include: IBI Group, 1990; Conservative Party of Ontario, 1995 (The Trimmer Report); GTA Task Force, 1996 (The Golden Report); Conservative Party of Ontario, 1996 (The Burnham Report); and the Crombie

Panel for the Ministry of Municipal Affairs and Housing (Ontario, "Who Does What" 1996). On the "Who Does What" Panel, see Graham and Phillips (1998a).

2 The claim that money would be saved depended entirely on a single report that the government itself had commissioned from the consulting firm, KPMG. The firm was given three weeks and $100,000 to "Estimate the potential savings that could arise from replacing seven governments ... with a single unified entity" (KPMG, 1996: 1). The report's authors were equivocal about the savings that would be realized from amalgamation. They suggest savings *could* be realized, but when interviewed, a representative of the firm acknowledged that "it's possible that the amalgamation could produce significantly lower savings than we have talked about or even a negative result, a net increase in expenditures" (cited in Vaughan, 1996). Several analyses of the KPMG report showed it had many holes. For example, one-third of the savings was attributed to the "consolidation" of governments while two-thirds were from "efficiency enhancements." No connection was made between the two. Therefore, Toronto could achieve "all these efficiencies with the existing municipalities and you could have amalgamation without gaining any of the efficiencies" (Sancton, cited in Barber, 1996: A11). The harmonization of differing service levels and collective labour agreements were not accounted for (Barber, 1996). Administrative savings were assumed to result from the consolidation of the seven bureaucracies into one; diseconomies of scale were not considered; and there is no evidence – anywhere – that savings emerge in monopolistic bureaucracies, especially big ones, according to the Wendell Cox Consultancy, which produced a report for the City of Toronto titled *Local and Regional Governance in the Greater Toronto Area: A Review of Alternatives*, 10 January 1997, cited in Barber (1997a). More substantive studies of the Canadian situation were available showing that savings from amalgamation are dubious (for example, Kushner et al., 1996; Sancton, 1996). Incidentally, Bill 103 was introduced in the legislature the day after the KPMG report was submitted so the government had obviously not intended to be guided by the consultants' findings or by careful analysis of them. This departed from earlier amalgamations and moments of establishing regional governments during the 1950s to 1970s, which had always been accompanied by "some measure of detailed research at both the provincial and local levels and there was provision made for some meaningful degree of systematic input on the part of those directly affected" (Downey and Williams, 1998: 212).

3 Announcing Bill 103 outside the legislature, and at the Board of Trade at that, was a double rebuke of the idea that the government is an ally in promoting civic values among all citizens. Choosing the Board of Trade

as the venue was a clear message that the provincial government was going over the heads of citizens to deliver the cities into the hands of business interests.

4 The electronic strategy was the work of Liz Rykert, a member of the C4LD steering committee, with help from others.

5 Two examples were: (1) A contempt of the legislature citation was levelled against the government by the opposition and upheld by the Speaker because a leaflet had been sent to every household in February 1997, suggesting that the amalgamation had already occurred before the Bill had been debated or passed; and (2) a few changes were made to the roles of the Financial Advisory Board and the Transition Team, which were to oversee the amalgamation process on behalf of the province from April 1997 until the new council took office 1 January 1998. Note that both these changes were achieved because the law was infringed. No changes were made to accommodate citizens' interests regarding the timing, process, or fact of amalgamation.

8 Signs of Life?
The Transformation of Two-tier Metropolitan Government

ANDREW SANCTON

Debates about municipal restructuring have occurred in virtually all of Canada's major urban areas in recent years. The most apparent unifying thread is the desire to save money (Sancton, 1996: 267–89; Vojnovic, 1998: 239–83.), but there is at least one other apparent point of agreement: two-tier urban governments of the type pioneered by Ontario in the 1950s and 1960s are part of the problem, not the solution. The desire to shun Ontario-style two-tier regional government has been so high in some provinces that all forms of two-tier government – even the flexible regional districts in British Columbia or the *municipalités régionales du comté* (MRCS) in Québec – have not been seriously considered. This chapter discusses the original model of two-tier urban government as it was worked out in Ontario, the sustained attack it has experienced almost everywhere in Canada during the 1990s, and its possible transformation – in a decidedly non-Ontario form – through the recent establishment of the Greater Toronto Services Board (GTSB).

TWO-TIER URBAN GOVERNMENT IN ONTARIO

The creation of the metropolitan government in Toronto (Colton, 1981: 66–73) in 1953 and of the various regional governments (Fyfe, 1975: 352–66) from 1968–75 has been described many times. For the purposes of this chapter the key point is that each of the newly created upper-tier authorities was to be considered a full-fledged municipality. Rural Ontario had been governed locally by two tiers of municipalities since the passage of the *Baldwin Act* in 1849, but two tiers of municipal government within cities was an entirely new experience. As in counties and school boards, the new upper-tier urban authorities did not tax citizens directly; instead the lower-tier municipalities collected for them whatever funds these upper-tier municipalities decided that they required. Like counties, the members of their councils generally sat on local councils as well and their chairs, unlike mayors and reeves, were not directly elected. In the Regional Municipality of Niagara, however, the original council consisted of twelve area mayors and sixteen other councillors elected at-large from each of the member municipalities to serve only at the regional level.

The theory behind the system was clear enough. Some functions were regional; others were local. A distinct level of municipal government was needed for each. By reducing the need for less formal mechanisms for intermunicipal co-operation, metropolitan and regional governments would insure that intermunicipal planning and infrastructure problems were addressed, that large-scale functions would be delivered more reliably and efficiently, and that costs would be apportioned in accordance with ability to pay.

It is universally acknowledged that the first decade of the Municipality of Metropolitan Toronto was an outstanding success. Indeed, its early success accounts for the fact that the regional governments in Ontario were so obviously modelled on the Metro experience. Early criticisms of Metro related primarily to process. Great accomplishments were acknowledged, but it was increasingly felt that important decisions were being taken in forums that were largely removed from the scrutiny of democratic politics. Voters knew little about Metro, in part because all its council members were elected primarily on issues of concern only within each of the local municipalities. Its first chair, Frederick Gardiner, was not elected by anybody (Colton, 1981: 136).

Presumably, fixing this perceived problem could have involved one of two options. One was to make Metro less like a government, to strip some of its functions away, especially as major infrastructure was eventually provided to most of its territory. Making Metro less of a government would have meant that issues of openness and direct accountability would have become less salient. Another benefit might have been that its territory perhaps could have been more easily extended.

But all the pressure was in the other direction: to make Metro even more like a distinct level of government. This was certainly the thrust of the Royal Commission on Metropolitan Toronto, headed by John Roberts, that reported in 1977. From that time onwards in Ontario,

conventional wisdom in the municipal world was that regional government needed to be made more accountable and linked more directly to its regional citizens, as in Niagara. In 1988, David Peterson's Liberal government finally implemented Robarts's recommendations for
direct election of the Metro council (Mellon, 1993: 38–56). Ten years
later, Mike Harris's conservative government abolished Metro's two-
tier system.

Meanwhile, regional governments throughout the province struggled with the issue of direct election. Hamilton-Wentworth, Waterloo,
and Sudbury all decided to elect their respective chairs directly, but otherwise to keep the representational system roughly the same. Ottawa-
Carleton took the most drastic steps: the chair became directly elected;
other councillors were elected directly from wards, some of which
crossed municipal boundaries; and local mayors were removed from
regional council altogether. In short, the Regional Municipality of
Ottawa-Carleton, as it has been configured since 1994, represents the
highwater mark for two-tier urban federalism in Canada. Ironically,
almost as soon as these new arrangements were in place, they came
under intense attack.

THE TWO-TIER MODEL UNDER ATTACK

The attacks began long before 1994. Indeed, the first sign that the two-
tier model might not be seen to be the universal solution came in 1971
when Premier Ed Schreyer's NDP government in Manitoba abolished
the ten-year-old upper-tier Corporation of Greater Winnipeg, replacing
it and the twelve local municipalities with a single City of Winnipeg,
the "unicity." One of the reasons the Corporation did not survive was
that its directly elected council was constantly battling with the local
municipalities, including the City of Winnipeg (Brownstone and Plunkett, 1983: 28-30).

Nova Scotia's Graham commission in 1974 made what was probably the most effective case against the desirability of two-tier metropolitan government ever articulated in a Canadian official government
document. All the arguments about conflict, complexity, and additional cost are fully explored. The report even includes the argument that
there is no rational way to allocate functions between the two tiers.

[B]ecause nearly all services would in fact be regional in nature, decisions as to
which should be provided locally and which regionally would be quite arbi-
trary ...

Were the provincial government to prescribe the allocation of functions
between the two levels of municipal government it would, we suggest, have no

logical basis on which to found its prescription, and even a purely pragmatic approach would encounter serious problems ...

Which level of government should provide police and fire services? If these two functions were allotted to the metropolitan authority together with water supply, sewerage, transportation, and parks services ... the functions remaining with the city and town councils would be few indeed. Conversely, there would seem to be little point in going to the trouble of creating metropolitan governments but continuing to maintain [separate] city and town police forces and ... fire forces ...

Land use planning is only part of a total planning process, which should not be seen as something that can be separated from social planning, financial planning and other planning functions. Every municipal unit that is responsible for providing a range of services should plan. In Ontario this was recognized to some extent when, with the new regional municipality established its own planning unit. The City of Ottawa, as one of the constituent municipalities, has continued, however, to maintain its own planning staff ... The inevitable result has been a considerably increased total expenditure on planning coupled with a fragmentation of the overall planning process (Nova Scotia, 1974: 62–4).

Although these passages make both explicit and implicit reference to Ontario's experience with two-tier regional governments, it is significant that, notwithstanding the report's otherwise exhaustive description and analysis, there is no reference whatever to the system of regional districts in British Columbia that had been established six years before.

Two-tier regional governments were never politically popular within Ontario, although they retained the support of most experts, both inside and outside government. The regional governments themselves became powerful political defenders of their own interests. But, in a review of the two-tier system in Hamilton-Wentworth as early as 1978, the Stewart commission concluded that the entire system should be replaced by a single municipality known as the City of Wentworth. The perceived problems were as follows:

there are serious conflicts between city and non-city politicians which interfere with and retard the development of policies to serve the citizens if the region; the structure blurs accountability and hinders accessibility, with the result that it cannot respond to the citizens easily; and finally, the structure of the system results in resources not being used as efficiently as possible (Ontario, 1978: 40–1).

The Stewart recommendations for a single city were never acted upon. Much more surprising was Harry Kitchen's conclusion in 1989 concerning the regional Municipality of Niagara. After more than 260 pages of analyzing the two-tier system and recommending relatively minor changes, he concluded that complete amalgamation was the preferred long-term (i.e., by 2000) option.

[M]oving to one level of government would eliminate the necessity of setting up similar departments at both the regional and area municipality level. This should eliminate the tension currently existing around the delivery of certain services where jurisdiction is shared between the two tiers.

Another advantage of this arrangement is that citizens would only need to deal with one level of government and hence, should not be confused about which level of local government is responsible for delivering which services. Instead of thirteen separate administrations as at the moment, only one would exist. Needless to say, this would almost certainly lower costs (Ontario, 1989: 270).

No action was taken on this aspect (or most others) of Kitchen's report. But, in 1999, the region and the area municipalities did establish a joint subcommittee on governance to update the report and to recommend structural changes.

During the 1990s, each of three Atlantic provinces – Nova Scotia, New Brunswick, and Newfoundland – addressed the desirability of two-tier municipal governmental arrangements. In each case the option was rejected, often with some form of negative reference to Ontario's experience. Events in the three provinces will be discussed briefly, beginning with Nova Scotia. Given the contents of the Graham report in the 1970s, it is perhaps not surprising that two-tier local government was never seriously considered as a restructuring option. The 1992 Task Force on Local Government once again rejected two-tier government for Nova Scotia, its "briefing book" specifically pointing to the analysis contained in the Graham report (Nova Scotia, 1992: 56). The report itself dismisses two-tier government in these words:

Rather than simplifying the structure, it complicates it. Understanding local government, and who is responsible for what, is more difficult. Lines of responsibility are blurred and conflict between the local and regional governments is probable. Total governmental costs will probably be increased rather than reduced. The defects are similar to those of shared cost programs (Nova Scotia: 32).

The recommendations of the task force for one-tier regional governments were adopted by the provincial government for Cape Breton and metropolitan Halifax.

In Halifax, the "municipal reform commissioner," C. William Hayward, revisited the two-tier option – but only to dismiss it.

The best known examples are the Ontario regional governments, such as metropolitan Toronto or Ottawa-Carleton.
A two-tier structure is more expensive: there are more elected officials, more administrators, and more facilities. It is more confusing to the taxpayer, since there are always questions about which of the two tiers is responsible for what. As a result, it is less responsive. Either the regional government is hampered in its ability to plan and provide services on a regional basis, or all units except the regional level become little more than tax gatherers for the regional government. If the regional level has any significant powers, public expectations insist that it be elected, apparently giving it some sort of moral ascendancy over the other units (Nova Scotia, 1993: 39).

Similar issues were addressed in New Brunswick at the same time, but in a seemingly more comprehensive manner. The province's 1992 discussion paper contained a quite detailed discussion of regional districts in British Columbia, pointing out that both New Brunswick and British Columbia have large expanses of land that are not incorporated municipally and that regional districts might be a mechanism for bringing better services (and taxes) to such areas. "It appears that the regional government concept has been less controversial and met with less opposition in British Columbia than elsewhere in Canada" (New Brunswick, 1992: 30). Despite such favourable comments, the paper rejected any form of two-tier model:

It is questionable whether a two-tier system of local government is appropriate for New Brunswick. It requires a large population to be effective and means putting in place more government at a time when the public is demanding more efficient and less government (ibid.: 39).

It concluded that two alternatives were preferable: "amalgamation and formalized regionalization," the latter involving special purpose bodies or formal intermunicipal agreements relating to particular services. In a quite remarkable example of hedging, the paper goes on to say:

The key to the success of this concept would be in the establishment of its structure. It would have to be structured in such a way as to retain the responsibility and autonomy of the municipal level of government and not create another level of government. At the same time, it would be more than a single-purpose, regional delivery agency (ibid.: 40).

Although the authors of New Brunswick's paper seemed unaware, this was exactly the feat that was attempted by the designers of British Columbia's regional districts. The reorganization process in New Brunswick spawned a series of reports. However, because their authors could choose only between amalgamation and "regionalization of services," none of them explicitly addressed the desirability of two-tier systems.

There have been numerous proposals in Newfoundland over the years to establish various forms of regional government. The latest comes from the 1997 Municipal Task Force on Regionalization. It ended up recommending a network of "regional county services boards" throughout the province governed by boards of directors comprising appointees from the councils of incorporated municipalities and directly elected members from unincorporated areas. Such institutions look very much like regional districts in British Columbia. The task force went out of its way to declare that they were not like two-tier municipal systems in Ontario.

Most of those who commented on the Regional Council model were of the view that it would impose a second level of government, would be expensive and highly bureaucratic, and would be remote from the people of the region. While some of this negative feeling might have been due to a misunderstanding of the Regional Council concept, there is ample evidence from elsewhere in Canada, particularly Ontario, that the standard two-tier regional government does lead to increased cost and bureaucracy (Newfoundland and Labrador, 1997).

Within Newfoundland's largest metropolitan area, the two most populous municipalities, St. John's and Mount Pearl both objected strenuously to the imposition of any kind of regional council or board. On 4 February 1998, the minister of municipal and provincial affairs announced that "regionalization of services in the two cities will apply only if it is requested and agreed to by both of the cities" (Newfoundland and Labrador, 1998).

In the prairie provinces there has been virtually no interest in anything resembling two-tier municipal structures, certainly not since the replacement of the Corporation of Greater Winnipeg by the unicity. In 1995–96 in Saskatchewan, the Romanow government introduced legislation to establish "municipal service districts," intermunicipal bodies that, on the surface at least, would seem quite unobjectionable, even to the most fervent advocate of local municipal autonomy. Apparently smaller municipalities feared that they would lose their managerial and administrative staff to the district service boards and that they would end up only "with a part time secretary to record the minutes of their meetings." Joseph Garcea also reports that municipal associations

were concerned that the creation of such boards, which they saw as a second level of government and not merely a multi-service authority, was likely to compromise the level of accessibility, accountability, responsiveness, and autonomy that existed under the current system of service delivery (Garcea, 1997: 11–12).

In the face of concerted opposition from the municipalities, the government withdrew the bill.

In Alberta, the Klein government repealed legislation that had established relatively weak intermunicipal planning commissions. Although legislation remained in place for regional services commissions, such commissions do not serve the largest cities, Calgary and Edmonton. In December 1998 the Alberta minister of municipal affairs appointed the former provincial treasurer, Lou Hyndman, as project chair of the Alberta Capital Region Governance Review. One of his first public statements was that the options facing him do not include a megacity or regional government.

Ironically, it has been in Ontario itself where the Ontario-style two-tier municipal government has been most under attack in the 1990s. The first point to note is that not a single urban area has become part of a two-tier system since the City of Sarnia joined Lambton county's two-tier structure in 1991. Outside Toronto, there were three urban areas where the two-tier system was especially threatened: Hamilton-Wentworth, Ottawa-Carleton, and Chatham-Kent. Each will be discussed in turn.

In the municipal elections of 1994 – almost a year before the Harris conservatives came to office – Terry Cooke campaigned for election as regional chair in Hamilton-Wentworth on the platform of converting the entire region into a one-tier system. He won the election, but without significant support outside the City of Hamilton and town of Ancaster. He therefore proceeded cautiously with his amalgamation plan. The first step was to appoint a "constituent assembly" to study the matter (Palango, 1997: 17). In 1996, after an extensive public consultation process, the assembly recommended complete amalgamation. Explicit criticism of the two-tier system was remarkably muted. This is the extent of it:

There is a lack of clarity about the division of responsibilities between our regional and local area municipalities. The citizens' perception is that there is a lot of overlap and duplication between the two levels of municipal government ...

[T]he current system of dual representation where one politician is expected to represent the local perspective on one set of municipal responsibilities and the regional perspective on another is leading to many conflicts and one or the other interest (regional or local) ends up being compromised or secondary (Regional Municipality of Hamilton-Wentworth, 1996: 13, 16).

Most of the report is devoted to demonstrating how amalgamation can save money and how local communities will be able to preserve a form of local decision-making through the creation of community committees.

The resulting uproar has been described elsewhere (Palango, 1997: 17–21; Downey and Williams, 1998: 219–22). Even the opponents of amalgamation did not want to preserve the existing two-tier system. The first objective of the alternative plan, devised under the leadership of local conservative MPP Toni Skarika, involved "[e]liminating the Regional government in Hamilton-Wentworth (pursuant to p. 17 in CSR [Common Sense Revolution])" (Skarika, 1997). The relevant reference in the CSR is presumably this: "We must rationalize the regional and municipal levels to avoid the overlap and duplication that now exists" (Progressive Conservative Party of Ontario, 1994: 17). In any event, as of mid–1999, the main changes have been at the administrative level, not the political. The regional municipality and the city now share a common chief administrative officer and senior management team. Some administrative departments have been completely integrated. Such changes, though risky, might well turn out to be genuinely innovative.

The Ottawa-Carleton story is at least as tangled as the one in Hamilton-Wentworth. In September 1995, less than a year after the region's reformed two-tier system was implemented, the City of Ottawa was calling for change. A city report stated that

it is clear that the problems associated with local/regional government in Ottawa-Carleton have not been resolved, and that it may now be time to consider the merits of a one-tier system of local government. In fact, the changes recently adopted by the previous provincial government may have exacerbated the problems that have existed in the two-tier system. For example, the direct election of regional councillors has resulted in no representation by local councils on regional council and this has led to a more fragmented approach to governing in Ottawa-Carleton. There continues to be duplication in administration, and with two sets of elected officials representing similar areas within the local municipal boundaries, division of responsibilities remains unclear. For example, it is difficult, in a two-tier system, to integrate overlapping functions such as local and regional planning (City of Ottawa, 1995: 37).

Counter proposals to amalgamation.

Although the paper did not choose a preferred solution, the city council eventually opted for complete amalgamation (Travers, 1997: A13).

The city's position – combined with the Harris government's enthusiasm for mergers – provoked a blizzard of suburban counterproposals for amalgamations: Nepean and Kanata; Goulbourn Osgoode, Rideau, and West Carleton (the "rural alliance"); Gloucester, Kanata, and Nepean. The most ambitious proposal came in February 1997 from all the suburbs acting together. It involved dismantling the regional government and replacing it with four "service corporations." Such nomenclature presumably allowed the authors to state clearly that "It is recommended that the two-tier system of regional and municipal governments be replaced with a one-tier system of municipal government" *(Greater Ottawa,* 1997). About the only thing both sides could agree on was that two-tier municipal government had to go. In any event, as of the fall of 1999, no changes have been made. On 29 September 1999 the provincial government named a special restructuring advisor for Ottawa-Carleton giving him sixty days to consult with area residents and community leaders and to formulate a plan. The advisor is Glen Shortliffe, former federal Clerk of the Privy Council.

Prior to 1 January 1998, the City of Chatham and Kent county were not linked by any form of multipurpose municipality. There was no two-tier regional government. Restructuring talks within the area began in 1996, but no agreement was reached (Downey and Williams, 1998: 225). Under the terms of the provincial *Savings and Restructuring Act, 1996*, a commissioner was sent in with complete authority to determine a solution. The commission comprised one person, Peter Meyboom, a former senior federal civil servant who had served for a few months in late 1995 and early 1996 as interim chief administrative officer at the City of Ottawa, just at the time when its proposals for a one-tier system in Ottawa-Carleton emerged. In deciding for a complete amalgamation of the city and all the county municipalities, Meyboom explicitly rejected any form of two-tier system: "by establishing a simplified two-tier system for Chatham-Kent, too many objectives of restructuring will be sacrificed in the name of representation." In addition to listing the usual criticisms of two-tier systems, he included another that was more specific to Ontario in 1997:

the coming changes to municipal government in Ontario, as reflected in the proposed legislative framework of the new *Municipal Act* and the Who-does-What re-alignment of services, with the emphasis on strong local government and increased upper-tier responsibilities, puts the future role of lower-tier municipalities in doubt (Ontario, 1997).

The best known attacks on two-tier municipal government were made during the period 1995-97, when the future of the Municipality of Metropolitan Toronto was under intense debate. A Task Force on the Greater Toronto Area (GTA), chaired by Anne Golden, was appointed by the NDP government on 1 April 1995. After having its deadlines shortened by the Harris government, which came to office in June, the Golden report was made public in January 1996. Although the report called for the abolition of the five existing metropolitan and regional governments, it also proposed the creation of a new one covering the entire GTA. Since this part of the Golden report is crucial for understanding the potential revival of interest in two-tier urban government, it will be considered in the next section of this paper.

To everyone's surprise, the Harris government's initial response to the Golden report was to propose, late in 1996, that the two-tier Metro system be completely amalgamated into one municipality, a new City of Toronto. After its initial indication of its preference for the mega-city option, the government agreed to allow time for Metro's six mayors to develop an alternative. The mayors' alternative was just as critical of two-tier municipal system as the provincial government was: "Most of the services provided by Metro today can be delivered at the local level. We propose that the existing Metro level of government be eliminated. This will eliminate duplication, reduce costs, and simplify government" (Mayor's Proposal, 1996: 6). The government's case for the megacity was exactly the same – and was never expressed in any more sophisticated terms. The only difference was that the mayors wanted to solve the problem by eliminating Metro and the provincial government wanted to solve it by eliminating the mayors. The controversy that followed need not be discussed here. One point is clear: there is lots of evidence to support the claim made at the time by the minister of municipal affairs that "No one is really happy with the system the way it is" and that "the status quo is not acceptable any more" (Leach, 1996). Such was the apparent end of two-tier municipal government in Metropolitan Toronto.

In 1997 James Lightbody wrote the academic obituary for two-tier local government in Canada. He claimed that the "B.C. regional district hybrid is suspect" as a two-tier system and that the Greater Vancouver Regional District (GVRD) "works as well as it does" only because it is not a real government (Lightbody, 1997: 437). In Lightbody's view, it was time for provincial governments to accept direct responsibility for the big intermunicipal issues facing our major metropolitan areas:

[T]here is no longer any substantial case for the preservation of bi-level metropolitan institutions. It is indeed time to say that traditional metropolitan

government, as emperor, is without clothes; it is time to put provincial departments, communities and specialized agencies directly to work (ibid.: 454).1

TRANSFORMATION

There have been in the 1990s two major reports for Canadian cities –
one for Montreal and one for Toronto – that placed a new form of
two-tier municipal government back on the agenda. Ironically, they
both predated the Ontario government's megacity decision, but they
are both profoundly relevant to any attempt to understand the future
of Canadian urban government. Each report – Pichette for Montreal
and Golden for Toronto – will be examined in turn.

The Québec government acted first. In 1992 the Liberal minister of
municipal affairs appointed Claude Pichette to chair a twelve-person
Task Force on the Montreal Region. When it reported in December
1993, the task force recommended the creation of a new twenty-one-
member council for the Montreal Metropolitan Region, the territory of
which would cover the entire census metropolitan area. The report
itself did not analyze institutional alternatives. It simply asserted that
such a council was needed to take regional action with respect to planning and development, economic development, the environment, culture and the arts, transportation, and public safety.

The Metropolitan council will be made up of exclusively of municipal councillors. The choice is based on the need to achieve the best possible harmony
between regional and local issues. The [task force] ... therefore has decided
upon an indirect method of representation which gives the mayors and municipal councillors the main responsibility to oversee the metropolitan organization (Québec, 1993: 17).

Most of the council members were to be mayors of constituent
municipalities chosen by regional groups of mayors but, because they
are so populous, the cities of Montreal, Laval, and Longueuil were to
be directly represented by both their mayors and by some members of
their councils. Existing upper-tier authorities within the region, including the Montreal Urban Community (MUC), were to be transformed
into "intermunicipal service agencies" and were expected to be of less
importance than both the municipalities and the Montreal Metropolitan Region.

The Liberals took no action on the report prior to their electoral
defeat in 1994. The new Parti Québécois government appointed a *ministre de la métropole* who conducted his own set of public consultations on the issue. The end result was the passage of legislation in mid-

1997 establishing a forty-member *Commission de développement pour la métropole* (CDM). It was to be presided over by the minister. Of the remaining thirty-nine members, two-thirds were to be elected municipal politicians (half from within the territory of the MUC and half from other municipalities within the census metropolitan area) and the other one-third were to be appointed by the minister from among representative socio-economic groups. The CDM was to have advisory functions only, especially in relation to issues concerning economic development, planning, transportation, and the environment. All existing municipal organizations – including the MUC – were to remain in place, although the CDM itself was supposed to make recommendations for the streamlining of this remarkably cumbersome set of municipal structures (Trépanier, 1998: 107–12).

In January 1998 a new *ministre de la Métropole* announced that the implementation of the CDM would be suspended because there was too much discord relating to the Québec government's fiscal downloading, too much local opposition, and too much concern about the City of Montreal's fiscal problems. He felt that, if these problems were not dealt with first, they would completely overshadow the work of the CDM and create an atmosphere in which it would be impossible to address the major regional issues. Even Montreal's mayor, Pierre Bourque, originally a supporter of the CDM, agreed with the minister that it was best not to proceed.

Mayor Bourque's preferred option was to enlarge the Montreal Urban Community to take in Laval to the north and the MRC Champlain (Longueuil, Saint-Lambert, Greenfield Park, LeMoyne, Saint-Hubert, and Brossard) to the south. This appeared to be the government's preferred option for a few months, but no action was taken prior to the 1998 Québec election. After the election, yet another minister was appointed.

The Golden Task Force on Greater Toronto confronted almost exactly the same kinds of issues as the Pichette Task Force on Greater Montreal (Canadian Urban Institute, 1994) and arrived at many of the same conclusions. Like Pichette, Golden concluded that there needed to be a new form of metropolitan authority for the entire city-region. It needed to be able to take regional action with respect to planning, the environment, public transit, piped infrastructure, expressways and traffic, debenturing, certain forms of licensing (including taxis), and regional assets (such as the Metro Zoo). Unlike Pichette, the Golden report discussed institutional alternatives. There were five.

1 Stronger provincial leadership: This involved creating an Ontario version of the *ministère de la métropole*. It was rejected on the grounds that the provincial government, by definition responsible

for the entire province, "lacks the capacity to advocate freely and effectively on behalf of the city-region" (Ontario, 1996: 163).

2 Intermunicipal agreements: like the first option, it is not clear that anyone actually advocated this approach as a stand-alone solution. In any event, it was rejected.

3 Metro's "supercity" proposal: this involved extending the existing Metro system – including a directly elected Metro council – to the entire GTA, thereby eliminating the existing regional governments in the suburban areas. "The Task Force rejected this model on the basis that too many services [notably police and transit] would be delivered at the [new] regional level" and that "Growth management and planning in the supercity's urban shadow would also pose problems under this model" (ibid.: 164).

4 The consensual model: This is the label used by the task force to characterize the Greater Vancouver Regional District. The model was rejected in these words:

> While the GVRD has generated a noteworthy level of consensus on an over-all ecological vision for the Vancouver Region, this process took twelve years and the agreed-upon vision fails to coordinate regional planning decisions any more effectively than does the current structure in the GTA.
>
> Moreover, Ontario and British Columbia have very different political cultures and traditions of planning and governance. The voluntary consensual approach embodied in the GVRD structure would be a major departure from Ontario's planning system [but a footnote points out that the "British Columbia planning system has been amended to require conformity between regional and local plans"] ...
>
> As well, the GVRD differs significantly in the scope of its functions and budget. In British Columbia, transit and social services are provincially funded, which is not the case in Ontario (ibid.: 165).

5 Greater Toronto Council: the task force recommended that a council with approximately thirty indirectly elected members be established to make decisions relating to the GTA functions it had previously enumerated. The existing Metro and regional governments would be eliminated. Direct election to the Greater Toronto Council from wards crossing municipal boundaries (as in Ottawa-Carleton and the old Corporation of Greater Winnipeg) was rejected.

> [B]y creating a direct and separate entity that is not composed of members of constituent local councils, this system invites friction between the upper and lower tiers. Further, there is no evidence that electing councillors directly to a regional body reduces parochialism.

A system of direct (or double direct) election in which wards would not cross municipal boundaries would, given the relatively small population of some municipalities, have created a council that was deemed to be too large (ibid.: 169).

The great problem for both the Pichette and Golden task forces was that some existing upper functions could not easily be moved either upwards to the new city-region authority, nor downwards to the lower-tier municipalities. The most obvious were policing in the MUC and policing and municipal social services throughout the GTA. Similarly, strategic planning for piped infrastructure was a natural city-region function, but it seemed that there were significant problems in vesting the new authorities with the responsibility of actually operating existing sewage-treatment and water-purification plants. Both Pichette and Golden attempted to solve the problem by recommending that a new form of intermediate body ("intermunicipal service agencies" for Pichette and "flexible service districts" for Golden) be established. In many respects such bodies were to act as replacements for the Metro and regional governments in Toronto and the MUC and MRCs in Montreal.

The political implications of such recommendations were almost identical in both city-regions. Suburbs within the central two-tier systems (the MUC and Metro) supported the recommendations because they envisioned escape from a system they considered expensive, cumbersome, and (to varying degrees) dominated by central-city problems and costs. They preferred the idea of being associated with a less powerful city-region authority in which central-city interests would be diluted. The central city was mildly supportive, in the perhaps naive expectation that the new authority would help prevent further outer suburban growth. Some central-city advocates – notably John Sewell – were profoundly suspicious, however, of any political entanglement in which central-city interests could be so easily outvoted. Outer suburbs were adamantly opposed, wanting nothing to do with central-city costs and problems or with implied constraints on future growth. Institutional interests connected with the existing upper-tier units (some politicians and unions and almost all senior administrators) that were to be abolished were also fervent opponents of the Pichette and Golden recommendations.

In addition to these kinds of political difficulties, the relevant provincial ministers must have been profoundly concerned that, if they acted on the recommendations, they would be seen as moving toward a three-tier system of municipal government. In Montreal, the problem was partially solved by the enthusiasm of the inner suburban mayors to reduce the MUC to the status of an intermunicipal service district and by the fact that, because the MUC as an institution was relatively weak politically and functionally, there would be few to defend it. In Toronto, the issue of what to do about Metro (and the regional governments) could not be minimized, especially since, contrary to Golden's assumptions, upper-tier responsibilities for social services were to be increased, not decreased (Graham and Phillips, 1998: 175-209). Such considerations provided the opening for Metro's chief administrative officer to launch a withering attack on Golden's recommendations.

The task force recommendations involving flexible service districts and the devolution of services to local municipalities will introduce a degree of complexity that will make it difficult for even the most informed resident to understand who is responsible for which services. For example, the flow of recommendations from a local standing committee to their council to a GTC service district to a GTC standing committee to the GTC will be complex and slow. Significant staff resources will be required simply to route agendas and materials through the cumbersome bureaucracy that will grow (Municipality of Metropolitan Toronto, 1996: 12).

These were the kinds of concerns that caused officials in the ministry of municipal affairs to counsel against implementing the Golden recommendations (Walker, 1996: A1, A4). Given that Premier Harris had promised during the election campaign "that the Metro regional government in its current form must go" (Harris, 1995), the only viable alternative to the Golden plan for Metro was total amalgamation.

In Québec, where the government's action was not constrained by election promises, a different course of action was taken to try to avoid the "three-tier" problem. The MUC and the MRCs were left exactly as they were and the government introduced legislation to create a CDM that was purely advisory. This infuriated the MUC suburban mayors, such opposition being one of the many factors that eventually caused the government to abandon the entire plan after the legislation had already been approved. In the absence of election promises, the Québec government ended up doing nothing: the two-tier structure of the MUC remains in place and the legislation establishing the CDM remains on the books.

To the surprise of many, the Harris government in Ontario actually went ahead in late 1998 and established a Greater Toronto Services Board covering the entire GTA. In introducing the legislation, municipal affairs minister Al Leach stated the following:

The legislation would enable the board to prepare strategies on how GTA municipalities provide the sewer and water pipes, the roads and transportation systems their communities need, and how to make sure they are efficiently used. The board would manage GO [commuter] Transit through an authority that would be called GT Transit. It would help coordinate economic development and tourism ... It would help resolve disputes. It would be a forum for municipalities to discuss the administration and costs of social assistance and social housing programs (Ontario, 1998).

The legislation, which was approved in December, established a forty-person board, comprising at least one member from each constituent municipality (but eleven from Toronto and two from Mississauga) as well as the four chairs of the remaining regional municipalities. The regional chair of Hamilton-Wentworth is a member for commuter-transit purposes. There is a system of weighted voting so as to promote representation by population. Bylaws to establish GTA strategies would require a two-thirds majority in order to be approved.

Mr Leach claims that the GTTSB "will not be another level of government. It has no service delivery responsibilities other than overseeing the operation of GO Transit, and it has no direct taxing authority" (Ontario, 1999). In fact, however, the board has the authority to collect funds from the City of Toronto and the four regional municipalities in exactly the same way that regional municipalities collect funds from their constituent units.

On 22 January 1999 the Greater Toronto Services Board met for the first time. By a vote of 87–32, the forty members chose Alan Tonks, the last chair of the Municipality of Metropolitan Toronto as their first chair. All eleven representatives from the City of Toronto supported Mr Tonks. His first task is to prepare a budget, including a provision for his own annual salary, expected to be approximately $100,000. In accepting his position, Mr Tonks was quoted as saying: "We are a community. But even if we have the technical capability to identify shared problems and develop solutions, implementation will only be possible if we build the civic capacity to mobilize and focus our resources" (Rusk, 1999).

Meanwhile, in Montreal, the possibility of a quite different, older form of metropolitan government has recently re-emerged. In April 1999 the Québec government received the report of the *Commission nationale sur les finances et la fiscalité locales*. This nine-person commission – appointed one year previous in the aftermath of intense municipal opposition to fiscal downloading – was chaired by Denis Bédard, a former senior Québec civil servant. The vice-chair was

Jean-Pierre Collin, a professor at *l'Institut national de la recherche scientifique (urbanisation)* and a prominent academic authority on urban issues in Montreal.

The Bédard report is a remarkable document. The commission's mandate was to study municipal fiscal issues throughout Québec and to pay special attention to the particular problems of the most populous municipality, the City of Montreal. Although municipal structures and functions were not explicitly mentioned in the terms of reference, the commission decided that, given the breadth of the fiscal mandate, such matters could not be avoided (Québec, Pacte 2000: 3). The result was that the commission arrived at some startling recommendations. One was that education (primary and secondary), health (including hospitals), and personal social services should come under the direct control of restructured municipal institutions.

The Bédard report contains 346 pages of description and analysis; thirteen of them (pp. 182–8 and 273–8) relate directly to municipal structures in the Montreal metropolitan region, although dozens of others are concerned with related Québec-wide concerns about fragmentation and inequity. The report explicitly accepts the diagnosis of Montreal's problems contained in the Pichette report but makes no reference whatever to its prescriptions (or to the prescriptions of any other document, such as the Golden report). In its recommendations, the commission devotes only a few paragraphs to metropolitan Montreal. It urges that the government force amalgamations in the area so as to reduce the number of municipalities from 111 to about twenty and in the MUC from twenty-nine to five at the most (ibid.: 277). The commission also recommends that a new level of government be established for the entire metropolitan area. This new government would be allocated "*revenus autonomes,*" and its governing body would be directly elected.

The commission's willingness to accept a new directly elected metropolitan level of government is in contrast with the approach taken in both the Golden and Pichette reports. Another difference is that the Bédard report recommended that the existing metropolitan police force be dismantled and become the responsibility of the newly amalgamated lower-tier municipalities. The Bédard report was similarly alone in suggesting that the new metropolitan authority eventually become responsible for public education and for the health-care system.

Not surprisingly, initial reaction to the report has been mostly negative, although Vera Danyluk, the chair of the MUC's executive committee, has urged the government to move ahead with its recommendations. Her position favouring a stronger metropolitan authority parallels that of the leadership of Metro Toronto during the debate on the Golden report. In the immediate aftermath of the report's release, the minister responsible, Louise Harel, refused to commit the government to any particular course of action. In the late summer of 1999, *Le Devoir* leaked proposed government action, which included a directly elected body for the greater Montreal area. Intense opposition ensued and by the end of September, the minister announced that consultations would occur before any action was proposed.

CONCLUSION

James Lightbody would doubtless associate Montreal's aborted CDM and Toronto's GTSB with the "council-of-government typology, so much in vogue in American federalism" (Lightbody, 1997: 437). How one labels these institutions does not really matter. Nevertheless, it is true that they do not have clearly defined functional authority and that they are primarily advisory. The CDM does not even exist. But what the architects of these institutions were searching for was a mechanism between province and municipality for the articulation of a city-region perspective. Perhaps such a perspective is not needed everywhere. Lightbody acknowledges that Toronto is a special case (ibid.: 438); he scarcely mentions Montreal (ibid.: 451), and, as has already been noted, he acknowledges that the GVRD works well.[2] Toronto, Montreal, and Vancouver are Canada's three largest metropolitan areas. Although neither of the ministers who sponsored the CDM or the GTSB would likely have admitted it, both institutions look as though they were modelled at least in part on the GVRD.

Because of the Bédard report, Montreal is still facing a debate about whether the entire metropolitan area will obtain its own directly elected metropolitan government or whether some form of lighter structure will suffice. In Toronto two less sweeping questions remain outstanding. Will the GTSB evolve as an institution that has real impact on how the GTA develops and how GTA municipalities deliver services? If so, will the existing two-tier regional systems survive?

With Alan Tonks as its full-time, high-profile chair, the GTSB already has a more visible and prominent political leadership than the GVRD has ever had. If the GTSB does nothing else, it will provide a platform upon which Mr Tonks can articulate the needs of the GTA as a whole, needs that are quite distinct from those of both the new City of Toronto and the province of Ontario.[3] For a short time at least, we shall all have the dubious benefit of observing the operation of a partial (i.e., not within the City of Toronto) three-tier system of local government. Such an inherently unstable system means that debates about municipal structures within the GTA are far from over. Will the City of Mississauga be absorbed into the new City of Peel? Or will the regional municipalities somehow disappear? The latter possibility seems problematic as long as regions retain responsibility for delivering virtually all forms of social assistance (including workfare), a state of affairs that no-one could have predicted as recently as mid–1996.

Debating about whether or not the GVRD, GTSB, and a CDM-like body constitute genuine levels, or tiers, of government is a fruitless and meaningless activity. Except for James Lightbody, every other informed and interested observer believes that such a body, in one form or another, should exist for every multi-municipal metropolitan area. The usual argument – especially from land-use planners – is that such bodies need to be stronger. The problem with making them stronger is that we start going down the road toward a two-tier system of the type that is now generally discredited, except to the authors of the Bédard report. The alternative to the Bédard model is clear. We can see it in the Greater Vancouver Regional District, and there is every likelihood that we shall soon begin to see it in the Greater Toronto Services Board. What we shall eventually see in Montreal is still anyone's guess.

NOTES

This chapter was completed in late 1999. It therefore does not deal with changes, such as those proposed for Québec, that took place after this date.

1 Lightbody (1997: 454) generously acknowledges that my earlier writing on the subject advanced a similar case (see Sancton, 1992). For a vigorous defence of the GVRD and of proposals for new territorially comprehensive metropolitan governments for Montreal and Toronto, see Gilbert and Stevenson, 1999.

2 For my favourable assessment of the GVRD, see Sancton, 1994: 65–71, 98-101. See also Smith and Oberlander, 1998. For more critical assessments, see McMillan, 1997; Artibise, 1998; and Smith and Stewart, 1998: 47–9.

3 Writing months before the legislation was approved, Frances Frisken expressed much more skepticism about the GTSB than is presented here, see Frisken, 1998.

PART THREE

Planning and Economic Development

9 Community Economic Development in Canadian Cities: From Experiment to Mainstream

BARBARA LEVINE, SHERRI TORJMAN, and PAUL BORN

"Community is not something we have,
it is something we never finish doing."
Marilyn Waring (1989)

INTRODUCTION

Municipal governments throughout the industrialized world, including Canada, are facing the effects of globalization, economic restructuring, high unemployment and underemployment, and rising rates of poverty and inequality. In Canadian cities and towns, there are serious shortages of affordable housing, pressure on social assistance programs, and a lack of full-time, well-paid employment, frequently combined with the loss of human, built, and natural community assets.

While poverty and community disinvestment are national challenges, the effects of poverty are felt locally. However, municipalities face serious constraints in their ability to create or maintain community assets and to tackle unemployment and poverty. They do not control many of the levers – such as interest rates, international trade agreements, and global currency trading – that contribute to and can help alleviate these problems. They can, however, help to create frameworks that support or are hostile to community economic development.

This chapter sets out a range of actions that municipal governments can take to tackle the social and economic problems that directly affect the quality of life in their communities. It acknowledges that both federal and provincial governments, as well as international bodies, must play a role in finding solutions to growing social and economic pressures at the community level. However, while there are limits to what municipal governments can achieve in the face of complex international problems, there are a range of strategies that municipal authorities can adapt and use to address the issues of community disinvestment and marginalization. Chief among these are locally inspired solutions to economic development and poverty alleviation, known popularly in Canada as community economic development or CED.

In this chapter, we will describe CED and what it does, document the current experience of Canadian urban centres with CED, suggest strategies for enhancing its effectiveness at the municipal level and recommend potential roles for municipal governments.

WHAT IS MEANT BY CED?

Community economic development refers to a range of activities that integrate economic and social goals, with the objective of supporting lasting community renewal (Torjman and Battle, 1999). While CED has often been used, sometimes very effectively, as a local development strategy in rural communities in Canada and has been recognized as an official policy instrument for regional development purposes internationally, its potential in urban areas in Canada has never been fully tested.

What distinguishes CED from other development approaches is that its primary focus is on building communities from *within*, while governments, including those at the municipal level, conventionally look for economic development from without. Furthermore, it tends to avoid service- or charity-based interventions that regard individuals as dependent, problem-laden "clients" who are unable to help themselves. Instead, CED focuses on long-term, enterprise-based strategies that recognize and build on existing resources and talents in the community. CED invests in individuals, populations, and neighbourhoods that have traditionally been disadvantaged and seeks to develop their knowledge, skills, and assets. While an increasing number of governments in Canada and around the world use the language of CED (such as self-reliance and empowerment), most still focus their efforts on creating a positive environment for small businesses, especially those that emphasize innovative entrepreneurship and new technologies.

Historically, CED organizations have employed different strategies at different times and places. What they have in common is the mobilization of both local and outside resources into broad, community-based processes that use untapped resources and capacity in local communities (Lewis, 1999). The Institut de formation en développement économique communautaire (IFDEC) in Montreal defines CED as an integrated approach to development that:

- is long-term and endogenous;
- seeks economic "development" rather than only economic growth;
- links economic and social development;
- combats poverty and exclusion;
- respects locality-based approaches (i.e., there is a spatial dimension to CED);
- builds on participation and seeks to empower local communities;
- builds partnerships among different stakeholders.

Brodhead has identified similar themes, adding that CED is often a *response to* or *emerges from* underdevelopment and marginalization at the community level (Brodhead, 1994).

HISTORY OF CED IN CANADA

The origins of CED in English-speaking Canada are found primarily in rural communities and small towns, although there have been some noticeable exceptions such as New Dawn in Sydney, NS, and the community development corporations that emerged in Québec in the 1980s. In contrast to the American experience, which in the 1970s viewed CED as an instrument for rebuilding disinvested inner cities, CED in Canada was conceived primarily as an instrument for regional and rural development. Programs like the Community Futures (CF) program, introduced in 1986 and building on earlier federal regional development programs, were aimed at non-metropolitan communities faced with economic decline and chronic unemployment. Over two hundred communities have been involved with the CF program, which provides funding for services ranging from business counselling to the management of loan funds for investing in development initiatives.

Constitutional constraints have prevented the federal government from playing a major role in supporting urban CED; since provinces have responsibility for municipal affairs, direct federal involvement with cities has been largely precluded. When the federal government does get involved in cities, as it has over the years through financial support for specific projects developed by urban citizens' organizations, the involvement is usually ad hoc, reactive and short-term. It could be argued that federal assistance for the CED initiatives of marginalized groups, particularly in major urban centres, has had a largely reallocative function intended to counter-balance, in a small way, government policies that have generally favoured growth rather than equity.

Thus we find that CED organizations in urban areas have historically had more of a social purpose than an economic mandate. Many urban CED organizations have been set up by social agencies and receive financial support from government departments with health and welfare mandates in order to address the chronic problems of unemployment and marginalization of their target groups. They tend to have multiple objectives (such as training, settlement and integration of new Canadians, and reduced dependence of the disabled or psychiatric survivors), in addition to economic objectives. Unfortunately, their performance is often measured by a single bottom line that ignores or minimizes the non-economic benefits to individuals and communities.

Community economic development in Québec has had rather different origins. CED in that province "arose out of Quebec's social and communitarian movements, somewhat on the fringes of government programs" (Favreau and Ninacs, 1994). The economic crisis of the early 1980s and the restructuring of the Québec economy during the previous two decades partly explain the emergence of CED, but social traditions and cultural values have also been important. Although many CED initiatives in Québec were to be found in rural areas far from large urban centres, as in the rest of Canada, Favreau and Ninacs argue that CED in Québec was really launched in 1984 with the emergence of the first community development corporations in Pointe-St-Charles in Montreal (an urban neighbourhood) and in Victoriaville (a small city). The current policy of the provincial government to create local development centres (CLDs) is drawn in large measure from this history. While the implementation of the new policy has been uneven, it marks a departure in that it is being applied in both urban and rural settings.

THE CURRENT CONTEXT FOR CED

The current revival of interest in community-based economic development is partly due to the failure of past attempts to deal with income and employment disparities and to the withdrawal of federal and provincial governments from traditional program areas such as regional and social development. At the same time, as national identity becomes more diffuse and as state power is eroded, citizens in communities around the world are struggling for a sense of purposefulness and powerfulness. Governments and civil society are rethinking their conventional development approaches in favour of models that support local decision-making and that affirm local identity.

In the face of a global economic order that concentrates economic wealth and political power in a few hands, new development models are gaining currency. According to David Driscoll, Executive Director of the VanCity Foundation and former Mayor of Port Moody, BC, many community activists don't want to re-create the large, bureaucratic, government-financed institutions of the 1970s as a means to invest in communities. Rather they are advocating approaches that are:

- asset-based;
- developmentally oriented;
- risk sharing (through multi-sector partnerships);
- locally grounded;
- accountable to local citizens;
- inclusive;
- vision-driven (Driscoll, 1999).

Nowhere was this changing public attitude more evident than at an international meeting that took place in Sherbrooke, QC, in October 1998. More than eight hundred delegates from around the world met to discuss the challenges facing CED and the social economy (as it is often referred to in Québec and Europe). Inventing and strengthening local strategies to global problems was the primary theme, and participants exchanged best practice and current experience.

WHAT DOES CED *DO*?

The most successful community-based approaches to economic development are multifaceted in nature (Lewis, 1999). Typically, they combine a number of strategies: training and job placement, job creation and retention, the provision of technical assistance and training for self-employment and business startup, support for enterprise creation or expansion (often community- or co-operatively owned), community empowerment and local institution-building, and enhancing local access to capital.

For purposes of discussion, it is useful to group these various activities into three major categories: community asset development and ownership (wealth creation), community building and mobilization (also referred to as "empowerment"), and labour market and employment innovation (which includes programming to support entrepreneurship, self-employment, and microlending.) (Born, 1999).

CREATING COMMUNITY WEALTH

Community asset development and ownership is central to most CED organizations in Canada. This is often accomplished by supporting the development of locally owned or community-owned small enter-

Table 1
Basic CED Models

	Community Asset Development and Ownership	Community Building and Mobilizing	Labour Market and Employment Innovation
MISSION	• Create wealth • Build an economic base	• Community Empowerment	• Human Resource Development • Job Creation
OBJECTIVES	• Create or strengthen locally or community-owned businesses and co-operatives that create jobs • Identify enterprise opportunities • Generate profits or surplus to reinvest in the community • Operate local loan and investment funds	• Organize and animate large networks of people and resources • Strategic planning, organizing and financing • Conflict resolution	• Support innovative labour market programs, e.g., Entrepreneurship programs, mentoring and networking for small business owners • Implement training programs • Support business development centres • Access and match needs of employers
CEDO ROLE	• Owner / partner / Financier	• Convenor / Organizer	• Trainer / Advisor

prises, co-operatives, not-for-profit businesses, training businesses, and sectoral business and community networks. Organizations such as the Niagara Enterprise Agency, the Enterprise Centre (Revelstoke), Le Regroupement pour la relance économique et sociale du sud-ouest, better known as RESO (Montréal), New Dawn Enterprises (Sydney), Edmonton Recycling Society, and the Human Resources Development Association (Halifax) have created multi-million dollar businesses, employing and/or training hundreds of local people and developing broad-based networks of support to strengthen marginalized communities.

CED organizations help communities to identify and develop local opportunities, niche markets, local ownership, and the human resource potential of the poor, the less educated, and persons with disabilities. In each case, the organizations mentioned above have helped transform social needs into community assets and economic opportunities.

COMMUNITY MOBILIZATION

CED organizations know how to mobilize communities, including those that are undergoing significant economic and social stress. These are communities with higher than average unemployment rates, poverty rates, crime rates, and death rates and fewer social and economic supports.

Organizations like New Dawn in Cape Breton, Le Carrefour de relance de l'économie et de l'emploi du centre de Québec (CRÉECQ) in Québec City, Learning Enrichment Foundation (LEF) in Toronto, Quint Development Corporation in Saskatoon, and Lutherwood-CODA in Waterloo Region have mobilized large networks of people, financial and human resources, and a growing political will to develop the economic and social infrastructure of their communities. Their methods include organizing and animating, broad-based listening, group and organizational development, strategic planning, conflict resolution, developing leadership, and inclusion. What makes CED organizations different is not the use of any one of these skills. Rather, it is the constant use of many of these methods together, while remaining constant and present in the community.

SELF-EMPLOYMENT DEVELOPMENT AND MICROLENDING

CED organizations were on the forefront in recognizing the trend nationally toward self-employment. Many organizations, among them the Community Business Resource Centre (CBRC), Self-Employment Development Initiatives (SEDI) and the Learning Enrichment Foundation in Toronto, Lutherwood-CODA, Women in Rural Economic Development (WRED), Mennonite Central Committee in Calgary, the Community Economic Development Corporations (CDEC) of Montreal, SEED Winnipeg, the Centre for Community Enterprise in BC, and dozens of other community-based organizations, have developed training programs enabling thousands of unemployed people or welfare recipients to start their own businesses. These are business support programs with a difference. In addition to recognizing the need for small business training, the organizations developed or entered into partnership with a variety of community supports to enhance the success of their clients. These supports include microlending funds, business resource centres, mentorship programs, marketing networks, and culture-, gender-, and age-specific curricula.

CED organizations have also battled locally and nationally for welfare and unemployment eligibility policies that assist rather than discourage participants' initiative. Most programs are now considering second-stage development issues for their clients: capitalization to grow their businesses; growth-related training issues; and municipal bylaw changes for home-based businesses.

CED organizations were among the first to recognize the growing trend toward self-employment precisely because they are present in their community. It is this presence and commitment to local issues that makes them development organizations rather than simply small-business trainers.

ROLE OF MUNICIPALITIES

The temptation for local government is to follow the example of most senior governments and focus on economic efficiency at the expense of supports for social integration, inclusion, and cultural values (Lithwick, 1970). However, the fabric of communities is not based solely on economic efficiency. Healthy and prosperous communities are those that are built upon trust between the governed and those governing, where there is a capacity for citizens to act together, where there is a tolerance of diversity, and where people can relate to one another in a "civil" way. It is in the interest of local government to create "space" for the building of trust among its citizens, politicians, and bureaucrats, and CED is one instrument that helps nurture an inclusive and civil society at the community level. It can also be a mechanism for moderating and negotiating compromises among contending forces – for example, the business elites that seek to minimize government spending and taxes on the one hand, and those groups of citizens who feel increasingly hopeless and excluded from the economic opportunities they see being created around them.

There is one "caveat" that follows from these principles. Municipalities, or public institutions of any kind, don't "do" CED. By definition, communities and local citizens, acting together through their own organizations (whether they be neighbourhood associations, businesses and business groups, co-operatives and credit unions, or service agencies) are responsible for community economic development. Governments and public agencies can support and facilitate, and they should be active partners.

Municipalities can play several key roles with respect to supporting CED. They can:

1 convene diverse sectors;
2 create favourable conditions;

3 support job creation;
4 incorporate the concept of economic opportunity within all municipal programs;
5 remove barriers;
6 develop and maintain an information base (Torjman, 1999).

Each of these will be discussed in greater detail in the sections that follow.

1 Convening Diverse Sectors

Municipal governments are in a unique position to convene diverse sectors that need to be involved in tackling unemployment and developing a community economic development initiative. Key sectors that need to be involved include the private sector (specific companies, business development centres, and sectoral representatives), the education and training sector, representatives of stressed neighbourhoods or groups, social agencies and health centres, labour, community foundations, and other levels of governments where appropriate. In some localities, the municipal government should defer to another convener – such as a community foundation, social planning council, or economic development committee – while playing an active supporting role. Credibility of the convening agency with the broadest range of stakeholders should be the most important aspect considered when determining who should play this role.

Municipalities throughout the industrialized world increasingly are using partnerships to tackle complex problems that cut across various sectors. In Wisconsin, for example, municipal governments have established Community Steering Committees to forge partnerships among industry, nonprofit groups, and government agencies. Among other tasks, the committees are expected to create private and public sector jobs, address child care and transportation problems, and provide advice to program administrators and participants.

The OP2000 project in Waterloo Region, which was launched in May 1998 by Lutherwood-CODA, has set up a leadership roundtable that involves business, the social sector, low-income people, and regional government (Hodgson, 1998). The roundtable helps promote community change not only through its own initiatives, but also through the work carried out by each representative within his or her respective sector. For example, the business representatives involved in OP2000 are encouraging their peers to examine their employment practices around hiring, wages, working time, and layoffs. They are also encouraging broader involvement in the community through the contribution of expertise and funds; for example, the Royal Bank representative on the Roundtable was instrumental in finding a new building for the local Food Bank.

As important as the Roundtable's major activities is the composition of its membership. To be successful, Roundtable members require a combination of knowledge of the issue, the skills to reduce poverty, and sufficient influence within the community to mobilize a broader effort. As such, 40 percent of the Roundtable members are leaders from low-income communities. Another 40 percent are from the business sector: entrepreneurs with a proven track record of creating opportunities. The remaining 20 percent are professionals from other sectors such as government, labour, and funders required for their technical skills as well as their influence within and beyond the community (Source: www.op2000.org).

The importance of this function shouldn't be minimized. Without a broad public consensus about the need for and benefits of a CED strategy, community-based enterprises and activities are exceedingly vulnerable. Their success in the past has often been undermined by alliances among small business, media, and various political elites who resist co-operative activity for ideological reasons and who perceive CED as competitors with the private sector. One can observe this phenomenon whether on a First Nations reserve or in the inner core of Canada's largest cities. By legitimizing CED, by recognizing the direct economic benefits to excluded citizens as well as the non-economic benefits CED provides with regard to strengthening local leadership and enhancing people's sense of belonging, municipalities can play a pivotal role in the success of community economic development initiatives. Because various sectors are "in the same room" talking with each other, they are more likely to hear each other's needs and identify collective solutions.

2 Creating Favourable Conditions

Municipal governments can take steps to create favourable conditions for community economic development. They can promote the economic health of their region by developing internal market opportunities. Local sourcing of supplies and labour, for example, keeps more money in the community. Municipal governments can promote awareness about locally produced goods and services as well as the benefits of local purchasing (Torjman, 1999).

Municipalities should be able to offer incentives in the form of tax breaks, for example, by reducing or delaying the payment of property taxes for firms that make a special effort to hire unemployed workers or welfare recipients. Sacramento County, California, was highly successful with an aggressive job development effort focused on a single employer. When a major electronics firm announced that it was building an assembly plant in a local enterprise zone, the Country offered tax credits for hiring welfare recipients. County staff coordinated a major employment outreach, screening more than thirty thousand applications, matching applicants with positions, providing support services and following up on job leads. Of the plant's four thousand new jobs, five hundred went to people formerly on welfare; another three hundred recipients found temporary employment (Torjman and Battle, 1999).

Municipal governments can also create favourable conditions for economic development by protecting certain tracts of land for designated purposes. Community land trusts are nonprofit corporations that separate the ownership of land from the ownership of buildings. First developed in the US during the 1960s by the Institute for Community Economics, land trusts have enabled community development corporations in cities like Boston to develop affordable housing, build incubators for community businesses, and increase community assets. For example, the support of the City of Boston was critical to the Dudley Street Neighbourhood Initiative, a major community-based development project involving community-based planning, housing construction, and capacity-building. The city sold eighteen acres of city-owned vacant land to the DSNI for one dollar and provided the backing to secure a $2 million loan from the Ford Foundation. Eventually, federal agencies pledged $2.1 million to subsidize development and mortgage costs (Tuloss, 1996).

3 Employment Development

Job Creation. Job creation includes the development of small businesses, worker co-operatives, and self-employment. While there are far too many examples of job creation to describe here, there are some exemplary models that have attempted to integrate economic and social goals. The Human Resources Development Association (HRDA) of Halifax is one such example, started by the Halifax municipal government in 1978 with $275,000 from the municipal welfare budget. It has become a successful venture capital and business development group set up primarily to serve social assistance recipients, using welfare funds to capitalize the businesses it starts. To date, fourteen businesses have been set up. While four have failed (not a bad record compared to general small business startups), four have been sold to employees, and others are turning a profit. HRDA also operates a job training program that includes life skills training, work placements, and specialized skills training.

Access to Capital.   Access to capital is often identified as the single most important barrier to the development of small and community-based businesses and co-operatives. A variety of local community financing mechanisms have been developed in the past ten years to address the shortage of capital or the mismatch between supply and demand. Community loan funds, for example, raise capital from individuals, businesses, banks, credit unions, and private foundations to lend to "high risk" entrepreneurs or to enterprises that are unable to meet the conventional requirements for security. Microlending programs or peer lending are variations now found in cities across the country (Vancouver, Edmonton, Toronto, Québec City, and St. John to name but a few). Programs that match entrepreneurs with "angel" investors is another innovation; Ottawa-Carleton, in particular, has developed impressive mechanisms for this purpose.

Local governments can play an important role in promoting the development of community-based financing alternatives. They can provide loan funds directly to prospective entrepreneurs through community-based organizations, or contribute to their core costs. They can make available seed capital to community loan funds. These can then use this money as leverage to raise funds from other levels of government, local businesses, private donors, or foundations. Municipalities can match individual and corporate donations, or they can act as guarantors for community loans. The beauty of the loan guarantee mechanism is that it enables not-for-profits to leverage additional resources from market lenders, without requiring an actual disbursement of funds. Finally, as in the case of the Montreal Community Loan Association, municipalities can provide in-kind resources such as space and staff who specialize in the provision of technical assistance for business development.

Self-Employment and Community Business.   Municipal governments can promote self-employment in several ways. They can help set up entrepreneurship centres and mentorship programs themselves, or they can preferably subcontract these programs to local CED organizations working with at-risk groups and in disadvantaged communities.

4 *Incorporate the Concept of* CED *across all Municipal Programs*

Local governments can encourage other organizations and firms to incorporate elements of skill-building and economic development into their activities. For example, any service group or organization that receives financial support from local governments should be encouraged to review all its activities and programs with a view to building opportunities for skill enhancement, job creation, and business development. However, additional resources need to be made available to facilitate these shifts. This is particularly true for the voluntary sector, which is being asked to innovate and develop new programs and approaches while, at the same time, it has seen its funding base erode.

Municipal government should apply the same approach to its own programs, identifying opportunities to invest in people and neighbourhoods through the complete range of municipal spending, not just social service spending. It should ensure that support for CED is included within the mandate of municipally funded business development offices or economic development committees, and it must continue to work with community-based groups to make sure low-income residents are able to access the complete range of municipal programs (from arts and culture to entrepreneurship training and planning services). Municipalities can partner in business incubators (e.g., City of Toronto) and ensure that legislation and regulations do not create barriers for emerging businesses. Finally, municipalities can play a pivotal role in supporting community-owned businesses by:

- inviting community groups to bid when contracting out municipal services; several Canadian municipalities have shown leadership in this area, particularly in the provision of waste and recycling services (Halifax, Edmonton, Toronto); however, there are many more sectors where this kind of partnership could be developed including park and building maintenance, the maintenance of municipal infrastructure, and food services;
- informing potential opponents to community enterprises about the economic and non-economic benefits of CED, such as reduced welfare costs, reduced crime, and improved health.

5 Removing Barriers

Local governments can remove barriers that are often embedded in program designs or rules that keep the unemployed out of the labour market or that prevent underemployed workers from upgrading their skills. As the Report titled *Ottawa's Hidden Workforce* (Huntley, 1998) indicates, the un- and underemployed often face barriers that have nothing to do with their skills or the availability of jobs but that make them ineligible for a host of program supports and jobs.

Municipalities, often in partnership with other stakeholders, can provide transitional funding for child care, work-related costs (e.g., purchase of a license or equipment), transportation costs, and technical aids that are disability-related. In many Canadian jurisdictions, special-assistance budgets face severe constraints. Yet without these funds, many individuals who are able and willing to work are virtually tied to the welfare system, as there are no other sources for the required aids and equipment. Many American states now offer transit vouchers and mileage reimbursement for vehicle use.

Municipal zoning bylaws may prohibit the startup and operation of home-based businesses. Until recently, for example, it was illegal to teach piano lessons from a private home in Toronto (Nares, 1999). In rural areas, some municipalities have restrictive sign policies, making it impossible for rural businesses to promote their location to the public. Municipal governments, in collaboration with other stakeholders, can undertake a review of their entire package of bylaws and regulations to determine their impact (positive, negative or neutral) on community economic development. And where barriers arise from policies outside municipal jurisdiction, local governments can document the effects and inform appropriate authorities.

6 Developing and Maintaining an Information Base

Municipalities should ensure that all local agencies and groups, including nongovernmental organizations, are operating on the basis of up-to-date and relevant information. A solid information base should include comprehensive data on the local labour force. Ottawa's Hidden Workforce was path-breaking in that it looked beyond official statistics and inventoried the unofficially un- and underemployed. In so doing, it identified significant underutilised and untapped capacity, as well as considerable mismatch between existing programs and need. For example, the study suggests that 70 percent of the region's 145,000 unemployed and underemployed people are not eligible to participate in publicly funded workforce adjustment programs – they don't even show up on the public policy radar screen. Incomplete estimates of the size and composition of a municipality's un- and underemployed population make it difficult to design effective employment transition and integration programs. Better data, along with critical assessment of the strengths and limitations of existing programs, can encourage the establishment of effective locally based initiatives. CED organizations, because they are present in their communities, have much to offer in this regard.

Other key information is an inventory of job vacancies, as well as community-based "early warning" systems that can help identify companies that may be in trouble. RESO, a major CED organization in Montreal, developed a capacity with local stakeholders to detect firms in trouble and, through a broad community process, was able to stem the tide of exiting businesses and retain the jobs at risk (Perry, Lewis, and Fontan, 1993).

Third, information should include the various types of training, skill development, and CED supports available in the municipality. The list should include both traditional sources of training and non-traditional community-based supports. The information should be reviewed regularly by all stakeholders with a view to identify changing needs, emerging trends (both demographic and job-related), and gaps in service. Finally, all stakeholders should invest some resources in tracking best practice in other municipal jurisdictions. The Federation of Canadian Municipalities (FCM) could play a key role in disseminating best practice to its members, linking various municipal and other stakeholders, and highlighting lessons learned in different municipal contexts. This would be a logical extension of the leadership FCM has shown at an international level and would also build on its current policy statement on economic development.

POSSIBLE ROLES FOR MUNICIPALITIES

Markell (1998) identifies a range of roles for municipal governments, from minimal to extensive involvement. Table 2 was constructed from discussions with successful Canadian CED organizations and municipal officials and a review of the literature. She found Canadian examples at every level.

FROM PILOT PROJECTS TO DELIVERY SYSTEMS: WHAT WOULD AN URBAN CED SYSTEM LOOK LIKE?

Community economic development, whether in Canada or overseas, has moved beyond the experimental stage. Practitioners and decision-makers are recognizing that the myriad projects that have been "seeded" over the years, through charitable grant-making and publicly funded programs, are taking root, and the beginnings of a CED system are emerging. Recent experiences in Nova Scotia and Newfoundland sug-

Table 2

Municipal Government Role in CED	Canadian Examples
ENCOURAGE AND RECOGNIZE – – Write letters of support to funders – Recognize CED volunteers and organizations – Provide information	Most municipalities Victoria: Mayor wrote a letter of support for Youth Employment Pilot Project and spoke at Official Opening.
PLAN AND COLLABORATE – – Invite CED groups and community associations to participate in municipal economic planning – Facilitate planning among CED groups	City of York: Developed an economic strategy involving all community sectors Cambridge: CEO of CODA invited to sit on three major committees of council, including Economic Development Council. Revelstoke: Economic development strategy is called a "CED strategy."
PURCHASE GOODS AND SERVICES FROM CED BUSINESSES – – Ensure CED organizations are invited to tender on municipal contracts – Give priority to local businesses	Edmonton/Hamilton/Halifax: Purchased recycling services from CED groups Saskatoon: Purchased tree banding kits Halifax: Purchased janitorial services and painting of city buildings
INNOVATE WITH TRADITIONAL MUNICIPAL TOOLS – – Use zoning bylaws to preserve industrial land – Issue permits for street use – Enter into agreements with developers for training and employment programs	Vancouver: Agreements with developers of GM Place and Convention Centre for training and employment programs.
FACILITATE LINKAGES, CONVENE STAKEHOLDERS – – Bring groups together – Provide meeting space and publicity	Victoria: Youth Employment Pilot Project and CED Network Toronto: Kensington Market Vermi-Composting Project.
INVEST STAFF TIME IN CED PROJECTS - – Second or free up staff time to participate in CED projects – Enable staff to participate in committees or project advisory boards	Ottawa-Carleton: Funding for CED consultant within an economic development corporation. Toronto: Planning staff manages development corporation, housing business incubator, and CED projects. Victoria: Administered Phase One of Youth Employment Pilot Project. Halifax: Social planning staff time on HRDA in early years.

Table 2   continued

Municipal Government Role in CED	Canadian Examples
PROVIDE INDIRECT FUNDING FOR CED ORGANIZATIONS – – Make available municipal land or buildings for CED purposes – Issue charitable receipts for donations to CED groups – Reduce the cost of business licenses	Saskatoon: Free rent in municipal building for Quint Development Corporation Toronto: Use of two City buildings for incubator run by Toronto Community Ventures Victoria: Provided charitable receipt for donated rent of YEPP office (one month)
FUND LOCAL CED ORGANIZATIONS – – Provide core funding, preferably on a long-term basis	Montreal/Québec City/Sherbrooke: 33 percent of core funding of Community Development Economic Corporations (CDEC). Municipalities in Nova Scotia.
PARTNER WITH OTHER FUNDERS – – Enter into new funding arrangements with other levels of government, whether loans or guarantees	Montreal: Tripartite agreements to fund CEDCs (1984-92: $8.4 million) County of Cape Breton: Put up loan guarantee to enable New Dawn to purchase Sydney Radar Station. Revelstoke: Financed start-up costs of Revelstoke Community Forest Corporation

INNOVATE AND LEAD –

– Use a combination of instruments and tools including use of tax system, creation of local investment funds, and investments in electronic and communications infrastructure

gest a way forward. Through federal-provincial agreements, all levels of government, including municipalities, are contributing to the costs of creating and maintaining CED infrastructure. In Nova Scotia, Regional Development Authorities (RDA) receive modest core funding (one-third federal, one-third provincial, and the remainder split among the various municipalities within the administrative area served by the RDA). Incentives for local investment funds have been created through the provincial tax system, and the first of several local investment pools were created on Isle Madame in Cape Breton. Residents of the island were encouraged to invest a total sum of $150,000 in exchange for a 30 percent provincial tax credit, a 20 percent provincial guarantee if investments failed, and RRSP-eligible shares. More of these investment funds are being replicated in other parts of the province.

Recognizing the need for skilled CED practitioners, the province encouraged the creation of a diploma course in CED. Centres like Acadia University and St Francis Xavier University have a long tradition in CED and co-operative studies, while the University College of Cape Breton has launched an MBA specializing in CED. In addition to the development of courses in CED, it is hoped that the various educational institutions will continue to support applied research at the community level. While largely provincially supported, the most successful RDAs have worked hard to ensure municipal involvement and financial support.

FUNDING THE GROWTH OF CED
IN CANADA

If CED is to be effective and sustainable it must be adequately funded. A three-point strategy for funding CED in Canada would go a long way to ensuring the long-term sustainability of the sector (Born, 1999).

The first strategy is to help emerging CED organizations with *core administrative and development costs*. These costs would be covered for a renewable two-year term with a possible fifth year should there be unusual circumstances. In exchange for this funding, CED organizations would be required to evaluate their effectiveness using a standard evaluation tool, work with two mentor organizations, and have an approved development plan based on best-practice principles with measurable milestones. Two-thirds of the capital for this funding would be raised by various levels of government, including municipal governments, and one-third from private foundations or corporations. The net result is that CED organizations would be able to enhance their capacity in a strategic manner and achieve a sustainable scale.

The second strategy is to help CED organizations to access pools of *capital that would assist in starting or growing enterprises*, such as community loan funds for low-income entrepreneurs, capital to purchase the assets for a community-owned business, or capital to purchase an existing enterprise important to the development of a community. This fund would give CED organizations access to patient and understanding capital as they use the entrepreneurial talents of their community for the common good. The recent paper developed by Revenue Canada suggests foundations are able to use capital to back these types of investments. There are already some foundations or church-based investment organizations doing this type of work, and these groups could pool their efforts to achieve greater impact. However, the financial leverage of our major institutions – churches and other religious groups, pension funds, trade unions, foundations, municipal governments, credit unions, labour-sponsored venture capital funds, and large nonprofit organizations – have not been brought to bear to enable community-based investment funds to achieve critical mass (Jackson, 1998).

The third strategy is to help CED organizations raise *capital for reserves* and/or special projects. This would work in two ways. First, a pool of money needs to be made available to organizations embarking on a capital fundraising campaign. The money would equal no more than 10 percent of the projected campaign and would be repayable over the campaign pledge period. This would enable CED organizations to invest in fundraising and avoid the Catch-22 of needing money to raise money. The second approach would be to provide matching grants to create endowments for CED organizations, possibly under the leadership of a community foundation. The funder, for instance, might provide three dollars for every dollar the organization invests. This would encourage organizations to build reserve funds for future initiatives. Once again, municipal governments could be active funders. They can also use this model to fund other not-for-profit initiatives.

CONCLUSION

For much of the 1990s, businesses in the service, information, and communication technology sectors created thousands of new jobs and infrastructure in the largest Canadian cities, and they offer the potential for job creation in a number of rural towns and villages. But not all Canadian communities will have a call centre installed in their midst, and not all Canadians will participate in the promised prosperity. For those regions and neighbourhoods that find themselves excluded, the choices are stark. But by mobilizing the resources and assets they do have, and by negotiating trade-offs in a civil way among various sectors and stakeholders, community economic development can offer constructive development strategies for municipalities.

CED is a comprehensive approach to tackling the problems of exclusion and community disempowerment. Depending on the human and natural resources of a municipality, the specific challenges it faces as well as opportunities that present themselves, solutions can cut across a wide range of sectors. In addition to broad-based efforts to alleviate poverty (as in the example of Kitchener-Waterloo or St. John, NB), CED may be one of several mechanisms that municipalities can use to address issues such as urban food security (by linking rural food producers directly to large urban markets), the integration of diverse populations (New Canadians, First Nations, women, the disabled, and youth), homelessness, creating environmentally sustainable communities and mobilizing new sources of capital from within the community.

There is much that municipalities can do to support community economic renewal. They can:

- support networks of CED practitioners and join multi-stakeholder roundtables or CED committees;
- advocate new policies and regulations at the provincial and federal levels, introduce new policies and regulations within their own jurisdiction that remove barriers to CED, and promote jobs and the creation of community wealth;
- help create and sustain new funding and investment vehicles (loan loss reserves, guarantees, community loan, and investment funds) with other funding partners;
- show leadership and be prepared to take risks;
- commit to the long-term and learn from best practice.

Together, citizens from various backgrounds and with diverse interests need to revive a vision of cities that are inclusive places of democracy, where citizens can engage in meaningful economic and social activity. Creating strong and vibrant local economies that maintain and build upon local assets (including people) and that have something to trade in a global marketplace is a smart strategy for the new millennium.

10 Urban Issues and New
Public Policy Challenges:
The Example of Public
Consultation Policy in Montreal

PIERRE HAMEL

In the last few years, urban neighbourhoods and in particular city centres have been confronted with challenges that had not been anticipated either by planners or by elites. At a time when new responsibilities for the management of public services and for local economic development are being thrust upon municipalities, cities must reconsider their institutional framework in order to adapt to the new urban reality (Petitet, 1998). Moreover, cities have to redefine the terms of their involvement in urban affairs. How do these changes contribute to the development of a new type of management? If it is true that since the beginning of the 1980s, municipal leeway has had the tendency to increase, this phenomenon is part of a transformation of intervention. What role do citizens play in this regard? Does the issue of local democracy remain a pertinent issue when we review the prevailing institutional arrangements? Finally, what can we make of the institutional innovations elaborated by cities in order to encourage the involvement of citizens in urban development and planning? Do these mechanisms contribute to a democratization of public management?

In order to better situate these questions in their politico-institutional context, I have chosen to consider the example of the public consultation policy that was instituted by the Montreal municipal administration at the end of the 1980s. Similar to what has been seen in several cities in Europe and in North America, the City of Montreal put into place mechanisms of public debate in order to encourage the involvement of the local population in urban affairs. Although this initiative began considerably later in Montreal than in most other large North American agglomerations, it included, nonetheless, some interesting aspects. First, this policy answers a social demand that goes back to the beginning of the 1960s. In this way it allows us to assess the validity of the political choices – as well as some internal and external resistance within the politico-administrative system – in light of the social expectations. Furthermore, it is part of a reform process of the entire municipal administration of which it also illustrates the limits. Finally, by revising the prevailing rules, it reveals the tensions that characterize local power, allowing the main instigators of urban development and urban management – professionals, developers, municipal civil servants, representatives of the senior levels of government, the municipal elected officials, the community organizations – to compromise.

In order to shed some light on the issues related to the setting up of Montreal's public consultation policy as a tool of planning and citizen involvement, I have divided the following chapter into three parts. In the first place, I will specify some elements of the problematic in order to focus the relevance of the questions related to public consultation in relation to the emergence of a new type of management that rests on a "new political culture." Then, I will consider the political and institutional aspects of the Montreal public consultation policy. Finally, I will return to the question of policy management from a perspective of democratizing planning and urban development in order to provide possible interpretations and some hypotheses.

PUBLIC CONSULTATION IN THE NEW POLITICAL CULTURE CONTEXT

The socioeconomic and politico-institutional changes that marked the local stage during the 1990s contributed to reviving the debate on the new models of regulation and their political significance (Stoker, 1998). If the role of public agencies, and particularly of municipalities, remains important, researchers have been less interested in examining this importance than in understanding the nature and the functioning of the mechanisms that have been set up. The recent changes related to the urban landscape and its multiple components (Caulfield and Peake, 1996) as well as those regarding management – notably the diversification of management models for public services and territory, such as privatization, nation-production, partnership, dialogue, etc. (Decoutère, Ruegg, and Joye, 1996; Graham et al., 1998) – are well documented. These studies allow us to understand the complexity of the transformations in progress, by considering contradictions that nourish and limit them simultaneously. Yet they give little attention to the significance of these transformations for the democratization of public management.

Indeed, within the context of late modernity, with the assertion of the pluralism of identities and belongings, democracy and its most fundamental requirements are confronted with a new regime of "production of legitimacy" (Fourniau, 1997). This new regime challenges the capacity of nation-states to define alone the general interest. It actively calls on a widened involvement of actors of the civil society. In my opinion, it is, above all, in relation to these issues of democracy that we must situate the "new" institutional mechanisms of urban management (e.g., public consultation) that, in order to arbitrate divergences or conflicts between interests that are more and more specialized and varied, municipalities resort to increasingly.

Without entering, for the moment, into a detailed examination of the theoretical and political problems raised by the institutional arrangements aimed at facilitating the nation-existence of multiculturalism and democracy (Leca, 1996), in the arbitration of conflicts, we must recognize that they converge around the emergence of a "new political culture." According to Beck (1992), this new reality is expressed by various forms of resistance from citizens and social movements in opposition to models of management and to authoritarian conceptions of democracy. It also corresponds both to a wider openness and to a specialization of the political fields, thus promoting reflexivity and diversification of the professional practices. Finally, it is characterized by negotiation processes and collaboration between public and private agents acting in a pragmatic fashion from within horizontally organized networks.

In this perspective and in order to understand how exchanges and power relations take place in the setting of a concrete democracy, it is necessary to break with the fiction of the official representation in which the politico-administrative system is understood to be the centre of the political sphere. Even though the political sphere formally remains organized in a hierarchical manner, it appears subject to various processes of democratization that modify power relations and introduce new rules:

As a consequence, political decision-making processes, no matter on what level they occur, can no longer be understood as the enforcement or implementation of a model determined in advance by some wise man or leader, whose rationality is not open to discussion and must be enforced even against the will and "irrational resistance" of subordinated agencies, interests and citizen's groups. Both the formulation of the program and the decision-making process, as well as the enforcing of those decisions, must rather be understood as a process of collective action (Crozier and Friedberg), and that means, even in the best case, collective learning and collective creation. This implies, however, that the official decision-making authority of political institutions is necessarily decentralized. The political administrative system then can no longer be the only or the central locus of political events. In tandem with democratization, networks of agreement and participation, negotiation, reinterpretation and possible resistance come into being across the formal horizontal and vertical structure of authorizations and jurisdictions (Beck, 1992: 191).

The emergence of a "new political culture" acknowledges the shift between, on one hand, a certain tradition, or even an ideological representation of the centralized operation of the political system, and, on the other hand, experimentation with social transactions, mediations, and exchanges within an open political public space. This automatically raises the question of governmentality, of its forms, and of its concrete modes within the whole society in general, including the local and the urban scenes.

Within the field of urban studies, the "new political culture" has attracted the attention of researchers and given place to multiple approaches. We can think of the analyses defined in terms of political networks (Le Galès and Thatcher, 1995), from those that turn to notions of governance (Cox, 1997) and urban regime (Lauria, 1997) to those that appeal to neo-institutionalism (Clarke, 1995). Beyond their divergences, these approaches reveal the attempts to explain the multiplicity of institutional logics that clash on the ground of urban development management: private logic through the neoliberal discourse and the ideology of privatization versus administrative or communitarian logic (Williams and Matheny, 1995).

The "substantial margin of initiative" (Gaudin and Novarina, 1997) or the new opportunities (Kaplan, 1995) for local authorities, from the 1980s onwards, do not necessarily imply that the power of local actors and of the political class active on the local scene in particular are enhanced. The new rules of competition on the international scale and the relative decline of state sovereignty in relation to the implementation of supranational mechanisms of coordination and control have indeed had the effects of intensifying competition at the local level (Kaplan, 1995) and of increasing the responsibilities of municipalities. This said, the constituent rules of economic development that grants precedence to privileged actors (Beauregard, 1993: 280) prevail nevertheless.

On that matter, if the capacity to influence investors goes along with pressures that may be exerted on them by local collectivities, the grounds for democracy maintain their importance. Indeed, the possibility of changing the culture of urban policies, either concerning the decisions to invest or the definition of social priorities, first goes through the mutual recognition of socio-political actors, the expression of their preferences, the transformation of conventions, and collective learning. These constitute a set of elements or of factors that are submitted to public debate and for which local democracy continues to act as a catalyst while constituting a convenient locus for the expression and the organization of social mediation.

This widened conception of local democracy does not imply that the institutions in which democracy are rooted do not undergo blocks or delays – therefore seeing their socio-political relevance lessened – notably because of transformations of urban reality. At the moment, this is the situation that prevails in Montreal – similar to what has been observed in several other metropolitan regions of North America: a decline in the demographic, economic, and political weight of the urban core has followed in the wake of urban sprawl and the development of the periphery. In practice and in terms of social representations, this has resulted in a loss of power for the central city, with the political actors unable to reach an agreement on the development of a system of political decision that would be more adequate at the metropolitan level (Léveillée, 1998).

However, in Montreal, although the institutional gaps that we have mentioned between the urban reality and the system of political representation that prevails at the metropolitan scale have repercussions on the content of local democracy in limiting both the scope and the context, they have not yet completely emptied the central city of its vitality. This is probably due to the fact that, contrary to what has been observed in several other Northeastern American cities, in Montreal the central city continues to play an important economic role in relation to the dynamism of the entire agglomeration.

Moreover, considering the new problems of social integration with which the urban environments must cope in this turn of the century, the urban scene and its democratic expression take on a new significance. If we consider the nature of social inequalities generated by the socioeconomic restructuring of the last years and the forms of segregation, exclusion, or "secession" that they introduce into the urban space – calling into question the principle of solidarity that prevailed between social classes during the industrial era (Donzelot and Jaillet, 1997) – the space of the central city remains highly relevant in order to review the processes of social recomposition that are taking place.

In this context, it appears impossible to ignore modes of citizen involvement in urban affairs. Of course, we no longer consider citizen involvement with the innocence that prevailed in the 1960s (Kotler, 1969). Thus, we no longer imagine that it is sufficient to encourage the establishment of self-management structures on the local scene in order to increase citizens' power. Some recent studies stress the fact that the setting up of these structures at the urban neighbourhood level does not necessarily result in a larger involvement of citizens. However, these studies also show that citizen involvement does not have any negative effects on management and on governmental efficiency (Wolman, 1995). Indeed, as they are recognized by the political elites and the municipal administrations, associations of citizens acquire, understandably, the status of partners. In the past, authorities often perceived these associations as enemies, today they see them more and more as allies (Thomas, 1983). In this context, one may argue that co-operation has replaced confrontation.

In relation to urban planning, however, one cannot yet affirm that citizen involvement has overcome the ambivalences and the ambiguousness that characterized it in the 1960s. Although involvement remains an essential component of the planning process, in the sense that it contributes to guaranteeing legitimacy within a democratic regime – thus contributing in a concrete manner both to the definition of social preferences (to reduce uncertainty, to construct compromises, or even consensus) and to the rise of local resistances – yet, at the same time, involvement is opposed to the nature of planning itself, which is based on scientific rationality and implies a discretionary leverage for planners to be efficient (Day, 1997).

The ambivalence of involvement resumes Lourau's (1969) analysis on the political level in reference, on one hand, to the offer that is made by the leaders and, on the other hand, to what is claimed by citizens. In each case, the notion of involvement has a different significance. When the ruling class speaks of involvement, it does not consider calling into question power relations, although this is first and foremost what is requested by citizens.[1]

Starting with local democracy as a way of preventing exclusion and social regression – in accordance with a certain conception of justice (Donzelot, 1995) – the extension of democracy is achieved, at least in part, through citizen involvement in urban affairs. It is in this perspective that the utility of the public consultation mechanisms to which the local authorities had recourse in Montreal from the end of the 1980s may be questioned.

In the literature on public consultation that has been produced in North America, it is generally recognized that public consultation is the most traditional method of citizen involvement. It is also recognized that its use is increasing at all levels of public management. Public opinion tends to consider the mechanisms of public consultation as a means for citizens to express their points of view and to influence policies (Checkoway, 1981). However, the literature also emphasizes the limits of these mechanisms as a method of citizen involvement.[2]

In terms of analyzing the utility of mechanisms of public consultation as a method of citizen involvement, two points of view prevail within the literature. A first point of view, which does not question the utility of public consultation, although it emphasizes its limits and its requirements, stresses the practical difficulties encountered by public administrators as well as by citizens. In this respect, researchers (Thibault, 1986) look first of all for technical, administrative, or legal arguments in order to suggest modifications aimed at improving the efficiency of these mechanisms, in relation to decision-making processes and the quality of citizen participation. In general, the approach of these researchers can be qualified as instrumentalist.

The other point of view considers these mechanisms from the perspective of channelling collective action for the benefit of the elites and of the power holders (Checkoway, 1981). Here, consultation serves above all to deactivate social protest. It can even give place to false representations and manipulations if it leads citizens to believe that they will be heard whereas, in reality, these mechanisms open the door first and foremost to experts and professionals. Consequently, public consultations have become a tool controlled by specialists. In fact, public consultations often drive citizens to appeal to measures of auto-control that do not serve their interests.[3]

Even if these two points of view focus on important and complementary aspects concerning the scope and limits of public consultation, they do not allow us to grasp the entire complexity of sociopolitical relations in which citizens, when they participate in the consultation process, become enmeshed inside as well as outside the institutional setting. In using public consultations as a means to express preferences with regard to planning and to urban development, citizens enter a process of social recognition: they contribute to the construction of a public tribune where it is possible to elaborate negotiated compromises that may influence decisions (Fourniau, 1997). Furthermore, public consultation is not a unique or exclusive stage. It has to be linked to the overall framework of the "new political culture." Thus, public consultation puts forward a set of new institutional devices that serve to redefine the legitimacy of public action.

Yet, this does not mean that public consultation completely escapes the power of mediators, defined as "agents that achieve the construction of the referential of a given policy" (Muller, 1990: 50). However, the mediators can never fully control the institutional space of public debate. This probably explains why the actors of urban movements that were opposed to institutionalized forms of involvement in the 1970s agreed to participate in them in the 1980s. By opting for a more pragmatic model of action (Hamel, 1995), these actors adjusted to the new political conjuncture and to the transformation of public management models.

Does public consultation lead to a democratization of public management – allowing citizens to participate in the development of urban projects while taking an active part in crucial decisions concerning development and implementation – or is it limited to encouraging the acceptability of a decision (Fourniau, 1997) for the benefit, above all, of mediators? In order to provide some answers to this question, we will examine in greater detail the policy of public consultation implemented by the municipal administration of Montreal at the end of the 1980s.

THE POLICY OF PUBLIC CONSULTATION ELABORATED BY THE CITY OF MONTREAL FROM AN INSTITUTIONAL PERSPECTIVE

The policy framework on public consultation, as formulated by the administration of the Montreal Citizen Movement (MCM)[4] in 1988, had three major objectives: 1) to encourage citizens to participate in public debates in order to reaffirm their sense of belonging to their neighbourhood and to their city; 2) to ensure that public consultation mechanisms be made available to all citizens, while including these mechanisms in a statutory and systematic way in the decision-making process; 3) to guarantee citizens the permanent right to voice their concerns by establishing this right in the city charter and by the adoption of a bylaw to this effect by the city council (Ville de Montréal, 1988: 8-9). In order to implement its policy framework on public consultation, the municipal administration used three complementary mechanisms. The first involved the creation of standing committees within the city council. Five committees[5] were thus set up with the mandate of studying matters related to their field of expertise, to hold public meetings on drafts, general policy statements, or draft bylaws, and to make recommendations to the city council (Ville de Montréal, 1995).

The second mechanism involved the creation of district advisory committees (DACs). The territory of the City of Montreal was divided into nine planning units called districts. For each district, the consultation policy recommended the setting up of advisory committees made up of the municipal councillors representing the electoral wards included in the district. Their role was to publicize questions related to urban development, the management of public services, and urban planning. Thus, the items that were always to be transmitted for discussion by the DACs, which held statutory monthly meetings, were specific urban planning matters such as area development plans and municipal projects requiring zoning revisions (Ville de Montréal, 1988: 13). At the DAC meetings, citizens had the opportunity to express their views. They could also present requests. They were hence able to influence the agenda of the meeting. Finally, the DAC had to make recommendations to the city's executive committee, which could decide whether or not to present the project in question to the city council.

The third mechanism involved the creation of the Bureau de consultation de Montréal (BCM). The BCM was an independent municipal organization, which called upon commissioners to conduct public hearings on specific projects, taking place within city limits. The BCM was connected to the Secretariat for administrative matters and was directly responsible to the city's executive committee. Thus, the matters on which the BCM held public consultations were chosen specifically at the behest of the executive committee. Modeled on the Bureau d'audiences publiques sur l'environnement (BAPE), the BCM followed formal procedures – including a code of deontology for its commissioners – to inform the population, gather its opinion, and make recommendations to the executive committee.[6]

To fully understand the nature of these three mechanisms, going beyond their performance and the politico-administrative problems related to their implementation, we must take into account several contextual factors as well as the organizational environment in which they took place. In more precise terms, the political choices made regarding this policy framework for public consultation come from the compromise that results from the restrictions on the policy stemming from municipal administration activities on the one hand and, on the other, the interests of socio-political actors to widen the policy.

At the end of the 1980s, as in the case of other public authorities, the Montreal municipal administration was confronted with the requirements of modernization. This resulted in a review of the strategic alliances that the municipal administration was maintaining with various categories of actors. While counting, notably, on public-private partnerships, the local administrators entered into a process of reviewing the distribution of responsibility in regard to the management of urban affairs. In this context, the business community and senior levels of government showed a new and more open attitude toward issues that they had so far disregarded. We can think of the problems of poverty of the local population within the central city as well as the issue of support to local economic development.

Another important aspect stems from the socio-cultural and the socio-political contexts within which the institutional reform of the involvement in planning and in urban development took place. Among the contextual elements in general, two, in my opinion, have contributed more directly to the definition of the context for the policy on public consultation: first, the social demands concerning popular involvement that go back at least to the 1960s and, second, the professional expertise concerning public consultation that took various forms from the 1970s onward.

The social demands concerning involvement in local management and their evolution since the beginning of the 1960s in the context of Montreal are well known. They gave place to numerous studies (McGraw, 1978; Godbout, 1983; Hamel, 1991; Morin and Rochefort, 1998). These studies have shed light on the transformation of these demands, their radicalization, and their politicization. Researchers have also emphasized the transformation of the collective action model to which the social movement actors and the local community in general contributed, given the nature of the contradictions to which they were confronted, and the choices that they made concerning issues of local democracy.

Regarding this matter, we can say that there has been a radical transformation of the initial collective action model. Leaving aside some ideological convictions and strategies oriented according to a "revolutionarist" conception of change, social actors have elaborated a number of pragmatic approaches dominated by dialogue, partnership, and the reaching of compromises.

On the local political scene, the MCM has carried a large part of these demands, in particular since the 1980s. Indeed, since its foundation, when it was the opposition party, the MCM associated itself with the demands of these groups and elaborated a participatory vision of local democracy. Thus, once in power, the MCM could not easily ignore demands coming from its social base. This explains, at least in part, the elaboration and the implementation of the policy framework on public consultation as a means of bringing the municipal administration and the citizens closer to each other.

We can say that the existence of professional expertise concerning public consultation prior to the reform elaborated by the municipal administration constitutes another important contextual factor. The City of Montreal would have not taken the direction that it did if it could not have relied on both this expertise and the lessons learned from previous experiences, in particular those in the environment and the planning fields. Indeed, through the amendment to the law on the quality of the environment in 1978 and through the creation of the BAPE the following year, the government of Québec has developed an original approach to environmental assessment, which includes a very broad definition of the notion of environment and the organization of public audiences aimed at informing the population and encouraging its involvement in the development of projects (Gariépy, 1997). It was because it could rely on this experience that the municipal administration of the MCM chose to forge ahead with its policy framework on public consultation.

In this respect, we may say that there exists in Québec a real culture of public consultation that has its own mentality, its own system of professional recognition, its own rules, and its own traditions. At least, this is what emerges from a series of interviews that we held, within the framework of the present research, with experts on public consultation. In fact, these experts generally agree on the definition of public consultation. For them, public consultation is, above, all a "mechanism of public involvement that aims at collecting citizen's values and opinions in order to orient decisions of the elected representatives" (Trân, 1998: 2). From this point of view, there is no doubt that public consultation is above all a tool of management even while recognizing that it corresponds to the emergence of new social and cultural values, notably in the environmental field.

The expertise in public consultation developed through experience in the environmental and the urban planning fields[7] contributed to the emergence of a set of skills, methodologies, and procedures – what some experts call "rules of the art" – that can be transposed to various situations. The rules described by Yergeau and Ouimet (1984), which outline the main requirements of processes of public consultation (clear and known procedures, accessible, available and complete information, neutrality of commissioners, recognition of public audience results in the decision making), are now accepted by the majority of the experts interviewed and even form the object of a broad consensus.

These rules also merge, in general, with the conditions for successful public consultation, on which the majority of experts agree. On this matter, four main conditions have been identified by experts:

First of all, the process of public consultation must be credible. Otherwise citizens will feel that they are being manipulated. Secondly, initiators of the public consultation must appear sincerely committed. Their decision must consider the results of the public consultation. Otherwise, citizens will have wasted their time and their energy and will lose interest in the process. Thirdly, actors that take part in the consultation must show transparency. Discussions must focus on the proposed project rather than on the legitimacy of the proposition. Finally, there must be a follow-up of the public consultation, so that citizens feel that they brought a meaningful contribution to the development of the project (Trân, 1998: 9).

Furthermore, during our interviews, some experts mentioned that there has been a change of mentality regarding public consultation, on the part of the developers or promoters as well as from the community. Thus, among representatives of the business community, the possibility of gaining benefits from these processes is now willingly considered. As mentioned by one of the experts interviewed:

I think that firms participate with more serenity. Now, there is a whole industry that has been created around consultations. It contributes to help leaders of firms to be more serene when they are obliged to participate in public audiences. Regarding this matter, we can say that firms are more flexible than they were (Trân, 1998: 3).

For representatives of the community, public consultation modifies some strategies of action. Even though, in fact, public consultation does not eliminate power inequalities, it contributes, in a positive manner, to the formulating of compromises. Furthermore, public consultations can also encourage the mobilization of citizens.

These contextual elements do not, by themselves, explain the intentions of the political elite and of the municipal administrative officials nor do they explain the nature of the changes occurring concerning public management to which the policy framework on public consultation must be associated. However, they do permit the delineation of the relative conditions for the elaboration of this policy. The social demand for democratization of municipal management, on one hand, and the possibility of resorting to a certain expertise or even to the existence of a Québécois "culture" of public consultation, on the other hand, simultaneously provided the elected municipal representatives with both guarantees and objective interests to commit themselves to the path of institutional reform. However, as illustrated by the electoral results of 1994, these reforms were plagued by pitfalls.

PUBLIC CONSULTATION
AND ISSUES OF LOCAL DEMOCRACY

The MCM elaborated the policy framework on public consultation. The party remained in power for two terms, before being ousted from city hall by a new political party – Vision Montreal (VM) – after the autumn 1994 elections. Originally, the MCM had defined itself as a left-wing municipal party, with a socialist ideological orientation (Thomas, 1997). Even though, through time, its program and its perspectives of action gave place to – in the case of the principal leaders – a pragmatic attitude, the MCM nonetheless continued to pursue a model, if not an ideology, of a democratized municipal administration. In this respect, public consultation was seen by many members of the MCM as a privileged means to realize the objectives of bringing the municipal administration and the citizens closer to each other.

From the day Pierre Bourque stepped into the city hall in 1994, the new mayor put into question the policy framework on public consultation. He abolished the BCM. The DACs were replaced by sixteen district councils (conseils de quartier), whose mandate is more limited. For example, it is no longer obligatory for the district councils to examine zoning modifications. Nevertheless, they must hold public meetings on city programs, interventions, or activities that affect the neighbourhood and on any other document that the executive committee submits to them. Finally, the responsibilities of the city council's five committees have been reviewed and redistributed between two committees that continue to relate to the council and that focus on the following areas: 1) administration and services to citizens; 2) finances and economic development. In addition, a committee on urban development was created – which met on average twice a month – to examine all regulation projects related to urban development.[8] This committee is directly responsible to the executive committee, which sets its mandates. Even though the policy framework on public consultation has undergone a thoroughgoing review by the new municipal administration – the mechanisms set up by the MCM having been either abandoned or amended – public consultation has not disappeared from the area of local politics.[9] However, its concrete modes have been transformed by several factors, starting with that of the political orientations of the new administration.

Nevertheless, even though the policy framework on public consultation was only in effect for a relatively short period of time, it has generated unexpected effects in regard to the management of urban services and to urban planning. For instance, public consultation brings to light the limits of sectorial management in relation to the organization and the functioning of the municipal administration of Montreal. Indeed, it is mainly the results of the public consultation on municipal management that led the executive committee, in January 1994, to create a coordination committee considering local management in order to elaborate an integrated model of deconcentration, decentralization, and territorial management. The study completed by this committee has resulted in a major reform project that recommends a revision of "the general architecture of territorial management" in order to overcome the gaps between, on one hand, the "operational requirements related to the benefits of direct service to the population" and, on the other, constraints that come from the management system (Ville de Montréal, 1994), which is organized in a centralized manner.

If it is premature to establish a direct relation between a reform of this type and the effects of public consultation on the transformation of the politico-administrative organization of the municipality, it is difficult to ignore the ties that exist between them. Furthermore, we can hypothesize that the implementation of new institutional mechanisms of public consultation has contributed to the review of the normative framework of urban development, including the responsibilities of the municipal administration and the perceptions or representations of the population regarding the issues of urban development.

This ethico-political aspect, which results from the implementation of the policy framework on public consultation, is not the only one that must be taken into account. Several other aspects – internal as well as external to the municipal administration – deserve to be closely studied. Given the importance of the issues surrounding the democratization of public management, the experience of public consultation invites the review of the distribution of responsibilities between professionals hired by municipalities, consultants, elected representatives, and citizens. The "new political culture" evoked above entails a redefinition of the parameters of public management. It also results in a transformation of professional practices regarding urban planning and urban management.

If we go back to the middle of the nineteenth century and consider the transformation of urban agglomerations in North America, it is difficult to define a unique model of decision-making concerning urban policies (Monkkonen, 1988: 217). Compromises that prevail on the local scene call on multiple rationalities that encourage, most of the time, the economic elites. Yet, this is not always foreseeable.

How are compromises constructed in urban affairs? What role does the municipal administration play in this matter? In what measure have the institutional mechanisms of public consultation encouraged the emergence of coalitions that are less exclusive in terms of citizen involvement in urban affairs and in terms of social integration? Have these mechanisms really contributed to broadening the public debate? If so, what are the terms: principles of modernization or of democratization?

Just like the institutional innovations in citizen involvement that were set up in other municipalities, the policy of public consultation elaborated by the City of Montreal has proved to be fragile. Two contextual variables greatly limited its scope. First, it took place within a system of management organized in a sectorial way. This organizational model is, in large part, incompatible with "territorial" management, which corresponds better to the procedural requirements for public consultation. This is, in fact, what was seen by the general Secretariat of the municipal administration shortly before the elections of 1994 (Ville de Montréal, 1994). Second, concerning the political aspect, these mechanisms of public consultation exist within a centralizing system of hierarchized power in which the executive committee and the mayor in particular maintain prerogatives similar to those of the ministerial party in a parliamentary regime of the British type. The policy framework could not impose a modification of this centralized political system. Thus, the public consultation had to fit into the processes of traditional political representation rather than the opposite. Limits were thus inherent in the process from the start, notably with regard to the capacity of citizens to influence political decisions.

Within planning theory, the communicative approach (Forester, 1989) aims at understanding the transformations of planning practices that have occurred over the last years. While stressing the intangible aspects of these practices and while showing that within the context of advanced complex societies it is more and more difficult to express the general interest in an authoritative manner, the communicative approach emphasizes the relevance of the citizen and of public debate from a new perspective. Some insisted, however, on the fact that the communicative approach does not take sufficient account of the institutional context within which these practices take place (Innes, 1994). This point of view focuses our attention on the multiple dimensions bound up with the institutional issues and by institutionalization. In other words, planners' good intentions are not sufficient. The institutional setting within which planners evolve and its capacity to encourage some meaningful relations – not only with the municipal elected officials and with the developers but also with the associations of civil society – also need to be taken into account. In this respect, the ethics of the discussion calls for a political or associative public space (Offe, 1997) that cannot result only from initiatives or responsibilities of the municipal administration but to which the municipal administration must contribute in a meaningful manner.

From this perspective, concerning the concrete scope of the democratization of public management, the policy of public consultation elaborated by the municipal administration of Montreal under the guidance of the MCM includes both positive and negative aspects. For now, the assessment that can be drawn remains mitigated. The new institutional mechanisms from this policy constitute innovations whose scope remains uncertain. These mechanisms can help the expression of social identity but they can also contribute, above all, to the deployment of an instrumental rationality leading paradoxically to the reinforcement of the legitimacy of the political elite.

No single conclusion can be drawn from the experiences that followed the implementation of these mechanisms. Some requirements for the organization of public consultations are now well known: diffusion of information, the role and the importance of hearings in the organization of public debates, the kinds of technical and financial support that are necessary to provide to citizens in order to facilitate their involvement, the requirements concerning the transparency of the procedures, the role of expertise, etc. Our understanding of the ways in which public consultations should be organized has been greatly improved. At the same time, we are a lot less naive about what we may expect from public consultations.

If the public consultations that took place in Montreal since the end of the 1980s provided a new tribune for a number of local actors and hence contributed to the modernization of the management of urban affairs, they had a limited impact on the democratization of urban planning. It is probable that important ethical and cultural dimensions were set aside by the traditional vision of urban affairs management that lies at the heart of the public consultation policy. Nevertheless, the debates stimulated by the policy statement on public consultation, by the mechanisms created for its implementation, and by their questioning by the City of Montreal still contributed, albeit ironically, to putting urban affairs back on the agenda.

NOTES

1 The term "involvement" conceals and allows to not distinguish between two types of social demands: the first one issues from the power and the dominant ideology, the other coming from social layers in quest of

power. Behind a unique strategy, taken by the whole of society as a "community," "involvement" implies in fact two strategies: one aims at preserving and improving the existing order, the other is a request of excluded social layers to obtain their share of power (Lourau, 1969: 89–90).

2 "Public hearings are commonly viewed as a way for citizens to express their views and influence policies and plans of government agencies. In practice, however, this is not always the case. What research has been done on the subject indicates several shortcomings of public hearings as a participation method" (Checkoway, 1981: 567).

3 Regarding this matter, Richardson, Sherman, and Gismondi (1993: 13) recall Adam Ashfort's point of view: "Ashfort believes that governments establish public hearings to placate the public by making people believe they have power that they do not have. Thus, if citizens take part in a public hearing believing that they can influence its outcome, they unwittingly participate in their own subjugation."

4 This political party was created in 1974 with the support of the union movement, the social movements, the Parti Québécois, and various progressive forces. It remained the opposition party until November 1986, when it won the municipal elections.

5 These committees focused on the following areas: 1) planning and housing; 2) administration and quality of services; 3) economic development; 4) culture, recreation, and community development; 5) environment and public works. These committees had been set up in 1987. Their inclusion in the consultation policy confirmed their status and their importance within the municipal administration. "From June 1987 to November 1994, the committees held public meetings to examine general policy statements" (Ville de Montréal, 1995: 9).

6 Let's note that the BCM elaborated three different types of procedures according to the size of projects and to the issues at stake: a regular procedure, a simplified procedure, and a particular procedure. Moreover, it is necessary to mention that the regular procedure included four stages: announcing the public consultation; making the documentation of the project available to the public; a public hearing (which included a question period), usually following the filing of a brief on behalf of those who want to participate in the audition; the writing of a report by the commissioners, to be transmitted to the executive committee.

7 Since 1979, the Bill 125 regional development obliges the regional county municipalities (RCM) and municipalities to consult the population on the content of city plans.

8 Before, this was done by the DACs.

9 Before the refusal of the municipal administration in 1996 to organize a

public consultation in order to study a real-estate development project on the Villa Maria site in Notre-Dame-de-Grâce district, citizens decided to organize their own consultation. A similar process was also undertaken by citizens in 1997 in order to oppose the transformation of the Jean-Talon metro station into a supermarket by the Loblaw company.

11 From the National to the Local: Recent Lessons for Economic Development Policy

DAVID A. WOLFE

INTRODUCTION

Discussions of economic development policy in Canada seem locked to an unnecessary extent in past debates over industrial policy, especially those that occurred in the 1970s and 1980s. To an inexplicable degree, both advocates of a more interventionist role for government and their critics remain strongly attached to views that were common in this earlier period, but seem quite dated in the new century. The old debate on industrial policy probably reached its low point in the work of the Royal Commission on the Economic Union and Development Prospects for Canada, where the policy divisions were strongly reflected in the different views of the economics and the political science streams of the research program. The report itself was deeply ambivalent over the meaning of the term, with the final text presenting two radically different conceptions and, ultimately, rejecting the use of industrial policy.

Current perspectives on the question seem to overlook the degree to which perspectives on economic development policy have changed dramatically in the past decade, especially in Europe and the US, and the degree to which the locus of attention has shifted from the national to the regional and local levels. In the Canadian context, our overwhelming preoccupation with things federal has led to a tendency to overlook the considerable degree of experimentation that has occurred at both the provincial and the local level over the past decade. For the most part, these new initiatives have been interpreted as a new development

sui generis, or as part of the growing decentralization and fragmentation of the federation – itself the result of the decline of state capacity
in Canada generated by the broader forces of globalization and conti-
nentalization.

At the same time, the debate has failed to notice a subtle but important shift in the terms with which it is engaged in other countries, especially in Europe, but also in the US. Over the course of the past decade,
there has been a shift in focus (both in policy and in academic terms)
from industrial policy to innovation policy. This reflects a change in
both the relevant understanding of the process of economic growth
and industrial development and also a shift in thinking about the most
effective points of leverage for policy to influence that process.

In Europe, the shift has been matched by a growing interest in, and
involvement with, innovation policy at the regional, as opposed to the
national or supranational level. This reflects the growing interest in
and attention to a Europe of the Regions. One of the offshoots of this
development has been a series of initiatives launched co-operatively by
DGs[1] XIII and XVI of the European Commission. Under the terms of
Article 10 of the European Regional Development Fund (ERDF) and the
Fourth Regional Technology Development Framework Program, they
have sponsored a series of innovative actions to foster greater innovation at the regional level. These initiatives have evolved over the course
of the past decade from Regional Technology Plans (RTP) to Regional
Innovation Strategies (RIS) and Regional Innovation and Technology
Transfer Strategies (RITTS). The interest in innovation at the regional
level is matched to some degree by a growing fascination with the role
of clusters as incubators for dynamic and innovative industries at the
regional and local level in North America. This fascination has sparked
a growing interest in the question of how to seed the growth of new
clusters.

This paper examines the nature of these innovative actions and documents the implications of this double shift in focus – from industrial
policy to innovation strategies and from the national level to both the
regional level and the local level. It concludes with a brief evaluation
of the lessons Canada can draw from both recent European experience
and local North American experiments and with implications of such
examples for a rethinking of economic development policy in the
decentralized context of the Canadian federation.

THE DEBATE OVER INDUSTRIAL POLICY

The issue of industrial policy emerged at the centre of the policy agenda during the 1970s. Under the combined pressure of trade liberaliza-

tion from the successive round of GATT negotiations running from
1947 to the Tokyo Round of the 1970s, the industrial structure of
national economies was exposed to more intensive international competition. This occurred in tandem with the slowdown in the rate of economic growth, with declining productivity levels, and with rising
unemployment resulting from the exhaustion of the growth potential
in the postwar paradigm of standardized mass production (Wolfe,
1983). In the face of these trends, virtually all the industrial countries
became preoccupied with the issue of maintaining employment
through the difficult and costly process of structural adjustment. Furthermore, the declining efficacy of Keynesian macroeconomic policies
led many governments to explore a wide array of alternative policy
instruments in response to this challenge. The attraction of industrial
policies was also stimulated by the increasing fascination with the
more interventionist approach to economic recovery and growth – in
comparison to that of the Anglo-Saxon democracies – pursued after
the war in France and Japan (Chandler, 1986: 171).

Most commentators view industrial policies as involving some sub-
set of the broad range of economic policies pursued by government in
the industrial countries. In his overview of the subject for the Macdonald Royal Commission on the Economic Union and Development
Prospects for Canada, André Blais defined it as "the set of selective
measures adopted by the state to alter industrial organization." Blais
noted that this and similar definitions are usually applied to the manufacturing sector, but they should apply equally across the primary,
secondary, and tertiary sectors of the economy. The various instruments deployed to implement industrial policies include tax incentives,
direct financial subsidies, technical assistance, government procurement, import protection, and, occasionally, public enterprise (Blais,
1986a: 4–5; Leiss and Smith, 1990: 114).

While this definition is reasonably clear, further confusion arises
over the distinction between industrial policies and industrial strategy,
while other authors focus more on the problem of industrial adjustment for, or assistance to, declining sectors (Chandler, 1986; Trebilcock, 1986; Tupper, 1982). A useful analytical distinction between
these four terms is offered in a study done for the Ontario Economic
Council by Paul Davenport and his collaborators. They provide a helpful set of definitions for distinguishing between these various terms.
Industrial policy is "any government program that directly affects the
economic activity of an industry, company or plant. Industrial policies
are designed to change economic structures, behaviour, and/or performance." They distinguish between two types of industrial policies:
interventionist or non-interventionist. "Interventionist policies can be

classified as innovative, defensive and adaptive. Innovative policies promote growth and development, primarily by fostering the adoption and diffusion of new product and process technologies; defensive policies are reactive in their attempt to protect firms, sectors or regions against undesired economic changes; and adaptive policies attempt to ease the adjustment process by reallocating capital and human resources away from declining economic activities" (Davenport et al., 1982: 1–2).

Another definition that has attracted a great deal of attention is provided in Michael Atkinson and Bill Coleman's study of industrial policy. They reduce the broad typology outlined above to two basic categories: anticipatory and reactive. Anticipatory policy emphasizes intrusive policy instruments that are integrated with each other and focus on promoting a structural transformation of the economy, while reactive policy is organized around the immediate needs of specific firms and tries to promote a climate attractive to investment. The goal in industrial policy is to manage the changes faced by industry and allow for an orderly process of economic adjustment in response to the pressures of industrial restructuring.

The key issue faced by industrial policy, according to Atkinson and Coleman, is which aspect of the objectives to stress: anticipatory policy tries to stress the adjustment aspect, while reactive policy focuses more on the protectionist element. The second dimension along which industrial policies can be distinguished is the extent of intrusiveness. Reactive policy tends to operate more at the framework level, by deploying a broad range of general measures, including tax, subsidies, and protectionist trade programs to create an appropriate investment climate. Anticipatory policy focuses more on selective intervention to influence the process of industrial restructuring aimed at the needs or requirements of specific industrial sectors. Finally, the policy modes can be distinguished by their relative degree of integration. Reactive policy tends to consist of a series of ad hoc measures focused on individual firms or sectors as the case demands, while anticipatory policy is more comprehensive and attempts to evaluate all firms and sectors against a broad set of bureaucratic and political criteria. Atkinson and Coleman make it clear that they are describing ideal types that are not always found in the policy world in their pure or "ideal" form (1989: 23–5).

During the period of greatest economic adjustment in Canada, from the onset of the oil crisis in 1973 to the end of the post-free-trade recession in 1993–94, the question of industrial policy was debated intensely. In the eyes of most commentators, Canada primarily pursued the reactive option at the national or economy-wide level. The policy tools that were deployed consisted of various forms of assistance to facilitate industrial adjustment. However, this approach has been criticized from both sides of the political spectrum. From the left, the primary criticism focuses on the failure to adopt a more innovative or anticipatory approach and the repeated inability to formulate a more coherent industrial strategy, despite the series of consultative exercises launched in the late 1970s and the infamous mega-projects episode of the early 1980s.[2] In the words of one critic, the upshot of this failure indicated that successive federal governments in Canada "simply lacked the political will to bite the industrial strategy bullet and move beyond the traditional economic policies that ... shaped the present chronic export, balance of payments, and employments crises" (Williams, 1983: 166), a criticism that is not significantly different than the defence cited above.

The critique from the right is equally categorical in its judgement. Most of the industrial policies deployed in this period (aside from tariffs) were various forms of adjustment policies. The onset of stagflation in the 1970s increased the pressure on governments to provide more focused firm-based and sectoral adjustment policies. Among the most visible of these was the assistance afforded to large corporations on the verge of collapse, including Chrysler, Massey-Ferguson, and the notorious Maislin Trucking; the unending subsidies to Canada's two aircraft assemblers after their absorption into the Canada Development Corporation; and the broader assistance to restructuring in a number of vulnerable sectors, such as textiles, shipbuilding, and pulp and paper, under the auspices of the Industry and Labour Adjustment Program and the Canadian Industrial Renewal Board. In the eyes of the critics, the original rationale for creating many of these programs had been lost by the early 1980s, and the ability of government to control their cost abandoned (Ritchie, 1983: 43–5; Trebilcock et al., 1985).

Some academic analysts have pointed to a wider range of factors that constrained the scope for Canadian industrial policy in this period. In her analysis of the *political* factors that explain the pattern of state intervention in providing assistance to industry, Marsha Chandler concluded that Canada lacked most of the key institutional features, on both the public and private sides, found in those countries that adopted more effective forms of public assistance to industry. On the bureaucratic side, the federal government lacked both a single ministry with a strong interest in playing the lead in this area and an effective political constituency that would give it the incentive to do so. On the private side, the organization of the banking system did not provide the mechanism for the financial sector to play the lead role in promoting industrial adjustment the way it did in some European countries. The fragmented nature of both the business organizations and the labour movement also tended to produce endless "wish lists" of sector or firm-oriented subsidies, rather than a cohesive framework, as in the case of the Tier I and Tier II consultations of the late 1970s. In conclusion she argued

In sum, Canada's institutional structures, banking system and public-private sector relationship decrease the probability that a state-led adaptive capacity will be developed. Organization at the federal level, the absence of adequate federal-provincial arrangements, and the autonomous banking system make it less likely that restructuring policies will be supplied; the fragmented organization of private-sector interests makes it unlikely that such policies will be demanded (Chandler, 1986: 205).

Atkinson and Coleman effectively concur in their detailed study of industrial policy in the 1980s. The dominant factor in explaining the inability to forge a consensus around a broadly based, anticipatory industrial strategy is the weakness of what they term the "state tradition" in Canada's parliamentary system of government:

It is hard to overemphasize the importance of state tradition for the conduct of industrial policy. Where state tradition is weak, state institutions often reflect the interests of the strongest organizational forces in society. Much of the state's apparatus is devoted to transmitting and responding to these demands. And because these demands are conflicting, and state structure under these circumstances is generally inchoate, industrial policy is typically a confusing amalgam of reactive policy initiatives (1989: 56).

While the preceding analyses find no shortage of explanations to account for the failings of Canadian industrial policy in the 1970s and 1980s, a number of other commentators have observed most of these attempts also failed to account for the federal dimension of Canadian politics. In a paper prepared for the Science Council in 1979, Richard Simeon identified the "regional challenges to industrial policy." The Canadian economy is a highly regional one and the institutions of the federal system accentuate this dimension of public policy by structuring the political life of the country around the interplay between regional and national forces. Growing tensions between the two levels of government have led to a situation in which each advances its own competing development strategies, making the formation of a national strategy increasingly difficult. An additional factor complicating the situation is that no one government controls all the policy instruments needed to implement a cohesive strategy. In fact, it is the provinces rather than the federal government that exercise primary jurisdiction over a number of the areas crucial for industrial policy. This underlines the interdependent nature of federal and provincial jurisdiction. The clear implication of his analysis is that a national strategy cannot be the product of the federal government alone; it requires the co-operation of both levels of government. In concluding, he analysed the conditions to be met before a new, more collaborative form of industrial strategy could emerge, but recognized the difficulty of moving to this model (Simeon, 1979; Tupper, 1982: 79–92).

Many of these themes were expanded upon in Michael Jenkin's thorough review of federal and provincial industrial policies for the Science Council. He examined the growing range of industrial policies adopted by most of the provinces in the late 1970s and early 1980s in response to the process of economic restructuring. Over the decade, they became more expert at promoting the industrial expansion of their own economies. At the same time, this created a need for greater collaboration and coordination – federal/provincial, interprovincial, and bilateral. The most difficult level to manage effectively was the federal/provincial one for all the problems traditionally identified with respect to intergovernmental coordination. These trends underlined the need for new mechanisms to resolve conflicts in this area and new means to promote greater collaboration. Unfortunately, the measures he proposed tend to fall into the category of "more of the same" – a Council of Industry and Technology Ministers, with a small secretariat, coupled with a more activist role for the federal government. This in turn required that regional perspectives be reflected more adequately in federal policy initiatives and that industrial planning be given a more integrated institutional base within the federal government (Jenkin, 1983: 169–81).

Jenkin's analysis perceptively anticipated the increasing tendency for the provinces to expand their industrial and technology policies that occurred in the late 1980s and early 1990s. A representative sampling of these initiatives is found in the following provincial strategy documents. Among the most noteworthy efforts are the Premier's Council Report and the Technology Fund established in Ontario in the late 1980s (Premier's Council, 1988), along with the Industrial Policy Framework and the Sector Partnership Fund created in the early 1990s (Ontario, 1992).[3] For its part, Québec has stood out in its application of Michael Porter's ideas about the role of clusters to a framework for industrial policy (Gagné and Lefèvre, 1993). Similar initiatives have been advocated by the Science Council in British Columbia (British Columbia, 1995) and as part of a broader process of economic renewal in Saskatchewan (Saskatchewan, 1994), and an initiative launched in Nova Scotia. Unfortunately, this plethora of provincial initiatives has not been matched by a comparable effort to move beyond the initial step of the National Science and Technology policy to incorporate these provincial efforts into a national framework.

FROM INDUSTRIAL POLICY
TO INNOVATION STRATEGIES

An additional problem with most discussions of industrial policy in Canada during the 1970s and 1980s is that, by focusing on a dichotomous typology, anticipatory versus reactive or adaptive versus defensive, they tend to overlook what is valuable in the third category of policies – innovative policies. Since the period in which many of these accounts and analyses of Canadian industrial policy were written, the broader literature has undergone a significant shift. In the late 1980s, the focus moved away from the specific questions of targeting high growth sectors or facilitating adjustment out of declining sectors. The earlier interest in industrial policy has been replaced with a broader concern with the way in which the ongoing processes of technological change and economic integration affect all sectors of the industrial economies. This is supplemented by a concern with the broader issue of how the various institutions in these economies – both public and private – cohere into broader systems that support innovation.

What is meant by innovative industrial policy varies considerably in the literature, but it tends to be closely associated with a Schumpeterian perspective, recognizing that higher economic benefits flow to firms and industries that succeed in capturing the excess rents commanded by innovative products and processes in the market. The economic justification for a form of industrial targeting based on Schumpeterian criteria are reasonably clear. The process of innovation constantly introduces new technologies with the prospect to generate higher than average social and economic returns. However, both the long-time horizon required to reap the benefits of investing in these technologies and the fact that the social returns to investment in these technologies are likely to exceed the privately appropriable returns, result in an underinvestment. Furthermore, the enabling character of these technologies, i.e., their capacity to generate important economic benefits for other sectors of the economy, also raise the social benefits derived from them. Conversely, an inadequate rate of investment in these technologies as a result of purely market-based incentives will likely reduce the social benefits that they could bring. This dilemma provided the policy rationale for a form of innovation-oriented industrial policy focused on new technologies and industrial sectors with the potential to generate these social benefits (Dosi, Tyson, and Zysman, 1989: 24–5).

Most analyses of industrial policy in Canada – whether prescriptive or analytical – have been silent on this Schumpeterian dimension, with one or two notable exceptions. One of the earliest sources to develop some of these themes was the Science Council of Canada. In several background studies and a major report completed in the late 1970s, it identified technological sovereignty as the cornerstone for an industrial strategy. It argued that, "a nation can be said to be technologically sovereign when it has the ability to develop and control the technological capability necessary to ensure its economic, and hence its political, self-determination" (Science Council of Canada, 1979: 14). It specified four lines of action that would contribute to the formation of an industrial strategy based upon the goal of technological sovereignty:

1 increasing the demand for indigenous Canadian technology;
2 expanding the country's potential to produce technology;
3 strengthening the capacity of Canadian firms to absorb technology;
4 increasing the ability of Canadian firms to import technology under conditions favourable to Canadian industrial development (ibid: 48; Britton and Gilmour, 1978: 166).

In addition to the Science Council, the Schumpeterian perspective received a thorough exploration in a background study for the Macdonald Royal Commission by Richard Harris.[4] According to Harris, the Schumpeterian perspective on trade and economic development leads to a key conclusion: "The social incentive to subsidize Schumpeterian industries is greater in a small open economy than in the large closed economy" (Harris, 1985: 105). The small economy has more reason to be concerned with receiving its share of the benefits from technological spillovers related to innovation. Further, the smaller firm size on average, which results in a suboptimal industrial structure for the purposes of investing in R&D and innovation, indicates that the total resources devoted to these purposes in the economy may be less than is socially optimal. For these reasons, and because of the high barriers to entry that may exist in industries dominated by Schumpeterian competition, small open economies need to focus on promoting the growth of industries that specialize in product differentiation as opposed to scale economies. Policy should also provide substantial support for small and medium-sized enterprises, given the greater innovativeness of these firms. The most effective way to intervene is to provide support directly to individual firms, rather than sectors or consortia, just as they are entering export markets. The best policy instruments to achieve these goals were greater support for R&D through tax incentives, direct subsidies, loan guarantees or government procurement, and the explicit subsidization of lower-cost loans in the capital markets (ibid: 106, 138).

Although they differ in some notable respects, following the insights derived from the Schumpeterian perspective, both Harris's background study and the Science Council reports are consistent in advocating stronger support of the industrial science and technology base of the country. There is little doubt that their policy prescriptions were never adopted for many of the reasons outlined above by Chandler, Atkinson, and Coleman. They also tended for the most part to adopt a centralist perspective, rather than to build in the regional dimension of the country.[5] To have intervened on the scale that this perspective implied would have required a state with a cohesive bureaucratic structure capable of formulating a clear vision for the economy and the consensus required to implement it.

FROM NATIONAL TO REGIONAL SYSTEMS OF INNOVATION

Recent work on the subject of innovation strategies has expanded the focus beyond the question of firm-based innovation to examine how the broad array of national institutions that affect innovation contribute to the process. From this perspective, innovation and technical progress are sustained by a complex set of relationships among the institutions that produce, distribute, and apply various kinds of knowledge. The innovative performance of individual countries is influenced by the way elements of this institutional system interact with each other in the creation and application of knowledge. The central role of institutional structures in national responses to a new techno-economic paradigm has led to the recent interest in the concept of national systems of innovation.

The systems of innovation approach emphasizes the role of various institutional structures and social forces in influencing the innovation process. The first published discussion of the concept is found in Christopher Freeman's study of technological change in the Japanese economy. In his own work, Freeman initially defined national systems of innovation as "the network of institutions in the public and private sectors whose interactions initiate, import, modify and diffuse new technologies" (Freeman, 1987: 1). Freeman underlines the role of social and political institutions in supporting the adoption and dissemination of scientific and technical knowledge. In a 1988 article and in a 1992 collection, Lundvall provides a somewhat more inclusive definition of the concept. Lundvall starts from the premise that the most fundamental resource in the modern economy is knowledge and, consequently, that the most important process is learning. The learning process is an interactive one that must be understood in its institutional and cultural context. A significant aspect of his approach is the importance attached to the patterns of interaction between firms as part of a collective learning process in the acquisition and use of new technical knowledge. This flows from the belief that innovation is increasingly tied to a process of interactive learning and collective entrepreneurship, especially in terms of the relationships between producers and users of new technology. For him "a system of innovation is constituted by elements and relationships which interact in the production, diffusion and use of new, and economically useful, knowledge and ... a national system encompasses elements and relationships, either located within or rooted in side the borders of the nation state" (Lundvall, 1992: 2; Lundvall, 1988). The main elements of the system include the internal organization of firms, the network of interfirm relationships, the role of the public sector, the institutional set-up of the financial sector, and the degree of R&D intensity and the nature of R&D organization.

Stan Metcalfe provides a somewhat more synthetic and simple definition of the national system of innovation. According to him, "A national system of innovation is that set of distinct institutions which jointly and individually contribute to the development and diffusion of new technologies and which provides the framework within which governments form and implement policies to influence the innovation process. As such it is a system of interconnected institutions to create, store and transfer the knowledge, skills and artifacts which define new technologies" (Metcalfe, 1997: 285).[6]

Although most innovative activity in national economies occurs with the boundaries of the private firm, the role of the public sector in stimulating and sustaining innovative behaviour is critical. In most of the industrial countries, the government supported share of funding on research and development ranges from a low of 20 percent to in excess of 50 percent. Moreover, the public sector maintains a vast array of infrastructural supports critical for the innovation process in the form of the post-secondary educational system, public R&D facilities, and a wide range of institutions that support the process of technology transfer. The concept of a national system of innovation thus draws attention to the effectiveness of public policies in fostering the kinds of private sector activity necessary to develop and maintain a sustained innovative capacity (Niosi et al., 1993).

Much of the early work on systems of innovation was conducted at the national level, partly in response to the issue of whether the innovation process of globalization was undermining national sovereignty. However, recent efforts have stressed the importance of the regional dimension as well.[7] Industrial geographers have long observed that complex systems of technology, production processes, industrial organization, and their supporting infrastructures of social and political institutions frequently exhibit distinctive spatial characteristics. Patterns of production tend to aggregate over time among networks of firms drawing upon the distinctive skills and characteristics of local labour markets in specific regions. Geographer Michael Storper uses the term "territorialization," to describe the range of economic activity that depends on territorially specific resources. The types of resources involved can include specific assets that are only available in a certain place, or, more critically, assets whose real value emerges out of the context of particular inter-organizational or firm-market relations that depend upon geographic proximity. Relations based upon geographic proximity constitute valuable assets when they generate positive spillover effects in an economic system. The more grounded the economic activities of a region are to the specific assets of that region, the more fully territorialized are those activities (Storper, 1997: 170).

Within this context of regional studies, increasing attention has been devoted to the question of regional systems of innovation. While definitions may vary, central to the idea of the regional system of innovation (RSI) is the notion of how the institutional and cultural environment of a region either supports or retards the innovation process. This may be defined as "the set of economic, political and institutional relationships occurring in a given geographical area which generates a collective learning process leading to the rapid diffusion of knowledge and best practice" (Nauwelaers and Reid, 1995: 13; Cooke, 1998). However, this focusing of attention on the regional level raises the question of how to define a region. Recent work draws an important distinction between two types of regions: "cultural" and "administrative." Cultural regions share certain features in common with "the classical definition of nation as a people sharing a common culture, language and territory but which either have not become states (e.g. the Basque Country) or forfeited that status (e.g. Scotland)," while the latter category includes subnational areas of jurisdiction within larger federal systems, such as the German Länder or US states, or newer forms of regional government within traditionally centralized democracies, such as France or Italy. All such regions are defined as "territories smaller than their state possessing significant supralocal governance capacity and cohesiveness differentiating them from their state and other regions" (Cooke, Uranga, and Etxebarria, 1997: 479–80).

As in the case of national systems, the role played by the public sector is central to the operation of the RSI, although the relevant institutions and policies, and the way they are deployed, have changed considerably in recent years. The expanded role played by subnational governments in promoting these relations stems, in part, from the growing economic significance attached to geographically based networks of firms and knowledge-creating forces discussed above. In a growing number of instances, the regional level of governance is assuming the role of social animator or facilitator of the desired forms of innovative activity.

[T]he elaboration of regionalized or localized public-private interfaces adds substantially to the performance of regional economies by enabling SMEs (small and medium-sized enterprises) to meet more effectively the requirements of their customers in respect of technology, quality and training. Regional economies displaying dense inter-firm and public-private interactions of this kind may be expected to show better than average growth performance (Cooke and Morgan, 1993: 552).

The most dynamic regional levels of government have experimented over the past two decades with a wide range of innovation policies. Differences in economic performance between the relatively more or less successful regions has prompted a corresponding interest in the mix of regional innovation policies and institutions that foster this dynamism. While these studies are still in their infancy, their conclusions have begun to coalesce into a new heterodox policy framework. This framework has many different variants, reflecting the prescription that regional innovation policies must be context sensitive, i.e., they must reflect the multiple realities created by different industrial cultures and institutional milieu in different regions (Storper, 1996: 272).

A critical component of a region's system of innovation is the infrastructure of R&D institutions located within it as well as the internal and external networks of relationships within and between public agencies and private actors. A number of recent schematics have been proposed to describe the RSI. One of these suggests that the RSI of a region should be conceptualized in terms of both the demand and supply side for innovation. On the supply side are located the institutional sources of knowledge-creation in the regional economy. Closely linked to these are the institutions responsible for training and the preparation of highly qualified labour power. The demand side of the system subsumes the productive sector – firms that develop and apply the scientific and technological output of the supply side in the creation and marketing of innovative products and processes. Bridging the gap between the two is a wide range of innovation support organizations. These organizations play a role in the acquisition and diffusion of technological ideas and knowhow throughout the system of innovation. These may include technology centres, technology brokers, business innovation centres, organizations in the higher education sector that facilitate the interface with the private sector, and mechanisms of financing innovation, such as venture capital firms (Nauwelaers and Reid, 1995: 15–16).

Regions that exhibit many of the above features are described as being *associative* in their form of governance. This term signifies the growing shift from *hierarchical* forms of organization in both public and private institutions to more *heterarchical* ones in which network relations are based on conditions of trust, reciprocity, reputation, openness to learning, and an inclusive and empowering disposition. According to a number of different authors (Amin, 1996), this requires a shift from the reliance upon public authorities associated with the state to regulate economic affairs to a greater degree of self-regulation by autonomous groups in the economy and society. This in turn involves the transfer of authority and responsibility of some critical aspects of economic policy to a range of local organizations capable of providing the required services or programs (such as vocational training or technology transfer). It also necessarily involves a more decentralized, open, and consultative form of governing. It is closely associated with the process of institutional learning and adaptation within the region (Cooke, 1997).

The appeal of the associative model of governance, especially at the level of the more dynamic regional economies, derives from the insights afforded by this analysis. The associative model substitutes for the exclusive role of the public bureaucracy a mix of public and private roles, and it emphasizes the context of institutional structures and learning. It involves the devolution of greater degrees of autonomy and responsibility for the policy outcome onto those organizations that will both enjoy the fruits of the policy success or live with the consequences of its failure. According to Amin, the adoption of an associative model does not imply an abandonment of a central role for the state, but rather a rethinking of its role. In an associationist model, the relevant level of the state has to become one of the institutions of the collective order, working in relationship with other organizations, rather than operating in its traditional command-and-control fashion. The state in this model continues to establish the basic rules governing the operation of the economy, but it places much greater emphasis on the devolution of responsibility to a wide range of associative partners through the mechanisms of "voice" and consultation (Amin, 1996: 19).

The associative model, as described above, has the potential to overcome one of the key sources of traditional weakness ascribed to Canadian industrial policy, namely the lack of a strong state tradition and the inability to locate responsibility for industrial policy in a strong centralized bureaucracy or to forge an internal consensus over the direction of industrial policy. In fact, these insights suggest that the very factors that were perceived as sources of strength in the past may no longer hold and that previous sources of weakness may in fact be the opposite. Similarly new developments at the regional level in Europe and the local level in North America point the direction in terms of overcoming the traditional source of weakness in Canadian industrial policy: the regionalized nature of the economy and the inherent conflicts in the federal system.

REGIONAL INNOVATION STRATEGIES IN THE EUROPEAN UNION

The current framework for regional innovation strategies in Europe results from a long process of development in regional policy. It originated in 1975 with the establishment of the European Regional Development Fund (ERDF) as a response to the accession of the United Kingdom, Denmark, and Ireland to the European Community. Although the ERDF was initially set up as a community-level policy instrument, it was structured so that member states had control over the disposal of the funds in their own jurisdiction. The most significant change to the ERDF occurred with the passage of the Single European Act in 1986. The creation of the Single Market set in train a further set of reforms to the regional development funds, designed to ensure that the three Structural Funds (including the ERDF) tackled the problems of regional development in a more coordinated fashion (Armstrong, 1997: 41–50; Marks, 1992: 206–12). One aspect of these reforms was to devote a small proportion of the total funds available under the ERDF to support innovative actions favouring regional development – the Article 10 funds. The initial set of innovative actions was launched between 1989–93 to deepen thinking within the European Community about the nature and dynamics of regional development. The innovative nature of the projects funded under Article 10 lay not only in the type of activities supported but also in the partnerships they fostered by involving local and regional authorities with a wide range of private actors (European Union, 1995a: 7).

In the period leading up to and following the signing of the Maastricht Treaty in 1992, increased emphasis was placed on the issue of social cohesion and, particularly, the relation between the goals of increased competitiveness and innovation and the highly uneven fashion in which innovative capabilities were distributed across the less favoured regions (LFR) of Europe. One influential study released in 1992 highlighted the extent to which the research and technology development capacity of the Union was concentrated in a relatively small number of urban areas. It concluded that ten relatively small local areas, stretching in a band from Greater London through Paris-Ile de France, Rotterdam/Amsterdam, Lyon/Grenoble, Frankfurt, Munich, the Rhine-Ruhr region, and Stuttgart to Milan and Turin, accounted for the vast majority of laboratories and firms engaged in science-based innovation. These "islands of innovation" were marked by dense local networks of co-operation between scientific laboratories and the firms engaged in research and innovation. As well, they tended to be the principal participants in the Community's Research and Technology Development (RTD) programs, further contributing to the uneven distribution of innovative capabilities and accentuating the problem of cohesion (Hingel, 1992).

The identification of this concentration led to recommendations concerning the need for a stronger geographic dimension in the formulation of the Community's RTD and innovation programs. In a communication to the Council and the European Parliament in May 1993, the Commission noted that the differences in gross expenditure on RTD and in the availability of highly qualified personnel vastly exceeded the differences in standards of living among member states. Both the Fourth Framework Program and the new round of spending under the Structural Funds afforded an opportunity to integrate the Community's cohesion objectives regarding the LFRs into its broader objectives concerning innovation and competitiveness. It recommended that the Commission's services organize and support the design and evaluation of technology diffusion networks in the less prosperous regions, give special attention to regions in which SMEs are the predominant form of economic organization, and encourage the LFRs to exchange experiences with the more advanced regions on the design and implementation of measures to raise the capacity of their SMEs to absorb technology. It also urged the ERDF to adopt measures to improve the capacity of eligible regions to participate more fully in the RTD Framework Program (Commission of the European Union, 1993).

In response, the Regional Policy and Cohesion Directorate (RPC) and the Telecommunications, Information Society and Exploitation of Research Results Directorate (TISERR) announced the launching of pilot projects in a number of LFRs to draft Regional Technology Plans (RTPS). The objective of the pilots was to allow the regions to undertake a detailed analysis of the strengths and weaknesses of the industrial structure in the region. The RTP was to focus on the relationship between the supply of, and the demand for, technology within the region and its implications for economic development. Finally, the results were to be integrated into local, national, and Community programs and strategies, with the goal of improving the transfer of technology into networks of SMEs within the LFRs. The conduct of a complete RTP was to take eighteen months and the Commission would pay 50 percent of the cost, up to a maximum of ECU 200,000. In the initial phase, RTPS were undertaken in four pilot regions: Limburg (Netherlands), Lorraine (France), Wales (UK), and Saxony (Germany). Subsequently four more pilot projects were launched (European Union, 1995b) in Norte (Portugal), Macedonia (Greece), Abruzzo (Italy), and Castilla-Y-Leone (Spain).

The primary goal of the pilot projects was to overcome the traditional approach of most Community RTD programs as top-down and focused on technology push. In contrast, the strategies were to follow a bottom-up approach; they were to be demand-driven, based on the needs identified by firms within the region, emerging out of a dialogue between the firms, regionally based technology transfer organizations, and the public sector. The strategies were to reflect a regional approach by forging, among the principal actors at the regional level, a consensus on the priorities for action. They were to adopt a strategic approach by elaborating a set of short and medium-term objectives for enhancing the technological capabilities and innovativeness of the firms in the region. The approach was to integrate the roles of both the public and private sector in order to increase the overall productivity and competitiveness of the region. Finally, the strategy was to reflect an awareness of global economic trends to ensure that the actions taken promoted the objectives of the region in the international sphere (European Union, 1997: 17).

The early pilot projects launched under the RTP initiative were widely regarded as a success. An early evaluation of the first three projects drew preliminary conclusions about the lessons learned from the experience. The first lesson concerned the diversity of approaches used to implement a regional technology plan, yet the significant convergence in the priorities that were established at the end of the process. In Limburg, the RTP process was managed jointly by the

Economic Department and a regional consulting firm. The central thrust of the strategy developed was to "Reinforce the level of knowledge within industrial companies in Limburg, especially SMES, and improve their access to the knowledge and educational infrastructure and the extent to which this infrastructure meets their needs." In Wales, the RTP exercise was coordinated by a strong management structure, directed by an RTP coordinator with a small project group drawn from individuals within the Welsh Development Agency. The central thrust of the exercise was "to achieve a consensus amongst public and private bodies on the overall objectives and actions required to upgrade the technological base, skills content, innovative capacity, value-added performance and RTD expenditure of the Welsh economy." In the region of Lorraine, the RTP followed a different route, with the workplan being revised continuously through the process. The RTP was managed by a Directing Committee formed of key decisionmakers representing both the central government in the region and the Regional council. It concluded with a formal consultation of the regional actors around a number of options that emerged from the preceding analysis (Nauwelaers et al., 1996).

The evaluation of these pilot RTPs also noted a considerable variation in the course that the process followed. In Limburg, the strategy was relatively well defined from the outset; in Wales, there were major changes and developments introduced during the process itself; and, in Lorraine, there was a partial work plan set out at the beginning, but the process evolved in a "learning-by-doing" fashion. The relation between the conduct of research, the consultation process, and the development of the strategy also varied: in some cases they were carried out consecutively, in others simultaneously. Despite this considerable variation in the process, the results of the strategies displayed a significant convergence. A number of key themes emerged in all cases. Some of the themes that received the strongest emphasis included: the need to bridge the gap between institutions of higher education and industry; promoting clustering between firms; increasing the demand for innovation in SMES; providing adequate financing for innovation; adapting the programs for training and further education to the needs of SMES, among others. The evaluation concluded that the RTP process could be described as "path dependent" and "evolutionary," terms often applied to the innovation process itself. The process of consensus-building and innovation policy development in each region was strongly influenced by what had been done previously; differences in the priority given to different elements of the strategy reflected this as well. There was also a strong feeling that the development of the RTP did not end with the termination of the process led by the European

Union. The process of devising regional systems of innovation is constantly evolving. The key lesson drawn from the original round of pilot projects was the RTPs were fundamentally learning processes – both within the regions themselves and at the level of policy formation for the European Union (Nauwelaers et al., 1996).

During the same period, DG XIII also supported a number of complementary initiatives known as Regional Innovation and Technology Transfer Strategies and Infrastructures (RITTS). The RITTS were more limited in scope and more applied in their objectives than the RTPs. The goal was to support regional governments and development authorities in analyzing the state of the technology transfer infrastructure in the region and to determine what actions were necessary to optimize the infrastructure and policies for supporting innovation and technology transfer. The process used to develop RITTS was less complex and inclusive than that for the RTPs. The projects were not necessarily carried out by the regional authorities; they could be undertaken by an innovation agency or institution of higher education. The majority of the work could be carried out by consultants and the projects were carried out for their intrinsic benefits to the region. In the initial period five RITTS were undertaken in Flanders (Belgium), Thessaly (Greece), Aquitaine (France), Nord-Pas-de-Calais (France), and Iceland.

Based on the success of the initial pilot projects under both programs, the European Union extended and expanded the range of innovative projects supported during the next period. In September 1995 the two directorates issued a call for a next round of Regional Innovation Strategies (RIS)/Regional Innovation and Technology Transfer Strategies and Infrastructures (RITTS). The shift in name for the first activity reflected a concern with broadening the exercise beyond a narrow focus on competitiveness based on access to, or the capacity to develop, technology. The RIS projects are encouraged either to engage a broader definition of innovation that includes managerial, commercial, technical, and financial aspects that promote the introduction of new or improved products or processes or to enable a public or private organization to introduce or improve service delivery. In the period from 1996 to 2000, an additional twenty-four regions in the European Union engaged in Regional Innovation Strategies with partial funding under the ERDF, Article 10. In addition, another seventy projects are engaged in formulating RITTS with funding from the Innovation Program of the Fourth RTD Framework Program. Finally, six other pluriregional technology transfer projects (RTT) were also funded under the ERDF, Article 10 (European Union, 1999; Landabaso and Reid, 1999).

The Guide to Regional Innovative Actions issued by DG XVI provides a virtual how-to manual on the conduct of successful

RIS/RITTS. It specifies that the process should follow six basic steps or themes. The first step involves the building of a regional consensus. This begins with the formation of a Steering Committee that includes a balanced representation of the various stakeholders concerned with innovation and economic development – such as local politicians, development agencies, business interests, and providers of innovation support services, such as universities or technology transfer centres. The second theme involves an analysis of the key industrial and technological trends affecting the region. The third step involves an evaluation of the main strengths and weaknesses of firms in the region, while the fourth constitutes an assessment of the regional innovative capacities and the supply of technology. In effect these two stages represent a traditional SWOT (strengths, weaknesses, opportunities, threats) analysis that provides an assessment of how well the regional economy stands up in terms of the challenges it faces from other regions and its potential to take advantage of new innovative opportunities. This activity will involve such traditional tools as technology audits for analysing firm needs. In some regions, these capabilities will be relatively better developed, while in others, some of these concepts may be introduced for the first time. It recommends the use of focused working groups of entrepreneurs to ensure that the assessment is based on an accurate view of their concerns. The assessment of firm needs should be complemented by an analysis of the services available in the region to match these needs. The last two steps involve the elaboration of a strategic framework – including a concrete plan of action to implement the recommendations – and the ongoing monitoring and evaluation of the adopted strategy's effectiveness (European Union, 1997: 9–10).

While it is too early yet to provide a complete evaluation of the success of this second round of RIS/RITTS projects, it is clear from both the volume of activity and the level of support provided by the Commission that the approach has struck a responsive chord in the regions. Its great virtue is that it overcomes the traditional dichotomy between a grass-roots or bottom-up approach to local economic development and the top-down, bureaucratic approach that characterizes some of the Commission's other initiatives. It brings together interests from the regional, national, and Union levels to focus on both the opportunities for innovation in the regions and the need of the regions to facilitate their adoption. The successful implementation of the RTP/RIS process requires a number of key ingredients: the participation of legitimate animateurs to stimulate the process; the ability to surmount both individual and institutional rigidities, allowing for new forms of dialogue among the participants; and the presence of an innovative and strategic capacity within the public sector to support the process. The other key element that the process requires is time: it takes time to establish the sustained dialogue that the RTP/RIS process needs to let trust relations grow and develop. However, the eventual results can more than justify the investment involved (Nauwelaers and Morgan, 1999). In fostering a consensus-building approach, it reflects some of the best values of the associative model of governance discussed above and, in linking both the supply and demand sides of the innovation process at the regional level, it overcomes the traditional failure of the technology-push approach to innovation

CLUSTER DEVELOPMENT
IN THE REGIONAL ECONOMY[8]

This emphasis in Europe on the region as a locus of innovation and the success of recent experiments has its parallel in another phenomenon in North America – a fascination with the emergence of dynamic, regional clusters in key locales across the continent. Michael Porter defines a cluster as "a geographically proximate group of interconnected companies and associated institutions in a particular field, linked by commonalities and complementarities" (1998: 199). These clusters include concentrations of interconnected companies, service providers, suppliers of specialized inputs to the production process, customers, manufacturers of related products, and, finally, governmental and other institutions, such as national laboratories, universities, vocational training institutions, trade associations, and collaborative research institutes. Clusters can consist both of concentrations of high-tech firms, which often center around research-intensive universities (as is clearly the case in Silicon Valley), and of firms based in more traditional industries, such as the ones studied by Maskell and his colleagues in Denmark (Maskell et al., 1998).

Porter, best known for his work on competitive advantage, provides a compelling analysis of the way in which the existence of clusters affect competition. The first is by increasing the productivity of their constituent firms and industries. Location of a firm within a cluster contributes to enhanced productivity by providing it with superior or lower-cost access to specialized inputs, including components, machinery, business services, and personnel as opposed to the alternative, which may involve vertical integration or obtaining the needed inputs from more remote locations. Clusters also offer distinct advantages to firms in terms of the availability of specialized and experienced personnel. The cluster itself often acts as a magnet drawing the skilled labour to it. Conversely the location of specialized training and educational institutions with the cluster can provide a ready supply of new labour to the firms in the cluster. Clusters also enhance productivity through facilitating the complementarities that exist between member firms. Membership in the cluster makes it easier for participants to source needed parts and components, thus enhancing the technological and productive capabilities of member firms.

The mutually beneficial activities of the firms in a cluster generate a number of cluster assets that can be viewed as quasi-public goods. The general level of knowledge and information built up in the cluster can act as such a good, if the level of trust is sufficient to generate an easy and mutual exchange of both tacit and codified knowledge. Similarly, the mobility of personnel between firms in a cluster can constitute a similar source of knowledge flows. Even more important, the strength of the cluster can provide an important stimulus to public investment in specialized infrastructure, such as communication networks, joint training and research institutions, specialized testing facilities, and the expansion of public laboratories or postsecondary educational institutions. As the depth and value of such investments increase, so do the economic benefits flowing to firms located in the cluster. Thus the strength of the cluster and its supporting infrastructure of quasi-public goods and public institutions create a mutually reinforcing positive feedback loop (Porter, 1998).

This analysis of the key factors that underlie the presence of clusters is also borne out in a related corpus of policy related work done in Canada and the us. Research undertaken for the National Research Council situates the process of industrial clustering within the systems of innovation approach (Nordicity Group Ltd, 1996). Based on this analysis, the Planning and Assessment Branch of NRC has identified a set of eight factors that contribute to cluster development: the presence of local champions with greater vision than single firm success; the existence of a strong S&T knowledge infrastructure – which includes research universities, government laboratories, and co-operative research centres; a source of motivated learners and technology, knowledge and skills; the presence of at least one exporting firm with some global reach; involvement by local networking facilitators who promote the growth of relationships within the cluster; involved, knowledgeable local sources of innovation financing; sustained, aligned development strategies by local institutions and governments; and a business climate and policy conditions favourable for innovators.

Recent work by ICF Kaiser International for the Economic Development Administration of the us Department of Commerce identifies a

similar set of factors that contribute to regionally based cluster development. The ICF Kaiser analysis suggests that in addition to the basic
prerequisites for cluster development – a strong concentration of related industries, as well as specialized suppliers and services – clusters
benefit from access to specialized economic inputs that are referred to
as "economic infrastructure." There are seven major categories of economic infrastructure: adaptable skills, accessible technology, adequate
financing, suitable physical infrastructure, advanced communications
facilities, an acceptable regulatory and business climate, and an attractive quality of life (Information Design Associates and ICF Kaiser International, 1997). This last point is strongly reinforced in the recent
report prepared by Richard Florida for the National Governor's association in the US (Florida, 2000). The core elements of the economic
infrastructure that underlie and support the process of cluster development are virtually identical to those of the regional system of innovation discussed above.

However, the presence, or absence, of key institutional elements of
the local or regional system of innovation may affect both their innovative capacity and their potential to serve as nodes for cluster development. Similarly, the ability, or inability, of the local or regional economy to develop the underlying conditions of trust and social capital that
contribute to the presence of a learning economy may inhibit its capacity to sustain the growth of dynamic clusters. The critical question that
remains unexplored through most of this literature is whether the conditions that influence the trajectory of growth for a specific regional or
local economy can be altered by direct intervention, and, if so, how
effectively. Other experiences suggest that it may be possible for local
communities to formulate specific strategies to both alter their economic trajectory and improve their changes of cluster creation.

Despite the general characterization of Silicon Valley as being relatively weak in social capital, one recent initiative – the creation of
Joint Venture: Silicon Valley, and its subsequent impact on improving
the quality of civic engagement in the Valley – has drawn considerable
attention. Three of the key participants in this venture, in a recent
analysis of it and related local development initiatives in other metropolitan areas, argue that the concentration of a large number of firms
is not sufficient to transform a particular locale into a vibrant and
dynamic cluster linked into the global economy. What is required to
ensure this is the presence of an "economic community" – places with
strong, responsive relationships between the economy and community that afford both companies and the community a sustained advantage. These relationships are mediated by key people and organizations who bring the respective economic, social and civic interests in

the community together to collaborate on strategies for the community. According to these authors, "the distinguishing feature of economic communities is not just that they have clusters but that they have mechanisms to engage their clusters and understand what they need from the community" (Henton, Melville, and Walesh, 1997: 7).

Based on their experience of working with community-based initiatives such as Joint Venture: Silicon Valley, they agree that social capital is a critical ingredient in the success of the most dynamic clusters. But they reject the deterministic explanations offered by Putnam and Fukuyama (Putnam, 1993; Fukuyama, 1995). They argue that social capital can be created and the basis for doing so is the establishment of collaborative networks between various elements of the business and civic communities. The catalyst for doing so is a new breed of civic entrepreneurs, individuals who lay down the basis for social capital by finding the opportunities for individuals to work together on projects to promote the community's economic prospects. The essential criterion for their success is finding the appropriate mechanisms to engage key members of the community in a sustained effort to advance its opportunities. Not just Silicon Valley, but similar efforts in Cleveland, Austin, and other centres over the past decade provide strong illustrations of how this process works (Henton, Melville, and Walesh, 1997: 31; Gibson and Rogers, 1994).

LESSONS FOR CANADA

The experience of the RTP/RIS exercises undertaken in Europe during the past decade and of the more innovative community-based experiments in North America has important lessons to offer students of industrial and innovation policy in Canada. These lessons are noteworthy first and foremost for their effectiveness in overcoming two of the central weaknesses traditionally seen as the key shortcomings of industrial policy in Canada – the lack of a strong bureaucratic state tradition and the divisive effects of the federal system. The RTP/RIS exercises are valuable in pointing the way towards a process that overcomes these weaknesses; they adopt an approach that not only involves in a coordinated effort all three levels of governance in the European Union but also works outside the bounds of a traditional state structure.

The program of Regional Innovation Strategies run by DG XVI of the European Union is predicated on the notion that innovative policies can be developed using a bottom-up approach within a framework of multi-level governance (Landabaso, Oughton, and Morgan, 1999; Morgan and Henderson, 2002). Similarly, the brief discussion of the emerging role of civic entrepreneurs in the cases of Austin, Cleveland, and Silicon Valley mentioned above provides preliminary evidence that a similar process can be followed in North America, albeit in a radically different institutional form (Henton, Melville, and Walesh, 1997).

It should be noted, however, that neither process is a substitute for innovation and industrial policy at any of the three levels of government, but rather a complement. In fact, one of the key virtues of this approach is the emphasis that it places on involving key actors at the local level in thinking about how to design effective innovation strategies within the framework of existing national and regional policies. The value that they serve is as an integrating mechanism that can help to supersede some of the traditional divisions that characterize industrial policy.

The processes described above bear some features in common with the more recent efforts to develop provincial S&T strategies in Canada. Yet they also differ in important respects. One of the greatest short-comings of the provincial efforts has been the inability of individual strategies to survive the transition from one government to the next. The true test of an effective innovation strategy at both the regional and the local level is its ability to build a solid base of support that maintains its continuity from one regime to the next. The other major shortcoming of the recent provincial efforts has been the relative isola-tion from the federal government with which they have been devised. The challenge for the future of industrial and innovation policy in Canada is to learn from the best of alternative approaches at both the regional and the local levels in devising a means to overcome the tra-ditional weaknesses of Canadian innovation policy. This will require an approach that builds from the bottom up, employing an associative model of governance to overcome the traditional weakness of the state in Canada and integrates the perspectives of all three levels of govern-ment in a coordinated fashion to both increase national capabilities and reflect regional and local realities.

NOTES

1 DG stands for Directorate Generale.
2 A number of excellent accounts exist of the several rounds of deliberation over industrial policy that occurred at the federal level during this period. For more detailed accounts, cf. French, 1984: ch. 6; Brown, Eastman, and Robinson, 1981; Doern, 1983.
3 I have provided a more detailed overview of these policy initiatives in Ontario in Wolfe, 1999, and Wolfe, 2002a.

4 It is one of the many ironies of the Royal Commission that its final
report ignored this study completely; virtually all references to Harris's
work in the main report are to his 1979 study for the Ontario Economic
Council, rather than the study that they had commissioned themselves.
The political science, or institutions, research program was almost totally
devoid of any studies that looked at industrial or innovation policy from
a Schumpeterian perspective.

5 For an earlier attempt to integrate this perspective with a more regional
focus, cf. Gertler, 1991.

6 This reference provides a small sampling of the different approaches to
the national system of innovation. For a more comprehensive overview
and a useful distillation of the key features they share, cf. Edquist,
1997.

7 The following discussion draws upon my more detailed treatment in
Wolfe, 1997.

8 The following section draws substantially on my article, Wolfe, 2002b.

12 Postmodern Planning: All Talk, No Action?

PIERRE FILION

Planning discourse is becoming increasingly disconnected from implementation. This situation is the consequence of two contradictory trends. Fanned by the opening of the planning process to public participation and the active involvement of pressure groups, planning discourse has become a vehicle for increasingly ambitious proposals intended to reorient urban development. At the same time, implementation capacity is deteriorating due to fiscal stress, lack of consensus over planning matters, and the rising influence of a laissez-faire ideology. This imbalance questions the relevance of planning discourse in the present postmodern context, given this discourse's apparent inability to prompt the type of actions required to assure a realization of its objectives (see Beauregard, 1989). It also raises the issue of how to address urban environmental, social, and economic problems emphasized in the contemporary planning discourse. This disjunction between planning discourse and implementation capacity is a phenomenon of the present. Indeed, during the first two post-war decades, a close connection had prevailed between the transformative tone of this discourse and the colossal efforts undertaken to adapt the city to growing car use and rising space consumption on the part of all land uses. The relevance of this chapter's discussion extends well beyond the specificity of urban planning. There are compelling reasons to believe that the gap between discourse and implementation observed within the planning sphere is but one manifestation of a more general disconnection between postmodern discourses generated around different issues and governments' intervention willingness and capacity.

To bring historical perspective to the present context, the chapter sketches major planning mutations from the Second World War to the present. This leads to the identification – and comparison in terms of process, discourse, implementation capacity, and urban outcomes – of three phases: 1) the post-war transformation; 2) the participatory transition; 3) and the disjunction between discourse and development. The third, or contemporary, phase is the main object of this chapter and accordingly receives disproportionate attention. Many accounts of planning's evolution see the participatory transition as still relevant to the present context (Hodge, 1998; Kaiser and Godshalk, 1995; Wolfe, 1994). I depart from this view by distinguishing the present period from the participatory transition phase in order to explain why changes heralded in that phase have not materialized in accordance with the expectations of the time and why contemporary planning has not lived up to these expectations. Contrasts between the three phases highlight factors that account for the contemporary disjunction between discourse and implementation. The chapter ends by exploring actual and possible roles for planning within the postmodern context.

Most of the empirical substance for this chapter originates from the Greater Toronto Area (GTA), a metropolitan region that has experienced intense planning activity over the three periods under consideration due to a need to cope with persistent growth pressures since the Second World War. The need to tackle problems associated with size and rapid development accounts for Toronto's position at the forefront of planning's evolution over the three identified phases. Still, it is this chapter's contention that observations about the GTA concerning the evolution and the present state of planning can be generalized to most other Canadian cities, albeit with adjustments reflecting differences in the chronology of different planning trends and the intensity with which they manifest themselves.

THE POST-WAR TRANSFORMATION: 1945 TO THE LATE 1960S

The twenty-five years following the war enjoyed feverish demographic and economic expansion, happening mostly within a dispersing urban form – characterized by low densities, a high degree of land-use specialization, an absence of a central focal point, and a heavy reliance on the car. This contrasted markedly with the pre-war, concentrated city – a dense, transit-oriented form organized around a strong central business district (see Filion, 1999a; Filion, Bunting, and Curtis, 1996). Over these years, governments became increasingly interventionist in a climate of expanding public sector finances and far-reaching adherence to Keynesian principles. In conformity with modernist tendencies, this period exhibited a great deal of social-value uniformity. It was characterized by widespread adhesion to the ideology of progress – with an unrelenting faith in science and expertise – that replaced tradional points of view with scientifically inspired outlooks on social phenomena (Giddens, 1990: 83–4).

Over the early post-war years, planning evolved rapidly into an instrument well suited to the adaptation of the city to the profound technological and value changes then unfolding in an environment of rapid economic and demographic growth. The resulting planning process became an embodiment of modernist values (Gottdiener, 1995: 14). This process was labelled rational-comprehensive: rational, because it was comprised of a logical succession of steps beginning with a problem-definition stage and ending with the formulation of planning proposals; comprehensive, because it purported to address all aspects of land-use planning. It relied heavily on expertise and quantitative techniques (on this form of planning, see, for example, Alexander, 1991; Chadwick, 1971; Chapin, 1957; Faludi, 1973; McLoughlin, 1969).

Consistent with modernist values, proposals emanating from this process called for a radical transformation of the pre-war portion of the city, deemed to be out of step with then emerging business needs, consumer preferences, and transportation requirements. Planning documents of the time were replete with expressway and urban renewal proposals intended to adapt the central city to prevailing trends. But by virtue of its role in shaping peripheral urbanization over the last fifty-five years, it is the suburban development formula emanating from the rational-comprehensive process that has most influenced post-war urban development. This formula is based on the assignment of functionally specialized zones and the supply of plentiful road capacity to assure their interconnectivity (Atash, 1996: 51; Relph, 1987). High levels of intrazonal specialization authorize the juxtaposition of pretty much any zone, provided the allotment of sufficient buffering. Specialized zones within the suburban realm are distributed in a fashion that assures that most everyday necessities are met within a ten to fifteen minute drive (Baldassare, 1986; Fishman, 1987; Kling, Olin, and Poster, 1991; Rowe, 1991). This formula has routinized the practice of suburban planning. It can apparently be replicated endlessly – that is, until ineluctable environmental and economic limits are reached.

Compatibility between the planning process and society-wide values, prosperity, and resulting government spending capacity led to a widespread implementation of planning proposals. Peripheral development conformed to the suburban planning formula, and expressways and urban renewal transformed many central-city sectors, albeit not quite to the extent prescribed in planning documents. The post-war transformation phase came to an end in the late 1960s before the realization of all of its visions. In Toronto, the compatibility between modernity and urban development was supplemented by the existence, for a time, of an agency, Metropolitan Toronto, with metropolitan-wide planning jurisdiction, which played an active role in planning new developments and developing transportation networks (Rose, 1972). The determining influence these circumstances had on urban development is illustrated by the scope of transportation investments carried out in the 1950s and 1960s. In Toronto, the structuring elements of the contemporary GTA transportation system were put in place over these two decades – 184 of the 325-kilometre expressway system and 32 of the 60-kilometre subway system. Later additions (and widenings) equalled neither the scale nor the impact of the achievements of these two decades (Filion, 1999a).

Until the mid 1960s, residents' objections rarely challenged modern planning's mission. Indeed, most criticism concerned perceived dissonance between targeted interventions and this mission. When residents complained, it was generally because in their view local regulations or projects did not conform sufficiently to modern planning visions or that the implementation of the modern planning agenda was not proceeding swiftly enough (Filion, 1999b).

THE PARTICIPATORY TRANSITION: LATE 1960s TO THE MID-1970s

The public's generally favourable attitude towards rational-comprehensive planning contrasted with loud dissenting voices aired in the literature. This form of planning's urban outcomes were portrayed as impediments to community formation and social diversity and, overall, were seen as responsible for an urban environment lacking the rich texture of the pre-war city (for example, Doxiadis, 1960; Goodman, 1971; Jacobs, 1961; McHarg, 1969; Mumford, 1961; Relph, 1976). Other objects of criticism were the expert-driven nature of this planning process and its highly standardized proposals, expressways and urban renewal in the central city, and the suburban planning formula everywhere else (Boguslaw, 1965). From the mid-1960s, the planning literature became saturated with appeals for a reorientation of planning. Proposed alternatives to the rational-comprehensive process included: the transactive model, which advocates a dialogue between planners and residents, mostly through the inclusion of public participation in the planning process (see Friedmann, 1973; and, more generally on participatory planning, Arnstein, 1969; Fagence, 1977; Glass, 1979); the advocacy model, which, from a social justice perspective, stresses the need for a disproportionate attention to marginalized populations on the part of planners (Belcher, 1970; Davidoff, 1965); and the radical model, which is committed to a profound transformation of the role planning plays in society in order to make it an agent of social change (Kraushaar, 1987).

From the mid-1960s, adverse effects emanating from implementations of the rational-comprehensive process prompted citizens to question the values embedded in this form of planning. In Toronto, residents mobilized around a central-city (the Spadina) expressway, private high-rise redevelopment, public sector urban renewal, and threats to inner-city neighbourhoods. They also demanded the right to take part in planning decision-making (Fraser, 1972; Lorimer, 1970; Nowlan and Nowlan, 1970; Sewell, 1972 and 1993). In 1970, adherents to this movement gained sufficient political clout on Toronto City Council to replace expert-driven planning with a process that gives primacy to public participation (see, for Toronto, Caulfield, 1974; and, for similar movements across Canada, Higgins, 1986). Illustrative of this change of planning philosophy was the introduction of a secondary plan process for each City of Toronto neighbourhood, wherein, for all intents and purposes, planners assumed the role of consultants at the service of residents. Not surprisingly, this process resulted in a downzoning of neighbourhoods – which assured the preservation of the existing built environment – and in an improvement of their infrastructures and amenities.

Participatory planning spread rapidly to other central cities, partly under the impetus of the federal government, who in 1973 introduced the Neighbourhood Improvement Program across the country (Filion, 1988). Public participation was a central feature of this program whose purpose was to rehabilitate rather than replace the built environment of selected inner-city neighbourhoods.

The participatory transition induced substantial changes in planning outcomes. In the central city, expressway proposals were put to rest and neighbourhoods were protected (albeit with little prejudice to central-city redevelopment potential because of an abundance of former industrial sites awaiting reuse). In Toronto, for instance, no serious consideration was given to new Metro expressways south of Highway 401 after the 1971 provincial government rejection of the Spadina expressway proposal. One inner-city Toronto project that epitomized the planning ideals of the time was the St. Lawrence community redevelopment, which is street oriented and high density and mixes land uses and income groups.

By contrast, still guided by the planning formula evolved early in the previous phase, suburban development was largely impervious to the participatory transition. Mostly a central-city affair, the impact of this shift on metropolitan-wide urban development was thus limited. The less suburban involvement in participatory planning over this period can be accounted for by: 1) fewer resident objections against development since most of the growth takes place on greenfield sites, not within established inhabited areas; 2) a greater ease, in most agglomerations, to influence suburban administrations, which tend to be smaller and more responsive than central-city municipal governments to resident organizations; 3) a concentration in the central city of young educated individuals who took a disproportional interest in planning issues and municipal politics (Ley, 1996).

DISJUNCTION BETWEEN DISCOURSE AND DEVELOPMENT: THE MID-1970S TO THE PRESENT

From the 1970s onwards, planning documents increasingly championed alternatives to prevailing forms of urbanization. Most prominent among these alternatives was the urban intensification concept, which purports to make urban form more compact through a reurbanization of empty and underutilized sites within the urban perimeter and through higher density peripheral development (Bourne, 1992; D'Amour, 1991; Paehlke, 1991; Tomalty, 1993). Intensification also involves an encouragement of public transit, cycling, and walking at the expense of car use (Klaasen, Bourdrez, and Volmuller, 1981). Interest in intensification arose in part from concern over the state of the environment, more specifically about air pollution and an accelerating urbanization of rural and natural land.[1] Equally, it was perceived as a response to a lack of urbanity within the suburban realm due to a near-total reliance on the car and a hostile pedestrian environment. The case for intensification was not exclusively environmental. Some studies made an economic argument in favour of this form of urbanization, linking higher urban density with reduced infrastructure and service costs (for example, Blais, 1996; Tomalty, 1997).

As early as 1970, the Toronto-Centred Region Plan proposed means to reduce sprawl within the Toronto metropolitan area (Ontario, 1970 and 1973). But subsequent policies, yielding to pressures from developers and peripheral municipalities, assured the persistence of prevailing sprawling urbanization patterns (Frisken, 1993: 174–5; Sewell, 1993: 200–12). Still, intensification did not vanish from Toronto planning rhetoric. To the contrary, by 1985 planning documents within the

GTA were nearly unanimous in voicing their adherence to this principle (Filion, 1996).[2]

The importance given to environmental concerns stems from the disproportional influence of certain groups within the participatory process set up in the 1970s (on uneven access to the planning participatory process, see Day, 1997: 428; Kweit and Kweit, 1990). The scene within this process has been disproportionately occupied by NIMBY (Not In My Back Yard) groups mobilized around local issues and, with most relevance to the present argument, advocacy organizations, particularly those upholding environmental values. These organizations have shown a great deal of skill in using the planning platform to broadcast their views. What is more, the intensification principle has special appeal for a certain category of municipalities: fully urbanized municipalities that would benefit economically from the redevelopment of underused sites. As expected, therefore, it is older, centrally located municipalities – in particular the former City of Toronto and Metro Toronto – that demonstrated the earliest and staunchest commitment to intensification.

The importance planning rhetoric gives to intensification is also a function of the rise of the environment within provincial and federal governments' agendas from the mid-1980s to the mid-1990s. Over these years, the Ontario government used its power over recalcitrant suburban jurisdictions, still wedded to the post-war low-density model of suburbanization, to enforce conformity between their official plans and its intensification objective. This situation was reversed, however, when the Conservative Party took power in June 1995, with a political platform of tax reduction, deficit elimination, deregulation, and overall public sector retrenchment. The environment is a far lower priority for this government than it was for its predecessors, as evidenced by sharp budget cutbacks for the Ministry of the Environment. More specifically, urban intensification is of little interest to the Conservative government. It is still too early to measure the effect of this change of provincial perspective on plans emanating from the GTA, however. Only one regional plan (to which municipal official plans must conform) has been adopted since the 1995 change of government, and this plan was prepared under the previous government and adhered to then-prevailing provincial guidelines.

The post-1970 period has witnessed some developments that conformed to intensification objectives. In particular, efforts were successful in bringing additional housing to Toronto's central area. Resident population in and around downtown Toronto rose thanks to condominium construction, mixed-used developments such as the St. Lawrence community, the residential redevelopment of industrial sites,

Table 1
Population Change in the Toronto CMA 1986–96

	1986	1996	Change 1986–96 (%)
Toronto CMA	3,431,981	4,263,757	24.24
City of Toronto			
(formerly Metro Toronto)	2,192,724	2,385,421	8.79
Rest of CMA	1,239,257	1,878,336	51.57

Sources: Statistics Canada, 1988, Census Tracts, Toronto: Part 1, Profiles, Ottawa, ON: Minister of Supply and Services, Cat. 95-163; Statistics Canada, 1997, A National Overview: Population and Dwelling Counts, Ottawa, ON: Minister of Industry, Cat. 93-357-XPB.

and the recent relaxation of zoning bylaws meant to encourage the reuse of former industrial buildings (Bourne, 1993; Nowlan and Steuart, 1990; Valpy, 1999). The February 1999 *Toronto Life* issue listed fifty-six central Toronto loft conversions of industrial buildings at different stages of completion (Lypchuk, 1999).

The central-city intensification strategy was not an outright success, however. Certain proposals intended to advance intensification within the inner city failed to reach completion. This was notably the case of the Ataratiri project meant to create a fourteen-thousand-resident neighbourhood on underused industrial land located two kilometres from downtown Toronto. This project fell victim to spiralling costs due, in part, to higher than expected soil decontamination expenses, fiscal stringency, and a deflating housing market, all of which compromised the possibility for this project to break even.

It is in the suburbs, however, that the distance between planning discourse and implementation is the greatest. Since the brunt of metropolitan growth took place within the suburban realm, most urban development was left largely unaltered by the intensification principles advanced in planning documents. This assured the persistence of a low-density and, most importantly, functionally segregated and car-dependent form of urbanization, still broadly in conformity with development norms dating from the immediate post-war period. Table 1 underscores the suburban nature of recent Toronto census metropolitan area (CMA) growth. While the City of Toronto (that is, the former Metro Toronto) grew by 8.8 percent between 1986 and 1996, in part in suburban like subdivisions erected on its few remaining greenfield sites, population increased by 51.6 percent in the remainder of the CMA. Suburbs outside the (new) City of Toronto accounted for 76.8 percent of the metropolitan region's demographic growth over the period. This development pattern tilts the population balance ever more in

Table 2
Modal Transportation Split, City of Toronto and GTA Regions (24 hrs), Percentages

		City of Toronto (new boundaries)	Durham	York	Peel	Halton
Auto Driver	1986	53	69	69	68	71
	1991	54	72	71	68	73
	1996	53	71	70	68	73
Auto Passenger	1986	13	17	14	15	15
	1991	14	16	14	16	13
	1996	15	16	16	16	16
Local Transit	1986	25	3	6	6	2
	1991	22	2	6	5	2
	1996	22	3	5	5	1
GO (train and bus)	1986	0	2	1	2	2
	1991	0	2	1	2	3
	1996	0	2	1	2	2
Walk and Cycle	1986	7	6	5	6	6
	1991	8	5	5	7	6
	1996	8	6	5	5	5
Other	1986	1	3	4	3	3
	1991	1	3	5	3	3
	1996	1	4	3	3	3

Source: Toronto Transportation Survey/Transportation Tomorrow Survey, www.jpint.utoronto.ca, retrieved April 1999.

favour of the dispersed realm, thus further entrenching the auto-use/low-density dynamic with detrimental consequences for metropol-itan-wide levels of public transit ridership (Miller, Steuart, and Jea, 1990: viii). Table 2 demonstrates that as growth occurs in outer sub-urbs (that is, those within the regions of Durham, York, Peel, and Halton), it takes place in car-oriented areas where public transit use is minimal and, if anything, is falling as urbanization unfolds.

Efforts to introduce intensification to suburbs have failed to meet their objectives. This was the case, for example, for the foremost such initiative, the creation of suburban downtowns. Many GTA jurisdictions encouraged the creation of such downtowns (for example, Metro Toronto, 1976: 4–6) with the goal of bringing to suburbs centres of activity that would replicate, at a smaller scale, the high level of transit use, pedestrian movement, and interactivity synergy characteristic of the central business districts of large cities. Although three of these suburban districts – the suburban downtowns of North York (labelled Downtown and Uptown), Scarborough (Town Centre) and Missis-

Table 3
Suburban Centres' Land-Use Allocations, Percentages

	Built-Up Area (building footprint)	Space Devoted to the Car (road and parking)	Other Open Land Uses (squares, parks, other green spaces, unoccupied lots)
Downtown Toronto	56	26	18
North York Downtown and Uptown	20	42	38
Scarborough Town Centre	22	53	25
Mississauga City Centre	22	57	21

Source: Calculations from digitized aerial photographs.

sauga (City Centre) – have been highly successful in attracting civic centres, office employment, and retail, their record regarding transit use, pedestrian movement, and inner-synergy is less positive. This strategy was effective in creating hubs of activity at a density exceeding the suburban norm, but failed in its attempt both to replicate the dynamic of traditional downtowns and to contribute to a reduction of suburban auto dependence. Table 3 highlights stark differences in the land-use patterns between suburban downtowns and that of downtown Toronto. As shown, these distinctions are in large measure a function of the vast amount of space required in suburban downtowns to accommodate the car. Their land-use allocations are detrimental to pedestrian movement and, therefore, to interactivity synergy. In the same vein, table 4 displays the modal transportation split discrepancy between downtown Toronto and suburban downtowns and their difficulties in becoming transit hubs as intended. In Mississauga City Centre, transit use is only slightly above average suburban values. Even Downtown and Uptown North York's public transit modal split, the highest among the three suburban downtowns, is less than half that of downtown Toronto.

The transportation side of the intensification strategy also encountered major difficulties. The ambitious $5 billion "Let's Move" program – which would have involved the construction of three new subway lines, as well as busways and an extension of two existing subway lines, a light rail transit line, and commuter rail services (Toronto Transit Commission, 1990) – fizzled out when confronted with the 1989-92 recession and resulting fiscal squeeze. The main public transit investment of the 1990s is the new 6.4-kilometre Sheppard subway line, which will cost approximately $1 billion. Present density within

Table 4
Total Journeys to, and Modal Transportation Split, Downtown Toronto, Three GTA
Suburban Centres (For a 24-Hour period, 1996)

	All Modes	Auto Driver (%)	Auto Passengers (%)	Public Transportation (%)	Walk (%)	Cycle (%)	Other (%)
Downtown Toronto	341,245	32.2	8	48.8	8.9	1.7	0
North York Downtown and Uptown	72,239	58.8	14	22.4	3.7	0.6	0.2
Scarborough Town Centre	45,297	66	17	15.4	0.9	0.2	0.1
Mississauga City Centre	50,372	71.7	18	9.3	1.2	0.1	0.2

Source: Transportation Tomorrow Survey, special tabulations.

the subway corridor is too low to justify this investment and resident opposition has restricted redevelopment possibilities along the new line (Barber, 1997). Thus, in all likelihood, this line will at best make a modest contribution to the transit and intensification objectives laid out in official planning documents. A more flagrant departure from these objectives is the ongoing extension and widening of expressways within the GTA's suburban realm. In contrast to the land-use impact of the Sheppard subway line, that of the newest GTA expressway, the 69-kilometre Highway 407, which crosses the entire metropolitan region, is not in doubt. Like all expressways, Highway 407 will contribute to further extension of the agglomeration's car-oriented, low-density realm.

What of the relevance of the planning system as a whole in the face of this inability to implement intensification objectives? Ironically, given the tone of its discourse, the leading urban development impact of the contemporary planning process lies in its coordination and design of sprawling suburban development. Official plans and zoning persist in their segmentation of land into monofunctional, mainly low-density, zones and in the provision of sufficient road capacity to cater to (and encourage) heavy reliance on the car. Thus the reality is that planning is far more effective in maintaining the present urban development trajectory than in redirecting it.

The dichotomy between planning's intensification ideal and its active involvement in the low-density suburban development process is embedded in the very architecture of official plans. Recently, these documents have been divided into two parts that lack consistency with each other. The prelude to most official plans consists of statements of environmental and, in the GTA, intensification objectives, but these themes are downplayed in the remainder of the documents, whose purpose is to prescribe specific land uses and which has force of law (albeit with possibility for amendments).

Contemporary planning has not lost its idealism as argued by writers such as Beauregard (1990) and Knox (1993). Rather, this idealism has been confined to a planning discourse that is increasingly divorced from planning practice.

UNDERSTANDING THE GAP BETWEEN DISCOURSE AND URBAN DEVELOPMENT

What has caused the disconnection between planning discourse and implementation to become a defining feature of contemporary planning? This dissonance proceeds in large part from the coincidence between an ambitious planning discourse – imprinted by vocal environmental advocacy groups that excel at making use of the participation process – and an impairment of governments' intervention capacity. Debilitated public agencies in the throws of a fiscal crisis, a rise of neoliberal ideology and economic globalization (which enhances firms' mobility and thus impedes possibilities of regulating them) are poorly positioned to actualize this discourse. These circumstances make it difficult for governments to impose the restrictive development regulations and proceed with the costly infrastructure required to accomplish the urban development turnaround called for in contemporary planning discourse. For example, a tight public purse prevents governments from putting in place high-quality public transportation systems in advance of peripheral urbanization so as to promote developments registering higher density and less car reliance than the run-of-the-mill suburb. The planning of new developments around high-quality transit systems could be particularly favourable to neo-traditional neighbourhoods by enabling them to operate as pre-war railway commuter villages, and thus reduce their car dependence in accordance with the principles of neo-traditionalism (on the goals of the neo-traditional planning movement, see Katz, 1994). Not only do public sector financial difficulties rule out such a profound rethinking of peripheral urbanization but, as noted, they have also blocked transit and intensification proposals formulated over the last fifteen years.

Insufficient government intervention capacity to meet the objectives of planning discourse are equally attributable to a maladjustment of the institutional structure as to the implementation of planning objectives, especially on the metropolitan scale. There is an absence in the GTA, and for that matter in other Canadian agglomerations, of agencies with the capacity to plan at the scale of the metropolitan region. The Organization for the Greater Toronto Area had such a mandate, but bereft of implementation capacity was limited to an advisory role (Farrow, 1997; Frisken, 1993: 170). In January 1999, the Ontario Conservative government set up the Greater Toronto Services Board, which, in addition to its role in welfare revenue redistribution, was originally meant to coordinate urban development within the GTA. But, bowing to pressures from municipal and regional administrations, the province devised a weak agency whose planning responsibilities are confined to promoting (not enforcing) the coordination of infrastructure, service, and economic development and the operating of the GO commuter train and bus system. Reaction on the part of the municipal and regional governments of the GTA is typical of the reception given everywhere to attempts to create powerful metropolitan-wide planning agencies. Local and regional governments, particularly suburban jurisdictions, are suspicious of any encroachment on their planning responsibilities, fearing limitations on their development potential – and hence of their potential assessment base.

Apprehension of the peripheral GTA municipalities about a metropolitan planning agency is not without ground. One of the main justifications for the existence of such an administration is the pursuit of metropolitan-wide planning objectives such as intensification. Meanwhile, the actualization of this concept entails a redirection of much of the growth from greenfield sites to locations within the urbanized perimeter (thus within the more centrally located municipalities). Municipal administrations also dread that a metropolitan agency might impose types of land use such as high-density and/or affordable housing, which are susceptible to anger by their residents (Tomalty, 1996). Note that, while intensification necessitates coordinated intervention at the scale of an agglomeration precisely to channel much of the development within the built perimeter, sprawl unfolds equally well within regions that are administratively centralized or fragmented. For the production of the suburban patchwork of monofunctional zones, it does not make much difference whether planning is carried out by a single metropolitan, a few large, or many small administrations. Whatever the local government institutional set up, provincial responsibility for major arterials and expressways, and occasionally for other structuring infrastructures, provides sufficient coordination to assure a measure of metropolitan-wide integration.

The concern of municipalities about residents' reactions to intensification initiatives imposed by overarching agencies brings us to the

NIMBY syndrome, another factor inhibiting the actualization of the planning discourse. The tendency for residents to oppose density elevations for fear of changes in the character of their neighbourhood, overtaxed services, and a fall in property values, represents a formidable challenge to intensification (Hulchanski, 1993: 20; Kanter, 1993: 6).

There is also in place a system of mutually reinforcing interests – comprising suburban municipalities, developers, and consumers – which perpetuates urban sprawl. In its enduring post-war form, suburban type development generates profits for developers, satisfies the preference of a majority of households for the single family home, and provides local governments with a predictable stream of revenue (on housing preferences, see Mary McDonough Research Associates, 1994).[3] These three groups of actors are thus interlocked in an urban development process driven by shared expectations and the furthering of their respective interests. The enduring influence of these groups is evidenced in the persistence of low-density, car-oriented suburban development, despite the alignment of official plans on provincially imposed intensification objectives.[4] A recent study has shown how local administrations successfully circumvent these provincial directives through their day-to-day planning decisions in order to carry on with dispersed forms of development (Tomalty, 1996).

Perhaps the most influential factor accounting for the entrenchment of dispersed patterns is the dynamic that prevails between, on the one hand, their low-density and highly specialized zones and, on the other, a nearly universal reliance on the automobile. This reliance, combined with massive road and expressway investment, reduces accessibility gradients, multiplies potential locations for all activities, and thereby lessens the attraction of the core while elevating that of the periphery. What is more, the resulting need to accommodate large numbers of cars hinders efforts to intensify urban sectors (Barnett, 1995: 25–9). For example, after parking requirements were factored in, the "Main Street" program, which purported to increase density along Metro Toronto arterials by lining them with six-storey residential buildings providing ground-level shops, ceased to be economically viable. The program was forestalled by pressures from residents of abutting neighbourhoods worried about the possible use of their street for the parking needs of the new apartment buildings and the refusal of the City of Toronto Land Use Committee to amend the requirement for each unit to be provided with one parking space (Farncombe, 1993; Gilbert, 1993). In a similar vein, as seen, the need to accommodate large amounts of cars on high-capacity roads and surface parking lots is key to suburban downtowns' inability to evolve as intended into pedestrian and transit-conducive environments capable of generating a high level of inner synergy.

The prevailing transportation/land-use dynamic forces certain behaviour patterns on urban residents, such as a reliance on the car for commuting and shopping purposes. It is indeed difficult in this urban context to function without a car. These imposed behaviours can be sources of cognitive dissonance for individuals whose values would have steered them towards other options, either made difficult, or simply ruled out, by current transportation and land-use patterns (Skelton et al., 1995).

PLANNING IN THE POSTMODERN ERA

As the label implies, postmodernism can be defined by what differentiates it from modernism (Cooke, 1990; Featherstone, 1988: 197).[5] Indeed, many prominent features of postmodernism derive from reactions against modernism. This is the case of the modernist cult of technological progress confronted with the postmodern emphasis on the environment and nostalgia. Likewise, modernism's "unidimensionality" makes way for the postmodern diversity of values and discourses (Marcuse, 1964).[6] This diversification is mirrored in an intense preoccupation with symbols of identity, another trait of postmodernism. Postmodernism is also characterized by the loss of confidence in the criteria that served to establish the superiority of certain forms of discourse over others (Bauman, 1988; Foster, 1985; Gibbins, 1989: 15; Jameson, 1984; Lyotard, 1984). Views sanctioned by science or by experts enjoyed disproportional influence over the modernist period (Dear, 1986: 377; Harvey, 1989: 66; Soja, 1989: 180–1). Postmodernism, in contrast, produces a much wider spectrum of discourses in the absence of broadly recognized validation criteria. This multiplication of points of reference gives rise to a cacophony of discourses that carries the threat of a trivialization of the entire discourse sphere (Bauman, 1985; Jacoby, 1987).[7] Direct experience of the adverse consequences of realizations emanating from expert and scientifically derived discourses also feeds postmodern scepticism towards such discourses (Goodchild, 1990: 131–3; Goodman, 1971; Ravetz, 1980).

Postmodern diversity is not confined to the discourse sphere. It manifests itself equally in the growing number of lifestyles, which find expression in increasingly differentiated consumption of goods and services. In this context, consumption takes on a strong symbolic dimension by assuming an important role in establishing one's link to a lifestyle category (Baudrillard, 1983; Bourdieu, 1984). Diversification of lifestyles is not alone in fostering a growing distinction between social groups. Distance between groups is further increased by income polarization associated with the passage from Fordism to post-Fordism, which has brought massive deindustrialization and public sector cutbacks, both resulting in a contraction of the middle class (Economic Council of Canada, 1990; Rifkin, 1995; Yalnizyan, 1998). With direct relevance to planning's recent evolution, certain individuals have adopted an environmentally friendly lifestyle, for example, by engaging in organic gardening and minimizing their use of the car. However, reflective of postmodern pluralism and equally pertinent to contemporary planning is the contrasting present predilection for energy-voracious sport utility vehicles and various forms of gas-powered recreation equipment. Postmodernism is also tied to manifestations of diversity as regards identity – visible in multiculturalism, the rise of nationalisms, and the affirmation of sexual preferences (Bauman, 1988). This differentiation carries the risk of communication breakdowns between social groups set apart by growing cultural distance. Under pressure from the NIMBY reactions it prompts, this cultural distance often translates into spatial distance.

The respective influence of the numerous discourses that crowd the postmodern scene is uneven. This lopsided impact is tied to the nature of the venues they invest. Some media, conveying certain types of discourses, reach a wide audience. By contrast, other discourses are confined to media with a much narrower reach and are thus restricted to small audiences. Planning is one venue for discourses. Since the participatory transition, environmental and social advocacy groups have been particularly active in influencing the planning discourse. Relative to many other discourses, the planning discourse enjoys prestige because it is formulated with the purpose of shaping decisions. As a result, it can draw on the resources required to conduct background studies, accommodate public participation and prepare visually appealing documents. But, as argued here, this prestige is increasingly out of step with this discourse's waning influence on decisions affecting urban development.

The scant impact of certain postmodern discourses, such as the contemporary planning discourse, reflects the persistence of power structures inherited from the modernist era, which have remained in large part impervious to the postmodern explosion and relativity of discourses and lifestyles. The evolution of planning since the late 1960s has demonstrated that the discourse sphere can be swayed in different directions, with little consequence for urban form. For all its harsh criticism of prevailing urban development trends, the postmodern planning discourse has had little impact on the urban power structure (that is, the categories of actors who are rewarded by prevailing forms of development) or on this development itself. Developers do not need to be active on the planning discourse scene in order to determine the form urbanization takes. Municipal governments' fiscal dependence on growth assures their attentiveness to developers' requests. Developers are also known to finance generously local politicians who support their ventures – another potential source of ascendency on municipal government decisions. The ability of the urban power structure to produce sprawling development without feeling the need to broadcast a discourse to counter that of intensification testifies to both this power structure's direct channels of influence on decisions and the limited impact of planning discourse. While strong arguments are voiced about the need to reverse present development trends, there appears to be no need to explain or justify staying the low-density suburbanization course.

This observation regarding the persistence of power structures within cities can be generalized to other levels of society. There is no need to insist here on the endurance, some would say strengthening, of power relations grounded in the capitalist system. Society-wide political structures have also retained much of their modern configuration. This has created the paradox that, as discourses, values, and lifestyles diversify, governments dilute the meaning of their discourse to the point of relying on a few vague slogans in attempts to appeal to as large an electorate as possible. Clearly, government rhetoric is one form of discourse that resists the postmodern tendency towards differentiation. In this same vein, governments find it difficult to adjust their interventions to the postmodern plurality of needs and preferences. The debate over the amalgamation of Metro Toronto cities into a new City of Toronto provides a vivid illustration of the clash between a modern political power structure and manifestations of the postmodern values of identity and difference. On one side of the debate stood a Conservative provincial government bent on reducing municipal expenditure through standardization and economies of scale by amalgamating Metro Toronto municipalities. Confronting this government were the local municipalities and numerous citizens groups upholding intermunicipal diversity regarding identity, built environment, planning, and services. Opponents rallied a strong majority of votes in municipal referendums. Yet, the province used its constitutional power to enforce amalgamation. In sum, the effect of postmodern discourses on society can be likened to that of waves on the sea, while the impact of power structures resembles that of underwater currents.

Attempts to create new power structures that implement proposals voiced in the postmodern planning discourse encountered severe impediments. Reform coalitions, which for a time assumed power in a number of central cities where they were instrumental in ushering in participatory planning, lacked stability because they were torn between opposing interests. It soon became apparent that these coalitions' perspective on urban conflicts was oversimplified. The neat fault lines – between left and right wing agendas or between residents and developers – that were at the core of the reform movement's tenets did not do justice to the variety of interests on the urban scene and the multidirectional character of urban conflicts. These coalitions' political aspirations were further thwarted by the nature of the institutional structures within which they operated, in particular by the fiscal dependence of municipal governments. To maintain and expand their municipality's assessment base, reform councils were compelled to spare or lure wealthy residents, private firms (especially the development industry), sometimes at the expense of demands from groups with less capacity to prop up municipal budgets (see Thomas, 1997, for an account of how this dilemma was felt within Montreal Citizens' Movement).

In this context of greater distance between planning rhetoric and the nature of urban development, planning participation and the attendant discourse formulation process may appear to be losing relevance, with a consequent risk of demobilization (see Grant, 1994: 217–8). This gap has brought discredit on political administrations that have actively encouraged participation. These administrations have been branded as ineffective, because they were more interested in public participation and political rhetoric than in concrete policies susceptible to improve living conditions. This type of criticism played no small part in the 1995 defeat of the Ontario NDP government and in that of the Montreal Citizens' Movement in 1994. In Ontario, immediately after taking power, the Conservative government curtailed planning participation, invoking the high cost of the planning process and the delays it inflicts on development (Ontario, 1996).

The discussion of planning's position within postmodernism begs the question: What can planning achieve in this context? This is not an idle question. Difficulties in actualizing the planning rhetoric do not imply that the environmental, economic, and social themes that pervade planning documents lack relevance. Environmental degradation at both the urban and global levels, social polarization, and problems in meeting urbanization expenses all call for policy responses. There are two possible approaches to meeting objectives embedded in the planning discourse. One approach would involve a direct challenge of the power structure and urban dynamic that underlie present forms of urban development. It would call for a profound transformation of society given the entrenchment of this structure and dynamic. While unlikely to muster sufficient support in present circumstances, major environmental, economic, or social crises could raise the impetus for such a course of action. For a time in the 1970s, in the wake of the oil crisis, governments did give serious consideration to policies aiming at augmenting densities and inducing a shift from car to transit use. In many metropolitan regions, this was indeed a time of major public transportation investment. The other approach, represented by the options listed below, comprises urban changes feasible within the bounds of the prevailing power structure and urban dynamic.

One could envisage the creation of high-density corridors that would be well served by efficient transit services (rail or busways). These corridors would appeal to individuals who seek pedestrian and transit-oriented alternatives to prevailing forms of suburbanization and who cannot live in the inner city due to housing-cost and work-proximity issues. The corridor option would avoid the head-on confrontation – with interests associated with prevailing types of development – that would inevitably ensue from blanket reliance on regulations in order to intensify all peripheral development. In addition, initiatives could also be taken with the deliberate intent of diversifing development patterns in a fashion that would jive with the postmodern explosion of values and lifestyles. Rather than using, as is presently the case, housing cost and life cycle as the primary, or only, factors of suburban neighbourhood differentiation, the physical layout of new residential areas could be particularized according to the lifestyle and values of their residents. There could be, for example, environmental communities provided with pedestrian and cycle paths, energy conservation devices, organic gardens, and advanced recycling programs; mutual help communities where the accent would be placed on networks of care involving volunteer providers; or, perhaps, clusters of artisans occupying live-work units and taking advantage of proximity to exchange ideas and products.

To be sure, these options fall well short from full compliance with planning discourse recommendations. The corridor approach would induce intensification, but only in certain areas. Its impact on agglomeration-wide density and transit use would therefore be slim. Meanwhile, if consistent with the growing distinction between social groups characteristic of postmodernism, the creation of distinctive communities does not constitute such an intensification strategy. Still, these options would represent a first major step away from the highly standardized car-oriented post-war suburbanization formula. In their early stages, they would play the role of demonstration projects, displaying the possibility of accommodating various ways of living within a more physically diversified suburban realm. These projects could occasion changes of preferences on the part of a number of consumers and a focusing of these new preferences on concrete models of urbanization. By devising planning processes that are conducive to alternative forms of suburbanization, giving rise to new markets and eventually raising the interest of developers for this emerging consumer demand, such demonstration projects could prompt a realignment within the urban power structure that produces the city's built environment.

CONCLUSION

This chapter has related the evolution of planning from a period when a great deal of consistency prevailed between a transformative discourse and planning outcomes to the present situation, when discourse and practice have become dissociated from each other. The chapter has discussed the circumstances that have provoked the present gap by, on the one hand, emboldening the planning discourse and, on the other, undermining government intervention capacity and encouraging the status quo as regards urban development. It has also insisted on adverse outcomes of this situation, more specifically, a difficulty in reorienting prevailing urban development trends and addressing their environmental sequels. The loss of discourse impact on planning practice may well occasion a demobilization of individuals and groups participating in the planning process. This would curb the production of a discourse that is critical – if not very effective at bringing change – of the prevailing planning formula, which is instrumental in the *ad infinitum* replication of the post-war suburban model of development.

By focusing on the links between the evolution of the planning process and postmodern societal transitions, this chapter has downplayed other possible perspectives on this evolution. An area of investigation that would have merited further treatment is the power dimension of the narrated planning transitions. According to this approach, recent planning predicaments would signal above all the scant political clout enjoyed by the social groups adhering to the values conveyed by the planning discourse, by comparison to the weighty influence of interests behind the production of the built environment.

NOTES

1 The environmental focus of planning documents over this period extended beyond the intensification concept to include a variety of other measures, such as recycling and the protection of environmentally

significant areas (on the widening scope of issues addressed in these plans, see Kaiser and Godschalk, 1995).

2 These included documents commissioned by, or originating from, the Office for the Greater Toronto Area (OGTA) (BLG, 1991; IBI Group, 1990a, 1990b; GTA 1991a, 1991b), the report of the Royal Commission on the Future of the Toronto Waterfront (1992), the report of the GTA Task Force (1996), and official plans from the City of Toronto (former boundaries) (1992), Metro Toronto (1994), as well as from all other GTA regions (Miller, Emereau, and Farrow, 1997; Tomalty, 1997).

3 Suburban municipalities do not readily subscribe to the view that intensification reduces municipal expenses and is thus favourable to municipal budgets. They prefer to rely on the predictability of proven formulas over experimentation and on commonplace models, so as to accelerate development. Municipal scepticism about the equation between intensification and reduced expenditure is echoed in the literature (for example, Gordon and Wong, 1985).

4 On restrictions placed on urban design principles by market trends, see Ellin, 1996: 156–61.

5 The present account of postmodernism is admittedly sketchy and fragmentary. Beacons within a rather confounding literature include Featherstone, 1991; Kellner, 1988; Lyotard, 1984.

6 Nowhere has the postmodern reaction against modernism been as evident as in the field of architecture, where stylistic eclecticism and playfulness took over in the 1970s from the austere international style (see, for example, Davis, 1985; Jencks, 1984; Venturi, 1966; Venturi et al., 1977).

7 On planning's recent efforts towards conceptual pluralism, see Friedmann, 1996; Friedmann and Kuester, 1994; and Thomas, 1996.

PART FOUR

Fiscal Challenges

13 Emerging Trends in Urban Affairs – A Municipal Manager's View

W. MICHAEL FENN

Throughout the 1990s, there has been a subtle but significant change in the self-defined and publicly acknowledged role of municipal politicians and other local "opinion leaders." Democratic political processes at the local level have traditionally encouraged and rewarded advocacy by municipal politicians on behalf of individuals and groups in the community. This traditional role sought to attract more fiscal and program resources for the issues and programs that favoured specific individuals and groups in the community. As a general statement, there has always been enough capacity in the budgets of moderately prosperous municipalities to respond positively, if only partially, to such advocacy.

With increased fiscal and budgetary pressures, however, municipal leaders find themselves in a new and less comfortable role. Their electors demand stable or reduced levels of taxation, at a time when real fiscal resources are declining. This places municipal politicians and other local officials in a position where they can no longer protect many existing programs and levels of service, much less accommodate new demands. They find themselves increasingly in a position of deciding on the "greater need" or the "greater good," in allocating declining fiscal resources among existing and new demands for municipal services. In the face of competing local groups and their needs, most municipal politicians have gone from being advocates to being arbiters and referees.

A NEW LABOUR RELATIONS ENVIRONMENT

This need to find resources to maintain support for municipal services has also encouraged many municipal politicians to target expenditures that do not obviously translate themselves into program activity with a direct impact in communities and neighbourhoods. In the parlance of business, they are challenging "non-value added" expenditures and practices. Local elected representatives are more frequently seen to challenge both municipal managers and public sector workers, whether during collective bargaining or when considering alternative ways of delivering municipal services at lower cost or with a higher degree of customer satisfaction.

Many municipalities, especially in older centres, are encountering the limits of conventional collective bargaining in the public sector. Post-Second World War public sector unions developed in an environment of monopoly service-delivery and expanding public revenues, without the disciplines of either profitability or competition. The strength and degree of public-sector unionization in Ontario was further accelerated in the past three decades, in parallel with increased unionization of the provincial and federal public services and Ontario Hydro.

During the same three decades, however, private sector unions facing "market place" pressures have hammered out, with company management across North America, new and creative approaches to work rules, compensation, competition, and productivity. Where this productivity-based labour-management accommodation has failed, so too have many of the companies that could not find that accommodation.

In the public sector, neither labour nor management, including political leadership, has faced this challenge in a serious way until very recently. For the most part, labour legislation, union contract provisions, and work practices still reflect an environment that has largely disappeared in the competitive industrial and commercial workplaces of Canada.

THE CITIZEN AS CONSUMER

Until recently, municipal government often existed, as did senior levels of government, in a political and managerial environment where organizational, political, and union elites were the primary influences. With a captive monopoly market and with a revenue guaranteed by the sanction of seizure of property for non-payment of municipal property and utility charges, it was not surprising that the consumer's voice was not paramount. Citizens often grew to expect (and to joke about) the inefficiency and poor quality of services from "city hall."

As cable television companies, telephone systems, and energy providers have learned, however, even the customers of captive monopolies can become demanding if they are taken for granted too long, or if they discover their power as retail consumers. In the 1990s, the retail phenomenon of the "demanding customer" made its appearance on the municipal scene. The effect on municipal decision-makers was immediate: for in a municipal monopoly, virtually every "consumer" of municipal services is also a municipal taxpayer and a municipal elector.

With the advent of municipal "customer" came another feature of 1990s consumerism: the "disconnect" between price and quality. Experience with "new format" retailers and financial services, computers, electronic equipment, and food products had taught consumers that prices did not have to rise to maintain or increase quality, quantity, availability, or choice. This experience struck at two basic municipal "truisms": "more services must equal more taxes" and "annual inflation means municipal services must always cost more." Citizens now feel little inconsistency in demanding restraint in property tax increases, while demanding that the range, quality, and level of community services be maintained or even expanded. These developments create significant problems for those elected to leadership roles in local government.

COMMUNITY LEADERSHIP AND AUTHORITY

Societal change is also having a significant impact on the role of the elected representative at the local government level and on other local opinion leaders and officials. For generations, the task of the municipal politician in North America had traditionally been to ensure that the groups in society with which he or she was associated would receive their share of the community's public resources. A key corollary to this role was the notion that society, including local communities, tended to organize themselves into community groups with strong affinities, based on geography, ethnicity, religion, economic circumstances, or their primary focus of community interest (business, labour, transportation, women's issues, health care, housing, etc.).

Community groups, in turn, put forward leaders in whom they invested their trust and on whom they conferred the authority to represent them in resolving public policy issues. These community leadership roles reflected the reality that group affiliations were strong. These roles were also reinforced by the media, by convention, and by electoral politics (underpinning "machine politics" in older US cities). As a result, average citizens in a municipality could expect their community group leader to represent their interests and to have that representation respected and reported upon by the political leadership and the local media.

With the gradual erosion of strong affiliations among the general population, however, came an important change in the local political landscape. In the eyes of municipal officials, community leaders were less obviously speaking authoritatively for the people that they nominally represented. Even when community leaders professed to speak for a broad constituency, local politicians, who typically know their communities very well, recognized that the spokesperson for some community interest might not be speaking for much more than a small executive group with limited influence in the broader constituency.

Municipal politicians certainly knew that very few community leaders were any longer in a position to "deliver" their constituency, nor did those community leaders continue to make such a claim. Community leaders might give useful insights into their views of the people with whom they were associated, but they were increasingly reluctant to act independently as leaders, preferring the safe role of delegated spokesperson.

Demographics are also having their effect. As the "baby boom" generation ages, larger numbers than anticipated are taking early retirement, at an age that allows them, many for the first time, to become more involved with civic issues. This constituency – whose impact on all other areas of North American society has been decisive for the past generation – will have the numbers, the skills, the time, and in many cases the resources to influence opinion and to make demands on the municipal service-delivery system.

THE ROLE OF THE MEDIA

Part of the problem was that many electors were no longer looking to traditional affiliations as their primary source of information and opinion on civic affairs. Opinion leaders might not only be the local clergy, service club president, or union official but also, just as easily, the neighbour who was involved in Neighbourhood Watch or the community newspaper columnist. With the declining importance of church, ethnicity, extended family and voluntarism in a busy commuter society, the media became a primary influence on decision-making for the mass of the local electorate.

The fragmentation of the media and the emerging dominance of broad-based electronic media news sources also made it increasingly difficult for a local or regional municipality to reach the whole community with a common message and to engage that community in civic affairs. Outside of major centres, the problem of communication was further complicated both by the loss of adequate coverage of municipal news in local daily or community newspapers and by the metropolitan media's preoccupation with metropolitan politics.

Intense commercial competition in the news media has taken its toll on the nature of municipal coverage. As journalists sought local news stories with "entertainment" value, they often neglected "city hall" altogether, awarded attention to "colourful" personalities, or avoided the complex issues associated with service restructuring or fiscal reform until the impacts became sensationalistic. With the rising influence of the electronic media came the preoccupation with the sixty-second "clip" and the "photo op," which tended to trivialize complex issues that, in the past, would have been the focus of detailed analysis by widely read and influential print journalists.

These two developments (loss of group affiliation and media relevance) led Ontario municipal governments to initiate a wave of new, direct-communication, and citizen-consultation measures. Municipal politicians and school trustees increasingly wondered (and occasionally asked aloud) if the community representatives facing them at public meetings really represented the community. The need for municipal leaders to look beyond the "community representative" and the media to confirm the views of the broader community, and to find ways to understand and to influence the community's views, led to a steady erosion in the role of interest-group leadership and the effort to open new channels of communication with the broader community. With the loss of a media-reinforced community leadership, however, came a loss of the municipal politician's ability to rely on brokerage politics – at a time when it was in greatest demand – to deal with reconciling competing interests in an environment of declining resources.

The rapid increase in personal computer ownership, supplemented by the internet, will also influence community decision-making. Since municipal government, by its nature, reacts more quickly and directly to customer demands and citizen input, a proliferation in the ability to express an informed opinion on civic issues – from tax rates to service quality – will place more burden on local governments than on the inevitably more remote governments at Queen's Park or in Ottawa. Virtually every municipality now maintains a public website and email

access. Civic authorities will soon find this new and ready access attracting larger numbers of active users.

EARLY RESPONSES

Among the early responses to the societal changes outlined above was a more widespread use of local and commissioned polling – along with the use of "focus" groups of targeted or randomly selected citizens – to deal with specific municipal issues. This information was used both to gauge and to guide public opinion. Rather than going through "community representatives," it guides the effort to make a direct appeal to citizens. Municipal councillors and other community leaders increasingly view their leadership role as one of framing and enunciating issues, rather than acting as "trustees" in deciding issues on behalf of the constituencies that they represent most directly.

As municipalities have increasingly been seen (and increasingly see themselves) to be service-delivery corporations as well as government institutions, they have supplemented political processes with techniques drawn from the consumer marketplace. For example, in fields such as municipal recreation or economic development, civic interests are governed by "marketing" plans and there is frequent use of commercial electronic communications.

Just as industry and the commercial service sectors have been forced to embrace restructuring and consolidation to improve productivity and reduce costs, so too have municipal governments. In recent years, large numbers of smaller Ontario municipalities have consolidated their operations. Similar pressures have been felt on major municipalities, although in the absence of legislative direction, fiscal pressures alone seem insufficient to generate institutional reform.

Many municipalities have undertaken measures that have attempted to increase the level of marketplace competition in the delivery of municipal services. The selective use of privatization of services and facilities complemented by the more widespread use of competitive contracting, or contracting-out, have become routine features of municipal efforts to promote commercialization of municipal service-delivery and service-financing.

One other interesting development that has appeared, primarily in the economic development sphere, is the increasing realization that urban economies (not national or provincial economies) are the basis of comparison in the global marketplace for job-creating industrial and commercial investments. The emergence of the so-called "city-state" or regional urban economy will inevitably add pressure to harmonize municipal licensing and trade regulations across regional trading areas, perhaps under the auspices of municipal governments with wider geographic mandates.

Investors also target regions with a "business-friendly" political and regulatory environment, including competitive levels of property taxation and utility rates. With the recent implementation of current value assessment and electricity deregulation in Ontario, those comparisons are easily done among Ontario municipalities and economic regions.

RISKS AND OPPORTUNITIES

With the pervasiveness and influence of the electronic media, municipalities will find themselves increasingly drawn to use electronic broadcast media to communicate their message. Along with increased use of public opinion polling and focus groups, electronic media offers the attractive political option of "going over the heads" of community leadership and media journalists to speak directly to the municipal "customer." Consistently marginalizing traditional participants in the decision-making process carries risks, however, even if traditional community leaders themselves recognize that their roles have been altered or diminished by a changing society. A sense of loss of power among traditional local elites can contribute to opposition for opposition's sake and to conflict between established and new voices within particular segments of the community.

Advances in electronic communications and consumer market research also make feasible, perhaps for the first time in this century, the Athenian ideal of direct democracy. The increasing interest in referendums and the use of full-membership voting by political parties illustrate this interest. Direct democracy offers a greater opportunity to meet customer needs and to engage citizens. However, the criticism of the electronic media for trivializing civic issues could be equally applied to direct democracy measures. As the saying goes: for every complex issue, there is an answer that is simple, straightforward, and wrong. Direct democracy measures can, by turning public policy questions into "favourite toothpaste" questions, undermine the balance that underpins the satisfactory resolution to every complex societal issue.

A POSITIVE APPROACH TO
THE NEW REALITIES

In the municipalities of the City of Burlington and the Regional Municipality of Hamilton-Wentworth, a five-point strategy was developed to deal with these "new realities." It draws on the same private sector experience that senior municipal officials observed within their local business communities. The five elements of the strategy sought to: (1) employ market research techniques to understand better the expectations of citizens; (2) apply value analysis, to determine where municipal operations could "add value" (or not); (3) introduce competition into public services by exposing municipal operations to the test of commercial competitiveness; (4) make municipal governments the "governor" of service delivery to the community through the use of commercial and non-profit contracts, rather than as the direct deliverer of municipal services; and, (5) build community loyalty and support by marketing a relationship between the community and its community government that extends beyond individual service transactions, i.e., "relationship marketing."

MARKET RESEARCH IN THE PUBLIC SECTOR

In these two municipalities, the use of commercial techniques to improve the effectiveness and cost-efficiency of municipal services began with market research. Objective analysis had to go beyond the traditional representatives of the community, whether elected or institutional, to deal with "average" citizens in the home. Municipal government activities needed to be recast as a defined set of several dozen products and services. They also had to be described in a fashion and in a language that allowed the consumer of those products and services to identify them easily, as a prelude to evaluating their quality, cost, availability, and importance. "Product knowledge" also required the citizen-consumer to understand the nature of the municipal service and to base an opinion on customer interaction, rather than mere perception. If a consumer rarely or never used a service, the consumer's view on the quality of that service had to be weighted accordingly. Likewise, links could be made between the priority of a service, the perceived need for improvements in quality, the willingness to see it privatized, and the higher "user fee" charged for its delivery by the municipality.

VALUE ANALYSIS

The value analysis process aimed to move beyond the superficial preoccupation with cheerful "customer service." The ability of those delivering the service to meet the real needs of the client (including a capacity to alter the delivery of the service "at the counter or at the curb-side" while still respecting the consistently applied public interest) came to be a true test of "added value." Hours of operation and access proved important in a society of commuters and two-income families. The ability to count unit-costs for delivering services and to compare them with last year's cost, or with the cost of similar services in similar municipalities, was another test of "value-added" service. In Burlington, this led to an interest in "activity-based costing" or "ABC" and, in Hamilton-Wentworth, to an interest in financial, social, and environmental performance indicators.

One of the ways that "value" was determined was the degree to which resources were devoted to direct customer service, as distinct from the many corporate and political activities that are part of any bureaucratic activity and that add to "non-value-added" or "overhead" costs. By employing a methodical "re-engineering" analysis to the production of municipal services, it was often possible to eliminate wasted effort and duplication. In some cases, responsibility for ensuring quality service delivery could be placed directly with the consumer by "up-streaming" key elements of an activity (like encouraging taxes to be paid by automatic monthly bank withdrawals or requiring development applications and recreation registrations to be substantially completed before presentation at "city hall" or by email). New technologies also provided municipalities with the opportunity to reduce labour costs by the introduction of productivity-enhancing equipment and computer technology. Re-engineering identified opportunities for standardizing the most popular service delivery formats, thus offering the benefits of economies of scale and mass production, while preserving a degree of consumer choice.

The last elements of the commercial marketplace to be imported into the municipal sector were the use of multi-year business strategies and strategic planning and the related use of business plans to guide the development of budgets and the coordination of corporate objectives. These efforts have produced a great interest in defining more clearly the true cost of municipal products and services, through the development of cost-performance indicators and other measures of program performance. In some cases, the interest in performance indicators has led to a documentation of "benchmarks" or organizational "best practices" that account for the ability of some organizations to out-perform others in the same or analogous fields. Of special interest are the efforts to look beyond the usual comparators to other, similar lines of activity, some of which are drawn from the commercial sector, rather than the public sector.

Best practice analysis has had a particular impact on the appetite for municipal restructuring. Long resisted by municipal institutions, on the premise that large bureaucracies are inherently more inefficient than small organizations, municipal restructuring has had a sudden resurgence, at least in Ontario. The widespread consolidation of business corporations and the attendant improvement in their performance and profitability has led to a general discrediting of the notion that bigger is never better.

SERVICE BY CONTRACT

In municipalities the consolidation at the political level has been matched, through devices such as shared services bureaux, by widespread efforts to consolidate a range of transactional services such as accounting, printing, computer systems, payroll, fleet management, and others. Municipal efforts to promote privatization have seen considerable, if isolated, success. In Hamilton-Wentworth, the privatization of water and waste-water collection and treatment, solid waste management, and international airport operations have saved taxpayers millions, although not without considerable ongoing political debate, led in large measure by the labour movement. In Hamilton-Wentworth, the joint delivery of information technology, financial services, and human resources services also contributed materially to the decision to amalgamate the administrations and service delivery operations of the Hamilton city government and the regional municipality in 1998.

In other instances, the application of business principles led municipal governments like the Regional Municipality of Hamilton-Wentworth to offer service delivery contracts with neighbouring regional municipalities and to provide services that those municipalities could not provide as efficiently on their own or where an existing capacity was underutilized. A long-term contract to provide water services to an adjoining region, at a price that earned a modest profit for the municipality, was one example. In another, a number of municipalities contracted to have emergency planning and business-continuity services provided by a not-for-profit corporation established by the Regional Municipality and the local college. In many cases, contract service delivery was seen to be superior to outright service privatization or to retaining in-house delivery, since contracts combined competitive pressures, the reduction of in-house staffing and equipment requirements, and the ability to retain effective public control over key issues like fees and to insist on an enforceable quality of service.

It became obvious to many municipalities that longer-term contracts held many advantages. Long-term business partners, if they could depend on the business and amortize their investment over a longer term, were more inclined to invest in new technology and to assume the risks associated with public sector agreements. Conversely, however, municipalities began to realize that long-term contracts tended to make them more responsible for the economic health and profitability of their contractor. This "business relationship" could place the municipality in a difficult position if there were later changes in the economic assumptions on which both sides entered into the contract. Likewise, the importance of preserving control over the revenue element of long-term or privatization contracts and the ability to respond to subsequent business amalgamations involving the prime contractor have been issues with many solid-waste management contracts. As the field of available providers diminishes, moreover, a municipality that has been "out of the business" of direct delivery for some time can find that it does not have the expertise, equipment, or human resources to take back a function that has been contracted out for an extended period.

RELATIONSHIP MARKETING

With the rapid turnover in products and technology, many large multinational commercial enterprises have recognized that they must compete with other firms, not just with competitive products. The demanding product competition among suppliers, as seen most readily in the automotive parts industry, has put many firms at risk of losing long-time, business-sustaining contracts for products and services. As a result, firms like Nortel and Dofasco have borrowed the Japanese industrial practice of developing a long-term business relationship in which the purchaser and the supplier see their interests in common and as mutually supportive. This relationship allows firms to weather economic downturns or periodic reverses in the marketplace.

In the public sector, the general impatience of taxpayers put governments at all levels in competition with one another for the increasingly begrudged taxpayer dollar. For regional municipalities, like Hamilton-Wentworth, this represented a special challenge. In common with most regional municipalities across Ontario, polls said that regional government services were widely recognized for their quality and importance (police, water, major roads, public health, etc.). The regional government providing those services was, by contrast, seen as unresponsive and remote. The experience of Burlington, on the other hand, was that the local municipality could find itself the beneficiary of a considerable degree of good will if the services for which it was responsible were well regarded by the citizens and the direct link between those services and the people at "city hall" was recognized by the citizens.

In the case of Hamilton-Wentworth, a business-like effort was made to document the quality and importance of its services (and to link them in the public mind to the regional municipality), to understand the customer, to respond to the needs of that customer, and to market the role of the regional municipality in meeting those customer needs. Over time, the relationship was enhanced, although labour-relations and municipal restructuring issues periodically eroded the effort to build that customer responsiveness. During collective bargaining and at other strategic points, however, the region's management reinforced the notion that the best way to protect employment and to "earn" extra compensation was to prove to a skeptical taxpayer that regional services were important, efficiently delivered relative to the competitive alternatives, and deserving of continued taxpayer support in a climate of reduced fiscal resources.

COMPETING DEMANDS AND NEW ACCOUNTABILITIES

The process of public decision-making is always a matter of choosing between social "goods." By applying "consumer products" techniques to municipal service delivery, it proved possible to improve the value and efficiency of municipal services to the taxpayer. However, this broad-based approach continued to run the risk that special clienteles might be ignored because they could not fit into mainstream service delivery. Reflecting the political dimension of municipalities, there were also concerns that vested interests could marshal their constituencies to offset the identified best interests of the broader public in order to preserve some traditional benefit, level of service, or collective agreement provision.

"When the water-hole shrinks, the animals view each other differently": in a period of fiscal restraint, public authorities increasingly compete with each other for the scarce public dollar. Municipalities have found themselves in a competition for limited revenue sources, in a fiscal environment where senior levels of government and crown corporations have traditionally had more ready access to broader and less conspicuous public revenues than the property tax.

The same might be said of the competition for public support. While local municipal governments apparently enjoy a higher level of public support than other governmental bureaucracies, municipal services would likely not do as well in competition for public revenues against other major public priorities such as health care and public education, paying down the deficit and debt, or reducing taxes.

An important element in public support is the public's willingness to allow municipal governments to "commercialize" their activities on a realistic schedule, before losing patience and responding to the pressure to transfer public functions and public finances to private hands to enjoy the cost-efficiency proffered by the private sector. Finally, all governments, but especially those providing local community services, face the task of distinguishing their governmental, regulatory, and taxation roles from their roles as providers of a range of commercial-type products, facilities, and services.

CONCLUSIONS: NEW ACCOUNTABILITIES

If municipalities are to prevail in this environment, their focus should likely be – as in any "consumer products" environment – on accountability. Municipalities must be able to demonstrate "value" in their delivery of products and services. To ensure that the message gets to their various publics and is understood, municipalities also need to recruit to their cause the voices of those in the broader community and in the private sector who can add credence to municipal claims of being "business-like" in the discharge of both their service delivery and their governmental responsibilities.

Municipalities must be attuned to the changing marketplace in which they operate. A period of prolonged fiscal restraint can lead to a siege mentality, where the tendency in the public sector is to "circle the wagons" and to focus on preservation rather than innovation. It would make more sense, however, for local governments to anticipate and to explain emerging trends and new developments. They cannot simply continue to cut back and to deliver the same products and services in the traditional fashion. They must develop the confidence to abandon or reprice some services when their value can no longer be justified by fiscal priorities or consumer needs. Of equal importance, they must continue to develop and offer products and services that meet the emerging needs of the community that they serve – most likely within the ambit of existing resources.

Municipal bureaucracies should recognize that commercializing their activities means that new and different skills are required. Lower unit-cost and commercial contracts require greater emphasis on the skills of project management, "enabling" specification writing, and contract administration. This entails a fundamental change in the municipal public service built on in-house policy development and direct program delivery. Municipal councils and senior managers will have to learn to redouble the conscious effort to balance the needs of the community and the needs of particular interests – and to do so in a fashion that is most easily integrated with a low-cost business environment and an ability to standardize the range and quality of municipal services.

Finally, all municipalities are coming to realize that it is not enough simply to do well in relation to last year or their neighbouring municipality. Economic regions, often more than provinces or countries, are competing with one another in the global economy. Municipal governments must project an approach that says they understand the need to be competitive and to be accountable for that competitive position in a way that satisfies any objective observer, critic, or investor.

14 Some Puppets; Some Shoestrings! The Changing Intergovernmental Context

KEN CAMERON

There are two questions to be answered here. How has the intergovernmental context for urban affairs changed since the 1970s? How has this change affected the place of urban affairs on the policy agenda?

THE 1970S PARADIGM

Urban affairs policy and practice in the early 1970s were the outgrowth of the postwar spirit of reconstruction that dominated the 1950s (physical reconstruction) and 1960s (social reconstruction). The ambitious role the federal government created for itself was reflected in the establishment of the welfare state programs. These had significant implications for local and community government. It was confidently assumed that Canada's governments collectively had the financial wherewithal and expertise to provide a wide range of health, education, and social services based on need. The distribution of these resources among levels of governments, however, was flawed to the point of threatening effective program implementation. The commonly accepted diagnosis of the capability of local governments was that they were too fragmented in their jurisdiction both geographically and structurally to play an effective role and that they lacked appropriate revenue sources to develop and deliver programs equitably and efficiently.

The prescriptions developed by provincial governments to respond to these issues were comprehensive and impressive, as exemplified in the report of the Smith Committee on Taxation in Ontario (Ontario, 1967), the Graham Commission in Nova Scotia (Nova Scotia, 1974), and New Brunswick's Equal Opportunity Program. Common themes in these responses were: the restructuring of local government, the creation of regional entities, the reform of property assessment and taxation, and the enhancement and reform of provincial grant and revenue sharing programs. The overall approach was to fix up local government and then transfer power and fiscal capacity to this level to enable programs to be delivered locally with efficiency and equity. Whether the residents of the localities involved supported or even understood these measures was a question seldom asked and even more seldom answered. The federal government also got in on the act, in the face of massive suspicion from the provinces, by creating a Ministry of State for Urban Affairs to coordinate both the traditional activities of the federal government that affected cities (e.g., housing, ports, and airports) and the newer programs in multiculturalism, unemployment insurance, and the arts.

While local governments enjoyed all the attention, their fundamental demand was "show me the money." Efforts to respond to this demand produced tri-level meetings on national and provincial scales and new provincial-municipal mechanisms within provinces, in which local government tried to get money, the federal government tried to get influence, and the provinces tried to defend their dominance against both. On the national level, one result of this process was the first comprehensive study of the financial relationships between levels of government ever conducted in Canada, which was commissioned by the second (of two) national tri-level conferences in 1973 (Tri-Level Task Force, 1976). The Canadian Federation of Mayors and Municipalities (CFMM), now called the Canadian Federation of Municipalities (CFM), summarized and projected the trends in these relationships in a 1976 paper titled "Puppets on a Shoestring: the Effects on Municipal Government of Canada's System of Public Finance." The CFMM stated that the paper: "foreshadows the decline and fall of municipal government as we know it in Canada within five years." These trends suggest that autonomous municipal government will not survive without: 1) huge increases in property taxes or 2) unacceptable cutbacks in services city residents now demand – or both.

The outward signs of this projected trend were the steady loss of municipal power and increasing financial constraints. Grants from provincial and federal governments came with so many strings attached and represented such a large part of municipal budgets that municipalities were becoming puppets in a show run mainly by provincial governments (CFMM, 1976).

The report went on to deplore the fact that federal and provincial transfers had risen to 32 percent of municipal expenses in 1974–75 from 27 percent in 1969-70. For local government, this would turn out to be a lesson in being careful what to wish for.

THE PUNDITS FOILED AGAIN

Anyone looking at the situation in 1976 would have predicted one of two outcomes. Either the CFMM's dire prediction of the demise of local government would occur, or there would be a continued and reinvigorated effort to reform the financial and jurisdictional arrangements to meet modern needs. As it turned out, neither happened. In fact, nothing much happened at all. Why? The two reasons have their roots in national politics.

The first was the 1976 election of the Parti Québécois government in Québec, which quickly ended the federal government's adventure in urban affairs and in other fields where federal involvement could be exploited by Québec or other provinces as intrusion in provincial jurisdiction. This, in turn, reduced some of the sense of urgency felt by the provinces that they should be seen to be handling their responsibilities for urban affairs competently.

The second was the development in Canadians of an appetite to pursue what was considered the politically impossible: the reduction and elimination of federal and provincial deficits and a return to balanced budgets and manageable debt loads. The process started with reduction in federal direct expenditures, then moved on, under the Mulroney government, to the capping of transfers to the provinces and, under the Chretien government, to the drastic reduction of these transfers. A significant part of the provincial response was to cut back or eliminate transfers to local governments. In more extreme cases, provinces tampered unilaterally with local autonomy by transferring responsibilities to local government without funding or altering the value of the property tax base, often with little or no consultation.

THE NASTY NINETIES

By the mid 1990s, this retrenchment within the overall framework of the existing system had pretty well run its course, and public attention began to focus on the governmental system itself. Governments in several provinces and councillors in many municipalities were elected on platforms based on back-to-basics minimalism in government and included in their interpretation of their mandates a responsibility to do something about the number of local governments and the number of local elected representatives and staff needed to provide local public services. This led to a number of restructurings and amalgamations, ranging in scope from the provincially directed amalgamation of the municipalities of Metropolitan Toronto (1998) and the creation of the Regional Municipality of Halifax (1995) to the voluntary mergers of two municipalities and three regional districts in British Columbia's Fraser Valley (Vojnovic, 1998). Although administrative efficiency and cost savings were always cited as primary reasons for undertaking these changes, there has been little evidence produced, before or since, that demonstrates unequivocally that the benefits are anywhere equal to the cost of disruption and confusion endured by the local governments and their residents (Sancton, 1996).

URBAN AFFAIRS AND THE CURRENT POLICY AGENDA. WHAT DOES ALL THIS MEAN FOR URBAN AFFAIRS AS AN ITEM ON THE POLICY AGENDA?

Meaner Streets

The social problems of Canadian cities are significantly more serious than they were twenty-five years ago. The elimination of funding for many support and assistance programs has come at a time when cities have been trying to cope with poverty, drug and alcohol abuse, and new health challenges such as AIDS. There is a growing realization of the shortsightedness of measures such as the withdrawal of federal and provincial governments from the housing field and a growing understanding of the unintended side-effects of initiatives such as deinstitutionalization of mental-health services. With the federal government and most provinces moving from deficits to surpluses, there is an interest in finding appropriate mechanisms for senior-government intervention.

A Greater Appetite for Community-based Solutions

A good deal has been learned about ways of helping communities to help themselves. The provision of urban social services has been irrevocably changed by the experience of food banks, neighbourhood-watch programs, and similar initiatives that offer a different model from the 1970s-style megaprograms of senior governments.

Local Governments Have Lost Ground Financially but Gained Ground Politically

Although the financial capacity of local government has generally deteriorated, the skill, creativity, and stature of local elected representatives has grown to the point that they are a force to be reckoned with by provincial governments. With public opinion polls consistently showing local governments enjoying the highest levels of trust and support of all the orders of government, and with the level of downloading having reached a point beyond which it cannot go much farther, local governments have seized opportunities to craft solutions and have dared provincial governments to interfere. Intelligent puppets can learn how to cope with weak shoestrings. This pattern has been assisted by the decreasing relevance of nation-states in human affairs and the growing recognition of the semi-autonomous urban region or city-state as a logical scale at which to address the current challenges of social, economic, and environmental sustainability.

The Importance of New and Ancient Rights

The codification of rights in the Canadian Charter of Rights and Freedoms has created new challenges to delivering government services in ways that cannot be challenged as discriminatory. At the same time, the recognition of Aboriginal rights in the Canadian constitution, strengthened by a growing body of jurisprudence, has redefined the role of aboriginal Canadians in urban as well as rural contexts.

The Provinces Are Still in Charge

Above this whole picture of shifting dynamics sit the provinces, with their virtually total control over the terms and conditions under which cities are governed and their demonstrated willingness to intervene when they deem it necessary. Over time, the Charter requirements for equal representation will provoke a stronger interest in urban policy on the part of provincial governments. However, this interest may be just as likely to take the form of direct provincial intervention to win urban votes as it is to take the form of strengthening urban government institutions (Sancton, 1992).

This brings us back to a different way of formulating the questions that began this chapter: Who governs Canada's cities? The experience of the past twenty-five years has confirmed that, in the formal sense, the answer to that question is: the provinces; but the same experience suggests that, in the political sense, the answer is: the people who live there and their local elected representatives. It is the interplay between these two ways of understanding urban governance that has produced the greatest successes and the most tragic failures of the country's recent urban history.

15 Have Fiscal Issues Put Urban Affairs Back on the Policy Agenda?

ENID SLACK

Municipalities across Canada are facing increasing demands for local services: better roads, transit, waste disposal, fire and police protection – and the list goes on. At the same time, transfers to municipalities from senior levels of government have been falling as these governments have attempted to address their own fiscal problems. Pressure for zero property tax increases, which began with Proposition 13 in California and has recently spread to this country, has prevented many municipalities from increasing property taxes to finance growing service demands. Provincial restrictions on revenue raising tools for local governments have made alternative revenue sources somewhat difficult to find. Municipalities are left largely with property taxes (which are virtually frozen) and user fees (which have never been popular) to pay for a wide range of services.

Urban affairs is definitely back on the policy agenda, and mounting financial pressures have put it there. The provincial response to fiscal problems at both provincial and municipal levels has been to undertake three broad policy initiatives: changing the allocation of responsibilities to municipal governments, restructuring municipalities, and reforming the main source of local government revenue – the property tax.[1] In 1998, Ontario, for example, undertook all of these initiatives at the same time. Although some of these policies have been more controversial than others, they each provide evidence that municipalities – particularly urban public finance – are back on the policy agenda.

Table 1
Comparison of Municipal Government Expenditures per Capita and as a Percent of
Gross Domestic Provincial Product (GDPP), 1988 and 1997

	1988			1997		
	Expenditures ($,000)	Per Capita	Percentage of GDPP	Expenditures ($,000)	Per Capita	Percentage of GDPP
Newfoundland	324,312	563	4.0	346,133	624	3.2
PEI	32,671	252	1.8	45,063	332	1.5
Nova Scotia	678,496	865	4.5	984,891	1,053	4.8
NB	403,776	551	3.3	524,672	669	3.1
Québec	6,874,930	1,002	4.9	9,344,398	1,277	5.0
Ontario	11,677,653	1,181	4.6	16,367,189	1,483	4.7
Manitoba	962,659	871	4.5	1,395,375	1,144	4.8
Saskatchewan	840,117	814	4.5	952,015	916	3.4
Alberta	3,217,350	1,306	5.2	4,063,571	1,348	4.0
BC	2,596,148	830	3.8	4,915,631	1,273	4.5
Yukon	31,649	1,177	3.6	54,467	1,632	4.8
NWT	102,233	1,816	4.6	39,177,429	1,308	4.6
Canadian Total/Average	27,741,994	1,035	4.6	39,177,177,429	1,308	4.6

Source: calculated from data provided by Statistics Canada, Public Institutions Division, Financial Management System (FMS), November 1998.

This chapter reviews the finances of municipalities over the last ten years and describes the three major activities that have been ongoing in the municipal finance field across Canada. The chapter concludes with a discussion of the fiscal challenges for municipalities in the future, with special emphasis on the issues faced by city-regions.

EXPENDITURES AND REVENUES
OF CANADIAN MUNICIPALITIES OVER
THE LAST DECADE

In 1997, municipalities across Canada spent almost $39.2 billion, compared to about $27.7 billion ten years earlier (see table 1).[2] Municipal expenditures increased from $1,035 per capita in 1988 to $1,308 in 1997. When compared to the overall growth in the economy – notwithstanding changes in service responsibilities over the last ten years, the decline in provincial-municipal grants, and other fiscal factors – municipal expenditures as a percentage of Gross Domestic Provincial Product (GDPP) did not change: they accounted for 4.6 percent of GDPP in 1988 and 4.6 percent again in 1997.[3]

Table 1 shows some differences in municipal expenditures in 1988 and 1997 across provinces. In 1997, municipal government expenditures relative to GDPP were highest in the Northwest Territories followed by Québec, Manitoba, Nova Scotia, and the Yukon.[4] The largest increase in municipal expenditures relative to GDPP over the ten-year period occurred in British Columbia and in the two territories; decreases occurred in Newfoundland, Prince Edward Island, New Brunswick, Saskatchewan, and Alberta.

Municipalities in Canada mainly spend on roads and transit (transportation and communications), police and fire (protection of persons and property), water and sewers (environment), and recreation and culture. Table 2 shows the distribution of municipal expenditures by function for each province for 1997. There is an important difference across provinces in spending on social services. This function is a provincial responsibility in most Canadian provinces; the main exceptions are Ontario and Manitoba.[5] Nova Scotia is currently moving to full provincial funding of social services even though this is not evident from the 1997 data in table 2. In most provinces, elementary and secondary education is provided by school boards and funded by the province or a combination of the province and school boards. Only in Nova Scotia are municipalities responsible for funding a significant portion of education. Table 2 also highlights significant differences in the use of debt to fund capital projects[6] by province with debt charges ranging from a high of 19 percent of expenditures in Newfoundland to a low of 1.3 percent in the Yukon. In most provinces, debt charges relative to operating expenditures have declined over the last twenty years (see Kitchen and Slack, 1993).

The main sources of revenue to municipalities are shown in table 3. Property taxes accounted for 51.2 percent of municipal revenues in 1997, followed by user fees at 21.2 percent, and transfers from other levels of government at 20.2 percent. Table 3 also shows considerable variation in the distribution of municipal revenue sources across the country: property taxes range from a low of just over 15 percent of municipal revenues in the NWT to a high of 68.5 percent in Québec. Transfers are as low as 8.2 percent of municipal revenues in Prince Edward Island and as high as 51.3 percent in the NWT. Very few transfers come directly from the federal government, and these are all specific purpose transfers that are required to be spent on designated functions. General purpose, or unconditional, grants represent a small proportion of transfers in most provinces with the exception of New Brunswick.[7] Finally, user fees range from 15.3 percent of municipal revenues in Québec to over 30 percent in Alberta and the NWT.

Table 2
Distribution of Local Government Expenditures, 1997 (percentages)

	NF	PEI	NS	NB	Qué	Ont	MB	SK	AB	BC	YK	NWT	Canada
• General services	15.1	12.1	6.0	9.5	11.9	8.7	12.4	13.6	10.9	8.6	19.2	16.7	10.0
• Protection of persons and property	8.8	24.5	14.8	24.5	16.8	15.6	15.9	16.3	14.4	18.1	8.0	4.4	16.1
• Transportation and communications	24.3	20.7	18.9	22.0	23.0	18.5	20.0	29.9	28.5	13.7	31.9	15.1	20.4
• Health	0.0	0.0	0.1	0.2	0.1	2.7	2.4	1.0	1.5	3.8	0.3	4.5	1.9
• Social services/social welfare	0.1	0.0	8.4	0.0	0.8	22.8	7.7	0.8	1.8	0.2	0.0	4.7	10.5
• Education – elementary and secondary	0.3	0.6	2.8	2.3	1.8	2.0	2.0	5.9	2.1	1.4	1.3	0.4	2.0
• Resource conservation and international development	18.8	23.3	17.7	21.1	16.5	12.7	17.3	13.7	13.2	22.2	19.0	30.6	15.4
• Environment	12.2	13.3	9.5	13.5	11.2	10.1	11.6	13.6	12.9	17.8	16.2	16.8	11.9
• Recreation and culture	0.5	0.0	0.7	0.3	3.5	1.4	0.2	0.2	0.4	0.7	0.0	3.2	1.6
• Housing	0.8	0.7	3.4	1.4	2.0	1.1	1.6	1.4	2.3	1.9	2.3	1.3	1.6
• Regional planning and development	19.1	4.6	3.8	5.2	12.1	3.8	8.7	2.8	11.0	10.5	1.3	1.8	7.7
• Debt charges	0.0	0.2	0.2	0.0	0.1	0.6	0.2	0.9	0.9	1.2	0.3	0.7	0.6
• Other expenditure													
Total general expenditure	100	100	100	100	100	100	100	100	100	100	100	100	100
School Board expenditure as a percentage of total local (municipal and school board) expenditure 1996.	61.4	73.5	43.2	0.0	44.0	44.6	46.9	52.1	43.8	45.5	0.0	16.9	44.6

Source: Statistics Canada, Public Institutions Division, Financial Management System (FMS), November 1998.

Table 3
Distribution of Municipal Government Revenue (excluding school bonds), 1997 (percentages)

	NF	PEI	NS	NB	Qué	Ont	MB	SK	AB	BC	YK	NWT	Canada
Property and related													
taxes	54.3	60.2	64.5	53.6	68.5	44.2	43.1	52.7	42.6	50.3	43.4	15.1	51.2
Other taxes	1.8	0.5	0.1	0.4	0.2	1.1	1.8	4.4	1.5	2.8	1.4	0.4	1.2
User fees	16.0	27.1	19.7	21.0	15.3	21.2	20.2	24.1	30.2	25.3	17.8	31.6	21.2
Investment income	1.9	2.5	2.6	0.9	2.1	4.3	6.3	7.8	10.9	8.5	5.4	1.3	5.0
Other own-source revenue	0.4	1.6	0.3	0.6	2.4	0.7	0.8	1.2	1.9	0.5	0.5	0.3	1.2
Total own-source revenue	74.4	91.9	87.2	76.5	88.5	71.5	72.2	90.2	87.1	87.4	68.5	48.7	79.8
General purpose transfers	8.6	3.3	1.7	16.0	1.3	4.2	6.5	3.9	1.7	3.0	7.0	6.6	3.3
Specific purpose transfers	17.0	4.9	11.1	7.5	10.2	24.4	21.3	5.9	11.4	9.7	24.4	44.7	16.9
– federal	3.1	1.4	2.3	1.5	0.1	1.2	2.3	0.8	1.8	1.7	0.2	1.2	1.2
– provincial	13.9	3.5	8.7	6.0	10.0	23.2	19.0	5.1	9.6	7.9	24.2	43.6	15.7
Total transfers	25.6	8.2	12.8	23.5	11.5	28.6	27.8	9.8	31.1	12.7	31.4	51.3	20.2
Total revenues	100	100	100	100	100	100	100	100	100	100	100	100	100

Source: Statistics Canada, Public Institutions Division, Financial Management System (FMS), November 1998.

Note: property and related taxes include real property tax, developers' contributions and lot levies, special assessments, land transfer tax, business tax, other property and relater taxes, and grants in lieu of taxes.

Note: other taxes include general sales tax, amusement tax, licences and permits, and other miscellaneous taxes.

Although municipal expenditures and revenues are controlled to a large extent by provincial governments, there are still some inter-provincial differences in the emphasis on various types of expenditures and the reliance on different revenue sources across the country. Most municipalities provide roads, transit, water, sewers, garbage collection and disposal, fire and police protection, and recreation and culture. There are differences, however, in the extent to which they fund social services. On the revenue side, property taxes remain the mainstay of municipal finance in all provinces and are likely to do so for some time to come.

LOCAL SERVICES REALIGNMENT

Sorting out provincial and local responsibilities across Canada has been going on since the 1970s. For example, BC and New Brunswick were among the earliest to undertake this exercise by placing the funding of "soft" services (social services and education) at the provincial level and "hard" services (such as roads, water, and sewers) at the local level. Nova Scotia in 1995 and Ontario in 1998 are the most recent provinces to undertake a local services realignment. The results have been somewhat different, however, in terms of how services responsibilities were reassigned among levels of government.

Generally the realignment of services (also known as disentanglement and "Who Does What") is based on a series of principles developed by panels or commissions appointed by provincial governments.[8] As an example, the Crombie "Who Does What" panel in Ontario applied the following principles to the disentanglement exercise:

- municipal governments should have a strong role in the provision and funding of hard services such as services to property (garbage collection, water, and roads, for example) and community infrastructure; the province should have a strong role in the provision of soft services such as health, welfare, and education;
- government programs primarily aimed at income redistribution should be funded by the province;
- only one level of government should be responsible for spending decisions, where possible, and the level of government making the spending decisions should have the responsibility for funding that service;
- there should be an appropriate balance between the allocation of responsibility and the financial resources available to support those responsibilities.

In its discussion of local governance, the "Who Does What" Panel also adhered to the subsidiarity principle, which requires that services be delivered by the lowest level of government that has the capacity to do so effectively. In this way, both efficiency and accountability to taxpayers can be achieved.[9]

The first two principles make it clear that provincial governments should fund social services because these are redistributive services. Also, the benefits of these services spill over municipal boundaries highlighting a need for provincial funding to ensure that the service is adequately funded. Social services are also services that benefit from having uniform standards across the province.

The third principle addresses accountability: where two levels of government share the funding of a services, it is easy to blame the other level for inadequate funding. There is more accountability in a system in which one level of government provides the services and, at the same time, pays for the service.

The fourth principle suggests that municipalities need appropriate financial resources to pay for the services assigned to them. For example, municipalities do not have the tools to fund social assistance because they cannot borrow funds to meet operating deficits. This means that, when the demand for social assistance increases, municipalities will be under great financial pressure to reduce payments, to increase property taxes, or to reduce other services. In the current fiscal environment of zero tax increases, the result is more likely to be lower social assistance payments or a reduction in the level of other municipal services than increased property taxes.

Consistent with these principles, as noted above, social services are funded at the provincial level in most Canadian provinces. The exceptions are Ontario and Manitoba. As will be noted below, where there is municipal funding of social services, there will be serious financial consequences, especially for large urban centres, which act as magnets for social service recipients.

The Québec government undertook a major services realignment in 1990 when it transferred the financing of a number of services, most notably public transit and road maintenance, to municipalities.[10] Local restructuring in Alberta in 1994 had the provincial government assuming full funding for elementary and secondary education and a reduction in the number of school boards by one half.

In Nova Scotia, the recent services realignment ("provincial-municipal service exchange") resulted from the recommendations of a 1992 Task Force report. The recommendations called for municipalities to be responsible for policing and roads in exchange for which the province would take over social services, justice, and health.

Since 1992, several changes to the service exchange have been made in response to concerns on the part of some municipalities. Full provincial funding of social services in Nova Scotia is gradually being implemented.

Ontario began the process of local services realignment in 1998 following the reports of the "Who Does What" Panel.[11] Notwithstanding the advice of the Panel, the province chose to download social services further onto municipalities along with a number of other services (such as water, sewers, roads, transit, social housing, the administration of provincial offences, property assessment, policing, and farm tax rebates) in exchange for taking over full funding of elementary and secondary education.

Why has the process of local services alignment been so controversial? In part it is because change of any sort is difficult. Municipalities are accustomed to providing the services they have been responsible for historically and do not want to change. In large part, however, it is because provincial governments have generally made the commitment that rationalizing service provision between the two levels of government would be revenue neutral. In other words, the service exchange would not change the overall expenditure levels of the province or of local governments. It rarely turns out that way, however.

Even if the impact is revenue neutral province-wide, the impact will be different in different municipalities. For example, in Ontario, rural municipalities have been particularly hard hit by the downloading of provincial highway maintenance costs, policing costs, and the elimination of the farm tax rebate. In large urban centres, the downloading of social assistance and social housing has placed an undue burden on these municipalities. As with all reforms of this type, the winners are quiet but the losers make a lot of noise.

Furthermore, even if the service exchange is revenue neutral at the time of the swap, the impact will change over time. For example, changing demographics mean that there will an increase in the demand for social services by the aging population over time and a reduction in the demand for education, other things being equal. A shift of education to the province and social services to municipalities will have significant financial consequences for municipalities in the future.

Notwithstanding the controversial nature of local services realignment, overall it is a good thing for governments to sort out "who does what." It can improve both efficiency and accountability and has the potential to improve equity. As part of the disentanglement process, it may still be necessary to ensure that all municipalities have the fiscal capacity (generally measured by the size of their tax base) to meet the responsibilities that have been assigned to them. In New Brunswick, for example, the province gives an equalization transfer to municipalities. It is an unconditional transfer, based on a formula, that is designed to ensure that each municipality can provide at least an average level of service (when compared to similar municipalities in terms of size and services provided) by levying an average tax rate. Few provinces still maintain equalization transfers to municipalities; most have moved away from this type of funding.

MUNICIPAL RESTRUCTURING

Municipal restructuring often goes hand in hand with the rationalization of municipal functions because of the need to create municipalities with a large enough tax base to provide the services assigned to them. Municipal restructuring is another reform that has swept the country.

Perhaps the most notable example is the creation of the "megacity" of Toronto in 1998 through the amalgamation of six lower-tier municipalities and the metropolitan government. The Halifax amalgamation has also received a lot of attention as have amalgamations in Moncton and Miramichi in New Brunswick. Successive amalgamations in Edmonton have made it the largest city in Canada geographically. Restructuring has also taken place in Québec following financial incentives from the province to municipalities to initiate amalgamations locally. British Columbia is the only province that is not encouraging municipalities to amalgamate in the 1990s, in large part because of the creation of regional districts in the 1960s.[12]

Several reasons for restructuring have been expounded by provincial governments, municipalities, the media, consultants, and academics. These generally include: the potential to achieve cost savings by reducing waste and duplication, the ability to coordinate services across municipal boundaries, and the need to spread the costs of local government across a broader tax base. There are also concerns about how amalgamation and restructuring affect accountability, local responsiveness, and access to local government.

Although service coordination and sharing local costs over a larger tax base are valid reasons for amalgamation, cost savings are not. The argument in favour of amalgamation is that a number of politicians and administrators can be eliminated when two or more governments are amalgamated. While this may be true, it is also true from past experience with amalgamations that expenditures tend to equalize up to those of the highest expenditure municipality. When municipalities with different service levels and different wage scales have amalgamated, expenditures rose.[13] This means that most of the cost savings are offset by this tendency to equalize all remaining salaries up to the highest level.

There are also increased transitional costs associated with a consolidation of municipalities. A review of the transitional and short-term impacts of consolidation in three Canadian cities (Abbotsford, BC, Miramichi, NB, and Halifax, NS) concludes that these costs can be significant (see Vojnovic, 1998). Transitional costs ranged from $180,000 in Miramichi (or $8.60 per capita) to over $25 million in the Halifax Regional Municipality (or $75.56 per capita).

Equalization of service levels is not necessarily a bad thing. If some municipalities cannot provide an adequate level of service because they do not have adequate resources, amalgamation allows them to provide the same level of service as other municipalities in the region. But this means that costs are likely to rise, not fall.

As noted above, amalgamation may be justified on a number of grounds, but probably not on the basis of cost savings. Indeed, cost savings are likely to be less for large urban centres because diseconomies of scale can set in. In short, the bureaucracy can simply become too large to be efficient.

A review of American empirical evidence on fragmented versus consolidated local governments (see Boyne, 1995) concluded that lower spending is a feature of fragmented local government systems; consolidated structures are associated with higher spending. For some municipalities seeking to increase efficiency and effectiveness of service delivery, other options include inter-municipal agreements or contracting out service delivery to the private sector.

Why has municipal restructuring been controversial? Perhaps the main reason is the opposition to change on the part of residents in small communities that have been consolidated with larger municipalities. The feeling of a loss of community identity coupled with the possibility of increased service costs has driven many citizens and politicians to oppose any change in municipal government structure. Perhaps it is because the promised cost reductions have not materialized.

In designing a new municipal structure, there is a need to balance efficiency and equity objectives with local accountability and responsiveness. In the past, two-tier systems of local government have been very successful at achieving these objectives: the upper tier provided services of a region-wide nature and coordinated services throughout the region; lower tiers provided local services and ensured local responsiveness. Examples include the former Metropolitan Toronto, the Greater Vancouver Regional District, and the Montreal Urban Community.

In the current context, there has been more concern with waste and duplication and the need to have larger government units to be able to finance the increasing number of services being downloaded to municipalities. It is important not to lose sight of the need for local responsiveness and accountability and, at the same time, to ensure that municipalities are sufficiently large to be able to coordinate planning and infrastructure investment.

PROPERTY TAX REFORM

Perhaps the most controversial municipal finance reform in this country is property tax reform. In all provinces, legislation requires that properties be assessed at their market value, usually defined as the price that would be struck between a willing buyer and a willing seller in an arm's length transaction. In reality, however, the implementation of assessment has meant that property values in many provinces have been out of date at certain times in their history.

When property values are out of date, three types of inequities can arise: within classes of property, between classes of property, and across municipalities. For example, two residential properties may each have a market value of $100,000; one may be assessed at $100,000, and the other may be assessed at $50,000. That is a within-class inequity. Comparable valued properties may be assessed at a different proportion of market value if they are in different property classes, for example, an apartment compared to a single-family home. That is a between-class inequity. Finally, two comparable properties may have different assessed values in two different municipalities resulting in an inequity across municipalities. A move to a uniform assessment system will, other things being equal, result in shifts in property taxes: those properties that were relatively over-assessed will enjoy tax decreases; those properties that were relatively under-assessed will face tax increases.

Why has property tax reform been so controversial? The reason is that property tax is a very visible tax and reforming it creates winners and losers. The property tax is a visible tax because, unlike the income tax, it is not withheld at source. With the exception of those who pay their property taxes through their mortgages, people pay property taxes directly in a lump sum to the municipal government. For this reason, they are aware of how much they are paying. At the same time, the property tax finances many services that are visible: roads, snow removal, garbage collection, for example. It is easy to relate the amount of taxes paid to the services received. Although this link between taxes and services promotes accountability, it makes it difficult to increase or change property taxes in any way.

In all provinces, municipalities have undergone property tax reform at some time in recent history. In British Columbia, for example, a major property tax reform was implemented in the late 1970s. Market value assessment has generally worked well but there have been problems in Vancouver arising from the volatility in real estate values. Effective in January 1997 a new property assessment system was introduced by the Saskatchewan Assessment Management Agency (SAMA). This new system updates values from 1965 to 1994. The province established property classes and determines the percentage of value that will be taxable in each class.

The history of property tax reform in Ontario is long and tortuous. The province took over the assessment function from municipalities in 1970 and made a commitment to implement market value assessment. Since then, there have been numerous studies of property tax reform in Ontario but not much was done until 1998. Ironically, after the province introduced current value assessment (another term for market value assessment), it returned the assessment function to municipal control under the Ontario Property Assessment Corporation (OPAC).

Since there were so many inequities in the assessment system, a move to a uniform system meant tax shifts within property classes, between classes of property, and across municipalities. For this reason, the province has introduced successive pieces of legislation to cushion the impact of the reassessment. The result is that the original goals of property tax reform – to achieve equity and simplicity – were quickly replaced by the goal of stability. In 2001, with a new reassessment, the tax reform process will be revisited.

It is essential for municipalities to have a credible property tax. Taxpayers need to perceive that the property tax is fair. For this reason, an up-to-date market value assessment system is needed. Unfortunately, reform of the most visible tax is always difficult as is increasing the tax.

Property taxes have also put urban affairs back on the policy agenda because of the commitments made by municipal governments to freeze tax increases. These promises have prevented municipalities from maintaining the level and quality of services that they have in the past. With decreasing transfers from other levels of government, further commitments to zero tax increases can only mean further reductions in services.

FUTURE CHALLENGES

The three activities – local services realignment, municipal restructuring, and property tax reform – are essential ingredients to putting municipalities on a proper footing to meet the challenges of the next century. Although this chapter has highlighted problems with some of the specifics of implementation, overall these three activities can strengthen municipalities.

Municipalities need to be stronger to face the complex array of competing demands in the future. Among those demands are providing a range of services that residents want and that will attract businesses and employment growth, ensuring an adequate supply of affordable housing, reducing air and water pollution, providing open space, and instilling a sense of community among residents. Municipal governments need the resources necessary to provide this range of services.

THE ROLE OF LOCAL GOVERNMENT

The traditional role of local government, according to economic theory, is to provide goods and services whose benefits are enjoyed within a particular geographic area.[14] These include: transportation, water and sewers, police and fire protection, parks and recreation, and planning. Services that involve an element of redistribution should be funded by the province.

The efficient provision of goods and services requires local governments to charge directly for services wherever possible. In this way, the user of the service knows how much it costs to provide it and can make an efficient and informed choice on how much to consume.[15] User fees allow businesses to know how much they are paying for the services that they are receiving from local governments.[16] Based on the services provided and the cost incurred, businesses can make an efficient decision about where to locate.

The role of the property tax is to finance those services of general benefit to people in the community, such as parks and streetlighting.[17] Differences in property taxes between communities should reflect differences in the quantity and quality of services provided. To the extent that property taxes do reflect the cost of public services used by businesses, they are similar to other input costs, such as wages and salaries. To the extent that property taxes are not related to the costs of public services consumed, there will be an impact on location decisions because differences in taxes are not compensated for by differences in service levels.

Government structure should be designed to ensure that services that individuals and businesses want are provided throughout the region in a cost-effective manner. This means that restructuring should be used to share the costs of local government over a large tax base and to coordinate services over a broader area.

THE SPECIAL CASE OF CITY-REGIONS

City-regions present a special case for three reasons. City-regions are key to success in the new global economy. Urban sprawl in city-regions is increasing the cost of services such as roads, water, and sewers. And city-regions face higher demands for social service expenditures arising from a high concentration of special needs.

City-Regions and the New Global Economy

Studies on cities and global competitiveness suggest that city–regions are the best places to meet the requirements of the new competitive economy (see, for example, Blais, 1994). City-regions are places where "capital, workers, institutions, and infrastructure (hard and soft) come together to provide the foundations for successful economic activity" (Report of the Mayor's Homelessness Action Task Force, 1999: 257). Businesses will want to locate in city–regions where they have access to a highly qualified workforce – the "knowledge workers" – as well as access to business services, transportation, and communications networks.

Local governments, in providing goods and services, have an important role to play in attracting and retaining businesses. The provision of goods and services affects the quality of life in the city and influences where the knowledge workers will live. The range of housing choices and the quality of the education system, cultural and recreational facilities, and social services are all important factors in determining where people live.

The challenge for city-regions is to provide both the hard services and the soft services required to be competitive. All of the activities that have been undertaken to strengthen municipalities – local services realignment, municipal restructuring, and property tax reform – can potentially make this happen. Municipalities also need to look at how to reduce the cost of services through more efficient delivery and reducing the costs of urban sprawl (see below).

Urban Sprawl

Urban sprawl significantly increases the cost of services, in particular infrastructure. Research indicates that an urban form with relatively high densities, mixed land use, contiguous development, and a smaller urban envelope have lower infrastructure costs than communities with low density, discontiguous land-use patterns (see Blais, 1996: 39). Sprawl also results in high energy consumption costs, increased air pollution, loss of resource land, and inadequate access to employment opportunities for low-income households without cars.

Findings of the GTA Task Force indicate that, if development patterns in the GTA continue as they have over the past twenty-five years, an additional $55 billion of capital investment will be needed over the next twenty-five years for roads, water, and sewer infrastructure. An additional $14 billion will be needed for operating expenditures. With more compact urban development in the GTA, the Task Force estimated that over $12 billion in capital costs could be saved over twenty-five years and these savings do not include reducing the costs of pollution, policing, parking, and other costs.

The need to reduce urban sprawl is not only a municipal finance issue because it can reduce the costs of services and thereby reduce property taxes but also because the financing tools used to pay for growth have an important influence on how the growth will occur. Studies on development charges (levies charged by municipalities on developers to pay the growth-related capital costs associated with development) show that the design of the charge can influence land-use patterns.[18] Charges based on average cost pricing whereby all developments within a particular municipality pay the same charge per lot regardless of location, for example, actually promote sprawl. Since all developments pay the same charge regardless of the costs incurred by each individual development, there is no incentive to locate near existing services. Marginal cost pricing (where charges reflect the cost of each development) are neutral with respect to the location of development.

A significant reduction in service costs (capital and operating) can be achieved by promoting more compact urban development. This requires not only planning tools to prevent sprawl but also financial tools that do not encourage sprawl.

City-Regions Are Magnets for Special Needs

At the same time that city-regions are the key to global competitiveness, they face unique challenges. In particular, they act as magnets for special needs. For example, the Mayor's Task Force on Homelessness in Toronto found that, over a nine-year period, 47 percent of homeless people using Toronto's shelters and hostels originated from outside of Toronto. Similarly, in Calgary, Vancouver, and Montreal, the percentage from outside the city was more than 50 percent. In some cases, shelter users come from outside the city; in other cases, they originate from outside the province or outside the country. Large cities attract people seeking economic opportunity; they also attract people with high social-service needs.

Evidence on poverty in the Greater Toronto Area shows that poverty is increasingly concentrated in the City of Toronto. Toronto has a large number of low-income families and proportionately more than other municipalities in the GTA. This number has risen every year because of a loss in income in Toronto and an increase in the number of low-income households moving to Toronto.

There is also evidence that large city-regions are the main reception centres for immigration in Canada, especially recent immigrants. Toronto, for example, receives one-third of the total number of Canadian immigrants and refugees who come to Canada each year. Furthermore, the incidence of poverty for families headed by non-Canadian-born residents has increased dramatically over the last seven years (see Report of the Mayor's Homelessness Action Task Force, 1999: 257). Policies and practices for immigration are established by the federal government, but many of the costs associated with new immigrants and refugees are absorbed by the provinces and by local governments.[19] For example, cities provide emergency shelter to immigrants and refugees who are unable to make their own arrangements. These are generally cost-shared between the province and local governments. Local costs are borne on the property tax base.

Increasing income polarization in city-regions increases the risk that the problems affecting so many US cities could happen here – the flight of the middle class to the suburbs, the growing gap between urban and suburban residents, and cities faced with rising service needs, an eroding tax base, and falling revenues. At the very least, a regional response is needed to counteract this polarization.[20] A greater federal and provincial role is also needed to address income disparities.

ROLE FOR FEDERAL AND
PROVINCIAL GOVERNMENTS

As noted in table 3 above, the property tax is the main source of revenue to local governments. Although the property tax is appropriate to finance some goods and services such as parks, police, and fire protection, it is not appropriate to fund social services: welfare assistance, social housing, and child care, for example. These are services that are redistributive in nature and require uniform standards, if not across the country then at least across each province. For these reasons, there is an important role for both the federal and provincial governments to play.

Provincial governments have historically provided conditional and unconditional transfers to municipalities, but, as shown earlier, these transfers are falling in part because of a decline in provincial funding for municipalities and in part because of the local services realignment, which has reduced the need for conditional transfers. Some provinces fund social services and social housing, but some still share the costs of these services with municipalities. There is a key role for provinces to fund social services and social housing and to provide equalization transfers to municipalities to ensure that they can provide a standard level of services at standard tax rates.

The federal government has been much less involved historically with municipalities than the provinces and than the federal government in other countries such as the us. The constitutional argument is put forward to explain the lack of federal involvement in cities in this country. Since, constitutionally, cities are creatures of the provinces, efforts on the part of the federal government to aid cities are frowned upon by the provinces.

The federal government has worked around constitutional barriers in the past, however. One example is the Infrastructure Program, which involved tri-level funding: one third federal, one third provincial, and one third municipal. CMHC has funded social housing and provided mortgage insurance for market housing; social housing either has been or is in the process of being devolved to the provinces, however. The federal government provides funding through the Residential Rehabilition Program (RRAP), which allows property owners to make needed repairs or modifications without raising rents or going into debt.

There is a role to be played by the federal government in urban affairs, especially in large city-regions. This role derives from cities being the key nodes of the global economy (see Gertler, 1996: 124) and because many of the problems facing cities relate to issues that are under federal (or provincial) jurisdiction. For example, there needs to be a greater federal role with respect to services for recent immigrants and refugees. Property taxes and user fees are appropriate to fund many local services, but they are not sufficient nor appropriate to meet the complex challenges that municipalities are increasingly being asked to face.

SUMMARY

Urban affairs is definitely back on the policy agenda in Canada. Indeed, this chapter has argued that it has been fiscal issues that have put urban affairs back on the policy agenda. Global competition has also put urban affairs back on the policy agenda because it is increasingly being recognized that cities are the places where the requirements of the new global economy will be met.

Provincial governments have been addressing fiscal pressures both at the provincial and local levels by realigning local services between the two levels of government, encouraging municipal restructuring, and implementing property tax reform. Although these changes have in many instances been controversial, they have been necessary to strengthen municipalities and prepare them for the challenges of the next century.

These policies alone are not sufficient, however, to meet the complex needs of large city-regions. All three levels of government need to recognize and address the unique needs of large city-regions with respect to their role in the new global economy, their need to reduce service costs by containing urban sprawl, and their high concentration of special needs.

NOTES

1   The *Constitution Act* sets out the division of powers between the federal and provincial governments. Municipal governments are only mentioned in the Constitution to the extent that they are creatures of the province. This means that provincial governments can restructure municipalities, allocate responsibilities to them, and determine what taxes they can levy.

2   A consistent data series is only available back to 1988.

3   Table 1 does not include education expenditures by school boards. Although education funding is beyond the mandate of this chapter, it is worth noting the trend towards provincial funding of elementary and

secondary education in BC, Alberta, Ontario, New Brunswick, PEI, New-foundland, and the Yukon. Furthermore, in those provinces with provincial education funding, the provincial government levies a property tax.

4 Cost of living differences account for the much larger expenditures per capita in the Yukon and Northwest Territories.

5 The local services realignment in Ontario effective in 1998 is not evident in table 2, which is based on 1997 data. The realignment has resulted in higher municipal expenditures on social and other services in exchange for removing elementary and secondary education spending from the local level.

6 Municipalities in Canada are not permitted to incur debt for operating expenditures except to the extent that they are waiting for tax revenues. The amount of debt incurred for this latter purpose is often constrained by provincial statute or regulation. For a good discussion of municipal debt rules and regulations, see Tassonyi, 1994.

7 The main provincial transfer to municipalities is an unconditional equalization transfer.

8 See, for example, the Report of the Advisory Committee to the Minister of Municipal Affairs on the Provincial-Municipal Financial Relationship, 1991, in Ontario (the Hopcroft Report) and the Report of the Royal Commission on Finance and Municipal Taxation in New Brunswick, 1963 (the Byrne Report).

9 For a discussion of the subsidiarity principle, see Barnett, 1996.

10 For a good discussion of the controversy over this service transfer, see Andrew, 1995: 151.

11 See Graham and Phillips, 1998, for a review of the "Who Does What" process.

12 For a comprehensive view of municipal consolidations in Canada in the 1990s, see Vojnovic, 1997.

13 See, for example, the 1967 Toronto amalgamation, the creation of the unicity in Winnipeg, and the recent amalgamation in Halifax.

14 It is not appropriate for local governments to carry out monetary and fiscal policies designed to achieve full employment, stable prices, and a reasonable level of economic growth. It is also not appropriate for them to focus on programs that are directed at the redistribution of income among individuals. These functions are performed better by the federal and provincial governments. See Bird and Slack (1993: 16).

15 See Bird and Tsiopoulos, 1997, for a discussion of the potentials and problems associated with user fees.

16 In some cases, direct charging is not appropriate. Direct charging cannot be used where income distribution is an important consideration (such as with the provision of welfare services) or where there are spillovers in the provision of a service (such as education). To finance these services, it

may be necessary for the province to fund them out of its general revenues or for the province to give grants to local governments to provide them.

17 Charging is not possible for types of services where it is difficult to identify the beneficiaries or costly to exclude those who do not pay.

18 See Slack, 1993, for a discussion of the influence of municipal financial tools on land use.

19 This is true, except in Québec, where a bilateral agreement has been signed with the federal government; see Report of the Mayors' Homelessness Action Task Force, 1999: 74.

20 See Orfield, 1997, for a discussion of income polarization in US cities.

CONCLUSION

The City as the Hope of Democracy

WARREN MAGNUSSON

A hundred years ago, a prominent American scholar, Fredric C. Howe, spoke of the city as "the hope of democracy." It was a controversial claim then, and it is no less controversial now.

Howe was reacting against the anti-urbanism of American democratic thought: the Jeffersonian strain that identified democracy with agrarian life and treated cities as sources of corruption. It was not that Howe was satisfied with what he saw in the cities of his time: on the contrary, he deplored their many failures. On the other hand, he thought that the cities could and should become crucibles of a new democracy, appropriate to the urban-industrial age. He was inspired by the efforts that he saw around him in America and Europe, and he thought that there was a bright future to be won. We know now that the horrors of the Great War lay ahead, but Howe's optimism – and the optimism of other municipal reformers – was not entirely unjustified. Many of the things of which they dreamed have long since been achieved in the world's more prosperous cities, including the ones in Canada. Even so, there are few people today who would describe the city as "the hope of democracy."

Anti-urbanism is a persistent phenomenon. It would not be difficult to string commentaries together from the 1890s and the 1990s to show that anxieties about urban life have remained consistent. The city is anonymous; everything moves too quickly; people are massed together willy-nilly; there are no stable communities; families are breaking apart; the poor are condemned to lives of misery; old national and religious hatreds are nurtured in the ethnic ghettos; people care nothing for the community as a whole; etc. Such are the old canards. However often they may have been challenged by evidence from the social sciences and other sources, these ideas of the urban remain. They express some of our deepest anxieties. It is no secret that the suburban ideal of a detached house on its own lot in a quiet residential neighbourhood taps into a longing for small town life. Nor is it an accident that the latest movement in suburban design is called the "new urbanism." The "new" urbanism is yet another attempt to defeat "existing urbanism" by turning edge cities into assemblages of small towns. The cohesive neighbourhood is – and has been since the late nineteenth century – the standard solution to the problem of the city. We keep coming back to the idea that we have to fix the city by stabilizing it: by giving it a form that we can identify with farming communities, fishing villages, and small country towns. This constant return to an old ideal is obviously connected with particular social anxieties, but there is a political dimension to it as well. It is this political dimension that I want to consider in this chapter.

When we speak of "policy agendas," we always have politics in mind. Typically, we attribute policies to governments, and imagine that every government has an agenda. We suppose that governments have their own agendas: issues with which they want to deal and about which they have policy ideas. On the other hand, we also know that a government's agenda is often changed by force of circumstance, which includes what other actors do and say. We suppose that politics is about getting issues on the government's agenda and then inducing the government to act in particular ways. This conception of politics is state-centric, in the sense that it attributes to governments – that is, to the ensemble of agencies that make up the state – the capacity to make policies that will govern the society. Since politics is about the way we are governed – or so we suppose – it inevitably focuses on the state. Putting urban affairs back on the policy agenda would mean putting distinctively urban issues near the top of government concerns and near the centre of political debate about the things that governments should or should not do. It would also mean bringing the municipal authorities – the ones that have front-line responsibility for urban government – closer to the centre of both politics and government. At the moment, it seems, municipal authorities are a distant third in the Canadian political imagination: far behind the federal and provincial governments in the order of public concerns. Moreover, the big governments that capture the public imagination give most attention to issues like taxation and health-care spending that are only distantly related to the matters that we take to be central to the urban. To bring urban affairs back on the policy agenda would evidently involve a major shift.

Suppose, however, that "policy" was not something that emanated from governments. Suppose, further, that "government" was quite different from what we usually imagined it to be: that what we *call* governments were particular assemblages of governmental authority that existed alongside other assemblages that also exercised such authority. Suppose, also, that the urban was a way of life that encompassed the whole: in other words, that it transcended the particularities of settlement patterns, transportation systems, housing arrangements, and so on. And suppose finally that politics was not an activity confined to a particular sector, but rather a way of relating critically to everything and anything? How then could we think of policy, politics, and government in relation to the urban? How, in particular, could we think of bringing urban affairs *back* on the policy agenda, when it is always already there?

As I shall argue in the pages that follow, we do indeed need to think in new ways about policy, government, politics, and the urban. On the other hand, I will also be suggesting that these "new" ways of thinking were always already implicit in the "reform" tradition to which we are heirs. A key, but often unnoticed feature of that tradition is that it points away from the state as a centre of concern and induces us to think about policy, politics, and government in much more general terms. It also is a tradition that encourages us to embrace the urban as our own way of life, to move beyond our own nostalgia, and to find better ways of living in a *global* city that *must* be the hope of democracy, if there is to be any democracy (or indeed any hope) at all.

FROM MUNICIPAL REFORM
TO PROVINCIAL STATISM

Fredric Howe is not a well-known figure today, but he was prominent enough in his own time. He was of the generation that developed the new science of public administration in the United States, a science whose object was, in large degree, municipal government. So-called municipal reformers in the US played a huge part in developing standards for accounting and financial management, working out the best practices for the letting of contracts, establishing merit tests for entry into the civil service, and so on. These reformers generally thought of themselves as "progressives": people who were looking for ways to extend and improve public services. They were not opposed to positive government: on the contrary. They sought to root out corruption and inefficiency, and to bring the best standards to bear on the full range of government activities. If government could be made effective and efficient, they thought, then its activities could well be extended. If it were the municipalities rather than the state that took on the responsibility for positive government, then the dangers implicit in an increase of governmental activity could be mitigated. A truly liberal society would not be without active government, but the main agencies of government would be municipalities that lacked the scarier powers of the state. The leading municipalities would be urban. They would be the political organizations of cities: not sovereign, but sufficiently empowered to improve urban life continuously. Since it was already obvious that the democracy of the future would be an *urban* democracy, it was evident that the hope of democracy was in the municipality. Municipal government had to be reformed if it were to realize its promise.

The movement to make public administration into a science and to reform municipalities and other governments had a huge impact on Canada as well as the United States. As historians of local government in Canada have pointed out, municipal reformers in this country often applied American models without sufficient thought. Like their American counterparts, they were often more interested in business efficiency than in progressive social change. Nevertheless, we should not underestimate the impact of these reformers on the great initiatives that we now associate with the welfare state. The New Deal in the US was in large degree an effort to generalize the "best practices" that had been developed by local agencies. Later reforms in Canada followed the same logic. They made the provincial governments into agencies for health, education, and welfare (as well as for infrastructural development and resource management) and gave the federal government responsibility for social insurance and fiscal equalization. The reforms were intended to generalize "best practices" and thus to create a uniform space for daily life. Increasingly that space was conceived as an *urban* space to be developed and managed by the provinces. The federal role was to coordinate provincial activities so that Canadians could enjoy a common domain for daily life. The municipalities were relegated to a minor role, as the key decisions about best practices were worked out at the higher levels of government.

Although the Canadian experience was somewhat different from the American, in that the provinces emerged as exceptionally powerful agencies of government, the drift away from the municipality as a centre of initiative was similar in both countries. By the middle of the twentieth century, progressive thinkers on both sides of the US/Canada border – and on both sides of the Atlantic Ocean – had come to the view that cities were no longer self-contained units and that progressive reform had to be adumbrated on a larger scale. Although municipal reformers talked about creating metropolitan or regional governments – and a few measures were taken in that direction – it was generally easier to go up a notch or two in scale: that is, to demand action on the part of the state or provincial government, or better yet on the part of the national or federal government. To most progressives, the rescaling of government was a necessary consequence of the rescaling of society, and it was in any case a desirable step toward the extension of rights and opportunities to everyone. Whatever the advantages of small-scale government, such government could not provide for equality over a large domain. By contrast, the higher authorities, who had the benefit of "sovereignty" as well as of a wider geographic reach, seemed to have the necessary capacity.

One of the ironies of the present is that the most powerful state in the world – the USA – has had particular difficulty in managing cities. At least since the days of James Bryce – the English intellectual who was Britain's ambassador to Washington in the 1880s – observers have been complaining about American cities. The complaints have come from Americans as well as foreign observers. Some of these complaints are obviously unfair. People construct a model that takes all the best features from Paris, Milan, Amsterdam, Stockholm, London, and Berlin (with the hill towns of Italy, the islands of Greece, and the villages of Spain thrown in for good measure), and find Newark, New Jersey, and Orange County, California, sorely wanting. Canada provides a more pertinent contrast, since its cities were constructed under conditions akin to those in the US. The common observation (on both sides of the border and from observers both foreign and domestic) is that Canadian cities are safer and cleaner, better served by public transit, and generally more inhabited and habitable in their centres. Gated communities are less common, and cities generally retain the feel of public spaces, in which people can interact comfortably, despite their differences. That, certainly, is the image that Canadians play back to themselves. Hidden in this image is another, however. That second, and arguably more powerful, image is of a more successful *state*, a state that does a better job of providing domestic security and that is more effective at integrating minorities into the wider society. Gun control and medicare are the twin symbols of Canadian difference and Canadian success. Gun control symbolizes the relative effectiveness of Canada's security culture; medicare does the same with respect to the welfare state. Thus, in the Canadian imagination – and, I would say, in the imagination of observers more generally – the relative success of Canadian cities is attributable to the Canadian state.

A cynic might say that in Canada the state, rather than the city, has been the "hope of democracy." To the extent that we have had a vision of a vital urban democracy, it has generally been posed in statist terms. Lithwick and Paquet's hope was that the federal government would finally recognize that Canada was an urban nation and take an appropriate lead in developing policies that would be appropriate for such a nation. Their belief – and the belief of most other observers – was that policy leadership would have to come from Ottawa and the provincial capitals. What the municipalities could do was necessarily secondary, since cities were already part of a more complex urban system that had to be considered as a whole. The locus of initiative was of necessity transmunicipal. Of course, what everyone soon discovered – if they did not already know – was that transmunicipal initiative had to be provincial rather than federal in the Canadian context. The quiet revolution in Québec and the other provinces had forestalled the possibility of creating a Canadian national government on the West European model. Only the provinces could act with the vigour expected by advocates of a forceful "urban policy." Thus, the demand for an urban policy became one of the supports for provincial statism.

FROM URBAN POPULISM
TO PRIVATIZED GOVERNANCE

It was in this context that the urban reform movement of the 1970s developed. It tended to be localist and antistatist, but it was also supportive of an extension of public authority. The idea, roughly, was that urban residents had to be mobilized to reclaim public space and public authority. The enemy was privatization: that is, the process whereby, on the one hand, the urban was claimed as a domain for commercial investment and, on the other, public authority was mobilized in support of commercial development. Much of the critical literature of the period was intended to highlight the fact that the urban domain had already been commercialized – indeed that it had been conceived from the very beginning as a commercial space – and that the municipal authorities in particular had long ago been colonized by commercial interests. To free the municipalities from commercial domination, to reclaim urban space for other uses, and to democratize municipal government came to be the major objectives of the new municipal reformers. It seems ironic that democratization should have been so central to the reformers' aims, given that the municipalities were supposed to be closest to the ordinary people. It was obvious, however, that most people took little interest in municipal government and that municipalities were especially vulnerable to domination by private interests.

In the end, the new reformers had limited impact. If anything, their criticisms of existing government activities provided a spur to privatization. There was a remarkable ideological shift in the 1980s. Practices that had been described as *problems* a few years before – collusion between business and government, privatization of public authority, commercialization of public services, and so on – were now being touted as *solutions* to some of the problems that the new reformers had identified. These problems included bureaucratic inefficiency, political corruption, and general insensitivity to popular concerns. Exponents of privatization were able to convince many people that market discipline was necessary for making public services and regulatory activities effi-cient and responsive. In this view, consumer sovereignty was the key to democracy. By the 1990s, that had become conventional wisdom, and it fed into the idea that the state – including municipal governments and other local authorities – should draw back from direct regulation and provision of services. The implication was that governance should be privatized as much as possible. Although the state would remain at the centre of the system of governance, it would act "at a distance," and it would "steer rather than row."

citizens as consumer

This shift in thinking had unnoticed political implications. If steering rather than rowing were the issue, then traditional statecentric politics would continue to make sense. On the other hand, the effect of "hollowing out the centre" is to give more power to the rowers and thus to redirect political attention toward authorities in the private sector or in that shadowy region where government agencies, non-profit institutions, and private businesses "co-operate" to do things for the public benefit. Thus, the politicization of all sorts of places where authoritative decisions are made – be they classrooms and medical offices or recycling depots and inspection stations or scientific laboratories and research sites – is a logical consequence of privatization; not even shopping centres or shareholders' meetings are immune (as various private businesses are finding out).

The idea that "policy" is made by the state underpins a traditional conception of politics. The early municipal reformers honoured this traditional conception, as do contemporary advocates of privatization. In both instances, however, there is a clear recognition that problems of governance cannot be overcome by action at the centre only. The early reformers like Howe knew that key changes required action at every level, inside and outside the organizations concerned. Directives from the top would not produce the desired results. The reformers hoped for waves of change that would pass through many different organizations and induce initiatives from the bottom up, as well as from side to side. A new policy, in the sense of a new approach to solving standardized problems, could emerge anywhere, and it could spread by any number of means. For instance, it was not a matter of ordering everyone to adopt standardized accounting procedures; it was instead a matter of developing such procedures, implementing them somewhere, demonstrating that they could work and that they would produce desirable results, spreading the word about those results, embarrassing people into adopting the "best practices," and, finally, shunning or punishing those who failed to go along with the new standard. Accounting was certainly a matter of public policy, but changes in accounting policy could not be secured just by issuing orders. One sometimes suspects that latter-day reformers forget this. Nonetheless, the new literature on governance tends to repeat the insight of the earlier literature on public administration: namely, that policy inevitably has multiple origins and is circulated by many different means, especially in a system where authority is widely dispersed.

If, by urban affairs, we mean matters relating to people's dwelling places, then the policy networks at issue are obviously not confined to particular cities, or even to particular countries. In Howe's day, the Bureau of Municipal Research in New York had widespread influence. In our day, private firms like KPMG and Andersen Consulting seem to be ubiquitous in the urban arena. Who holds *them* to account? Their customers? Scarcely: organizations that can pay for such expensive advice are usually sophisticated enough to generate the advice that they want. In any case, the public is at several removes from the purchasers of consulting services. How can the public hold consulting firms to account? And how can the public influence the culture of the consulting firms? Do the consultants have no values of their own, no predisposed ways of looking at the world, no solutions looking for problems? Clearly there is a consulting culture, just as this as there is a culture of medicine, engineering, or accounting. Moreover, this culture is formed within international networks of corporations, trade associations, business schools, professional bodies, and so on. Such networks are in many ways beneficial, but the growing power of the private authorities that dominate these networks raises serious issues about democratic accountability and democratic influence. It seems that the centre from which we are to govern "governance" (or to do the steering) is flowing out through these networks into the private sector. Moreover, that private sector is international.

FROM NATIONAL ECONOMIES
TO GLOBAL CITY-REGIONS

If the domain of governance is complex and expansive, so too is the domain of the urban. Thirty years ago, people were struggling to understand that "urban systems" were regional or national. The idea that Toronto, Hamilton, and Oshawa were all part of the same urban system, and that the Toronto-Centred Region was to be conceived as a key node on the Windsor-Québec corridor, seemed like a revelation. It was also a revelation to think – following the work of Harold Innis, Donald Creighton, J.M.S. Careless, and others – that Canada as a whole could be conceived as a kind of urban system linked together on an east-west axis. Such notions made sense of the idea of a "national" urban policy. On the other hand, they could hardly be articulated without revealing other secrets: namely, that the Canadian urban system was related to the American and that such autonomy as it had depended heavily on linkages with Europe. As the European connection declined in importance, the relation with the US seemed ever more important. The free-trade debates of the late 1980s were implicitly about urban policy, even though they were usually articulated in other terms. The supposition of the free traders was that Canadian cities had to be reorganized, so that they could function more effectively within the American urban system. Barriers had to come down. Cities north of the line had to learn to cope with competition from the south and to take advantage of their opportunities in southern markets. This continentalist vision was soon inflected with the rhetoric of globalization. So, the aspiration of the 1990s was to turn Canadian cities into important nodes within a global network: not just "metropolitan areas," but global cities. But, again, the political implications of this were not well considered. How can a global city fit within a system of national governance?

By definition, a global city or city-region transcends the province or the nation. It exists within a *global* space and competes with other cities or city-regions for economic and cultural advantage. Successful cities attract both capital and talent. Such cities acquire their own cultural identities and come to influence cultures globally. They also become centres of economic initiative and extend their economic influence everywhere. New York and Los Angeles are paradigmatic, but places like Hong Kong, Bombay, Milan, Paris, London, and Frankfurt also seem to fit the model. Some analysts – Kenichi Ohmae, most notably – have argued that states are becoming irrelevant and that the optimal units of political organization within the new, globalized economy are actually city-regions with populations on the scale of 3 to 5 million people. On this logic, Megacity Toronto is actually a bit small: its boundaries ought to have been extended to include the outlying "905" suburbs. In any case, a city or city-region of this type is in principle outside or beyond the jurisdiction of a mere state or province. The city itself is supposed to be the polity that establishes appropriate linkages, facilitates strategic decision-making, and enables the population to develop. The state is necessarily at one remove, because it is an embodiment of national or provincial identities, rather than of urban identities that transcend such narrow limits.

One sign of globalization is that the major cities have become sites of diasporic intersection. Many, if not most, nationalities are now global, in the sense that the peoples concerned have spread across the world and established themselves in many different places. These peoples may or may not have internationally recognized homelands. If they are engaged in struggles for recognition, they are likely to carry those struggles with them. The same is true of religious conflicts. So, a globalized city may become a site of struggles that have little to do with the place itself but that nonetheless have much to do with the way the place is situated within global cultural networks. This is a commonplace observation, but it helps us to see that a city is more than just a unit within an economic order. It is a "space of flows" of all sorts, and the eddies and currents do not create regions with definite boundaries. Vancouver, for instance, is linked to the markets for BC forest products, markets that are partly European and partly Asian, but preponderantly American. Vancouver is also Hollywood North. But, then, it is a *China* as well: a centre for Chinese life and Chinese business in Canada, linked with other "overseas" centres like Los Angeles and Sydney and tied into "homeland" cities like Hong Kong, Taipei, Singapore, and Shanghai. Vancouver is also a centre of the Sikh world, and the Tamil world, and many other worlds. So, if it is at the heart of a "city-region," the region in question is very complex and not simply Canadian.

The crude idea of a global city or city-region – the one articulated by Chambers of Commerce, Economic Development Commissions, and International Trade Offices in cities all over the world – is of an economic entity competing with other such entities for the favour of investors. Fortunately, there is a growing recognition that "human capital" is as important for business as other kinds of capital and that humans need to be properly educated if they are to serve modern business. There is also a recognition that humans need decent places to live and have to have good public services. As the IMF, the World Bank, and the OECD all now acknowledge, people – and the businesses they serve – need good governance. Despite all the pressures upon us to think about governance in a business-oriented way, we do still express cultural, spiritual, and other concerns. Our many-sided humanity, including our compassion for others and our concern for the world, as well our ornery selfishness, self-righteousness, and clannishness, do get expressed in our demands about governance. They are also articulated in our ways of governing ourselves and the people around us. So-called free societies are *self-governing* societies, and so the global concerns that people have are expressed in activities that govern the conduct of everyday life. The globalism of the global city-region is not a set of relations that can be governed by trade offices and development commissions. It is instead a set of relations implicit in the day-to-day activities and day-to-day consciousness of ordinary people. Globalism is a mode of cultural participation in sports, music, food, fashion, chat rooms, shopping, and entrepreneurial activity. Global entrepreneurship is not just a matter of selling software in China. It is also a matter of linking up with activists to stop construction of the Three Gorges Dam.

Although it may seem that global city-regions nest more easily within the global market than within the nation-state, that is probably an illusion – as the WTO found out in Seattle. The term, "global city-region" is itself indicative of a certain collapse. City, region, and globe were supposed to be in a hierarchy, with cities at the bottom, the globe at the top, and regions in between. But each city is a world in itself: not so much in the old sense of being a space apart, but in the sense of being particular place that, in distinctive ways, spans the whole world and brings the whole world *in*. Each city is its own region, but the region has no definite external boundaries. So, to speak of a global city-region is to speak of a place that is all three: "world," region, and city. And to say that, is in effect to admit that the categories that we have used in the past no longer make much sense. The local and the global no longer relate to one another as inside and outside, small and big, particular and universal. The economic, social, cultural, and political relations that we experience on a day-to-day basis no longer have the form that enabled us to say that *this* was a purely local matter and *that* was something bigger. The Public Utilities Commission in Walkerton dealt with a global issue in relation to the town's drinking water (and did it rather badly). Did they have any idea that they were acting in a global political space, dealing with fundamental issues of global governance? Probably not, but they evidently were. How can we think and act politically in a world where the familiar spatial coordinates have already been displaced?

FROM THE NEW URBANISM
TO DEMOCRATIC POLITICS

Fredric Howe and the others of his generation spoke of the city, but Louis Wirth and others of the next generation – the generation of the 1920s, 30s, and 40s – spoke of urban life, urbanism, or urban society. Wirth in particular recognized that the way of life that had developed in America and elsewhere was increasingly urban. It was already obvious in the 1930s that the vast majority of people would live in cities in the not-too-distant future and that the way of life of such people was inevitably different from that of agriculturalists, pastoralists, hunters, fishers, and gatherers. Cities are obviously nodes within a wider urban reality. A key question is whether the urban can be territorialized: that is, whether the dynamics of urban life can be contained within spaces that are given by an external authority. Territorialization was the key to agricultural colonization in North America: farms were laid out on the authority of the state. Similar authority was used to lay out cities. Nevertheless, it was always clear that urban life tended to develop in accordance with its own logic and to flow beyond the boundaries established for it. Although Wirth and his contemporaries tended to identify the urban with concentrations of population, they also noticed that cities tended to spread out and link up with one another. In fact, these early theorists of the urban were frightened and entranced by the rapid movements within and between cities. It was the unsettled, almost nomadic character of urban life that seemed most distinctive, especially when it was compared with life in farming communities. Sixty or seventy years on, non-urban life is at best an ancestral memory for most Canadians. It is the life that their grandparents or great-grandparents lived: a life to be recalled through nostalgic television programs.

If urbanism is a deterritorializing movement (as it seems to be), and if the vast majority of us are caught up in it (whether we like it or not), then the question of urban policy is not secondary. It is the key policy question to be posed. On the other hand, to say policy is to presuppose a politics: that is, to assume that there is a process by which policy is generated and people are induced to abide by it. As we have already noted, traditional ideas about who is making policy, how, and for whom presuppose a certain relation between state and society. But, the relation is not as imagined. Thus, the locus of politics is not what we imagined either. The politics within which policies are generated has different origins, a different shape, and different impacts from the ones we have traditionally expected. And this has much to do with the nature of urbanism as a way of life. Originally, cities were compact and could easily be imagined as contained spaces. According to the ancient Greeks, politics proper was only possible within territorially delimited spaces. The modern theory of the state incorporates that idea. On the other hand, urbanism as *a way of life* spills out of contained spaces. It deterritorializes, reterritorializes, and deterritorializes again. The futility of drawing definite urban boundaries is indicative of this. A democratic urban politics would have to flow from the movements characteristic of urbanism, and not be imposed, as it were, from outside.

The "new urbanism" is a scheme for territorialization, in that it posits imagined communities to be secured by structures that fix people to particular territories. It is doubtful whether the new urbanism will be any more successful than its predecessors in this respect. It will be sold as a design scheme, and as such it will appeal to people who think that existing urbanism defeats our aspirations to community and polity. These aspirations are nicely expressed in the work of Jane Jacobs, who has inspired many of the new urbanists. Jacobs has been associated with a group who have been attempting to apply the "citistate" idea to Toronto and other major Canadian urban centres. Although Jacobs certainly recognizes the fluidity of urban life and is herself suspicious of statist forms of government, the ideal of the *polis* still shadows her understanding of democratic possibility. She and other city-centered intellectuals still regard the suburbs, the small towns, and the outlying rural areas as places distinct from the city proper. Thus, the ideal of civic democracy is connected in the minds of these intellectuals with an ideal of urban autonomy. In a way, this is an articulation of the new urbanism on a larger scale. At the neighbourhood level, we are to redesign our communities, so that they become real places with a public life of their own. At the city-regional level, we are to make our urban centres into politically autonomous places, free from the strictures of suburbanites and small town people.

Such schemes appeal to us because they tap into our nostalgia for small town life, face-to-face politics, and communal autonomy. In the third quarter of the twentieth century, it seemed to many people that the nation-state could provide for democracy on a reasonable scale, democracy of a kind that allowed for effective popular sovereignty. But, the idea that every nation can be a self-governing community seems a bit of a pipe dream in an era of globalization. In this context, it is not surprising that some people have begun to think of smaller communities on the scale of a city-region as possible surrogates for the nation-state. If autonomy is necessarily limited, why not get the scale of political organization down to a more manageable level? Why not constitute the city as the focus of our loyalties, and let the nation and the state go? This is an idea that keeps resurfacing, but it never generates the popular enthusiasm that its advocates think it deserves. One of the reasons for this is that the idea of the city-state is simply a variant of the idea of the nation-state (and vice versa). Neither political plan comes to terms with the reality that most ordinary people sense: namely, that the world in which we live is deterritorialized. The problem we have is not to rescale our political units, but rather to invent a politics appropriate to a deterritorialized existence.

A generation ago, Manuel Castells drew our attention to urban social movements and hence to the fact that cities were the sites at which political challenges were likely to develop. The challenge implicit in an urban social movement is directed at the whole system of government. The system of government is not just a set of public policies in the narrow sense. It is instead an array of practices that "govern" our gender identities, our ethnicities, our economic relations, our modes of environmental occupation, and indeed our understandings of what human life entails. Ultimately, everything is at issue in movement politics. This is as it must be, because movements respond to the ensemble of practices implicit in urbanism as a way of life. We cannot say beforehand how, when, where, or why the urban is to be called into question, for everything is always at stake. Efforts to fix us in particular places, or to put our politics in particular forms, are likely to be stifling, but they will never be entirely successful. Urban politics keeps breaking out, and reposing problems in unexpected ways. In this sense, urban affairs is always already on the policy agenda, even if it is not exactly where our managers would like it to be.

Bibliography

INTRODUCTION

Bourne, L.S. and D.F. Ley, 1993. *The Changing Social Geography of Canadian Cities*. Montreal and Kingston: McGill-Queen's.

Campbell, R.M. 1999. "The Fourth Fiscal Era: Can There Be a 'Post-Neo-Conservative' Fiscal Policy?" in *How Ottawa Spends 1999–2000: Shape Shifting: Canadian Governance Toward the 21st Century*, Leslie A. Pal (ed.). Don Mills: Oxford University Press: 113–49.

Canadian Journal of Regional Science, Special Issue – Metropolis, vol. 20, no. 1-2, 1997.

Canadian Journal of Regional Science, Special Issue – Comparative Development in Montreal and Toronto, vol. 22, no. 1–2, 1999.

Collingwood, R.G. 1946. *The Idea of History*. New York: Oxford University Press.

Dennis, M. and S. Fish, 1972. *Housing in Canada: Programs in Search of a Policy*. Toronto: Hakkert.

Doern, G.B. 1996. "The Evolution of Canadian Policy Studies as Art, Craft and Science," in *Policy Studies in Canada: The State of the Art*, Laurent Dobuzinskis, Michael Howlett, and David Laycock (eds). Toronto: University of Toronto Press: 15–26.

Feldman, L.D. and K.A. Graham, 1979. *Bargaining for Cities*. Montreal: Institute for Research on Public Policy.

Garigue, P. 1956. "French Canadian Kinship and Urban Life," in *American Anthropologist*, vol. 58, no. 6: 1090–101.

Gibbins, R. 1999. "Taking Stock: Canadian Federalism and Its Constitutional Framework," in *How Ottawa Spends 1999-2000: Shape Shifting: Canadian Governance Toward the 21st Century*, Leslie A. Pal (ed.). Toronto: Oxford University Press: 197–220.

Graham, K.A. and S.D. Phillips, with A.M. Maslove, 1998. *Urban Governance in Canada: Representation, Resources and Restructuring*. Toronto: Harcourt Brace.

Howlett, M. and M. Ramesh, 1995. *Studying Public Policy: Policy Cycles and Policy Subsystems*. Don Mills: Oxford University Press.

Ibbitson, J. 2000. "Deaths Cast Tories into Chaos," in *The Globe and Mail*, 3 June 2000: A3.

Lewis, O. 1966: "The Culture of Poverty," in *Scientific American*, vol. 215, no. 4, October 1966: 19–25.

Lithwick, N.H. 1970. *Urban Canada: Problems and Prospects*. Ottawa: Central Mortage and Housing Corporation.

Lithwick, N.H. and G. Paquet (eds), 1968. *Urban Studies: A Canadian Perspective*. Toronto: Methuen.

Mayer, M. 1991. "Politics in the Post-Fordist City," in *Socialist Review*, no. 21: 105–24.

Sancton, A. 1992. "Provincial-Municipal Disentanglement in Ontario: A Dissent," in *Municipal World*, July 1992.

Siegel, D. 1992. "Disentangling Provincial-Municipal Relations in Ontario," in *Public Management*, Fall 1992.

Simeon, R. 1972. *Federal:Provincial Diplomacy: The Making of Recent Policy in Canada*. Toronto: University of Toronto Press.

– 1976. "Studying Public Policy," in *Canadian Journal of Political Science*, vol. 9, no. 4, December 1976: 548–80.

Tosh, J. 1991. *The Pursuit of History. Second Edition*. London: Longman.

Wirth, L. 1938. "Urbanism as a Way of Life," in *On Cities and Social Life:Selected Papers*. Chicago: Univesity of Chicago Press, 1964: 60–83.

CHAPTER ONE

Abu-Laban, Y. 1997. "Ethnic Politics in a Globalizing Metropolis: The Case of Vancouver," in *The Politics of the City: A Canadian Perspective*, T.L. Thomas (ed.). Scarborough: International Thomson Publishing, Nelson, 77–95.

Badets, J. and L. Howatson-Lee, 1998. "Recent Immigrants in the Workforce," in *Canadian Social Trends*, Spring 1998: 16–22.

Balakrishnan, T.R. and F. Hou, 1996. *Immigration and the Changing Ethnic Mosaic of Canadian Cities*, paper prepared for presentation at the National Symposium on Integration: New Challenges. Winnipeg, October 1996.

Basch, L., N.G. Schiller, and C. S. Blanc, 1994. *Nations Unbound: Trans-*

national Projects, Postcolonial Predicaments, and Deterritorialized Nation States. Langhorne, PA: Gordon and Breach.

Bernhard, J.K., M. Freire, F. Torres, and S. Nirdosh, 1998. "Latin Americans in a Canadian Primary School: Perspectives of Parents, Teachers and Children on Cultural Identity and Academic Achievement," in *Canadian Journal of Regional Science*, no. 20: 217–36.

Brunet, R. 1997. "Farewell to the Lotusland Lifestyle: BC's Immigration-Driven Population Boom is Transforming the Province," in *British Columbia Report*, no. 8: 30–3.

Carey, E. 1999a. "Chinese Community Feels Prejudice," in *The Toronto Star*, 10 May 1999: A1.

– 1999b. "'The City That Works' Could Be Even Better," in *The Toronto Star*, 1 May 1999: A1.

Citizenship and Immigration Canada, 1998. *Canada – A Welcoming Land*, 1999 Annual Immigration Plan. Ottawa: Minister of Public Works and Government Services Canada.

Croucher, S. 1997. Constructing the Image of Ethnic Harmony in Toronto, Canada: The Politics of Problem Definition and Nondefinition," in *Urban Affairs Review*, no. 32: 319–47.

Darroch, G.A. and W.G. Marston, 1971. The Social Class Basis of Ethnic Residential Segregation: The Canadian Case," in *American Journal of Sociology*, no. 77: 491–510.

DeVoretz, D. 1995. *Diminishing Returns: The Economics of Canada's Recent Immigration Policy*. Toronto: C.D. Howe Institute.

Economic Council of Canada, 1991. *New Faces in the Crowd*, Ottawa: Economic Council of Canada.

Evans, R.S. 1997. "New Spaces in a Decentralizing Welfare State: Local Politics and Local Decision-Making," in *The Politics of the City: A Canadian Perspective*, T.L. Thomas (ed.). Scarborough: International Thomson Publishing, Nelson: 173–90.

Fincher, R. 1997. "Gender, Age, and Ethnicity in Immigration for an Australian Nation," in *Environment and Planning A*, no. 29: 217–36.

Frisken, F. 1997. "Jurisdictional and Political Constraints on Progressive Local Initiatives," in *The Politics of the City: A Canadian Perspective*, T.L. Thomas (ed.). Scarborough: International Thomson Publishing, Nelson: 151–72.

– 1999. *Toronto at a Crossroads, and How It Got Here*, paper prepared for the course "Urban and City Management: Challenges for the Next Century." Toronto: York University.

Garcia, S. 1996. "Cities and Citizenship," in *International Journal of Urban and Regional Research*, vol. 20, no. 1: 7–21.

GTA Task Force, 1996.

Hiebert, D. 1998. " Interpreting Segregation," in *Metropolis Year II, The*

Development of a Comparative Research Agenda, M. McAndrew and N. V. Lapierre (eds). Montreal: Immigration and Metropolis, Inter-University Research Centre of Montréal on Immigration, Integration, and the Urban Dynamics, 240–8.

Henry, F. 1994. *The Caribbean Diaspora in Toronto: Learning to Live with Racism*. Toronto: University of Toronto Press.

Henry, F. and E. Ginzber. 1985. *Who Gets the Work?: A Test of Racial Discrimination in Employment*. Toronto: Urban Alliance on Race Relations and The Social Planning Council of Metropolitan Toronto.

Hulchanski, D. 1998. " Immigrants and Access to Housing: How Welcome are Newcomers to Canada?" in *Metropolis Year II, The Development of a Comparative Research Agenda*, M. McAndrew and N.V. Lapierre (eds). Montreal: Immigration and Metropolis, Inter-University Research Centre of Montréal on Immigration, Integration, and the Urban Dynamics, 263-74.

Immigration Legislative Review, 1997. *Not Just Numbers: A Canadian Framework for Future Immigration*. Ottawa: Minister of Public Works and Government Services Canada.

Infantry, A. 1999. "Opportunity Knocks ... But Not for All," in *The Toronto Star*, 2 May 1999: A1.

Jacobs, J.M., 1998. "Staging Difference: Aestheticization and the Politics of Difference in Contemporary Cities," in *Cities of Difference*, R. Fincher and J.M. Jacobs (eds). New York and London: Guilford Press, 252–78.

Kazemipur, A. and S.S. Halli,1997. "Plight of Immigrants: The Spatial Concentration of Poverty in Canada," in *Canadian Journal of Regional Science*, no. 20: 11–28.

Knowles, V. 1992. *Strangers at Our Gates: Canadian Immigration and Immigration Policy, 1540-1990*. Toronto: Dundurn Press.

Lehrer, U. and J. Friedmann, 1997. "Urban Policy Responses to Foreign In-Migration: The Case of Frankfurt-Am-Main, Germany," in *Journal of the American Planning Association*, 63.

Ley, D. 1995. Between Europe and Asia: The Case of the Missing Sequoias," in *Ecumene*, vol. 2, no. 2: 185–210.

Ley, D. and H. Smith, 1997. "Immigration and Poverty in Canadian Cities, 1971–1991," in *Canadian Journal of Regional Science*, no. 20: 29–48.

Li, P. 1998. *Chinese in Canada, Second Edition*. Don Mills: Oxford University Press.

Lo, L. and S. Wang, 1997. "Settlement Patterns of Toronto's Chinese Immigrants: Convergence or Divergence?" in *Canadian Journal of Regional Science*, no. 20: 49-72.

Lungren, P. 1997. "Racist Attitudes in Toronto Greatest in Canada: Report," in *Canadian Jewish News*, no. 38: 5.

Madonapour, A., G. Cars, and J. Allen, 1998. *Social Exclusion in European*

Cities: Processes, Experiences, and Responses. London and Philadelphia: Regional Studies Association.

Man, G. 1997. "Women's Work is Never Done: Social Organization of Work and the Experience of Women in Middle-Class Hong Kong Chinese Immigrant Families: An Inquiry into Institutional and Organizational Processes," in *Asian and Pacific Migration Journal*, no. 4: 303–25.

Marshall, T.H. 1964. *Class, Citizenship and Social Development.* Westport, CT: Greenwood Press.

Massey, D.S. and N.A. Denton, 1993. *American Apartheid: Segregation and the Making of the Underclass. Cambridge,* MA: Harvard University Press.

Mercer, J. 1995. Canadian Cities and Their Immigrants: New Realities," in *The Annals of the American Academy of Political and Social Science,* no. 538: 169–84.

Municipality of Metropolitan Toronto, 1995. *Filling in the Future: Social Prospects in Metro.* Toronto: Social Development Division, Metro Community Services.

– 1997. Municipality of Metropolitan Toronto Submission to the Immigration Legislative Review Advisory Group. Toronto: Municipality of Metropolitan Toronto.

Murdie, R.A. 1993. "Blacks in Near-Ghettos? Black Visible Minority Populations in Metropolitan Toronto Housing Authority Public Housing Units," in *Housing Studies,* no. 9: 437–57.

Mwarigha, M.S. 1997. "The Future of Settlement Services in the New City of Toronto," in *The Joint Centre of Excellence for Research on Immigration and Settlement – Toronto, Newsletter,* no. 1: 1.

Nolin-Hanlon, C.L. and A. Kobayashi, 1998. "Rewriting Canada: Transnationalism as a Challenge to Canadian Public Policy," paper presented at the annual meeting of the Canadian Association of Geographers, Ottawa.

Ng, R. 1996. *The Politics of Community Services, Immigrant Women, Class and State.* Halifax: Fernwood Publishing.

Palmer, D.L. 1997. *Canadians' Attitudes Towards Immigration: November 1996 and February 1997 Surveys.* Ottawa: Program Support, Strategic Policy, Planning and Research Branch, Citizenship and Immigration Canada.

Peach, C. 1998. "The Measurement and Meaning of Immigrant and Minority Segregation," in *Metropolis Year* II, *The Development of a Comparative Research Agenda,* M. McAndrew and N.V. Lapierre (eds). Montreal: Immigration and Metropolis, Inter-University Research Centre of Montréal on Immigration, Integration, and the Urban Dynamics, 217–34.

Permezel, M.J. 1999. "Shaping Citizenship in Local Communities: Community Activism in Neighbourhood Houses of Melbourne," paper presented at the annual meeting of the Association of American Geographers, Honolulu, Hawaii.

Preston, V. and L. Lo, 1997. "Conflicts in the New Chinatowns: 'Asian

Malls' in Toronto," paper presented at the annual meeting of the Canadian Association of Geographers, St. John's, Newfoundland.

Preston, V. and G. Man, 1999. "Employment Experiences of Chinese Immigrant Women: An Exploration of Diversity," paper presented at the annual meeting of the Association of American Geographers, Honolulu, Hawaii.

Qadeer, M. 1997. "Pluralistic Planning for Multicultural Cities: The Canadian Practice," in *Journal of the American Planning Association*, no. 63: 481–95.

– 1998. Ethnic Malls and Plazas: Chinese Commercial Development in Scarborough, Ontario," working paper. Toronto: Joint Centre of Excellence for Research on Immigration and Settlement – Toronto.

Ray, B.K., 1998. "The Measurement and Meaning of Segregation in Montréal," in *Metropolis Year II, The Development of a Comparative Research Agenda*, M. McAndrew and N.V. Lapierre (eds). Montreal: Immigration and Metropolis, Inter-University Research Centre of Montréal on Immigration, Integration, and the Urban Dynamics, 249–59.

– 1999. "Negotiating Identity and Integration: Experiences of Haitian Women in Rene Goupil," in paper presented at the annual meeting of the Association of American Geographers, Honolulu, Hawaii.

Ray, B.K., G. Halseth, and B. Johnson, 1997. "The Changing 'Face' of the Suburbs: Issues of Ethnicity and Residential Change in Suburban Vancouver," in *International Journal of Urban and Regional Research*, no. 21: 73–99.

Reichold, S. 1998. "Le Rôle et l'action des organismes communautaires," paper presented at Séminaire Conjoint France-Canada sur l'Immigration et l'Integration, Montreal.

Reitz, J.G., 1997. "Institutional Structure and Immigrant Earnings," paper presented at the annual meetings of the American Sociological Association, Toronto.

Richmond, T. 1996. Effects of Cutbacks on Immigrant Service Agencies, Results of an Action Research Project. Toronto: City of Toronto Public Health Department

Rose, D. and B.K. Ray, 1998. The Role of 'Weak Ties' in the Settlement Experience of Immigrant Women with Young Children: The Case of Central Americans in Montreal," working paper. Toronto: Joint Centre of Excellence for Research on Immigration and Settlement – Toronto.

Rutherford, T. 1997. "The Socio-Spatial Restructuring of Canadian Labour Markets," in *Canada and the Global Economy: The Geography of Structural and Technological Change*, J. Britton (ed.). Montreal and Kingston: McGill-Queen's University Press, 407–32.

Sassen, S. 1996. *Losing Control? Sovereignty in an Age of Globalization*. New York: Columbia University Press.

Smith, D.M. and M. Blanc, 1996. "Citizenship, Nationality and Ethnic

Minorities in Three European Nations," in *International Journal of Urban and Regional Research*, vol. 20, no. 1: 66–82.

Social Planning Council of Metropolitan Toronto, 1997. *Profile of a Changing World: 1996 Community Agency Survey.* Toronto: Social Planning Council of Metropolitan Toronto.

Stasiulus, D. 1997. "Participation by Immigrants, Ethnocultural/Visible Minorities in the Canadian Political Process," in *Immigrants and Civic Participation: Contemporary Policy and Research Issues.* Ottawa: Multiculturalism Program, Department of Canadian Heritage, 12–29.

Statistics Canada, 1997. "1996 Census: Immigration and Citizenship," in *The Daily*, Tuesday, 4 November 1997: 1–14.

– 1998. "1996 Census: Sources of Income, Earnings, and Total Income, and Family Income," in *The Daily*, Tuesday, 12 May 1998: 1–16.

Teixeira, C. 1996. "The Suburbanization of Portuguese Communities in Toronto and Montreal: From Isolation to Residential Integration?" in *Immigration and Ethnicity in Canada*, A. Lapierre, V. Lindstrom, and T.P. Seiler (eds). Montreal: Association for Canadian Studies, 181–201.

Thompson, S., K. Dunn, I. Burnley, P. Murphy, and B. Hanna, 1998. *Multiculturalism & Local Governance, A National Perspective.* Sydney: New South Wales Department of Government, Ethnic Affairs Commission of New South Wales, University of New South Wales.

Wayland, S.V., 1992. "Political Participation: Immigrant and Visible Minority Associational Movements in Toronto," paper presented at the American Political Science Association meetings, Chicago.

Weinfeld, M. 1997. "Dilemmas of 'Ethnic Match' in Health and Social Services," paper presented at the monthly research seminar series, Joint Centre of Excellence for Research on Immigration and Settlement – Toronto, Toronto.

Wilson, W.J. 1996. *When Work Disappears: The World of the New Urban Poor.* New York: Knopf.

Wong, M. 1998. "Ghanaian Women in Toronto's Labour Market: Negotiating Gendered Work and Transnational Household Strategies," paper presented at the annual meeting of the Canadian Association of Geographers, Ottawa.

Yuval-Davis, N. 1996. "Women, Citizenship and Difference," background paper for the Conference on Women and Citizenship, University of Greenwich, Greenwich.

CHAPTER TWO

Armstrong, J. 1985. *Slash.* Penticton: Theytus Books.

Asimi, A.P. 1967. "The Urban Setting," in *Resolving Conflicts – A Cross-*

Cultural Approach. Winnipeg: Department of University Extensions and Adult Education, University of Manitoba, 89–96.

Barron, F.L. and J. Garcea, 1999. *Urban Indian Reserves: Forging New Relationships in Saskatchewan*. Saskatoon: Purich Publishers.

Best, J. 1989. *Images of Issues: Typifying Contemporary Social Problems*. New York: Aldine de Gruyter.

Berkhoffer, R.F. 1979. *The White Man's Indian: Images of the American Indian from Columbus to the Present*. New York: Vintage Books.

Boek, W.E. and J.K. Boek, 1959. *The People of Indian Ancestry in Greater Winnipeg*. Winnipeg: Department of Agriculture and Immigration, Queen's Printer.

Bond, J.J. 1967. *A Report on the Pilot Relocation Project at Elliot Lake, Ontario*. Ottawa: Indian Affairs Branch, Department of Indian Affairs and Northern Development.

Braroe, W.W. 1975. *Indian and White: Self-Image and Interaction in a Canadian Plains Community*. Stanford: Stanford University Press.

Breton, R. and G. Grant, 1984. *The Dynamics of Government Programs for Urban Indians in the Prairie Provinces*. Montreal: The Institute for Research on Public Policy.

Brody, H. 1983. *Maps and Dreams: Indians and the British Columbia Frontier*. New York: Penguin Books.

Buckley, H. 1992. *From Wooden Ploughs to Welfare: Why Indian Policy Failed in the Prairie Provinces*. Kingston: McGill-Queen's University Press.

Canada, Department of Indian Affairs and Northern Development, 1957. *The Indian News*, vol. 2, no. 4: 3.

– 1991. *Quantitative Analysis and Socio-Demographic Research, Basic Departmental Data*. Ottawa: Minister of Supply and Services.

Canada, Joint Committee of the Senate and the House of Commons on Indian Affairs, 1960a. *Brief of the Indian-Eskimo Association of Canada, Minutes of Proceedings and Evidence, vol. 5*: 363–427.

– 1960b. *A Submission by the Government of Saskatchewan, Minutes of Proceedings and Evidence, vol. 12*: 1029–90.

Canadian Corrections Association, 1967. *Indians and the Law*. Ottawa: The Canadian Welfare Council.

Clatworthy, S.J. 1980. *The Demographic Composition and Economic Circumstances of Winnipeg's Native Population*. Winnipeg: Institute of Urban Studies, University of Winnipeg.

Clatworthy, S.J. and J.P. Gunn, 1981. *The Economic Circumstances of Native People in Selected Metropolitan Centres in Western Canada*. Winnipeg: Institute of Urban Studies, University of Winnipeg.

Clatworthy S.J. and J. Hull, 1983. *Native Economic Conditions in Regina and Saskatoon*. Winnipeg: Institute of Urban Studies, University of Winnipeg.

Clatworthy, S.J., J. Hull, and N. Loughran, 1995. "Urban Aboriginal Orga-
nizations: Edmonton, Toronto and Winnipeg," in *Self-Government for
Aboriginal People in Urban Areas*, E.J. Peters (ed.). Kingston: Institute of
Intergovernmental Relations, Queen's University, 25–81.

Comeau P. and A. Santin, 1990. *The First Canadians: A Profile of Canada's
Native People Today*. Toronto: James Lorimer.

Culleton, B. 1983. *In Search of April Raintree*. Winnipeg: Pemmican.

Currie, W. 1966. *Urbanization and Indians*. Lakehead University: unpublished address to the Mid-Canada Development Corridor Conference,
Indian-Eskimo Association.

Davis, A.K. 1965. *Edging Into Mainstream: Urban Indians in Saskatchewan*.
Bellingham: Western Washington State College.

Dunn, M. 1986. *Access to Survival: A Perspective on Aboriginal Self-Government for the Constituency of the Native Council of Canada*. Kingston:
Institute of Intergovernmental Relations, Queen's University.

Elias, P.D. 1975. *Metropolis and Hinterland in Northern Manitoba*. Winnipeg: Manitoba Museum of Man and Nature.

Falconer, P. 1985. *Urban Indian Needs: Federal Policy Responsibility and
Options in the Context of the Talks on Aboriginal Self-Government*. Winnipeg: unpublished discussion paper.

– 1990. "The Overlooked of the Neglected: Native Single-Mothers in Major
Cities on the Prairies," in *The Political Economy of Manitoba*, J. Silver
and J. Hull (eds). Regina: Canadian Plains Research Centre, University of
Regina, 188–210.

Francis, D. 1992. *The Imaginary Indian: The Image of the Indian in Canadian Culture*. Vancouver: Arsenal Pulp Press.

Frideres, J.S. 1984. "Government Policies and Programs Relating to People
of Indian Ancestry in Alberta," in *The Dynamics of Government Programs
for Urban Indians in the Prairie Provinces*, R. Breton and G. Grant (eds).
Montreal: The Institute for Research on Public Policy, 321–517.

– 1988. *Canada's Indians: Contemporary Conflicts. Third Edition*. Scarborough, Ontario: Prentice-Hall.

– 1993. *Native Peoples in Canada: Contemporary Conflicts, Fourth Edition*.
Scarborough, Ontario: Prentice Hall.

Gerber, L.M. 1977. *Trends in Out-Migration from Indian Communities
Across Canada. A Report for the Task Force on Migrating Native People*.
Ph.D. thesis, Harvard University.

Goldie, T. 1989. *Fear and Temptation: The Image of the Indigene in Canadian, Australian and New Zealand Literature*. Kingston: McGill-Queen's
University Press.

Goldman, G. 1993. *The Aboriginal Population and the Census: 120 Years of
Information – 1871 to 1991*. Ottawa, Statistics Canada: unpublished
paper.

Graham, K.A. 1999. "Urban Aboriginal Governance in Canada: Paradigms and Prospects," in *Implementing Aboriginal Self-Government in Canada*, J.H. Hylton (ed.). Saskatoon: Purich Publishers, 377–91.

Hawthorn, H.B. 1966–67. *A Survey of the Contemporary Indians of Canada – A Report on Economic, Political and Educational Needs and Policies*, two volumes. Ottawa: The Indian Affairs Branch, Ottawa.

Hawthorn, H.B., C. Belshaw, and S. Jamieson, 1958. *The Indians of British Columbia*. Toronto: University of Toronto Press.

Helgason, W. 1995. "Urban Aboriginal Issues, Models and Stakeholders Relative to the Transition to Self-Government," in *Self-Government for Aboriginal Peoples in Urban Areas*, E. Peters (ed.). Kingston: Institute of Intergovernmental Relations, Queen's University, 131–40.

Hirabayashi, G.K. 1962. *The Challenge of Assisting the Canadian Aboriginal People to Adjust to Urban Environments: Report of the First Western Canadian Indian-Metis Seminar*. Edmonton: University of Alberta.

Indian-Eskimo Association, 1960. *National Research Seminar on Indians in the City*. Kingston, Queen's University: unpublished proceedings.

Indian-Eskimo Association, 1971. *Final Report: Indians and the City*. Toronto: Contract with Secretary of State.

Kastes, W.G. 1993. *The Future of Aboriginal Urbanization in Prairie Cities: Select Annotated Bibliography and Literature Review on Urban Aboriginal Issues in the Prairie Provinces*. Winnipeg: Institute of Urban Studies, University of Winnipeg.

Krotz, L. 1980. *Urban Indians:The Strangers in Canada's Cities*. Edmonton: Hurtig Publishers.

Lagasse, J.H. 1958. *A Study of the Population of Indian Ancestry in Manitoba: A Social and Economic Study*. Winnipeg: The Social and Economic Research Office, Manitoba Department of Agriculture and Immigration.

Lithman, Y.G. 1984. *The Community Apart: A Case Study of a Canadian Indian Reserve Community*. Winnipeg: University of Manitoba Press.

Lurie, N.O. 1967. "The Indian Moves to an Urban Setting," in *Resolving Conflicts – A Cross-Cultural Approach*. Winnipeg: Department of University Extensions and Adult Education, University of Manitoba, 73–86.

MacLean, J. 1889. *Indians of Canada: Their Manners and Customs*. Toronto: William Briggs.

– 1896. *Canadian Savage Folk: The Native Tribes of Canada*. Toronto: William Briggs.

Maidman, F. 1981. *Native People in Urban Settings: Problems, Needs and Services*. Toronto: A Report of the Ontario Task Force on Native People in the Urban Setting.

Maracle, L. 1992. *Sundogs*. Penticton:Theytus Books.

McCaskill, D.N. 1981. "The Urbanization of Indians in Winnipeg, Toronto,

Edmonton and Vancouver: A Comparative Analysis," in *Culture* vol. 1, no. 1: 82–9.

Melling, J. 1967. *Right to a Future: The Native Peoples of Canada.* Toronto: T.H. Best Printing Co. Ltd.

Morse, B. 1989. "Government Obligations, Aboriginal Peoples and Section 91(24)," in *Aboriginal Peoples and Government Responsibility: Exploring Federal and Provincial Roles*, D.C. Hawkes (ed.). Ottawa: Carleton University Press, 59-92.

Morse, B.W. 1993. *A Legal and Jurisdictional Analysis of Urban Self-Government.* Ottawa: Native Council of Canada Royal Commission Intervenor Research Project, 59–92.

Nagler, M. 1970. *Indians in the City.* Ottawa: Canadian Research Centre for Anthropology, St. Paul University.

Native Council of Canada, 1992. *Decision 1992: Background and Discussion Points for the First Peoples Forum.* Ottawa: NCC.

– 1993. *The First Peoples Urban Circle: Choices for Self-Determination. Book 1.* Ottawa: Native Council of Canada.

Neeginan Development Corporation, 1999. *Neeginan "Our Place"* (pamphlet). Winnipeg: Neeginan Development Corporation.

Opekokew, D. 1995. "Treaty First Nations Perspectives on Self-Government for Aboriginal Peoples in Urban Areas," in *Self-Government for Aboriginal Peoples in Urban Areas*, E. Peters (ed.). Kingston: Institute of Intergovernmental Relations, Queen's University, 168–72.

Penner, K. 1983. *Indian Self-Government.* Ottawa: Supply and Services.

Peters, E.J. 1991. "'Urban' and 'Aboriginal': An Impossible Contradiction?" in *Critical Approaches to Canadian Urbanism*, J. Caulfield and L. Peake (eds). Toronto: University of Toronto Press, 47–62.

– 1994. "Geographies of Self-Government," in *Implementing Aboriginal Self-Government in Canada*, J. Hylton (ed.). Saskatoon: Purich Publishers.

– 1995. *Self-Government for Aboriginal Peoples in Urban Areas.* Kingston: Institute of Intergovernmental Relations, Queen's University.

Price, J.A. and D.N. McCaskill, 1974. "The Urban Integration of Canadian Indians," in *Western Canadian Journal of Anthropology*, vol. 4, no. 2: 29–45.

Ray, B.K. 1992. *Immigrants in a "Multicultural" Toronto: Exploring the Contested Social and Housing Geographies of Post-War Italian and Caribbean Immigrants.* Ph.D. Thesis, Kingston: Department of Geography.

Reeves, W. 1986. "Native Societies: The Professions as a Model of Self-Determination for Urban Indians," in *Arduous Journey: Canadian Indians and Decolonization*, J.R. Ponting (ed.). Toronto: McClelland and Stewart, 342-58.

Reeves, W. and J. Frideres, 1981. "Government Policy and Indian Urbanization: the Alberta Case," in *Canadian Public Policy*, vol. 7, no. 4: 584–95.

Regina Welfare Council, 1959. *Our City Indians: Report of a Conference.* Regina: Saskatchewan House.

Reiber-Kremers and Associates, 1977. *A Preliminary Overview of Native Migration into the City of Winnipeg. A Discussion Paper Prepared for the City of Winnipeg.* Winnipeg: Environmental Planning Department.

Richardson, B. 1994. *People of Terra Nullus: Betrayal and Rebirth in Aboriginal Canada.* Vancouver: Douglas & McIntyre.

Robertson, H. 1970. *Reservations Are for Indians.* Toronto: James Lewis & Samuel.

Rothney, R.G. 1992. *Neechi Foods Co-op Ltd.: Lessons in Community Development.* Winnipeg: Winnipeg Family Economic Development Inc.

Royal Commission on Aboriginal Peoples, 1993a. *Aboriginal Peoples in Urban Centres: Report of the National Round Table on Aboriginal Urban Issues.* Ottawa: Minister of Supply and Services.

– 1993b. *Partners in Confederation: Aboriginal Peoples, Self-Government, and the Constitution.* Ottawa: Minister of Supply and Services.

– 1993c. *The Electronic Series: Public Hearings,* CD-ROM. Ottawa: Minister of Supply and Services.

– 1996. *Volume 4: Perspectives and Realities.* Ottawa: Canada Communications Group.

Ryan, J. 1975. *Wall of Words: The Betrayal of the Urban Indian.* Toronto: Peter Martin Associates Limited.

Saskatchewan, Government of Saskatchewan, 1979. *The Dimensions of Indian and Native Urban Poverty in Saskatchewan.* Regina: The Social Planning Secretariat.

Shimpo, M. and R. Williamson, 1965. *Socio-Cultural Disintegration Among the Fringe Saulteaux.* Saskatoon: Centre for Community Studies, University of Saskatchewan.

Shorten, L. 1991. *Without Reserve: Stories from Urban Natives.* Edmonton: NeWest Press, Edmonton.

Sibley, D. 1981. *Outsiders in Urban Societies.* New York: St. Martin's Press.

Spector, M. and J.I. Kitsuse, 1987. *Constructing Social Problems.* New York: Aldine de Gruyter.

Stymeist, D. 1975. *Ethnics and Indians.* Toronto: Peter Martin Associates.

Tizya, R. 1992. "Comments on Urban Aboriginals and Self-Government," in *Aboriginal Governments and Power Sharing in Canada*, D. Brown (ed.). Kingston: Institute of Intergovernmental Relations, Queen's University, 45–52.

Tobias, J.L. 1983. "Protection, Civilization, Assimilation: An Outline History of Canada's Indian Policy," in *As Long as the Sun Shines and Water Flows: A Reader in Canadian Native Studies*, A.L. Getty and A.S. Lussier (eds). Vancouver: University of British Columbia Press, 29–38.

Trudeau, J. 1969. "The Indian in the City," in *Kerygma*, vol. 3, no. 3: 118–23.

Vincent, D.B. 1971. *The Indian-Metis Urban Probe*. Winnipeg: Indian-Metis Friendship Centre and Institute of Urban Studies, University of Winnipeg.

Weinstein, J. 1986. *Self-Determination Off a Land-Base*. Kingston: Institute of Intergovernmental Relations, Queen's University.

Young, D. 1995. "Some Approaches to Urban Aboriginal Governance," in *Self-Government for Aboriginal Peoples in Urban Areas*, E.J. Peters (ed.). Kingston: Institute of Intergovernmental Relations, Queen's University, 153–62.

Zeitoun, L. 1969. *Canadian Indians at the Crossroads: Some Aspects of Relocation and Urbanization in Canada*. Ottawa: unpublished study for the Manpower Utilization Branch, Department of Manpower and Immigration.

Zentner, H. 1973. *The Indian Identity Crisis*. Calgary: Strayer Publications Ltd.

CHAPTER THREE

Ahrentzen, S. 1997. "The Meaning of Home Workplaces for Women," in *Thresholds in Feminist Geography: Difference, Methodology, Representation*, J.P. Jones III, H.J. Nast, and S.M. Roberts (eds). Lanhan, MD: Rowman & Littlefield Publishers.

Andrew, C. 1992. "The Feminist City," in *Political Arrangements: Power and the City*, Henri Lustiger-Thaler (ed.). Montreal: Black Rose Books, 109–22.

Armstrong, P. and H. Armstrong, 1994. *The Double Ghetto: Canadian Women and Their Segregated Work, Third Edition*. Toronto: McClelland & Stewart.

Birkeland, J. 1991. "An Ecofeminist Critique of Manstream Planning," in *Trumpeter*, vol. 8, no. 2: 72–84.

Birkeland, J. 1993. "Ecofeminism: Linking Theory and Practice," in *Ecofeminism: Women, Animals, Nature*, G. Gaard (ed.). Philadelphia: Temple University Press: 13–59.

Bondi, L. 1991. "Gender and Gentrification: A Critique," in *Transactions of the Institute of British Geographers*, no. 16: 190–8.

Bookchin, M. 1992. "The Meaning of Confederalism," in *Putting Power in its Place: Create Community Control*, J. Plant and C. Plant (eds). Philadelphia: New Society Publishers, 59–67.

Burman, D. 1997. "Enhancing Community Health Promotion with Local Currencies: The Local Employment & Trading System (LETS)," in *Eco-City Dimensions*, M. Roseland (ed.). New Haven, CT: New Society Publishers, 51-63.

Canadian Mortgage and Housing Corporation (CMHC), 1997. *Changing Values, Changing Communities: A Guide to the Development of Healthy, Sustainable Communities*. Hygeia Consulting and REIC Ltd.

Castells, M. 1989. *The Informational City: Information Technology, Economic Restructuring, and the Urban-Regional Process*. New York: Blackwell.

Dalal-Clayton, B. 1996. *Getting to Grips with Green Plans: National-Level Experience in Industrial Countries*. London: Earthscan Publications.

Davis, M. 1990. *City of Quartz*. London: Verso.

Dobson, A. 1995. *Green Political Thought , Second Edition*. London: HarperCollins.

Eichler, M. (ed.) 1995a. *Change of Plans: Toward a Non-Sexist Sustainable City*. Toronto: Garamond Press.

– 1995b. "Designing Eco-City in North America," in *Change of Plans*, M. Eichler (ed.). Toronto: Garamond Press, 1–23.

Esser, J. and J. Hirch, 1994. "The Crisis of Fordism and the Dimensions of 'Post-Fordist' Regional and Urban Structure," in *Post-Fordism: A Reader*, A. Amin (ed.). Oxford: Blackwell: 71–97.

Fincher, R. and J.M. Jacobs (eds), 1998. *Cities of Difference*. New York: Guilford Press.

Garber, J. 1995. "Defining Feminist Community: Place, Choice, and the Urban Politics of Difference," in *Gender in Urban Research*, J. Garber and R. Turner (eds). London: Sage, 24–44.

Gorz, A. 1993. "Political Ecology: Expertocracy versus Self-Limitation," in *New Left Review*, no. 202: 55–67.

Gurstein, P. and J. Curry, 1993. "Implementing Concepts of Sustainable Community Planning: A Case Study of Bamberton, British Columbia," in *Plan Canada*, March 1993: 8–15.

Hayden, D. 1980. "What Would a Non-Sexist City be Like? Speculations on Housing, Urban Design and Human Work," in *Signs*, vol. 5, no. 3, supplement, Spring 1980: S170–87.

– 1981. *The Grand Domestic Revolution*. Cambridge: MIT.

Hough, M. 1995. *Cities and Natural Process*. New York: Routledge.

Huxley, M. 1994. "Space, Knowledge, Power, and Gender," in *Suburban Dreaming: An Interdisciplinary Approach to Australian Cities*, L.C. Johnson (ed.). Geelong, Victoria: Deakin University Press, 181–92.

– 1997. "Ecologically Sustainable Cities, Environmentally Friendly Transport, or Just 'More Work for Mother'?" in *Women on the Move: Maintaining the Momentum*, Conference Proceedings, Second National Women on the Move Conference, TransAdelaide and South Australian Department of Transport, Adelaide: 1–4.

International Council for Local Environmental Iniatives (ICLEI), 1996. *The Local Agenda 21 Planning Guide*. Toronto: ICLEI and Ottawa: IDRC.

Jezierski, L. 1995. "Women Organizing Their Place in Restructuring Economies," in *Gender in Urban Research*, J. Garber and R. Turner (eds). London: Sage, 60–76.

Kanter, R.M. 1972. *Commitment and Community: Communes and Utopias in Sociological Perspective*. New York: The Free Press.

Keil, R. 1995. "The Environmental Problematic in World Cities," in *World Cities in a World System* , P. Knox and P. Taylor (eds). Cambridge: Cambridge University Press: 280–97.

– 1996. "World City Formation, Local Politics and Sustainability," in *Local Places in the Age of the Global City*, R. Keil, G. Wekerle, and D.V.J. Bell (eds). Montreal: Black Rose Books, 37–44.

Kipfer, S., F. Hartmann, and S. Marino, 1996. "Cities, Nature and Socialism: Towards an Urban Agenda for Action and Research," in *Capitalism, Nature, Socialism*, vol. 7, no. 2: 5–19.

Kofman, E. 1998. "Whose City? Gender, Class, and Immigrants in Globalizing European Cities," in *Cities of Difference*, R. Fincher and J.M. Jacobs (eds). New York: The Guilford Press, 270–300.

Lehrer, U. and R. Milgrom, 1996. "New (Sub)Urbanism: Countersprawl or Repackaging the Product," in *Capitalism, Nature, Socialism*, vol. 7, no. 26: 49–64.

Lipietz, A. 1992. *Towards a New Economic Order: Postfordism, Ecology, and Democracy*. London: Oxford University Press.

MacGregor, S. 1995. "Deconstructing the Man-Made City: Feminist Critiques of Planning Thought and Action," in *Change of Plans: Towards a Non-Sexist Sustainable City*, M. Eichler (ed.). Toronto: Garamond Press, 25–49.

– 1997. "Feeding Families in Harris's Ontario: Women, the Tsubouchi Diet, and the Politics of Restructuring," in *Atlantis: Journal of Women's Studies*, vol. 21, no. 1: 93–110.

– 1998. "It's Not Easy Being Green: Feminist Thoughts on Planning for Sustainability," in *Planners Network*, no. 129, May 1998: 7–9.

Marcuse, P. 1998. "Sustainability is Not Enough," in *Planners Network*, no. 129, 1 May 1998: 10.

Massey, D. 1991. "Flexible Sexism," in *Environment and Planning D: Society and Space*, no. 9: 31–57.

McLaren, V. 1992. *Sustainable Urban Development in Canada: From Concept to Practice*. Toronto: ICURR Press.

Mellor, M. 1992. *Breaking the Boundaries: Towards a Feminist Green Socialism*. London: Virago Press.

Milroy, B.M. 1996. "Women and Work in a Canadian Community," in *City Lives and City Forms: Critical Research and Canadian Urbanism*, J. Caulfield and L. Peake (eds). Toronto: University of Toronto Press, 215–38.

– 2002. "Toronto's Legal Challenge to Amalgamation," in this volume.

Mouffe, C. 1992. "Feminism, Citizenship and Radical Democratic Politics." in *Feminists Theorize the Political*, J. Butler and J. Scott (eds). New York: Routledge, 376–84.

Nozick, M. 1992. *No Place Like Home: Building Sustainable Communities*. Ottawa: Canadian Council on Social Development.

O'Brien, M. 1986. "Feminism and Revolution," in *The Politics of Diversity*, R. Hamilton and M. Barrett (eds). Montreal: Book Centre, 424–31.

O'Hara, B. 1993. *Working Harder Isn't Working: How We Can Save the Environment, the Economy, and Our Sanity by Working Less and Enjoying Life More*. Vancouver: New Start Books.

Paehlke, R. 1994. "Possibilities for and Limitations on Environmental Protection in the Changing Metropolis," in *The Changing Canadian Metropolis: A Public Policy Perspective, vol. 1*, F. Frisken (ed.). Toronto: Canadian Urban Institute, 106–22.

– 1998. "Work in a Sustainable Society," in *Political Ecology: Global and Local*, R. Keil, D.V.J. Bell, P. Penz, and L. Fawcett (eds). New York: Routledge, 299–304.

Perks, W. and D. Van Vliet, 1993. "Sustainable Community Design: Restructuring and Demonstration," in *Plan Canada*, November 1993: 30–6.

Peterson, R. 1979. "Impacts of the Conserver Society on Women," in *Conserver Society Notes,Special Issue: Women and the Conserver Society*, vol. 2, no. 1: 4–8.

Pietila, H. 1997. "The Triangle of the Human Economy," in *Ecological Economics*, no. 20: 113–27.

Plant, J. and C. Plant (eds), 1995. *Putting Power in its Place: Create Community Control*. Philadelphia: New Society Publishers.

Plumwood, V. 1994. "Ecosocial Feminism as a General Theory of Oppression," in *Ecology: Key Concepts in Critical Theory*, C. Merchant (ed.). Atlantic Highlands, NJ: Humanities Press, 207–19.

Rees, W. and M. Roseland, 1991. "Sustainable Communities: Planning for the 21st Century," in *Plan Canada*, vol. 31, no. 3, May 1991: 15–24.

Rifkin, J. 1995. *The End of Work*. New York: Tarcher/Putnam.

Roberts, W. and S. Brandum, 1995. *Get a Life! Dance Around the Dinosaurs*. Toronto: Get a Life Publishing.

Rogers, R. 1995. *The Oceans are Emptying: Fish Wars and Sustainability*. Montreal: Black Rose Books.

Roelofs, J. 1996. *Greening Cities: Building Just and Sustainable Communities*, A TOES Book. New York: Bootstrap Publishing.

Roseland, M. (ed.) 1997. *Eco-City Dimensions: Healthy Communities, Healthy Planet*. New Haven, CT: New Society Publishers.

– 1998. *Toward Sustainable Communities: Resources for Citizens and Their Governments*. Philadelphia: New Society Publishers.

Royal Commission on the Regeneration of Toronto's Waterfront (RCTW), 1990 *Watershed:Interim Report* (David Crombie, Commissioner). Toronto: RCTW.

– 1992. *Regeneration: Toronto's Waterfront and the Sustainable City*. Toronto: Queen's Printer of Ontario.

Sale, K. 1992. "Free and Equal Intercourse: The Decentralist Design," in *Putting Power in its Place: Create Community Control*, J. Plant and C. Plant (eds). Philadelphia: New Society Publishers, 20–7.

Sandilands, C. 1993. "On 'Green Consumerism': Environmental Privatization and 'Family Values,'" in *Canadian Women's Studies/Les Cahiers de la Femme* vol. 13, no. 3, Spring 1993: 45–7.

Sassen, S. 1991. *The Global City: New York, London, Tokyo*. Princeton, NJ: Princeton University Press.

Schor, J. 1997. "Utopias of Women's Time," in *Feminist Utopias in a Postmodern Era*, A. Van Lenning et al. (eds). Tilburg, Netherlands: Tilburg University Press, 45–54.

Schultz, I. 1993. "Women and Waste," in *Capitalism Nature Socialism* vol. 4, no. 2: 51–63.

Spain, D. 1995. "Sustainability, Feminist Visions and the Utopian Tradition," in *Journal of Planning Literature*, vol. 9, no. 4, May 1995: 362–9.

Stoeker, R. 1992. "Who Takes Out the Garbage? Social Reproduction and Social Movement Research," in *Perspectives on Social Problems*, no. 3: 239–64.

Taminga, K. 1996. "Restoring Biodiversity in Urbanizing Regions: Towards Pre-emptive Ecosystem Planning," in *Plan Canada*, July 1996: 10–15.

Tomalty, R., R. Gibson, D. Alexander, and J. Fisher, 1994. "Ecosystem Planning for Canadian Urban Regions," in *Intergovernmental Committee on Urban and Regional Research*. Toronto.

Trepl, L. 1996. "City and Ecology," in *Capitalism Nature Socialism*, vol. 7, no. 2: 226–56.

Vodden, K. 1997. "Working Together for a Green Economy," in *Eco-City Dimensions*, M. Roseland (ed.). New Haven: New Society Publishers, 80–94.

Waring, M. 1989. *If Women Counted: A New Feminist Economics*. San Francisco: Harper & Row,

Wackernagel, M. and W. Rees, 1996. *Our Ecological Footprint: Reducing Human Impact on the Earth*. Gabriola Is., BC: New Society Publishers.

Wekerle, G. 1980. "Women in the Urban Environment," in *Signs: Journal of Women in Culture and Society*, vol. 5, no. 3, supplement 1: s188–214.

– 1993. "Responding to Diversity: Housing Developed By and For Women," in *Shelter, Women and Development: First and Third World Perspectives*, H. Dandekar (ed.). Ann Arbour, MI: George Wahr Publishing, 178–86.

– 1996. "Reframing Urban Sustainability: Women's Movement Organizing and the Local State," in *Local Places in the Age of the Global City*, R. Keil et al. (eds). Montreal: Black Rose Books, 137–45.

Wekerle, G. and L. Peake, 1996. "New Social Movements and Women's

Urban Activism," in *City Lives and City Forms*, J.Caulfield and L. Peake (eds). Toronto: University of Toronto Press, 263–81.

Wekerle, G. and C. Whitzman, 1995. *Safe Cities: Guidelines for Planning, Design and Management*. New York: Van Nostrand Reinhold.

White, R. and J. Whitney, 1992. "Cities and the Environment: An Overview," in *Sustainable Cities: Urbanization and the Environment in International Perspective*, R. Stren, R. White, and J. Whitney (eds). Boulder, CO: Westview Press, 8–51.

Whitzman, C. 1995. "What Do You Want to Do, Pave Parks? Urban Planning and the Prevention of Violence," in *Change of Plans*, M. Eichler (ed.). Toronto: Garamond Press, 89–109.

– 2002. "The 'Voice of Women' in Canadian Local Government," in this volume.

Wilson, E. 1995. "The Rhetoric of Urban Space," in *New Left Review*, no. 209, January-February 1995: 146–60.

World Commission on Environment and Development (WCED), 1987. *Our Common Future*. London: Oxford University Press.

Young, Iris Marion, 1990. *Justice and the Politics of Difference*. Princeton, NJ: Princeton University Press.

Zillman, K. 1996. "Gender-Sensitive and Sustainable Urban Development: A Report from the German National Round Table of Women Planners and Architects for the Second United Nations Conference on Human Settlements," in *Capitalism Nature Socialism*, vol. 7, no. 2: 147–54.

CHAPTER FOUR

Adamson, N., L. Briskin, and M. McPhail, 1988. *Feminist Organizing for Change: the Contemporary Women's Movement in Canada*. Toronto: Oxford University Press.

Andrew, C. 1992. "The Feminist City," in *Public Arrangements: Power and the City*, Henri Lustiger-Thaler (ed.). Montreal: Black Rose Books, 109–22.

Andrew, C. and B.M. Milroy (eds), 1988. *Life Spaces: Gender, Housing, Employment*, Vancouver: UBC Press.

Briskin, L. 1991. "Feminist Practice: A New Approach to Evaluating Feminist Strategy," in *Women and Social Change: Feminist Activism in Canada*, Jeri Wine and Janice Ristock (eds). Toronto: James Lorimer and Company.

Burnett, P. 1973. "Social Change, the Status of Women and Models of City Form and Development," in *Antipode*, no. 7: 57–62.

Canadian Panel on Violence against Women, 1993. Report.

Catallo, R. 1994. *Lessons from Success Stories: Making Communities Safer*. Toronto: City of Toronto Safe City Committee.

Chouinard, V. 1999. "Body Politics: Disabled Women's Activism in Canada and Beyond," in *Mind and Body Spaces: Geographies of Illness, Impairment and Disability*, R. Butler and H. Parr (eds). London and New York, Routledge, 269–94.

City of Montreal Standing Committee on Urban Planning, 1989: "Women and the City: Report of the Committee on the Problems of Women in an Urban Environment."

City of Saskatoon, 1993. "Reports on the Focus Group on Women's Issues in the Community."

City of Toronto Task Force on the Status of Women, 1976: "Final Report."

City of Toronto Parks and Recreation Department, 1987. "High Park User Survey."

City of Toronto, 1988: *The Safe City: Municipal Strategies for Preventing Public Violence Against Women*.

City of Toronto Committee on the Status of Women, Older Women's Network, and Women Plan Toronto, 1997: "Make Women's Needs Heard November 10, 1997: Information about Issues that may Impact Women in the 1997 Municipal Election" (booklet).

City of Toronto Task Force on Community Safety, 1999: *Toronto, My City, a Safe City: A Community Safety Strategy for the City of Toronto*.

Coates, L., C. Guberman, and D. Orsini, 1992. *Planning, Designing and Maintaining Safer Parks*. Toronto: City of Toronto Parks and Recreation Department.

Eichler, M. (ed.) 1995a. *Change of Plans: Towards a Non-Sexist Sustainable City*. Toronto: Garamond Press.

– 1995b. "Designing Eco-City in North America," in *Change of Plans: Towards a Non-Sexist Sustainable City*, M. Eichler (ed.). Toronto: Garamond Press, 1–23.

Enjeu, C. and J. Save, 1974. "The City: Off-Limits to Women," in *Liberation*, vol. 18, no. 9: 9–13.

Federation of Canadian Municipalities, 1993. *How to Build Safer Communities for Women: A Handbook for Community Leaders*. Ottawa: FCM.

Federation of Canadian Municipalities International Office and Femmes et Ville Montreal, 1997. *A City Tailored to Women: The Role of Municipal Governments in Achieving Gender Equality*. Ottawa: FCM.

Grant, A. 1989. *Planning for Sexual Assault Prevention: Women's Safety in High Park*. Toronto: METRAC.

Greater London Council, 1985. *Changing Places: Positive Action on Women and Planning*. London: GLC Women's Committee.

Guberman, C. 1995. "Sowing the Seeds of Sustainability: Planning for Food Self-Reliance," in *Change of Plans: Towards a Non-Sexist Sustainable City*, M. Eichler (ed.). Toronto: Garamond Press:

Halford, S. 1992. "Feminist Change in a Patriarchal Organization: The

Experience of Women's Initiatives in Local Government and Implications for Feminist Perspectives on State Institutions," in *Gender and Bureaucracy*, Mike Savage and Ann Witz (eds). Oxford: Blackwell Publishers/Sociological Review.

Hallatt, S. and T. Dame, 1999. Presentation at BC Coalition for Safer Communities Forum on "What's Happening, What's Working."

Hayden, D. 1981. *The Grand Domestic Revolution: A History of Feminist Designs for American Homes, Neighbourhoods, and Cities*. Cambridge, MA: MIT Press.

– 1984. *Redesigning the American Dream: The Future of Housing, Work, and Family Life*. New York: WW Norton.

Hendler, S. 1994. "Feminist Planning Ethics," in *Journal of Planning Literature*, vol. 9., no. 2: 115–27.

International Union of Local Authorities, 1998. Worldwide Declaration on Women in Local Government. Harare, Zimbabwe.

Jacobs, J. 1961. *The Death and Life of Great American Cities*. New York: Random House.

Klodawsky, F., C, Lundy, and C. Andrew, 1994, "Challenging 'Business as Usual' in Housing and Community Planning: The Issue of Violence Against Women," in *Canadian Journal of Social Research*, vol. 3, no. 1: 40–58.

Korn, Y. 1993. *Inspirations for Action: A Practical Guide to Women's Safety*. Swindon, Wiltshire: Crime Concern.

Lahaise, M.-D. and C. Whitzman, 1990. "London Inspires Montreal Which Inspires Toronto Which Inspires London ..." in WEB: *Women and the Built Environment*, no. 15-16: 22–3.

Little, J. 1994. *Gender, Planning, and the Policy Process*. Oxford: Elsevier Science/Pergamon Press.

Little, M. 1998. *No Car, No Radio, No Liquor Permit: The Moral Regulation of Single Mothers in Ontario 1920–1997*. Toronto: Oxford University Press.

London Edinburgh Weekend Return Group. 1979. *In and Against the State*. London: Pluto Press.

Lugones, M. and E. Spelman, 1983. "Have We Got Theory for You! Feminist Theory, Cultural Imperialism and the Demand for 'The Women's Voice,'" in *Women's Studies International Forum*, vol. 6, no. 6: 573–81.

MacGregor, S. 1994. "Feminist Approaches to Thought and Action: Practical Lessons from Women Plan Toronto." Master's Thesis, School of Urban and Regional Planning, Queen's University.

– 1995. "Deconstructing the Man Made City: Feminist Critiques of Planning Thought and Action." in *Change of Plans: Towards a Non-Sexist Sustainable City*, M. Eichler (ed.). Toronto: Garamond Press, 25–49.

Mackenzie, S. and D. Rose, 1983. "Industrial Change, the Domestic

Economy and Home Life," in *Redundant Spaces in Cities and Regions*, J. Anderson, D. Simon, and R. Hudson (eds). London: Academic Press.

MacLeod, L. 1989. *The City for Women: No Safe Place*. Ottawa: Corporate Policy Branch, Secretary of State Canada

Manakau Safer Community Council. Series of Reports on Safety Audits of Wards, January–May 1995.

Matrix, 1984. *Making Space: Women and the Man-Made Environment*. London: Pluto Press.

McClain, J. and C. Doyle, 1984. *Women and Housing: Changing Needs and the Failure of Policy*. Ottawa: James Lorimer and Company/Canadian Council on Social Development.

McDowell, L. and R. Pringle, 1992. "Defining Public and Private Issues," in *Defining Women: Social Institutions and Gender Divisions*, L. McDowell and R. Pringle (eds). Milton Keynes: Open University Press.

METRAC, 1989a. *Moving Forward: Making Transit Safer for Women*. Toronto: METRAC, Toronto Transit Commission, Metro Toronto Police Department.

– 1989b: *Women's Safety Audit Guide* (booklet; modified in 1992).

– 1990. *Special Issue on Women's Safety. Women and Environments*, vol. 12, no. 1, Fall 1989/Winter 1990.

Michelson, W. 1985. *From Sun to Sun: Daily Obligations and Community Structure in the Lives of Employed Women and Their Families*. Totawa, NJ: Rowman and Allanheld.

Milroy, B.M. 1991a. "Feminist Critiques of Planning for Work: Considerations for Future Planning," in *Plan Canada*, vol. 31, no. 6: 15–22.

– 1991b. "Taking Stock of Planning, Space and Gender," in *Journal of Planning Literature*, vol. 6, no. 1: 3–15.

Modlich, R. 1988. "Planning Implications of Women Plan Toronto," in *Plan Canada*, July 1988: 120–31.

Novac, S. 1995. "Seeking Shelter: Feminist Home Truths," in *Change of Plans: Towards a Non-Sexist Sustainable City*, M. Eichler (ed.). Toronto: Garamond Press.

Organisation for Economic Co-operation and Development (OECD), 1995. *Women in the City: Housing, Services and the Urban Environment*. Paris: OECD.

Paquin, S. 1998. *Pour un quartier plus sur: les interventions en matière d'amenagement sécuritaire du Comité femmes et sécurité de la Petite Patrie*. Montreal: City of Montreal.

Penrose, J. 1987. "Women and Man-Made Environment: The Dutch Experience," in *Women and Environments*, vol. 9, no. 1, Winter 1987: 12–13.

Planning Ourselves In Group of Women in Planning. 1994. *Planning Ourselves In: Women and the Community Planning Process: A Tool Kit for Women and Planners*. Vancouver: Social Planning and Research Council of BC.

Planning Theory, 1992: *Special Issue on Feminist Planning Theory.*

Ritzdorf, M. 1986. "Women and the City: Land Use and Zoning Issues," in *Journal of Urban Resources*, vol. 3, no. 2: 23–7.

– 1992. "Feminist Thoughts on the Theory and Practice of Planning," in *Planning Theory*, no. 7–8: 13–19.

Ross, B.L. 1995. *The House that Jill Built: A Lesbian Nation in Formation.* Toronto: University of Toronto Press.

Sandercock, L. and A. Forsyth, 1990. *Gender: A New Agenda for Planning Theory.* University of California at Berkeley Institute of Urban and Regional Development Working Paper 521.

– 1992a. "A Gender Agenda: New Directions for Planning Theory," in *Journal of the American Planning Association*, vol. 58, no. 1: 49–59.

– 1992b. "Feminist Theory and Planning Theory: the Epistemological Linkages," in *Planning Theory*, no. 7–8: 45–9.

Sterner, B. 1987. *The WISE Report: Women in Safe Environments.* Toronto: Women Plan Toronto, York University Faculty of Environmental Studies, METRAC.

Stimpson, C. et al. 1981. *Women and the American City.* Chicago: University of Chicago Press. (Originally published in 1980 as a supplement to *Signs*, vol. 5, no. 3.)

Taylor, B. 1985. "Women Plan London: The Women's Committee of the Greater London Council," in *Women and Environments*, vol. 7, no. 2: 4-6.

Toronto Transit Commission, 1988. "The Accessibility of the TTC: Women's Issues," in *Background Report #9, Transit Services for the Disabled and Elderly to the Year 2000.*

Valentine, G. 1990. "Women's Fear and the Design of Public Space," in *Built Environment*, vol. 16, no. 4: 288-303.

– 1992. "Images of Danger: Women's Sources of Information about the Spatial Distribution of Male Violence," in *Area*, vol. 24, no. 1: 22–9.

Valverde, M. 1991. *The Age of Light, Soap, and Water: Moral Reform in English Canada, 1885–1925.* Toronto: McClelland and Stewart.

VCCAV (Victorian Community Council Against Violence), 1995: *Safety Audits: Past Experiences and Future Strategies. Notes from a Forum Held March 7, 1995.*

WACAV (Women's Action Centre Against Violence), 1995. *Safety Audit Tools and Housing: The State of the Art and Implications for CMHC.* Ottawa: Canada Mortgage and Housing Corporation.

Watson, S. 1990. "The State of Play," in *Playing the State: Australian Feminist Interventions*, S. Watson (ed.). Sydney: Allen and Unwin.

– 1992. "Femocratic Feminisms," in *Gender and Bureaucracy*, M. Savage and A. Witz (eds). Oxford: Blackwell Publishers/Sociological Review.

Wekerle, G. 1984. "A Woman's Place is in the City," in *Antipode*, vol. 6, no. 3: 11-19.

- 1986. "Lessons Learned from a Municipal Taskforce on Public Violence Against Women and Children," paper presented at the conference Planning to End Violence Against Women, University of California at Los Angeles.
- 1991. "Gender Politics in Local Politics," paper presented at the Annual Meeting of ACSP/AESOP, Oxford England.
- 1997. "Canada, United States, Germany:Gendering the Local State " in FCM 1997.
Wekerle, G. and L. Peake, 1996. "New Social Movements and Women's Urban Activism," in *City Lives and City Forms: Critical Research and Canadian Urbanism*, J. Caulfield and L. Peake (eds). Toronto: University of Toronto Press, 263–81.
Wekerle, G., R. Peterson, and D. Morley (eds), 1980. *New Space for Women*. Boulder, CO: Westview Press.
Wekerle, G. and C. Whitzman, 1995. *Safe Cities: Guidelines for Planning, Design and Management*. New York: Van Nostrand Reinhold.
Whitzman, C. 1992. "Taking Back Planning: Promoting Women's Safety in Public Places – The Toronto Experience," in *Journal of Architectural and Planning Research*, vol. 9, no. 2: 169–79.
- 1995. "What Do You Want to Do? Pave Parks? Urban Planning and the Prevention of Violence," in *Change of Plans: Towards a Non-Sexist Sustainable City*, M. Eichler (ed.). Toronto: Garamond Press, 89–109.
Wise-Harris, D. 1991. *A Safer City: The Second Stage Report of the Safe City Committee*. City of Toronto Safe City Committee.
Women Plan Toronto, 1986: *Shared Experiences and Dreams*.
- 1987: *What Can We Do? Lots! City Planning Issues for Women*.
- 1988: *Do You Know?*
- 1990: *Our Needs, Our Communities, Let's Plan: A Community Planning Manual for Women in Metro Toronto and Ontario*.
Young, I.M. 1990. "The Ideal of Community and the Politics of Difference," in *Feminism/Postmodernism*, L. Nicholson (ed.). New York: Routledge.
Zielinski, S. 1995. "Access Over Excess: Transcending Captivity and Transportation Disadvantage," in *Change of Plans: Towards a Non-Sexist Sustainable City*, M. Eichler (ed.). Toronto: Garamond Press.

CHAPTER FIVE

1000 Friends of Oregon, 1997. *Making the Connections: A Summary of the LUTRAQ Project*. Portland, Oregon: 1000 Friends of Oregon.
Babcock, R. and F.P. Bosselman, 1973. *Exclusionary Zoning: Land Use Regulation and Housing in the 1970's*. New York: Praeger.
Baker, K., S. Hinze, and N. Manzi, 1991. *Minnesota's Fiscal Disparities Program*. St Paul: Minnesota House of Representatives, Research Department.

Blais, P. 1996. *The Economics of Urban Form*. background paper. Toronto: Greater Toronto Area Task Force.

Block, W. and E. Olsen, 1981. *Rent Control: Myths and Realities: International Evidence of the Effects of Rent Control in Six Countries*. Vancouver: Fraser Institute.

Bourne, L.S. 1996. "Reurbanization, Uneven Urban Development, and the Debate on New Urban Forms," *Urban Geography*, vol. 17, no. 8: 690-713.

Canada Mortgage and Housing Corporation, 1994. "CMHC Announces Housing Affordability Grants," press release, 2 February 1994.

Clatworthy, S.J. 1987a. *Final Evaluation of the Winnipeg Core Area Agreement Housing and Community Improvement Area Programs*. Winnipeg: Winnipeg Core Area Initiative.

– 1987b. *Final Evaluation of the Winnipeg Core Area Agreement Employment and Affirmative Action Program*. Winnipeg: Winnipeg Core Area Initiative.

DeGrove, J.M. with D. Miness, 1992. *The New Frontier for Land Policy: Planning and Growth Management in the States*. Cambridge, MA: Lincoln Institute of Land Policy.

Downs, A. 1988. "The Real Problem with Suburban Anti-Growth Policies," in *Brookings Review*, vol. 6, no. 2: 23-9.

Enchautegui, M.E. 1997. "Latino Neighbourhoods and Latino Neighbourhood Poverty," in *Journal of Urban Affairs*, vol. 19, no. 4: 445–67.

Epstein Associates Inc., 1987. *Final Evaluation of the Winnipeg Core Area Agreement Economic Stimulus Programs*. Winnipeg: Winnipeg Core Area Initiative.

Essiambre-Phillips-Desjardins Associates Ltd, J.L. Richards and Associates Ltd, C.N. Watson Associates Ltd, and A. Nelessen Associates Inc., 1995. *Infrastructure Costs Associated with Conventional and Alternative Development Patterns: Final Report (Vol. 1)*. Ottawa: Canada Mortgage and Housing Corporation, August 1995.

Fischel, W.A. 1990. *Do Growth Controls Matter? A Review of Empirical Evidence on the Effectiveness and Efficiency of Local Government Land Use Regulation*. Cambridge, Massachusetts: Lincoln Institute of Land Policy.

Harrell, A.V. and G.E. Peterson, 1992. *Drugs, Crime and Social Isolation: Barriers to Urban Opportunity*. Washington, DC: The Urban Institute.

Holloway, S.R., D. Bryan, R. Chabot, D.M. Rogers, and J. Rulli, 1998. "Exploring the Effect of Public Housing on the Concentration of Poverty in Columbus, Ohio," in *Urban Affairs Review*, vol. 33, no. 6, July 1998: 767–89.

Isard, W. and R.E. Coughlin, 1957. *Municipal Costs and Revenues Resulting from Growth*. Wellesley, Mass: Chandler-Davis.

Leo, C. 1995. "The State in the City: A Political Economy Perspective on Growth and Decay," in *Canadian Metropolitics: Governing Our Cities*, James Lightbody (ed.). Toronto: Copp Clark, 27–50.

– 1998. "Regional Growth Management Regime: The Case of Portland, Oregon," in *Journal of Urban Affairs*, vol. 20, no. 4.

– 1999. "Regional Growth Management Regime: The Case of Portland, Oregon," in *Journal of Urban Affairs*, forthcoming.

Leo, C. with M.A. Beavis, A. Carver, and R. Turner, 1998. "Is Urban Sprawl Back on the Political Agenda? Local Growth Control, Regional Growth Management, and Politics," in *Urban Affairs Review*, forthcoming.

Leo, C. and W. Brown, with K. Dick, 1998. *Urban Development in A Slow-Growth City: The Case of Winnipeg*. Winnipeg: Canadian Centre for Policy Alternatives.

Logan, J.R. and M. Zhou, 1989. "Do Suburban Growth Controls Control Growth?" in *American Sociological Review*, no. 54, June 1989: 461–71.

Mallach, A. 1984. *Inclusionary Housing Programs: Policies and Practices*. New Brunswick, NJ: Center for Urban Policy Research, Rutgers.

Marcuse, P. 1997a. "The Enclave, the Citadel, and the Ghetto: What Has Changed in the Post-Fordist US City," in *Urban Affairs Review*, vol. 33, no. 2: 228–64.

– 1997b. "The Ghetto of Exclusion and the Fortified Enclave: New Patterns in the United States," in *American Behavioural Scientist*, vol. 41, no. 3, November/December: 311–26.

Marshall, W. 1987. *Final Evaluation of the Winnipeg Core Area Agreement Community Facilities and Services Programs*. Winnipeg: Winnipeg Core Area Initiative.

Martin, N. 1994. "Develop Land Or Watch for Rural Exodus: Councillor," in *Winnipeg Free Press*, 31 March 1994: B9.

Massey, D.S. and N.A. Denton, 1993. *American Apartheid: Segregation and the Making of the Underclass*. Cambridge: Harvard University Press.

Mincy, R.B. and S.J. Wiener, 1993. *The Underclass in the 1980s: Changing Concept, Constant Reality*. Washington: The Urban Institute.

Orfield, M. 1997. *Metropolitics: A Regional Agenda for Community and Stability*. Washington, DC: Brookings.

Patterson, E.B. 1991. "Poverty, Income Inequality, and Community Crime Rates," in *Criminology*, no. 29: 755–76.

Real Estate Research Corporation, 1974. *The Cost of Sprawl: Environmental and Economic Costs of Alternative Residential Development Patterns at the Urban Fringe*. Washington, DC, April 1974.

Redekop, B. 1996a. "Insurers Say No to Core," in *Winnipeg Free Press*, 2 March 1996: A1.

– 1996b. "Living Scared in the No-Zone," in *Winnipeg Free Press*, 2 March 1996: A4.

Rosen, K.T. and L.F. Katz, 1981. "Growth Management and Land Use Controls: The San Francisco Bay Area Experience," in *Journal of the American Real Estate and Urban Economics Association*, vol. 9, no. 3: 321–44.

Smith, P.J., 1996. "Restructuring Metropolitan Governance: Vancouver and BC Reforms," in *Policy Options*, vol. 17, no. 7: 7–11.

Social Planning Council of Winnipeg, 1995. *Demographic Insights into Winnipeg's Past, Present and Beyond*. Winnipeg.

Stone, P.A., 1973. *The Structure, Size and Costs of Urban Settlements*. Cambridge, UK: Cambridge University Press.

Turner, R.S., 1990. "New Rules for the Growth Game: The Use of Rational State Standards in Land Use Policy," in *Journal of Urban Affairs*, vol. 12, no. 1: 35–47.

Van Kempen, E.T., 1997. "Poverty Pockets and Life Chances: On the Role of Place in Shaping Social Inequality," in *American Behavioural Scientist*, vol. 41, no. 3, November/December: 430–49.

Wacquant, L.J.D. and W.J. Wilson, 1993. "The Cost of Racial and Class Exclusion in the Inner City," in *The Annals of the American Academy of Political and Social Science*, no. 501: 8–25.

Weiss, M.A. 1987. *The Rise of the Community Builders: The American Real Estate Industry and Urban Land Planning*. New York: Columbia University Press.

Wheaton, W.L. and M.J. Schussheim, 1955. *The Cost of Municipal Services in Residential Areas*. Washington, DC: US Dept of Commerce.

Wilson, W.J. 1987. *The Truly Disadvantaged: The Inner City, the Underclass, and Public Policy*. Chicago: University of Chicago Press.

– 1991. "Studying Inner-City Social Dislocations: The Challenge of Public Agenda Research," in *American Sociological Review*, no. 56: 1–14.

– 1996. *When Work Disappears: The World of the New Urban Poor*. New York: Alfred A. Knopf.

Winnipeg Core Area Initiative, 1992. *Final Status Report of Programs and Projects to December 31, 1991*. Winnipeg: Winnipeg Core Area Initiative.

CHAPTER SEVEN

Andrew, C. 1995. "Provincial-municipal Relations; Or Hyper-fractionalized Quasi-subordination Revisited," in *Canadian Metropolitics: Governing our Cities*, J. Lightbody (ed.). Toronto: Copp Clark Ltd, 137–60.

– 1997. "Affidavit," in *Citizens' Legal Challenge Inc. v. Attorney General of Ontario*. 9 May 1997. Court File No. 97-CU-122492.

Attorney General of Ontario, 1997a. "Factum of the Respondent," in *Corporation of the Borough of East York et al. v. Attorney General for Ontario; Corporation of the City of Scarborough et al. v. Attorney General of Ontario; Citizens' Legal Challenge Inc. et al. v. Attorney General*

for Ontario. Ontario Court (General Division). Court File Nos.
97-CU-122390, 122393, 122492.

– 1997b. "Factum of the respondent", *Citizens' Legal Challenge Inc. et al.* v. *Attorney General of Ontario.* Ontario Court of Appeal. Court File No. 97-CU-122492.

– 1998. "Memorandum of Argument of the Respondent," *Citizens' Legal Challenge Inc. et al.* v. *Attorney General of Ontario.* Supreme Court of Canada. Court File No. 97-CU-122492.

Barber, J. 1996. "Promised Spending Cuts Ephemeral When Compared with Harsh Realities," in *The Globe and Mail* 18 December 1996.

– 1997a. "Consultant Finds Megacity Plan "Beyond Belief," in *The Globe and Mail,* 10 January 1997.

– 1997b. "Megacity Legislation Has Broken Civic Spirit," in *The Globe and Mail,* 22 April 1997.

Bourne, L.S. 1997. "Affidavit," in *East York et al.* v. *A.G.Ont.,* 23 May 1997. Court File Nos. 97-CU-122390, 122393, 122492.

Citizens' Legal Challenge Inc., 1997a. "Factum of the applicants," in CLC *Inc. et al.* v. *A.G.Ont.,* Ontario Court (General Division). Court File No. 97-CU-122492.

– 1997b. "Appellants' Factum," in CLC *Inc. et al.* v. *A.G.Ont.* Ontario Court of Appeal. Court File No. C27925.

– 1997c. "Memorandum of Argument [of the Appellant]," in CLC *Inc. et al.* v. *A.G. Ont.* Supreme Court of Canada.

Citizens' Legal Challenge Inc. et al. v. *Attorney General of Ontario.* , 1997. [Indexed as: *East York (Borough)* v. *Ontario* (1997), [1998] 36 O.R. (3d) 733, [1998] 47 C.R.R. (2d) 232 (Ont. C.A.), Abella, Rosenberg and Moldaver JJ.A.]

City of Toronto Act, 1997 (formerly Bill 103): "An Act to Replace the Seven Existing Municipal Governments of Metropolitan Toronto by Incorporating a New Municipality to Be Known as the City of Toronto," ch. 2, S.O. 1997. Proclaimed in force 1 January 1998.

Conservative Party of Ontario, 1994. *The Common Sense Revolution.* Toronto: Conservative Party.

– 1995. "The Metro Task Force Summary" (chaired by Joyce Trimmer). Toronto: Conservative Party.

– 1996. The Review Panel on the Greater Toronto Area Task Force Report (The Burnham Panel). 17 April 1996.

Cooper, R. 1996. "Municipal Law, Delegated Legislation and Democracy," in *Canadian Public Administration,* vol. 39, no. 3: 290–313.

Corporation of the Borough of East York et al. v. *Attorney General for Ontario; Corporation of the City of Scarborough et al.* v. *Attorney General for Ontario; Citizens' Legal Challenge Inc. et al.* v. *Attorney General for Ontario* [Indexed as: *East York (Borough)* v. *Ontario (Attorney General)*

(1997), 34 O.R. (3d) 789, 45 C.R.R. (2d) 237 (Ont. Ct. (Gen. Div.)), Borins J.]

Courchene, T.J. 1998. *From Heartland to North American Region State.* Toronto: University of Toronto, Faculty of Management.

Downey, T.J. and R.J. Williams, 1998. "Provincial Agendas, Local Responses: The 'Common Sense' Restructuring of Ontario's Municipal Governments," in *Canadian Public Administration*, vol. 41, no. 2: 210–38.

Drainie, B. 1998. "Them Against Us," in *Toronto Life*, May 1998: 76–82.

East York et al., 1997. "Factum of the Applicants," in *East York (Borough) et al. v. A.G.Ont.* Ontario Court (General Division). Court File No. 97-CU-122390.

Frisken, F. 1993. "Planning and Servicing the Greater Toronto Area: The Interplay of Provincial and Municipal Interests," in *Metropolitan Governance: American/Canadian Intergovernmental Perspectives*, D.N. Rothblatt and A. Sancton (eds). Berkeley, CA: Institute of Governmental Studies Press, 171–217.

Graham, K.A. and S.D. Phillips, 1998a. "Who Does What' in Ontario: the process of provincial-municipal disentanglement," in *Canadian Public Administration*, vol. 41, no. 2: 175–209.

Graham, K.A. and S.D. Phillips, with A.M. Maslove, 1998b. *Urban Governance in Canada: Representation, Resources and Restructuring*, Toronto: Harcourt Brace & Co.

Harrison, J. 1998. "New Municipal Roles," in *Municipal World*, vol. 108, no. 8: 14–18.

Ibbitson, J. 1997. *Promised Land: Inside the Mike Harris Revolution.* Scarborough: Prentice Hall.

IBI Group, 1990. *Greater Toronto Area Urban Structure Concepts Study.* Prepared for Ontario Ministry of Municipal Affairs, Greater Toronto Coordinating Committee.

Isin, E.F. 1992. *Cities Without Citizens: Modernity of the City as a Corporation.* Montreal: Black Rose Books

Jacobs, J. 1997a. "Affidavit," in CLC *Inc. et al. v. A.G. Ont.*, 8 May 1997. Court File No. 97-CU-122492.

– 1997b. "Reply affidavit," in CLC *Inc. et al. v. A.G.Ont.*, 27 May 1997. Court File No. 97-CU-122492.

KPMG, 1996. *Fresh Start: An Estimate of Potential Savings and Costs from the Creation of Single Tier Local Government for Toronto.* 16 December 1996.

Kushner, J., I. Masse, L. Soroka, and T. Peters, 1996. "Are Municipal Expenditures Affected by Factors Such as Regionalization and City Size?" in *Municipal World*, vol. 106, no. 11, November 1996: 11–12. (A précis of their 1996 study, "The Determinants of Municipal Expenditures in Ontario," in *Canadian Tax Journal*, vol. 44, no. 2: 451–64.)

Leo, C. 1998. "Regional Growth Management Regime: The Case of Port-land, Oregon," in *Journal of Urban Affairs*, vol. 20, no. 4: 363–94.

Lidstone, D. 1998. "Donald Lidstone Compares New and Proposed Municipal Legislation," in *Municipal World*, vol. 108, no. 8, August 1998: 9–12.

Machimura, T. 1998. "Symbolic Use of Globalization in Urban Politics in Tokyo," in *International Journal of Urban and Regional Research*, vol. 22, no. 2: 183–94.

Mayors' Proposal, 1996. "Change for the Better: A Framework for Re-structuring Local Government." Toronto, 28 November 1996.

Milroy, B.M., P. Campsie, and R. Whittaker, with Z. Girling, 1999. "Who Says Toronto Is a Good City?" in *World Class Cities: Can Canada Play?* C. Andrew and P. Armstrong (eds). Ottawa: Carleton University Press.

Municipal World, editorial: "Megacity Madness?" vol. 107, no. 2: 2.

Ontario, Greater Toronto Area Task Force (Golden Report), 1996. *Report*. Toronto: Queen's Printer.

Ontario, "Who Does What" Panel (Crombie Panel), 1996. *Report*. Toronto: Ministry of Municipal Affairs and Housing.

Rusk, J. 1997. "Amalgamation Risky Political Strategy," in *The Globe and Mail*, 13 January 1997.

Sancton, A. 1996. "Reducing Costs by Consolidating Municipalities: New Brunswick, Nova Scotia and Ontario," in *Canadian Public Administration*, vol. 39, no. 3: 267–89.

– 1997. "Affidavit," in *Scarborough et al. v. A.G. Ont.*, 7 May 1997. Court File No. 97-CU-122393.

– 1998. "Amalgamations, Service Realignment, and Property Taxes: Did the Harris Government Have a Plan for Ontario's Municipalities?" Paper presented at the "Governing Ontario Conference," University of Western Ontario, 20 November 1998.

Scarborough, 1997. "Factum of the Applicants," in *Corporation of the City of Scarborough and Alan Carter v. Attorney General for Ontario*. Ontario Court (General Division). Court File No. 97-CU-122393.

Sewell, J. 1998., "Helping the Public to Participate in Planning," in *Lessons in Participation from Local Government*, K.A. Graham and S.D. Phillips (eds). Toronto: Institute of Public Administration of Canada, 78–93.

Tindal, C.R. 1997. "Sex, Lies and Amalgamations?" in *Municipal World*, vol. 107, no. 2: 6–9.

Tindal, C.R. and S.N. Tindal, 1995. *Local Government in Canada, 4th ed.*, Toronto: McGraw-Hill Ryerson Ltd.

Vaughan, C. 1996. "Little Proof Megacity Will Save Money," in *The Globe and Mail*, 23 December 1996.

CHAPTER EIGHT

Artibise, A. 1998. "Regional Governance without Regional Government: The Strengths and Weaknesses of the Greater Vancouver Regional District," revised background report prepared for the Regional Municipality of Ottawa-Carleton, April 1998.

Brownstone M. and T.J. Plunkett, 1983. *Metropolitan Winnipeg: Politics and Reform of Local Government.* Berkeley: University of California Press.

Canadian Urban Institute, 1994. *The Future of Greater Montreal: Lessons for the Greater Toronto Area? Conference Proceedings.* Urban Focus Series 94–1, Toronto.

City of Ottawa, Office of the Chief Administrative Officer, 1995. *Municipal Government in Ottawa-Carleton,* September 1995.

Colton, T.J. 1981. *Big Daddy: Frederick G. Gardiner and the Building of Metropolitan Toronto.* Toronto: University of Toronto Press.

Downey, T.J. and R.J. Williams, 1998. "Provincial Agendas, Local Responses: The 'Common Sense' Restructuring of Ontario's Municipal Governments," in *Canadian Public Administration,* vol. 41, no. 2: 210–38.

Frisken, F. 1998. "The Greater Toronto Area in Transition: The Search for New Planning and Servicing Strategies," in *Metropolitan Governance Revisited: American/Canadian Intergovernmental Perspectives,* Donald N. Rothblatt and Andrew Sancton (eds). Berkeley, CA: Institute of Governmental Studies Press at the University of California. 199–200.

Fyfe, S. 1975. "Local Government Reform in Ontario," in *Urban Problems, rev. ed.,* R. Charles Bryfogfle and Ralph Krueger (eds), Toronto: Holt, Rinehart and Winston, 352–66.

Garcea, J. 1997. "Saskatchewan's Aborted Municipal Service Districts Act (Bill 33): Pegasus or Trojan Horse," paper presented to the annual meeting of the Canadian Political Science Association, St. John's, Newfoundland, June 1997.

Gilbert, R. and D. Stevenson, 1999. "Governance and Economic Performance: The Montreal, Toronto, and Vancouver Regions," in *Better Governance for More Competitive and Liveable Cities: Report of the OECD-Toronto Workshop, Toronto, October 22–24, 1997.* Toronto: City of Toronto, 1999, 73–96.

Graham, K. and S. Phillips, 1998. "Who Does What in Ontario: The Process of Provincial-Municipal Disentanglement" in *Canadian Public Administration,* vol., 41, no. 2: 175–209.

Greater Ottawa: A Partnership for the Future, February 1997.

Harris, M. 1995. "Mike Harris: 'Within 180 days of taking office, my government will act,' " in *The Toronto Star,* 4 April 1995: A14.

Leach, A. 1996. Partial text of speech to the Toronto Board of Trade, 17

December 1996, as reproduced in *The Toronto Star*, 18 December 1996: A27.

Lightbody, J. 1997. "A New Perspective on Clothing the Emperor: Canadian Metropolitan Form, Function, and Frontiers," in *Canadian Public Administration*, vol. 40, no. 3: 436–56.

Mayors' Proposal, 1996. "Change for the Better: A Framework for Re-structuring Local Government," Toronto, 28 November 1996.

McMillan, M.L. 1997. "Taxation and Expenditure Patterns in Major City-Regions: An International Perspective and Lessons for Canada: An International Perspective and Lessons for Canada," in *Urban Governance and Finance: A Question of Who Does What*, Paul A.R. Hobson and France St-Hilaire (eds). Montreal: Institute for Research on Public Policy, 47–9.

Mellon, H. 1993. "Reforming the Electoral System of Metropolitan Toronto," in *Canadian Public Administration*, vol. 36, no. 1: 38–56.

Municipality of Metropolitan Toronto, Chief administrator's Office, 1996. "Review of GTA Task Force Report – A Metro Perspective," 27 February 1996.

New Brunswick, Department of Municipalities, Culture, and Housing, 1992. *Strengthening Municipal Government in New Brunswick's Urban Centres*, 30 December 1992.

Newfoundland and Labrador, Department of Municipal and Provincial Affairs, Task Force on Municipal Regionalization, 1997. *Final Report*, 10 September 1997. <http://www.gov.nf.ca/mpa/publicat/taskforce/region1.htm>.

Newfoundland and Labrador, Department of Municipal and Provincial Affairs, 1998. "Press Release: The Southlands Feasibility Study," 4 February 1998. <http://www.gov.nf.ca/releases/1998/mpa/0204n01.htm>.

Nova Scotia, Royal Commission on Education, Public Services and Provincial-Municipal Relations, 1974. *Report, vol. 5*. Halifax: Queen's Printer.

Nova Scotia, Department of Municipal Affairs, Task Force on Local Government, 1992. *Report to the Government of Nova Scotia*.

Nova Scotia, Department of Municipal Affairs, 1993. *Interim Report of the Municipal reform Commissioner (Halifax Metropolitan Area)*, 8 July 1993.

Ontario, 1978. *Report of the Hamilton-Wentworth Review Commission*. Toronto.

Ontario, GTA Task Force, 1996. *Greater Toronto*, January 1996.

Ontario, Ministry of Municipal Affairs, Niagara Region Review Commission, 1989. *Report and Recommendations*. Toronto: Queen's Printer.

Ontario, Ministry of Municipal Affairs and Housing, County of Kent and City of Chatham Restructuring Commission, 1997. "Final Restructuring Proposal for Kent County and the City of Chatham and Order of the Commission," 28 April 1997.

Ontario, Legislative Assembly, 1998. *Debates*, 25 November 1998.

Ontario, 1999. *Debates*, 25 November 1999.

Palango, P. 1997. "An Undone Deal: Too Much Cooke Incurs This Maverick MPP's Wrath," in *Hamilton Magazine* Spring 1997: 17–21.

Progressive Conservative Party of Ontario, 1994. *The Common Sense Revolution*.

Québec, Ministry of Municipal Affairs, Task Force on Greater Montreal, 1993. *Montreal: A City Region*, December 1993.

Rusk, J. 1999. "Tonks Voted Head of Service Board," in *The Globe and Mail*, 23 January 1999.

Sancton, A. 1992. "Canada as a Highly Urbanized Nation: New Implications for Government" in *Canadian Public Administration*, vol. 35, no. 3: 281–98.

– 1994. *Governing Canada's City-Regions*. Montreal: Institute for Research on Public Policy.

– 1996. "Reducing Costs by Consolidating Municipalities: New Brunswick, Nova Scotia and Ontario," in *Canadian Public Administration*, vol. 39, no. 3: 267–89.

Skarika, T., MPP, 1997. "Press Release: MPP Recommends Local Plan for Local Government," 23 February 1997.

Smith, P.J. and H.P. Oberlander, 1998. "Restructuring Metropolitan Governance: Greater Vancouver-British Columbia Reforms," in *Metropolitan Governance Revisited: American/Canadian Intergovernmental Perspectives*, Donald N. Rothblatt and Andrew Sancton (eds). Berkeley, CA: Institute of Governmental Studies Press at the University of California, 371–405.

Smith, P.J. and K. Stewart, 1998. "Making Local Accountability Work in British Columbia: Report 2 – Reforming Municipal Electoral Accountability," Report for the British Columbia Ministry of Municipal Affairs and Housing, June 1998, <http://www.sfu.ca/igs/report/assets/report2.pdf>.

Travers, J. 1997. "Ottawa More Layered than an Onion," in *The Toronto Star*, 27 January 1997: A13.

Trépanier, M.O. 1998. "Metropolitan Governance in the Montreal Area," in *Metropolitan Governance Revisited: American/Canadian Intergovernmental Perspectives*, Donald N. Rothblatt and Andrew Sancton (eds). Berkeley, CA: Institute of Governmental Studies Press at the University of California, 107–12.

Vojnovic, I. 1998. "Municipal Consolidation in the 1990s: An Analysis of British Columbia, New Brunswick, and Nova Scotia," in *Canadian Public Administration*, vol. 41, no. 2: 239–83.

Walker, W. 1996. "The Inside Story: How Harris Built Megacity," in *The Toronto Star*, 21 December 1996: A1, A4.

CHAPTER NINE

Born, P. 1998. "Confessions of a Pilot Project Junky," in *Making Waves: Canada's Community Economic Development Magazine*, vol. 9, no. 4: 6–9.

Brodhead, D. 1994. "Community Economic Development in Canada," in *Community Economic Development – Perspectives on Research and Policy*, B. Galaway and J. Hudson (eds). Toronto: Thompson Educational Publishing, Inc.

Driscoll, D. 16 February 1999. *Presentation to the Senate Standing Committee on Social Affairs, Science and Technology*. Ottawa.

Favreau, L. and W.A. Ninacs. "The Innovative Profile of Community Economic Development in Quebec," in *Community Economic Development: Perspectives on Research and Policy*, Burt Galaway and Joe Hudson (eds). Toronto: Thompson Educational Publishing, 1994.

Hodgson, D. 1998. *Opportunities 2000: A Community-Based Program to Reduce Poverty*. Caledon Institute.

Huntley, S. 1998. "Ottawa's Hidden Workforce." Ottawa: Ottawa Economic Development Corporation.

Jackson, E.T. 1998. "Development Finance: An Agenda for Action," in *Making Waves*, vol. 9, no. 3, Autumn 1998. Port Alberni, BC: Centre for Community Enterprise, 4–6.

Lewis, M. 1999. "Community Economic Development," in *Employment Policy Options*, Ken Battle and Sherri Torjman (eds). Ottawa: Caledon Institute of Social Policy, 181–214.

Lithwick, N.H. 1970. "Urban Canada: Problems and Prospects". A Report prepared for the Honorable R. Andras, Minister Responsible for Housing. Government of Canada.

Markell, L. November 1998. "The Municipal Role in Urban Community Economic Development," a report to the City of Victoria. Victoria: CEDCO.

Nares, P. 1999. "Self-Employment," in *Employment Policy Options*, Ken Battle and Sherri Torjman (eds). Ottawa: Caledon Institute of Social Policy, 357–83.

Perry, S.E., M. Lewis, and J.-M. Fontan, 1993. *Revitalizing Canada's Neighbourhoods: A Research Report on Urban Community Economic Development*. Vancouver: Centre for Community Enterprise.

Torjman, S. 1999. *Strategies for a Caring Community: The Local Government Role*. Ottawa: Caledon Institute of Social Policy, September 1999.

Torjman, S. and K. Battle, 1999. "Good Work: Getting It and Keeping It." Caledon Institute: Ottawa.

Tuloss, J. 1996. "Transforming Urban Regimes – A Grassroots Approach to Comprehensive Community Development: The Dudley Street Neighbourhood Initiative." University of North Carolina at Greensboro. (Later version of a paper delivered to the 1996 Annual Meeting of the American Political Science Association, San Francisco.)

Waring, M. 1989. *If Women Counted: A New Feminist Economics*. San Francisco: Harper & Row.

CHAPTER TEN

Beauregard, R.A. 1993. "Constituting Economic Development: A Theoretical Perspective," in *Theories of Local Economic Development: Perspectives from Across the Disciplines*, R.D. and R. Mier (eds). Newbury Park, London: Sage, 284–304.

Beck, U. 1992. *Risk Society: Towards a New Modernity*. London: Sage.

Caulfield, J. and L. Peake (eds), 1996. *City Lives & City Forms. Critical Research & Canadian Urbanism*. Toronto: University of Toronto Press.

Checkoway, B. 1981. "The Politics of Public Hearings," in *The Journal of Applied Behavioral Science*, vol. 17, no. 4: 566–82.

Clarke, S.E. 1995. "Institutional Logics and Local Economic Development: A Comparative Analysis of Eight American Cities," in *International Journal of Urban and Regional Research*, vol. 19, no. 4: 513–33.

Cox, K.R. "Governance, Urban Regime Analysis, and the Politics of Local Economic Developement," in *Reconstructing Urban Regime Theory: Regulating Urban Politics in a Global Economy*, M. Lauria (ed.). Thousand Oaks: Sage, 99–121.

Day, D. 1997. "Citizen Participation in the Planning Process: An Essential Contested Concept?" in *Journal of Planning Literature*, vol. 11, no. 3: 421–34.

Decoutère, S., J. Ruegg, and D. Joye (eds), 1996. *Le Management territorial*. Lausanne: Presses Polytechniques et Universitaires Romandes.

Donzelot, J. 1995. "De la consultation à l'implication," in *Informations sociales*, no. 43: 21-32.

Donzelot, J. and C. Jaillet, 1997. "Séminaire sur les zones urbaines défavorisées en Amérique du Nord, 1995-1996. Esquisse de synthèse pour introduire à une seconde phase de la recherche." Paris: CDSM/OTAN, Plan Urbain.

Forester, J. 1989. *Planning in the Face of Power*. Berkeley: University of California Press.

Fourniau, J.M. 1997. "Figures de la concertation 'à la française,'" in *Ces réseaux qui nous gouvernent?*, M. Gariépy and M. Marié (eds), Paris and Montreal: L'Harmattan, 371–402.

Gariépy, M. 1997. "L'évaluation environnementale 'à la québécoise' dans le déploiement d'infratructures d'Hydro-Québec," in *Ces réseaux qui nous gouvernent?*, M. Gariépy and M. Marié (eds). Paris and Montreal: L'Harmattan, 425–52.

Gaudin, J.-P. and G. Novarina, 1997. *Politiques publiques et négociation: Multipolarités, flexibilités, hiérarchies*. Paris: CNRS Éditions.

Godbout, J. 1983. *La Participation contre la démocratie*. Montreal: Les Éditions Saint-Martin.

Graham, K.A., S.D. Phillips, with A.M. Maslove, 1998. *Urban Governance in Canada: Representation, Resources, and Restructuring*. Toronto: Harcourt Brace & Company.

Hamel, P. 1991. *Action collective et démocratie locale: Les mouvements urbains montréalais*. Montreal: Les Presses de l'Université de Montréal.

– 1995. "Collective Action and the Paradigm of Individualism," in *Social Movements and Social Classes: The Future of Collective Action*, L. Maheu (ed.). London: Sage, 236–57.

Innes, J. 1994. "Planning Institutions in Crisis," in *Planning Theory*, no. 10-11: 81-98.

Kaplan, M. 1995. "Urban Policy. An Uneven Past, An Uncertain Future," in *Urban Affairs Review*, vol. 30, no. 5: 662–80.

Kotler, M, 1969. *Neighborhood Government: The Local Foundations of Political Life*. Indianapolis and New York: The Bobbs-Merrill Company.

Lauria, M. 1997. "Introduction: Reconstructing Urban Regime Theory," in *Reconstructing Urban Regime Theory: Regulating Urban Politics in a Global Economy*, M. Lauria (ed.). Thousand Oaks: Sage, 1–9.

Leca, J. 1996. "La Démocratie à l'épreuve des pluralismes," in *Revue française de science politique*, vol. 46, no. 2: 225–79.

Le Galès, P. and M. Thatcher, 1995. *Les Réseaux de politique publique: Débat autour des policy networks*. Paris: L'Harmattan.

Léveillée, J. 1998. "Développement des régions, redressement de Montréal et affirmation de la capitale: est-il possible de faire les trois démarches en même temps?" in *Revue Organisation*, Winter 1998: 5–13.

Lourau, R. 1969. "Critique du concept de participation" in *Utopie*, no. 2–3: 99–119.

McGraw, D. 1978. *Le Développement des groupes populaires à Montréal (1963–1973)*. Montreal: Les Éditions Coopératives Albert St-Martin.

Monkkonen, E.H. 1988. *America Becomes Urban: The Development of U.S. Cities & Towns 1780–1980*. Berkeley: University of California Press.

Morin, R. et M. Rochefort, 1998. "Quartier et lien social: des pratiques indi-viduelles à l'action collective," in *Lien social et politique – RIAC*, no. 39: 103-14.

Muller, P. 1990. *Les Politiques publiques*. Paris: PUF.

Offe, C. 1997. *Les Démocraties modernes à l'épreuve*. Paris: L'Harmattan.

Petitet, S. 1998. *Histoire des institutions urbaines*. Paris: PUF.

Richardson, M., J. Sherman, and M. Gismondi, 1993. *Winning Back the*

Words: Confronting Experts in an Environmental Public Hearing. Toronto: Garamond Press.

Stoker, G. 1998. "Theory and Urban Politics," in *International Political Science Review/Revue internationale de science politique*, vol. 19, no. 2: 119-29.

Thibault, A. 1986. "La Consultation du public, au-delà du symbole," in *Loisir et Société/Sociey and Leisure*, vol. 9, no. 1: 11-32.

Thomas, J.C. 1983. "Citizen Participation and Urban Administration: From Enemies to Allies?" in *Journal of Urban Affairs*, vol. 5, no. 3: 175-82.

Thomas, T.L. 1997. *A City With a Difference: The Rise and Fall of the Montreal Citizen's Movement.* Montreal: Véhicule Press.

Trân, C. 1998. *Compte-rendu des entrevues exploratoires menées auprès d'experts de la consultation publique* (Working Paper). Montreal: Institut d'urbanisme, Université de Montréal.

Ville de Montréal, 1988. *Un Dialogue à poursuivre: la consultation publique. Énoncé de politique.* Montreal: Ville de Montréal.

– 1994. *Le Choix de la gestion territoriale: de meilleurs services, une municipalité plus productive.* Montreal: Ville de Montréal, Secrétariat général.

– 1995. *Bilan administratif. Commissions permanentes et comités du Conseil 1987-1994.* Montreal: Ville de Montréal, Service du Greffe, Division des comissions et comités du Conseil.

Williams, B.A. and A.R. Matheny, 1995. *Democracy, Dialogue, and Environmental Disputes.* New Haven and London: Yale University Press.

Wolman, H. 1995. "Local Democratic Institutions and Democratic Governance," in *Theories of Urban Politics,* D. Judge, G. Stoker, and H. Wolman (eds). London: Sage, 134-59.

Yergeau, M. and L. Ouimet, 1984. "Pour que les audiences publiques aient un sens, " in *Le Devoir,* 14 July 1984: A7.

CHAPTER ELEVEN

Amin, A. 1996. "Beyond Associative Democracy, " in *New Political Economy*, vol. 1, no. 3: 309-33.

Armstrong, H.W. 1997. "The Role and Evolution of European Community Regional Policy," in *The European Union and the Regions*, Barry Jones and Michael Keating (eds). Oxford: Clarendon Press, 23-62.

Atkinson, M.M. and W.D. Coleman, 1989. *The State, Business, and Industrial Change in Canada*, The State and Economic Life Series. Toronto: University of Toronto Press.

Blais, A. 1986a . "Industrial Policy in Advanced Capitalist Democracies," in *Industrial Policy*, vol. 44: *Studies of the Royal Commission on the Economic Union and Development Prospects for Canada*, André Blais (ed.). Toronto: University of Toronto Press, 1-53.

– (ed.) 1986b. *Industrial Policy*, vol. 44: *Studies of the Royal Commission on the Economic Union and Development Prospects for Canada*. Toronto: University of Toronto Press.

British Columbia, Minstry of Employment and Investment, 1995. *Science and Technology: A Strategic Plan for British Columbia*, a report prepared by the Premier's Advisory Council on Science and Technology. Victoria.

Britton, J.N.H. and J.M. Gilmour, 1978. *The Weakest Link: A Technological Perspective on Canadian Industrial Underdevelopment*, Science Council of Canada, Background Study No. 43. Ottawa: Supply and Services Canada.

Brown, D., J. Eastman, and I. Robinson, 1981. *The Limits of Consultation: A Debate Among Ottawa, the Provinces and the Private Sector on Industrial Strategy*, prepared for the Science Council of Canada. Kingston: Institute of Intergovernmental Relations, Queen's University.

Chandler, M.A. 1986. "The State and Industrial Decline: A Survey," in *Industrial Policy*, vol. 44, *Studies of the Royal Commission on the Economic Union and Development Prospects for Canada*, André Blais (ed.). Toronto: University of Toronto Press, 171–218.

Commission of the European Union, 1993. *Cohesion and RTD Policy – Synergies Between Research and Technological Development Policy and Economic and Social Cohesion Policy*. COM(93) 203. Brussells.

Cooke, P. 1997. "Institutional Reflexivity and the Rise of the Regional State," in *Space and Social Theory: Interpreting Modernity and Post-Modernity*, G. Benko and U. Strohmayer (eds). Oxford: Blackwell, 285–301.

– 1998. "Introduction: Origins of the Concept," in *Regional Innovation Systems: The Role of Governances in a Globalized World*, H. Braczyk, P. Cooke, and M. Heidenreich (eds). London: UCL Press, 2–25.

Cooke, P. and K. Morgan, 1993. "The Network Paradigm: New Departures in Corporate and Regional Development," in *Environment and Planning D: Society and Space*, no. 11: 543–64.

Cooke, P., M.G. Uranga, and G. Etxebarria, 1997. "Regional Innovation Systems: Institutional and Organizational Dimensions," in *Research Policy*, no. 26: 475–91.

Davenport, P. et al. 1982. *Industrial Policy in Ontario and Quebec*, discussion paper series. Toronto: Ontario Economic Council.

Doern, G.B. 1983. "The Mega-Project Episode and the Formulation of Canadian Economic Development Policy," in *Canadian Public Administration*, vol. 26, no. 2, Summer 1983: 219–38.

Dosi, G. et al. (eds), 1988. *Technical Change and Economic Theory*. London and New York: Pinter Publishers.

Dosi, G., L. D'Andrea Tyson, and J. Zysman, 1989. "Trade, Technologies and Development: A Framework for Discussing Japan," in *Politics and Productivity: How Japan's Development Strategy Works*, Chalmers

Johnson, Laura D'Andrea Tyson, and John Zysman (eds). Cambridge, Mass: Ballinger, 3–38.

Edquist, C. 1997. "Introduction: Systems of Innovation Approaches – Their Emergence and Characteristics," in *Systems of Innovation: Technologies, Institutions and Organizations*, Charles Edquist (ed.). London: Pinter, 1–35.

European Union, Regional Policy and Cohesion, 1995a. *Guide to Innovative Actions for Regional Development (European Regional Development Fund – ERDF, Article 10) 1995-99.* Luxembourg: Office for Official Publications of the European Communities.

– 1995b. *Research and Regional Development.* Luxembourg: Office for Official Publications of the European Communities.

– 1997. *Practical Guide to Regional Innovation Actions.* Luxembourg: Office for Official Publications of the European Communities.

– 1999. *Article 10 ERDF Innovation Actions: Innovation Promotion.* Luxembourg: European Commission.

Florida, R. 2000. *Competing in the Age of Talent: Quality of Place and the New Economy.* Report Prepared for the R.K. Mellon Foundation, Heinz Endowments and Sustainable Pittsburgh. <http://www.nga.org/NewEconomy/rflorida.pdf>.

Freeman, C. 1987. *Technology Policy and Economic Performance: Lessons from Japan.* London and New York: Pinter Publishers.

French, R.D. 1984. *How Ottawa Decides: Planning and Industrial Policy-Making, 1968–1980, 2nd. Ed.* Toronto: James Lorimer.

Fukuyama, F. 1995. *Trust: The Social Virtues and the Creation of Prosperity.* London: Hamish Hamilton.

Gagné, P. and M. Lefèvre, with G. Tremblay, 1993. *L'Atlas industriel du Québec.* Montréal: Publi Relais.

Gertler, M.S. 1991. "Canada in a High-Tech World: Options for Industrial Policy," in *The New Era of Global Competition: State Policy and Market Power*, Daniel Drache and Meric S. Gertler (eds). Montreal and Kingston: McGill-Queens University Press.

Gibson, D.V. and E.M. Rogers, 1994. *R&D Collaboration on Trial: The Microelectronics and Computer Corporation.* Boston: Harvard Business School Press.

Harris, R.G. 1985. *Trade, Industrial Policy and International Competition.* Toronto: University of Toronto Press.

Henton, D., J. Melville, and K. Walesh, 1997. *Grassroots Leaders for a New Economy: How Civic Entrepreneurs Are Building Prosperous Communities.* San Francisco: Jossey-Bass Publishers.

Hingel, A.J. 1992. *Science, Technology and Community Cohesion: Research Results and RTD Policy Recommendations*, Monitor-FAST Programme,

Prospective Dossier No. 1. Brussels: Commission of the European Communities, February 1992.

Information Design Associates and ICF Kaiser International, 1997. *Cluster-Based Economic Development: A Key to Regional Competitiveness*. Washington, DC: Economic Development Administration, US Department of Commerce.

Jenkin, M. 1983. *The Challenge of Diversity: Industrial Policy in the Canadian Federation*, Science Council of Canada Background Study 50. Ottawa: Supply and Services Canada.

Johnson, C., L. D'Andrea Tyson, and J. Zysman (eds), 1989. *Politics and Productivity: How Japan's Development Strategy Works*. Cambridge, Mass: Ballinger.

Landabaso, M., C. Oughton, and K. Morgan, 1999. "Learning Regions in Europe: Theory, Policy and Practice Through the RIS Experience." Paper Presented to the 3rd International Conference on Technology and Innovation Policy, Austin, Texas.

Landabaso, M. and A. Reid, 1999. "Developing Regional Innovation Strategies: The European Commission as Animateur," in *Regional Innovation Strategies: The Challenge for Less Favoured Regions*, Kevin Morgan and Claire Nauwelaers (eds). London: Stationary Office, 19–39.

Leiss, W. and R. Smith, 1990. "Industrial Policy and Strategies for Research and Development," in *Managing Technology: Social Science Perspectives*, Liora Salter and David Wolfe (eds). Toronto: Garamond Press, 113–28.

Lundvall, B.-Å. 1988. "Innovation as an Interactive Process: Form User-Producer Interaction to the National System of Innovation," in *Technical Change and Economic Theory*, G. Dosi et al. (eds). London and New York: Pinter Publishers, 349–69.

– 1992. "Introduction," in *National Systems of Innovation: Towards a Theory of In novation and Interactive Learning*, Bengt-Åke Lundvall (ed.). London and New York: Pinter, 1–19.

Marks, G. 1992. "Structural Policy in the European Community," in *Euro-Politics: Institutions and Policymaking in the "New" European Community*, Alberta M. Sbragia (ed.). Washington, DC: The Brookings Institution, 191–224.

Maskell, P. et al. 1998. *Competitiveness, Localised Learning and Regional Development: Specialisation and Prosperity in Small Open Economies*. New York and London: Routledge.

Metcalfe, J.S. 1997. "Technology Systems and Technology Policy in an Evolutionary Framework," in *Technology, Globalisation and Economic Performance*, Daniele Archibugi and Jonathan Michie (eds). Cambridge: Cambridge University Press, 268–96.

Morgan, K. and D. Henderson, 2002. "Regions as Laboratories: The Rise of

Regional Experimentalism in Europe," in *Innovation and Social Learning: Institutional Adaptation in an Era of Rapid Technological Change*, Meric S. Gertler and David A. Wolfe (eds). Basingstoke, UK: Palgrave, 204–26.

Nauwelaers, C. et al. 1996. *Building Regional Innovation Strategies: RTPs in an Evolutionary Perspective*. Maastricht: Maastricht Economic Research Institute on Innovation and Technology.

Nauwelaers, C. and A. Reid, 1995. *Innovative Regions? A Comparative Review of Methods of Evaluating Regional Innovation Potential*, European Innovation Monitoring System (EIMS) publication no. 21. Luxembourg: European Commission, Directorate General XIII.

Nauwelaers, C. and K. Morgan, 1999. "The New Wave of Innovation-Oriented Regional Policies: Retrospect and Prospects," in *Regional Innovation Strategies: The Challenge for Less Favoured Regions*, Kevin Morgan and Claire Nauwelaers (eds). London: Stationary Office, 224–38.

Niosi, J., P. Saviotti, B. Bellon, and M. Crow, 1993. "National Systems of Innovation: In Search of a Workable Concept, " in *Technology in Society*, no. 15: 207–27.

Nordicity Group Ltd, 1996. *Regional/Local Industrial Clustering: Lessons from Abroad*. Ottawa: National Research Council Canada.

Ontario, Ministry of Industry, Trade and Technology, 1992. *An Industrial Policy Framework for Ontario*. Toronto: Queen's Printer for Ontario.

Porter, M.E. 1998. "Clusters and Competition: New Agendas for Companies, Governments, and Institutions," in *On Competition*, Michael E. Porter. Cambridge, MA: Harvard Business Review Books, 197–287.

Premier's Council, 1988. *Competing in the New Global Economy. Vol. 1*. Toronto: Queen's Printer for Ontario.

Putnam, R.D., with R. Leonardi and R.Y. Nanetti 1993. *Making Democracy Work: Civic Traditions in Modern Italy*. Princeton, NJ: Princeton University Press.

Ritchie, G. 1983. "Government Aid to Industry: A Public Sector Perspective," in *Canadian Public Administration*, vol. 26, no. 1, Spring 1983: 36–46.

Salter, L. and D.A. Wolfe (eds), 1990. *Managing Technology: Social Science Perspectives*. Toronto: Garamond Press.

Saskatchewan, Ministry of Economic Development, 1994. *Research and Technology Commercialization Strategy and Action Plan*, an initiative under the Partnership for Renewal. Regina.

Science Council of Canada, 1979. Forging the Links: A Technology Policy for Canada. Report 29. Ottawa: Supply and Services Canada.

Simeon, R. 1979. "Federalism and the Politics of a National Strategy," in *The Politics of an Industrial Strategy: A Seminar*, Science Council of Canada. Ottawa: Minister of Supply and Services, 5–54.

Storper, M. 1996. "Institutions of the Knowledge-Based Economy," in *Employment and Growth in the Knowledge-Based Economy*, OECD. Paris: Organisation for economic co-operation and development.

– 1997. *The Regional World: Territorial Development in a Global Economy.* New York and London: The Guilford Press.

Trebilcock, M. 1986. *The Political Economy of Economic Adjustment*, Studies of the Royal Commission on the Economic Union and Development Prospects for Canada, vol. 8. Toronto: University of Toronto Press.

Trebilcock, M. et al. 1985. *The Political Economy of Business Bailouts, Vol. 2.* Ontario Economic Council Research Studies. Toronto: Ontario Economic Council.

Tupper, A. 1982. *Public Money in the Private Sector: Industrial Assistance Policy and Canadian Federalism. Queen's Studies on the Future of the Canadian Communities.* Kingston: Institute of Intergovernmental Relations, Queen's University.

Williams, G. 1983. *Not for Export: Toward a Political Economy of Canada's Arrested Industrialization*, Canada in Transition Series. Toronto: McClelland and Stewart.

Wolfe, D.A. 1983. "The Crisis in Advanced Capitalism: An Introduction," in *Studies in Political Economy*, no. 11, Summer 1983: 7–26.

– 1997. "The Emergence of the Region State," in *The Nation State in a Global/Information Era: Policy Challenges*, Thomas J. Courchene (ed.). The Bell Canada papers on economic and public policy 5. Kingston: John Deutsch Institute for the Study of Economic Policy, Queen's University.

– 1999. "Harnessing the Region: Changing Perspectives on Innovation Policy in Ontario," in *The New Industrial Geography: Regions, Regulation and Institutions*, Trevor J. Barnes and Meric S. Gertler (eds). London: Routledge, 127–54.

– 2002a. "Negotiating Order: The Sectoral Approach to Industrial Policy in Ontario," in *Innovation and Social Learning*, Meric S. Gertler and David A. Wolfe (eds). London: Macmillan, 227–50.

– 2002b. "Social Capital and Cluster Development in Learning Regions," in *Knowledge, Clusters and Regional Innovation: Economic Development in Canada*, J. Adam Holbrook and David A. Wolfe (eds). Kingston: Queen's School of Policy Studies and McGill-Queen's University Press, 11–38.

CHAPTER TWELVE

Alexander, E.R. 1991. *Approaches to Planning: Introducing Current Planning Theories, Concepts, and Issues (2nd edition).* Philadelphia, PA: Gordon and Breach Science Publishers.

Arnstein, S.R. 1969. "A Ladder of Citizen Participation," in *Journal of the American Institute of Planners*, no. 35: 216–24.

Atash, F. 1996. "Reorienting Metropolitan Land Use and Transportation Policies in the USA," in *Land Use Policy*, no. 13: 37–49.

Baldassare, M. 1986. *Trouble in Paradise: The Suburban Transformation in America*. New York, NY: Columbia University Press.

Barber, J. 1997. "Mel's Megaproject Pure Folly," in *The Globe and Mail*, 29 October 1997: A11.

Barnett, J. 1995. *The Fractured Metropolis: Improving the New City, Restoring the Old City, Reshaping the Region*. New York, NY: Icon Editions.

Baudrillard, J. 1983. *Simulations*. New York, NY: Semiotext(e).

Bauman, Z. 1985. "On the Origins of Civilization," in *Theory, Culture and Society*, no. 2: 7–14.

– 1988. "Is There a Postmodern Sociology," in *Theory, Culture and Society*, no. 5: 217–37.

Beauregard, R.A. 1989. "Between Modernity and Postmodernity: The Ambiguous Position of US Planning,"in *Environment and Planning D*, no. 7: 381–95.

– 1990. "Bringing the City Back In," in *Journal of the American Planning Association*, no. 56: 210–15.

Belcher, E.M. 1970. *Advocacy Planning for Urban Development*. New York, NY: Praeger.

Blais, P. 1996. *The Economics of Urban Form* (background study for Greater Toronto Area Task Force Report). Toronto: Publications Ontario.

BLG Ltd, 1991. *Study of the Reurbanization of Metropolitan Toronto*. Toronto, ON: Berridge, Lewinberg, Greenberg Ltd.

Boguslaw, R. 1965. *The New Utopians*. Englewood Cliffs, NJ: Prentice Hall.

Bourdieu, P. 1984. *Distinction: A Social Critique of the Judgement of Taste*. London: Routledge and Kegan Paul.

Bourne, L.S. 1992. "Self-fulfilling Prophesies? Decentralization, Inner City Decline, and the Quality of Urban Life," in *Journal of the American Planning Association*, no. 58: 509–13.

– 1993. "Reurbanization Revisited: The Transformation from Concept to Planning Strategy," in *Plan Canada*, May 1993: 7–9.

Caulfield, J. 1974. *The Tiny Perfect Mayor*. Toronto, ON: James Lorimer.

Chadwick, G.F. 1971. *A Systems View of Planning*. Oxford: Pergamon.

Chapin, F.S. 1957. *Urban Land Use Planning*. New York, NY: Harper and Brothers.

City of Toronto (Planning and Development Department), 1992. *Cityplan, Final Recommendations*. Toronto, ON: City of Toronto.

Cooke, P. 1990. *Back to the Future*. London: Unwin Hyman.

D'Amour, D. 1991. *The Origins of Sustainable Development and its Relationship to Housing and Community Planning*. Ottawa, ON: Canada Mortgage and Housing Corporation.

Davidoff, P. 1965. "Advocacy and Pluralism in Planning," in *Journal of the American Institute of Planners*, no. 31: 331–8.

Davis, M. 1985. "Urban Renaissance and Spatial Postmodernism," in *New Left Review*, no. 151: 106–13.

Day, D. 1997. "Citizen Participation in the Planning Process: An Essentially Contested Concept?" in *Journal of Planning Literature*, no. 11: 421–34.

Dear, M. 1986. "Postmodernism and Planning," in *Environment and Planning D*, no. 4: 367–84.

Doxiadis, C. 1960. *The Death of Our Cities*. Athens: Doxiadis Associates.

Economic Council of Canada, 1990. *Good Jobs, Bad Jobs: Employment in the Service Economy*. Ottawa, ON: Economic Council of Canada.

Ellin, N. 1996. *Postmodern Urbanism*. Oxford: Blackwell.

Fagence, M. 1977. *Citizen Participation in Planning*. Oxford: Pergamon.

Faludi, A. 1973. *Planning Theory*. Oxford: Pergamon.

Farncombe, A. 1993. "Chronicle of Descent: Housing on Toronto's Main Streets," in *The Intensification Report*, no. 4: 11–15.

Farrow, M. 1997. *Getting Together: Report of the Special Advisor*. Toronto, ON: Office of the Special Advisor, Greater Toronto Services.

Featherstone, M. 1988. "In Pursuit of the Postmodern: An Introduction," in *Theory, Culture and Society*, no. 5: 195–215.

– 1991. *Consumer Culture and Postmodernism*. London: Sage.

Filion, P. 1988. "The Neighbourhood Improvement Plan, Montreal and Toronto: Contrasts Between a Participatory and a Centralized Approach to Urban Policy Making," in *Urban History Review*, no. 17: 16–28.

– 1996. "Metropolitan Planning Objectives and Implementation Constraints: Planning in a Post-Fordist and Postmodern Age" in *Environment and Planning A*, no. 28: 1637–60.

– 1999a. "Balancing Concentration and Dispersion? Public Policy and Urban Structure in Toronto," in *Environment and Planning C* (in press).

– 1999b. "Rupture or Continuity? Modern and Post-Modern Planning in Toronto," in *International Journal of Urban and Regional Research* (in press).

Filion, P., T.E. Bunting, and K. Curtis (eds), 1996. *The Dynamics of the Dispersed City: Geographic and Planning Perspectives on Waterloo Region*. Waterloo, ON: University of Waterloo, Department of Geography Publications Series.

Fishman, R. 1987. *Bourgeois Utopias: The Rise and Fall of Suburbia*. New York, NY: Basic Books.

Foster, H. (ed.) 1985. *Postmodern Culture*. London: Pluto Press.

Fraser, G. 1972. *Fighting Back: Urban Renewal in Trefann Court*. Toronto, ON: Hakkert.

Friedmann, J. 1973. *Retracking America*. New York, NY: Anchor-Doubleday.

– 1996. "The Core Curriculum in Planning Revisited," in *Journal of Planning Education and Research*, no. 15: 89–104.

Friedmann, J., and C. Kuester, 1994. "Planning Education for the Late Twentieth Century: An Initial Inquiry," in *Journal of Planning Education and Research*, no. 14: 55–64.

Frisken, F. 1993. "Planning and Servicing the Greater Toronto Area: The Interplay of Provincial and Municipal Interests," in *Metropolitan Governance: American/Canadian Intergovernmental Perspectives*, D.N. Rothblatt and A. Sancton (eds). Berkeley, CA: Institute of Governmental Studies Press, 153-204.

Gibbins, J.R. 1989. "Contemporary Political Culture: An Introduction," in *Contemporary Political Culture: Politics in a Postmodern Age*, J.R. Gibbins (ed.). London: Sage, 1–50.

Giddens, A. 1990. *The Consequences of Modernity*. Cambridge: Polity Press.

Gilbert, R. 1993. "The City of Toronto Main Street Program," in *The Intensification Report*, no. 2: 6–8.

Glass, J.J. 1979. "Citizen Participation in Planning: The Relationship Between Objectives and Techniques," in *Journal of the American Planning Association*, no. 45: 180–9.

Goodchild, B. 1990. "Planning and the Modern/Postmodern Debate," in *Town Planning Review*, no. 61: 119–37.

Goodman, R. 1971. *After the Planners*. New York, NY: Simon and Schuster.

Gordon, P. and H.L. Wong, 1985. "The Costs of Urban Sprawl: Some New Evidence," in *Environment and Planning A*, no. 17: 661–6.

Gottdiener, M. 1995. *Postmodern Semiotics: Material Culture and the Forms of Postmodern Life*. Oxford: Blackwell.

Grant, J. 1994. *The Drama of Democracy: Contention and Dispute in Community Planning*. Toronto, ON: University of Toronto Press.

GTA Task Force, 1996. *Report*. Toronto, ON: Queen's Printer of Ontario.

Harvey, D. 1989. *The Conditions of Postmodernity: An Inquiry into the Origins of Cultural Change*. Oxford: Blackwell.

Higgins, D. 1986. *Local and Urban Politics in Canada*. Toronto, ON: Gage.

Hodge, G. 1998. *Planning Canadian Communities: An Introduction to the Principles, Practice and Participants*. Scarborough, ON: ITP Nelson.

Hulchanski, J.D. 1993. "And Housing for It All: Opening the Door to Inclusive Community Planning," in *Plan Canada*, May 1993: 19–23.

IBI Group, 1990a. *Greater Toronto Area Urban Structure Concepts Study: Background Report No. 1, Description of Urban Structure Concepts*. Toronto, ON: IBI Group.

– 1990b. *Greater Toronto Area Urban Structure Concepts Study: Background Report No. 2, Comparison of the Urban Structure Concepts*. Toronto, ON: IBI Group.

Jacobs, J. 1961. *The Death and Life of Great American Cities: The Failure of Town Planning*. New York, NY: Vintage.

Jacoby, R. 1987. *The Last Intellectuals*. New York, NY: Basic Books.

Jameson, F. 1984. "Postmodernism or the Cultural Logic of Late Capitalism," in *New Left Review*, no. 146: 53–92.

Jencks, C. 1984. *The Language of Postmodern Architecture*. London: Academy.

Kaiser, E.J. and D.R. Godschalk, 1995. "Twentieth Century Land Use Planning: A Stalwart Family Tree," in *Journal of the American Planning Association*, no. 61: 365–85.

Kanter, R. 1993. "Legal and Financial Constraints Impede Intensification," in *The Intensification Report*, no. 3: 6–8.

Katz, P. 1994. *The New Urbanism: Toward an Architecture of Community*. New York, NY: McGraw-Hill.

Kellner, D. 1988. "Postmodernism as Social Theory: Some Challenges and Problems," in *Theory, Culture and Society*, no. 5: 239–69.

Klaassen, L.H., J.A. Bourdrez, and J. Volmuller, 1981. *Transport and Reurbanization*. Aldershot, Hants: Gower.

Kling, R., S. Olin, and M. Poster (eds), 1991. *Postsuburban America*. Berkeley, CA: University of California Press.

Knox, P.L. 1993. "The Postmodern Urban Matrix," in *The Restless Urban Landscape*, P.L. Knox (ed.). Englewood Cliffs, NJ: Prentice Hall, 207–36.

Kraushaar, R. 1987. "Outside the Whale: Progressive Planning and the Dilemmas of Radical Reform," in *Journal of the American Planning Association*, no. 54, 91–100.

Kweit, M.G. and R.W. Kweit, 1990. *People and Politics in Urban America*. Belmont, CA: Wadsworth.

Ley, D. 1996. *The New Middle Class and the Remaking of the Central City*. Oxford: Oxford University Press.

Lorimer, J. 1970. *The Real World of City Politics*. Toronto, ON: James Lewis and Samuel.

Lyotard, J.-F. 1984. *The Postmodern Condition: A Report on Knowledge*. Manchester: Manchester University Press.

Lypchuk, D. 1999. "Lust for Lofts," in *Toronto Life*, vol. 33, no. 2: 67–72.

Marcuse, H. 1964. *One-Dimensional Man: Studies in the Ideology of Advanced Industrial Society*. Boston, MA: Beacon Press.

Mary McDonough Research Associates, 1994. *Comprehensive Buyer Profile*. Toronto, ON: The Greater Toronto Home Builders Association.

McHarg, I. 1969. *Design with Nature*. New York, NY: American Museum of Natural History.

McLoughlin, J.B. 1969. *Urban and Regional Planning: A Systems Approach*. London: Faber and Faber.

Metro Toronto (Planning Department), 1976. *Plan for the Urban Structure of Metropolitan Toronto: Concept and Objectives*. Toronto, ON: Metro Toronto.

Metro Toronto (Metro Planning), 1994. *The Official Plan of the Municipality of Metropolitan Toronto: The Liveable Metropolis*. Toronto, ON: Metro Toronto.

Miller, E.G., G.N. Steuart, D. and D. Jea, 1990. *Understanding Urban Travel Growth in the GTA: Volume III*. Toronto, ON: Ontario Ministry of Transportation.

Miller, G., J. Emereau, and J. Farrow, 1997. *GTA Urban Structure: An Analysis of Progress Towards the Vision*. Toronto, ON: Canadian Urban Institute.

Mumford, L. 1961. *The City in History*. New York, NY: Harcourt Brace Jovanovich.

Nowlan, D. and N. Nowlan, 1970. *The Bad Trip*. Toronto, ON: Anansi Press.

Nowlan, D. and G. Steuart, 1990. *The Effects of Downtown Population Growth in Commuting Trips: Some Recent Toronto Experiences*. Toronto, ON: University of Toronto, Program in Planning, Paper 35.

Office for the Greater Toronto Area (OGTA), 1991a. *GTA 2021 – The Challenge of Our Future: A Working Document*. Toronto, ON: OGTA.

– 1991b. *Growing Together: Towards an Urban Consensus in the Greater Toronto Area*. Toronto, ON: OGTA.

Ontario (Government of) (Regional Development Branch of the Department of Treasury and Economics), 1970. *Design for Development: The Toronto-Centred Region*. Toronto, ON: The Queen's Printer.

Ontario (Ministry of Treasury, Economics and Intergovernmental Affairs), 1973. *Government Policy for the Parkway Belt West*. Toronto, ON: Government of Ontario.

– 1996. *Bill 20: An Act to Promote Economic Growth and Protect the Environment by Streamlining the Land Use Planning and Development System Through Amendments Related to Planning, Development, Municipal and Heritage Matters* (1st Session, 36th Legislature, Ontario, 45 Elizabeth II).

Paehlke, R. 1991. *The Environmental Effects of Intensification*. Toronto, ON: Ontario Ministry of Municipal Affairs, Municipal Planning Policy Branch.

Ravetz, A. 1980. *Remaking Cities: Contradictions of the Recent Urban Environment*. London: Croom Helm.

Relph, E. 1976. *Place and Placelessness*. London: Pion.

– 1987. *The Modern Urban Landscape*. Baltimore, MD: Johns Hopkins University Press.

Rifkin, J. 1995. *The End of Work: The Decline of the Global Labor Force and the Dawn of the Post-Market Era*. New York, NY: Putman.

Rose, A. 1972. *Governing Metropolitan Toronto: A Social and Political Analysis 1953–1971*. Berkeley, CA: University of California Press.

Royal Commission on the Future of the Toronto Waterfront, 1992. *Regeneration – Toronto's Waterfront and the Sustainable City: Final Report.* Ottawa, ON: Minister of Supply and Services Canada and Toronto, ON: Queen's Printer of Ontario.

Rowe, P.G. 1991. *Making a Middle Landscape.* Cambridge, MA: MIT Press.

Sewell, J. 1972. *Up Against City Hall.* Toronto, ON: James Lorimer.

– 1993. *The Shape of the City: Toronto Struggles with Modern Planning.* Toronto, ON: University of Toronto Press.

Skelton, I. et al. 1995. "Linking Urban Development and Environmental Concerns: Constraints and Opportunities," in *Canadian Journal of Urban Research*, no. 4: 228–47.

Soja, E.W. 1989. *Postmodern Geographies: The Reassertion of Space in Critical Social Theory.* London: Verso.

Thomas, J.M. 1996. "Educating Planners: Unified Diversity for Social Action," in *Journal of Planning Education and Research*, no. 15: 171–82.

Thomas, T.L. 1997. *A City with a Difference: The Rise and Fall of the Montreal Citizen's Movement.* Montreal: Véhicule Press.

Tomalty, R. 1993. *Urban Form and Sustainable Urban Development: An Ecosystem Approach to Growth Management.* Hull, QC: Environment Canada, Canadian Federal Environmental Assessment Review Office.

– 1996. *The Compact Metropolis: Planning for Residential Intensification in the Greater Toronto Area*, unpublished thesis. Waterloo, ON: School of Urban and Regional Planning, University of Waterloo.

– 1997. *The Compact Metropolis: Growth Management and Intensification in Vancouver, Toronto and Montreal.* Toronto, ON: Intergovernmental Committee on Urban and Regional Research.

Toronto Transit Commission (TTC), 1990. *Let's Move: Program Status Report.* Toronto, ON: TTC.

Valpy, M. 1999. "Breaking the Shackles of Ancient Planning," in *The Globe and Mail*, 27 February 1999: A11.

Venturi, R. 1966. *Complexity and Contradiction in Architecture.* New York, NY: Museum of Modern Art.

Venturi, R., D. S. Brown, and D. Izenour, 1977. *Learning from Las Vegas: The Forgotten Symbolism of Architecture Form.* Cambridge, MA: MIT Press.

Wolfe, J. 1994. "Our Common Past: An Interpretation of Canadian Planning History," in *Plan Canada*, no. 34: 12–34.

Yalnizyan, A. 1998. *The Growing Gap.* Toronto, ON: Centre for Social Justice.

CHAPTER FOURTEEN

Canadian Federation of Mayors and Municipalities, 1976. *Puppets on a Shoestring: The Effects on Municipal Government of Canada's System of*

Public Finance. Ottawa: Canadian Federation of Mayors and Municipalities.

Nova Scotia Royal Commission on Education, Public Services and Provincial-Municipal Relations. 1974. *Report of the Royal Commission on Education, Public Services and Provincial-Municipal Relations*. Halifax:
Queen's Printer.

Ontario Committee on Taxation, 1967. *The Ontario Committee on Taxation
Report*. Toronto: Frank Fogg Queens Printer.

Sancton, A. 1992. "Canada as a Highly Urbanized Nation: New Implications
for Government," in *Canadian Public Administration*, vol. 35, no. 3:
281–98.

– 1996. "Reducing Costs by Consolidating Municipalities: New Brunswick,
Nova Scotia and Ontario," in *Canadian Public Administration*, vol. 39,
no. 3: 267–89.

Tri-Level Task Force on Public Finance in Canada, 1976. *Report of the Tri-
Level Task Force on Public Finance*. Ottawa: Ministry of State for Urban
Affairs.

Vojnovic, I. 1998. "Municipal Consolidation in the 1990s: An Analysis of
British Columbia, New Brunswick, and Nova Scotia," in *Canadian Public
Administration*, vol. 41, no. 2: 239–83.

CHAPTER FIFTEEN

Andrew, C. 1995. "Provincial-Municipal Relations; or Hyper-Fractionalized
Quasi-Subordination Revisited," in *Canadian Metropolitics, Governing
Our Cities*, James Lightbody (ed.). Toronto: Copp Clark Limited: 137–60.

Barnett, R. 1996. "Subsidiarity, Enabling Government and Local Gover-
nance," in *Urban Governance and Finance: A Question of Who Does
What*. Hobson, Paul and France St-Hilaire (eds). Montreal: Institute for
Research on Public Policy.

Bird, R.M. and E. Slack, 1993. *Urban Public Finance in Canada. Second edition*. Toronto: John Wiley and Sons.

Bird, R.M. and T. Tsiopoulos, 1997. "User Charges for Public Services:
Potentials and Problems," in *Canadian Tax Journal*, no. 1: 25-86.

Blais, P. 1994. "The Competitive Advantage of City-Regions," in *Policy
Options*, vol. 15, no. 4: 15–19.

– 1996. "The Economics of Urban Form," report prepared for the GTA Task
Force. Toronto.

Boyne, G. 1995. "Local Government Structure and Performance," in *The
Government of World Cities: The Future of the Metro Model*, L.J. Sharpe
(ed.). Chichester: John Wiley and Sons.

Gertler, M.S. 1996. "City-Regions in the Global Economy: Choices Facing
Toronto," in *Urban Regions in a Global Context: Directions for the*

Greater Toronto Area, Judith Kjellberg Bell and Steven Webber (eds). Toronto: Centre for Urban and Community Studies and Program in Planning, University of Toronto.

Graham, K. and S. Phillips, 1998. "Who Does What in Ontario: The Process of Provincial-Municipal Disentanglement," in *Canadian Public Administration*, vol. 41, no. 2: 175–209.

Kitchen, H. and E. Slack, 1993. *Trends in Municipal Finance*. Ottawa: Canada Mortgage and Housing Corporation.

Greater Toronto Area Task Force. 1996. Greater Toronto. Report of the GTA Task Force. Toronto: Queen's Printer.

Orfield, M. 1997. *Metropolitics: A Regional Agenda for Community and Stability*. Washington, DC.: Brookings Institution Press and Cambridge, Mass.: Lincoln Institute of Land Policy.

Report of the Advisory Committee to the Minister of Municipal Affairs on the Provincial-Municipal Financial Relationship, 1991. Toronto: Queen's Printer.

Report of the Mayor's Homelessness Action Task Force, 1999. *Taking Responsibility for Homelessness. An Action Plan for Toronto*. Toronto.

Report of the Royal Commission on Finance and Municipal Taxation in New Brunswick, 1963.

Slack, E. 1993. *The Land Use Implications of Alternative Municipal Financial Tools: A Discussion Paper*. Toronto: Intergovernmental Committee on Urban and Regional Research.

Tassonyi, A. 1994. *Municipal Debt Limits and Supervision: The 1930s and 1990s in Ontario*. Kingston: Government and Competitiveness Project, School of Policy Studies, Queen's University.

Vojnovic, I. 1997. *Municipal Consolidation in the 1990s: An Analysis of Five Canadian Municipalities*. Toronto: Intergovernmental Committee on Urban and Regional Research.

– 1998. "Municipal Consolidation in the 1990s: An Analysis of British Columbia, New Brunswick, and Nova Scotia," in *Canadian Public Administration*, vol. 41, no. 2: 239–83.

Index

About the Authors

CAROLINE ANDREW Professor of political science and dean of the Faculty of Social Sciences, University of Ottawa

PAUL BORN Tamarack Institute for Community Engagement, Cambridge, Ontario

KEN CAMERON Manager, Policy and Planning, Greater Vancouver Regional District

W. MICHAEL FENN Former chief administrative officer, Regional Municipality of Hamilton-Wentworth (Ontario); now Ontario deputy minister of Municipal Affairs and Housing

PIERRE FILION Professor, School of Planning, University of Waterloo

KATHERINE A. GRAHAM Professor of public affairs and management and dean, Faculty of Public Affairs and Management, Carleton University

PIERRE HAMEL Professor of sociology, Université de Montréal

CHRISTOPHER LEO Professor of politics, University of Winnipeg, and adjunct professor of city planning, University of Manitoba

BARBARA LEVINE Director, social development, World University Service of Canada (WUSC)

SHERILYN MacGREGOR PhD, Faculty of Environmental Studies, York University

WARREN MAGNUSSON Professor and chair of the Department of Political Science, University of Victoria

BETH MOORE MILROY Professor, School of Urban and Regional Planning, Ryerson University

MERLE NICHOLDS Former mayor of Kenata, Ontario

EVELYN PETERS   Professor, Department of Geography, University of Saskatchewan

SUSAN PHILLIPS   Professor of public policy and administration, Carleton University

VALERIE PRESTON   Professor, Department of Geography, York University

ANDREW SANCTON   Professor and chair, Department of Political Science, University of Western Ontario

LISA SHAW   Researcher with the Canadian Centre for Policy Alternatives, Manitoba

ENID SLACK   President, Enid Slack Consulting Inc

SHERRI TORJMAN   Vice-president, Caledon Institute of Social Policy

CAROLYN WHITZMAN   Doctoral candidate, School of Geography and Geology, McMaster University

DAVID A. WOLFE   Professor of political science and co-director, Program on Globalization and Regional Innovation Systems, Monk Centre for International Studies, University of Toronto

MADELEINE WONG   Professor, Department of Geography, University of Wisconsin